Shakespeare's resources

Manchester University Press

Shakespeare's resources

John Drakakis

MANCHESTER UNIVERSITY PRESS

Copyright © John Drakakis 2021

The right of John Drakakis to be identified as the author of this work has been asserted by them in accordance with the Copyright, Designs and Patents Act 1988.

Published by Manchester University Press
Oxford Road, Manchester M13 9PL

www.manchesteruniversitypress.co.uk

British Library Cataloguing-in-Publication Data
A catalogue record for this book is available from the British Library

ISBN 978 1 5261 5786 7 hardback
ISBN 978 1 5261 7452 9 paperback

First published 2021
Paperback published 2023

The publisher has no responsibility for the persistence or accuracy of URLs for any external or third-party internet websites referred to in this book, and does not guarantee that any content on such websites is, or will remain, accurate or appropriate.

Typeset in 10/12.5pt Sabon LT Pro by
Cheshire Typesetting Ltd, Cuddington, Cheshire

In memory of Terry Hawkes

Contents

Acknowledgements — page viii

Introduction — 1
1 The legacy of Geoffrey Bullough — 42
2 Myths of origin — 92
3 Textual economies — 130
4 Trafficking in intertextuality — 164
5 The nature of con-text — 216
6 From formula to text: theatre, form, meme and reciprocity — 248
7 The Thorello Plays: Shakespeare, Jonson and the circulation of theatrical ideas — 289
8 Shakespeare as resource — 318
Conclusion: the elephant in the graveyard — 357

Bibliography — 367
Index — 379

Acknowledgements

Challenging orthodoxies is never a comfortable undertaking, and while the confrontations stimulated by the more nuanced theoretical discourses of the late 1970s and mid-1980s were designed to be comprehensive, a retrospective view of the trajectory of Shakespeare Studies reveals some significant omissions. Pre-eminent among these are Shakespeare biography, a combination of 'fact' and 'fiction' that has remained within established critical parameters, and the study of Shakespeare's 'sources'. Geoffrey Bullough's monumental eight-volume *Narrative and Dramatic Sources of Shakespeare* (1957–75) provided the template for a practical critical vocabulary, and the final volume set the conditions for reflection. Tentative though some of Bullough's categorisations were, they were bequeathed to future generations of scholars who sought to establish the relationship between Shakespeare and the texts (exclusively printed texts) that were thought to inform the making of his own plays, and non-dramatic poems. In the last eight years or so, there has been a growing dissatisfaction with the Bullough-derived vocabulary of 'sources', some of which has harmonised with my own unease. I am grateful to my colleagues at Stirling, Katie Halsey and Angus Vine, for inviting me to contribute to their volume on *Shakespeare and Authority* (2018) that allowed me to begin to rethink some of the issues relating to source study, and to Colin Burrow for sending me a copy of his paper that he delivered at the British Shakespeare Conference in 2014 at Stirling, which was the starting point for the Halsey–Vine collection of essays. I am also grateful to Dennis Austin Britton and Melissa Walter who had heard of my interest in the topic and who invited me to contribute an afterword to their edited collection, *Rethinking Shakespeare Source Study: Audiences, Authors, and Digital Technologies* (2018). This latter invitation came as a result of Routledge's decision to begin a revision of Bullough's *Narrative and Dramatic Sources*, itself a monumental undertaking, and to appoint me as general and contributing editor to the project.

These were the spurs to urge a reformulation of established procedures and they helped to focus a growing frustration with what had become an all-but-derided activity. I am also grateful to Matthew Frost at Manchester University Press for a prompt and informed expression of interest in the face of the current COVID-19 crisis, for his unfailing sense of adventure, and to the two anonymous readers for the press who expressed their enthusiasm for the project. In the final stages of the preparation of the manuscript for the press, I was fortunate to be able to call on the expertise of David Appleyard at MUP, to whom I owe a debt of gratitude for his willingness to guide and advise on matters of presentation and house style. I am also indebted to my copy-editor Joe Haining for his scrupulous attention to detail, for the clarity of his advice, for the speed of his responses and for his unfailing good humour; his invaluable help, and his extraordinary eye for detail, and his valuable suggestions for improvement contributed in no small measure to making this very important part of the process pleasurable.

I have also been fortunate to have had the opportunity of many conversations with friends and colleagues who listened attentively and with varying degrees of scepticism to my concerns over the last ten years or so, and against a background of a diminishing interest in what is now dismissively labelled 'theory'. For the most part, however, my main engagement – sometimes constructive, sometimes combative – has been with books and articles that comprise the formidable literature of 'source' and 'influence' but where the predominant evidence has ranged from the certainty and demonstrability of connection to the speculatively circumstantial. One day in early 2016 I sat down and formulated a plan that has culminated in the following chapters, and as I began writing, so I gradually came to think that the term 'source' was even more of a problem than I had thought, but that, at the time, very few others shared that concern.

Formulating a style and a trajectory has not been easy, but I have been fortunate in having a small circle of friends to whom I have been able to turn. Foremost among them was the late Terry Hawkes, with whom I had long discussions on the matter of 'sources' long before I began on this project, and to whose memory this book is dedicated. His own writings have been an inspiration, and I have long relied on his guidance. Indeed, it is a pleasure to acknowledge what has been a very long friendship, as well as a continued influence. At a more immediately practical level, I am grateful to Adrian Streete, now professor of English at the University of Glasgow, a formidably collegial interlocutor, for having read earlier drafts of the first three chapters, and for engaging constructively and critically with them; his many suggestions have made sometimes obscure and difficult arguments much clearer. To Susan Bassnett, Professor Emerita of the University of Warwick and a much-respected friend of longstanding, I am grateful for taking time out from a very busy schedule to read and comment constructively on an earlier version of Chapter 4. I have tried to take to heart all of their valuable comments, but it goes without saying that I accept full responsibility for any oversights and failures on my part.

At Stirling I am grateful to Angus Vine for numerous discussions over the past few years, and also to the staff at the university library for their unfailing help and support in securing books and articles. At home, my wife, Christine, and my daughters, Alexia and Helena, have maintained the role of a relentless Greek chorus with their persistent, impressively choreographed enquiries about the progress of the manuscript, and by their genial, if at times critical, demeanour that comes of years of, as they would have it, raising their eyebrows at my obsessions and telling truth to power. I have been fortunate nonetheless to have been the beneficiary of their varied, occasional culinary skills, and their formidable range of unfailing good humour; their most recent recruit, our now teenage granddaughter Elildh, shows all the signs of swelling this choral triumvirate into a quartet.

Introduction

Shakespeare in the library

Over a century ago, H.R.D. Andes prefaced his study of *Shakespeare's Books* (1903), with two startling observations. He first claimed that it was 'exceedingly improbable that Shakespeare was the owner of a private library of large dimensions' and that '[i]n the absence of public libraries in those days, it becomes natural to ask where the poet found the volumes he required'.[1] This essentially literary interpretation, concerned primarily with locating and retrieving and documenting, is followed by a second claim that is, in part, based upon the first. While we may be uncertain about the precise chronology of the *sources* that Shakespeare drew on, the fact that antecedent texts exerted a pressure on his own writing raises a question about the dramatist's 'originality':

> In conclusion one word about Shakespeare's sources and his originality. I look upon Shakespeare as the great architect, who gifted with a truly divine talent gave the materials their beautiful shape. The architect can never be made by the things. But he does not make the things either. The materials are given, not created by him. In so far, he is dependent on them. But more than this. His very conceptions and designs, however original they may be, are influenced by previously conceived plans and existent structures. In brief, originality is not creative production but novel combination.[2]

It is surprising how durable this formulation has remained. For example, in his biography *Shakespeare: A Life*, even Park Honan, who is on the whole sceptical about the precise breadth of

Shakespeare's reading, notes that, 'Learning by ear and memory, William would have read very little in the few, costly schoolbooks'.[3] But he quickly qualifies this heretical thought with the speculation that, 'from his father's friends, if not from the schoolmaster, [Shakespeare] could have borrowed, *at last*, as much of Terence or Plautus as he wished' (my italics),[4] and that, in addition to Ovid:

> William's chief guides for rhetoric were the *Ad Herennium* (then thought to be Cicero's) for general information, Quintilian for theory, Erasmus's *Copia* for variety and elegance, and Susenbrotus for tropes and figures of speech. It is not clear that he ever read a work by Cicero other than *Tusculan Disputations*; his texts at school were few.[5]

Honan's reference to Shakespeare's institutionally cultivated 'memory' raises a fundamental question to which we shall return, although the implication, from the list of books Honan assembles, affirms a modicum of formal training that, to some extent, stands in opposition to what 'learning by ear and memory' might suggest. Also, given the wide variety of originary texts that have been unearthed since Andes compiled his list, attention has sometimes turned to the provenance of the narratives that were available to Shakespeare. For example, in a noticeable broadening of the concept of origins, Emrys Jones's *The Origins of Shakespeare* emphasises the humanistic ethos into which Shakespeare was born, and he notes with astonishment a direct quasi-Eliotean 'ease and rapidity of commerce between literature and life, between literary texts and the life of spontaneous feeling'.[6] However, in addition to writers such as Euripides, Plautus and Erasmus, and educationalists such as Roger Ascham, Jones also includes the distinctly non-literary structural influence of the Mystery Plays. He does so on the grounds that there had been performances at Coventry in 1579 and that Stratford's proximity to Coventry – 20 miles – is sufficient reason to invent a connection:

> Living in Stratford-upon-Avon, Shakespeare would have found Coventry within easy reach. And Coventry was not only geographically close, it was by far the largest town in that part of England and had long been famous for its performance of mystery plays. As one whose boyhood was spent in Warwickshire, Shakespeare was

exceptionally well placed to catch by the tail the vanishing eel of medieval dramatic tradition.[7]

Jones then proceeds, through quotation from Hall's *Chronicles* to establish an explicitly structural connection between *2 Henry VI* where the fall of Duke Humphrey mirrors that portion of the Mystery Plays that deals with 'the Passion sequence itself, from the Last Supper to the Crucifixion', which 'stands out for its tragic or quasi-tragic impact'.[8] Some of the issues raised by Jones have since 2000 received emphasis as a new generation of scholars have taken up the business of expanding the contents of Shakespeare's hypothetical library.

Colin Burrow, in his book *Shakespeare and Classical Antiquity* (2013), has added substantially to this list, and in a thoroughly pragmatic way. He argues that the Cressida of Shakespeare's *Troilus and Cressida* may be 'a product of many different post-Homeric Cressidas', and that his depiction of Achilles may also be the product of 'Shakespeare's education [that] may have tumbled together and confused the sequence of texts which we regard as "primary" and "secondary" and that may have left him with a *creatively* confused sense of literary chronology' (my italics).[9] In the twenty-first century 'sources' have become pluralised and origins less dogmatically linear than they had been previously. Even so, Burrow's pragmatism appears to be that of the literary scholar faced with loose ends that simply refuse to submit to the demands of a linear explanatory narrative of the relation between texts. Behind, and sometimes alongside, each text is another, making straightforward linear retrieval difficult and thereby obscuring the archival record. Even so, whatever the strategy deployed, Burrow's pattern of identification and retrieval touches lightly on Shakespeare's hypothetical access to libraries and on the different facets of his memory, raising the question both of what was available in print and also the nature of the dramatist's cognitive ability to feed off existing non-literate materials that were available and that comprised what we might call 'folk memory'.[10] For the modern – or indeed post-modern – scholar, libraries, whether digitised or not, are the documentary repositories of a more or less specialist cultural memory, but in the early modern period printed texts were clearly not *sui generis*, although they offered, by comparison with the digitised archive, relatively restricted access. Indeed, living memory in its various forms competed with print technology as an alternative mode of cognition, and what was documented might easily have had another (initially oral) identity, circulating originally and/or contemporaneously by word of mouth as part of a shared memory. The Aristotelian explanation of 'memory' or 'remembering' that was transmitted in part through rhetorical and educational works was defined as 'the possession of an image as a copy of that of which it is an image', and it is 'the primary faculty of perception, that is, the faculty by which we perceive time'.[11] Also, the distinction that Aristotle drew between those who have good memories and those who are 'good at recollecting' also survived down into the early modern period in the distinction between 'natural' and 'artificial' memory.[12]

Sixteenth-century England had become what Adam Fox has called 'a highly documentary society',[13] even though, as he goes on to observe:

> there continued to be many aspects of life in which writing was irrelevant or unavailable, and elements of communication and exchange which always remained purely oral. In the small communities in which most people lived, what was important was the seasonal cycle of work, the operation of local custom, the lore and tradition of the neighbourhood, and the gossip about its inhabitants.[14]

The linguistic variations that resulted from a strong but residual orality challenged the impulse to standardisation that slowly became a determining feature of print technology. Even in burgeoning urban environments, 'early modern England was less a unified nation and more a constellation of communities, which while they may have shared some common cultural features, stubbornly clung to chauvinistic and exclusive ways of acting, perceiving and speaking'.[15] This is clear from an encounter in Shakespeare's *Richard III* between an aristocratic state functionary and a gathering of citizens; the entrance of a 'scrivener' with a written indictment against Hastings is followed by Buckingham's declaration to the King of his frustration at the lack of responsiveness of the citizens who 'spake not a word, / But like dumb statues or breathing stones / Stared at each other and looked deadly pale' (3.7.24–6).[16] Buckingham asks the Mayor, 'what meant this wilful silence?', and

> His answer was, the people were not used
> To be spoke to but by the Recorder.
> Then he was urged to tell my tale again:
> 'Thus saith the Duke; thus hath the Duke inferred' –
> But nothing spoke in warrant from himself.
>
> (3.7.29–33)

Fox treats in specific chapters the varieties of popular communication that subsumed into its aegis 'proverbial wisdom', 'old wives tales and nursery lore', 'ballads', the survival of primarily oral narratives subsequently committed to print, and 'Rumour and news'. In the case of 'proverbial wisdom', this found its way into the printed collections of 'adages' and commonplace sayings, but also into dramatic dialogue.[17] In such cases oral forms migrated into print where they mingled with quotations from books, and from thence were recuperated for theatrical performance. Thus, the products of lived experience were transported between different forms of communication, while local habits and customs were preserved in communal memory. Fox describes a custom of boundary-marking among Western Islanders, 'in which formal and binding regulations could exist nowhere but in memory and practice and in which symbolic objects were the "characters" of the people, ritual acts their "title deeds"'.[18]

At issue here is one of two different, but not entirely unrelated, conceptions of memory: natural, living or folk memory, and 'artificial cultural memory'. The former comprises the variety of material that was spontaneously available to Shakespeare in primarily non-textual form. From this perspective, the *oeuvre* is, in very large measure, dependent upon what, in purely cognitive terms, the literary theorist Aleida Assmann in her book *Cultural Memory and Western Civilization: Arts of Memory* (2013) argues might have been 'personal decisions and selections, on institutions and media'. The living memory might include details from the variety of printed texts that Honan and Burrow, among others, have identified as contents of the educated mind. In contrast, according to Assmann, artificial cultural memory 'brings together temporal extension with the threat of distortion, reduction, and manipulation that can only be averted through continuous public criticism, reflection and discussion'[19] – in short, the resulting self-reflection that is generated by the formal cultivation of the faculty of memorisation, and augmented by the requirements of print. Indeed, this formalised sort of memory involving reflection and evaluation is rooted in longstanding pedagogic practice and privileges, as Assmann contends, the processes that lead ultimately to a fully fledged historiography; but following the Nietzsche of 'On the uses and disadvantages of history for life', she seems to suggest that reflection on a large scale drives 'the history that serves life' indiscriminately towards the 'neutrality' of an 'antiquarian' history.[20] In Nietzsche's own words, 'the antiquarian sense of man' is dismissed out of hand in the following terms:

> The antiquarian sense of a man, a community, a whole people, always possesses an extremely restricted field of vision; most of what exists it does not perceive at all, and the little it does see it sees much too close up and isolated; it cannot relate what it sees to anything else and it therefore accords everything it sees equal importance and therefore to each individual thing too great importance. There is a lack of that discrimination of value and that sense of proportion which would distinguish between the things of the past in a way that would do true justice to them; their measure and proportion is always that accorded them by the backward glance of the antiquarian nation or individual.

Nietzsche's objection is both to the antiquarian preoccupation with unstructured fragments of the past at the expense of organic unity, and to the 'immortality' that is conferred upon 'antiquity' defined as 'an ancient custom of the ancestors, a religious belief, an inherited political privilege' that stands in the way of innovation or 'the strength to break up and dissolve a part of the past'.[21]

However, what remained of the past, as Adam Fox has observed, were unwritten 'fireside stories' and a sense of 'identity and pride' inscribed in the very landscape itself, all of which 'provided an imagined heritage which helped to underscore the emotional solidarity of the community'; these stories and sensibilities 'were expressed in the "common voice", "common fame", or "common report" of the inhabitants which antiquaries and travellers frequently encountered as they toured the country'.²²

Burrow's account stands between the competing forces of living or folk memory and antiquarian history, at the very point where the products of popular culture and those of the trained critical mentality collide. The result is a sharpening of the distinction between those elements of the past that can be incorporated into a living present, and those that remain in the past as an accumulation of inert 'facts' that are 'dead' but that can be retrieved through literary reconstruction. Indeed, Burrow is one in a long line of scholars whose discomfort with the methods of traditional source study have emerged in their recognition of the limitations of a linear approach to the problem, but who have not fully appreciated the tension between oral and literary language that might be involved.²³

Bruce R. Smith has observed that Shakespeare's contemporary Ben Jonson entertained a 'literate view' of language as 'a body'.²⁴ This is true, but only up to a point. However, the Jonsonian axiom that 'Language most shewes a man; speake that I may see thee', as Terence Hawkes demonstrated over a quarter of a century before Smith, draws attention to a function of spoken language that is expressive and evanescent but also affective, functions that are subsumed into Annabel Patterson's generalised unifying, term 'voice' in the title of her book.²⁵ In his attempt to align the aural habits of the Elizabethan mind with sound ('the O-factor'), Smith proposes a direct (although, perhaps, reductively material) connection between memory, utterance and the body. He suggests that

> memory mediates between the senses and bodily actions, between bodily actions and the senses. With respect to the sense of hearing in particular, memory transforms air waves into embodied action. It remembers sound in various parts of the human body: in the other ventricles of the brain, in the ears, in the hands, in the eyes, in the body as a kinaesthetic whole.²⁶

This recognisably Galenic physiological account, mediated through contemporary Elizabethan developments of the physiology of the brain, seems to miss the point of Jonson's axiom, which is as much moral and ethical as it is physiological. It is also, perhaps, reminiscent of some of the instructional works on rhetoric, such as Quintilian's *The Orator's Education* that placed considerable emphasis on the instrumental as opposed to the material 'body language' of the competent orator.[27]

In the light of these observations, the image of an elephant's graveyard that has often been associated with source study, speaks to an antiquarian ethos that has exerted a powerful influence on some aspects of historiography traditionally conceived. It is perhaps no accident that, contemporary with Shakespeare, early modern historiographers such as William Camden, or (more problematically) Holinshed, were beginning to extend in print the chronicle form that they had inherited from earlier centuries. As the historical narratives that they accumulated migrated into the public theatre they were transformed by what appears to have been a deliberate ambiguity consequent upon the collision of two distinctly opposed forms of dissemination: an early emergent archivalism, and a receding popular 'memory' that lived in and through repetition and oral circulation. Moreover, if Frances Yates's speculation that a theatre like Shakespeare's Globe could appear in distorted form in a text dedicated to the formal training of memory is at all plausible, then this testifies to the power of an image derived from the oral medium of performance to shape a literary and rhetorical understanding of cognitive processes.[28]

These processes are structurally aligned with the complex evolution of memory that entails different kinds of engagement with the past. In a chapter-long excursion into 'The battle of memories in Shakespeare's histories', Aleida Assmann demonstrates how the plays in the Second Tetralogy begin with an imperative to unlearn 'previous usages of historical memory',[29] 'endowing' facts 'with aesthetic form', and thereby 'with meaning that helps both to shape and to perpetuate memories'.[30] The result is 'the creation of a new national myth' that provides a 'context' in which 'the conflict between memories is settled by the construction of a collective memory that becomes a national possession'.[31] She goes on to suggest that what is at issue is the conflict between 'the constructivist, identity-forming character of memory' and a 'neutral historiography', where the one is active and formative, while the other is passive and obstructive.[32] This distinction points up the difference between the contract that Shakespeare makes with his early modern

Introduction 9

audiences (and readers) whereby what remains alive of the available past is shaped selectively in order to serve a collective identity, and the role of the modern critic as historiographer who seeks to identify and classify the genesis of Shakespeare's texts. One of Nietzsche's concerns was with how breaks with the dead hand of the past could be effected, whereas Assmann is concerned with the identification of the different ways in which 'memory', and 'cultural memory' in particular, operate, and with the conflict between 'embodied and disembodied, or inhabited and uninhabited: memory belongs to living beings with prejudicial perspectives, whereas history, because it "belongs to everyone and no-one" is considered to be objective and so without identity'.[33] It is hardly surprising that 'source-hunting' and its extensions into areas of 'influence' should have a whiff of Nietzsche about them, both in the unfortunate attempt they make to construct Shakespeare as some sort of literary superman and in the opprobrium they attract of being associated with the activity of rummaging in the elephant's graveyard. The question that source-hunters have set themselves is precisely how what appear to be dead remains may be reanimated, brought back to life in order to disclose the moment of their creation, and what they might contribute to an understanding of Shakespeare's dramaturgy. In short, how can we reconstruct the elephant from the bones?

The Shakespearean memory

The fragmented Shakespeare that emerges from attempts to trace the different kinds of memory implied in the narratives he deployed bears some similarity to cognitive investigations into the dramatist's 'brain'. In a challenge to structuralist and post-structuralist accounts of human agency and subjectivity, Mary Thomas Crane suggests that cognitive neuroscience's 'broader view of unconscious mental processes also means that speaking about Shakespeare's brain as one place of origin for his works does not imply complete conscious control over them'.[34] Crane is concerned to break free from the refinements of the Foucauldian focus of the connections between the human subject and discourse, and her focus is on the distinction between 'subject' and 'self', and on a politics that revolves around questions of ideological over-determination and resistance. Her account sets up a difference between definitions of 'subject', 'agent' and 'discourse' that resonates with a sense of the variety of resources (including textual traces) available to the practising dramatist. For her the issue revolves around the alternatives between 'multiplicity' and 'constructedness' in the formation of the human subject:

> Although *subject* seems to mean almost the opposite in these two sets of binaries, representing multiplicity and constructedness as opposed to a unified 'individual' in one case and representing the experience of unity and wholeness as opposed to multiple and constructed 'selves' in the other, the most crucial difference lies in the Marxist/psychoanalytic attempt to distinguish an illusory experience of wholeness from an 'actual' multiplicity of positions and the cognitive assumption that both *subject* and *self* are part of a metaphoric system through which we experience our subjectivity. For a cognitive theorist the question is not which is more accurate as a description of human selfhood but rather how we rely on both metaphors, and the difference between them, for our sense of ourselves as persons.[35]

There is much to quibble about in Crane's argument, not least its tendentious amalgamation of 'Marxism' and 'psychoanalysis' and its overlooking of the essentially *linguistic* basis of metaphor itself. But it does raise some fascinating questions about the Shakespearean 'subject', the Shakespearean 'self' and, of course, Shakespearean agency.

Shakespeare, it is often asserted, was not a literary or theatrical *inventor*, the original source of the plays that are attributed to him, but a *bricoleur*, one who assembled, in part purposefully, and in a creative way a variety of recollected elements of other texts, and memories, a general practice that he shared with a number of dramatists whose work appeared in print during the late sixteenth and early seventeenth centuries. But perhaps we need to view this process within a much wider context, imaginatively articulated in Edmund Spenser's allegorical account of the three rooms of Alma's 'stately Turret' in Book 2 of *The Faerie Queene*. Sir Guyon and Prince Arthur are offered a conducted tour of the Turret, where the occupants of the three rooms represent the future, the present and the past:

> The first of them could things to come foresee,
> The next could of things present best aduize;
> The third things past could keep in memoree,
> So that not time, nor reason could arize,
> But that the same could one of these comprise.
>
> (*The Faerie Queene*, Bk 2, Canto ix.49)[36]

The allegorical figure 'of infinite remembrance' (2.ix.55) who has outlived 'Nestor' and 'Mathusalem' is ensconced in a chaotic 'library' of documents:

> His chamber was all hangd about with rolles,
> And old records from auncient times deriu'd,
> Some made in books, some in long parchment scrolles,
> That were all worm-eaten, and full of canker holes.
>
> (2.ix.57)

Spenser's light-hearted evocation of a library could well have had the early organisation of the Society of Antiquaries in mind since, as Joan Evans suggests, it was the publication in 1580 of William Camden's *Britannia*, and the setting up shortly thereafter of the library of Sir Robert Cotton, that stimulated 'the interest of a little coterie of friends' who 'had fallen into the habit of regular meetings for discussion'.[37] The chaos of Spenser's fictional library is mitigated by the assistance of 'a little boy':

> Amidst them all he ['This man of infinite remembruance'] in a chair
>   was set,
> Tossing and turning them withouten end;
> But for he was unhable them to fet,
> A little boy did on him still attend,
> To reach whenever he for ought did send;
> And oft when things were lost, or laid amis,
> The boy them sought, and vnto him did lend.
> Therefore he *Anamnestes* cleped is,
> And that old man *Eumnestes*, by their propertis.
>
> (2.ix.58)

Both visitors chance on books that record *Briton moniments*: 'That of this lands first conquest did deuize, / And old diuision into Regiments, [independent kingdoms] / Till it reduced was to one mans gouernment' (2.ix.59), and also the *Antiquitie of Faerie* where Sir Guyon finds 'Th' offspring of Elues and Fairies ..., / As it deliuered was from hond to hond' (2.ix.60). These volumes appear to impose some sort of historical order on what is otherwise an unsystematic chaos of past events, and they contribute, as Andrew Hiscock has astutely observed, to the knights' 'search for cultural and personal origination'.[38] Here the poet as agency displaces onto his allegorical figures a conscious search for selfhood, while at the same time permitting the recognition of the chaotic experience that the library offers. Indeed, the record of the passage of information 'from hond to hond' suggests that the *Antiquitie of Faerie* represents something more than a straightforward written record. What may be at issue here is not a simple record of the transmission of written texts, but something tantamount to an inscription of an otherwise primary oral history. Thus, in the library in Alma's tower the products of orality and literacy, primary and secondary memory, collide as history and myth confront each other through allegorical representation.

Hiscock goes on to make the connection between Spenser's allegorical reconstruction of this early modern encounter with the past and Thomas Tomkis's comedy *Lingua: or The combat of the tongue* (1607) in which the figure of Memory appears as

> an old decrepit man, in a black Veluet Cassock, a Tafata Gowne furred, with white Grogaram, a white beard, Veluet slippers, a Watch, Staffe, etc., ANAMNESTES his Page, in a graue Sattin sute Purple, Buskins, a Garland of Bayes and Rosemary, a gimmall ring with one link hanging, Ribbands and Threds tyed to some of his fingers, in his hand a paire of Table-bookes etc.[39]

Here the 'white Grogaram' and 'gimmall ring' testify to the multiple identities of Memory and Anamnestes,[40] in line with the various forms of the records that they are charged with keeping. In Spenser and Tomkis, access to the past has not yet been systematised and relegated to a library solely of books. Thus, to live in the late sixteenth century was to live at a moment of transition between two competing modes of representation and preservation: the oral and the written. Patterson's insistence on a 'popular voice' seeks to address the substance of the former, while the instability of early modern print and in particular its transitional identity can be easily perceived in matters of appearance such as spelling variation and the quirks of punctuation in published texts.

Shakespeare's grammar-school education has been well documented, especially those elements that focused on the disciplines of rhetoric and memory. Quintilian's *The Orator's Education* contains an 'Art of Memory',[41] and the *Ad Herennium* has a section on 'Memory' that Frances Yates noted was a text constantly referred to 'as the main source of the tradition'.[42] Indeed, from Plato and Aristotle onwards, formal training in rhetoric involved specific training of the faculty of memory, but we should take care not to abstract this feature from a much larger context. In his *Preface to Plato* Eric Havelock situates Plato 'near the end of the great transition from oral to literate habits of communication',[43] and he later goes on to describe the philosopher's 'opposition to poetic experience' in *The Republic* as one that necessarily involved the destruction of 'the immemorial habit of self-identification with the oral tradition'.[44] How much of the detail of this debate filtered through into the pedagogic practices of early modern England is, of course, difficult to estimate, but in anticipating subsequent cultural-anthropological investigations of the larger structures of mental life of the habits of oral communities, Havelock observes a conservative politics that underpins oral poetry:

> Oral verse was the instrument of a cultural indoctrination, the ultimate purpose of which was the preservation of group identity. It was selected for this role because, in the absence of the written record, its rhythms and formulas provided the sole mechanism of recall and of re-use.[45]

What we can suggest, however, is that the rapid spread of print technology during the early modern period brought to the surface a debate about the different kinds of 'memory' that a classical education sought to simplify, if not obscure. Moreover, in a rapidly developing urban dramaturgy in which the forces of 'cultural indoctrination' and a new individual identity predicated upon the growth of literacy confronted each other, memory itself became a site of contestation. At one extreme, in what Walter Ong has described as 'primary oral cultures', learning does not depend upon 'study'; rather the acquisition of knowledge depends upon 'listening', repetition, 'mastering proverbs and ways of combining them, [and] by assimilating other formulary materials, by participation in a kind of corporate retrospection'.[46] In such an ethos the cognitive structures of the human brain represent capacities that are very clearly linked to the ways in which human subjects adapt to the metaphorical articulations of culture. The difference is between what Paul Ricoeur identifies as 'the famous distinction between *mémoire-habitude* (memory as habit) and *mémoire-souvenir* (memory as distinct recollection)', an opposition that he regards as 'two poles of a continuous range of mnemonic phenomena'.[47] As part of a culture that was on the cusp of a transition from orality to literacy, Shakespeare had available to him the formal practices of a sophisticated rhetorical education that subsumed an entire and evolved history of learned mental habits from Plato and Aristotle onwards, but also cultural materials and fictional narratives. Some of these materials and narratives were the products of print culture, while others were part of a collective, carefully calibrated, popular culture – an unconscious, even – that came into view piecemeal and especially at moments of crisis.

To take an example that found its way into a Shakespearean drama, the figure of Hamlet is positioned on the focal point of this transition when he is caught readjusting the contents of his 'memory' in relation to his mother and Claudius in particular. The ghost of his father provides an affective narrative of an 'experience' that forces the son to recalibrate his understanding of human behaviour, that he then proceeds to formulate in an aphorism that he notes, perhaps like Tomkis's Anamnestes, in his 'table-book':

O most pernicious woman,
O villain, smiling damned villain,
My tables! Meet it is I set it down
That one may smile and smile and be a villain –
At least I am sure it may be so in Denmark.

(1.5.105–9)

Within the context of the play the experience appears primary, and as such it forces a readjustment of prior knowledge, which is then recorded and added to memory as a habit. Rhodri Lewis has observed a connection between Hamlet's utterance and Cicero's observation in his *Three Bokes of Duties* (1556), especially in relation to issues such as 'hypocrisy' and the metaphor of hunting.[48] However, the idea of Vice 'often clothed in virtue's habit' has an independent colloquial existence that makes the direct link with Cicero less firm than the documentary evidence might imply.[49] For Hamlet, this stringently mediated narrative of the past is brought into the present in such a way that it exerts a pressure on an actual lived experience that the audience is invited to share, albeit provisionally, as a hypothetical truth: 'At least I am sure it may be so in Denmark.' This proverbial utterance will accumulate substantial meaning as the play progresses, but here its validity is speculative in a play where speculation and experience are constantly called into question. Here also a gap remains between veracity and doubt – 'I am sure' and 'it may be so' – that helps to steer the observation away from Hamlet as an individual thinking and acting subject and towards the community of spectators with whom, at this moment in the play, he is communicating. Hamlet's audience does not comprise a 'Twittersphere' of isolated individuals since it is made up of the recipients of an empirically derived communal knowledge, a regularly repeated everyday occurrence rather than the product of a momentary formulation of transient opinions that can be uncoupled at will from the past that generates them. In other words, cognitive and communicative functions operate in unison to generate and disseminate a shared communal perception. At the very beginning of a play that is obsessed with 'memory' the past is transported into the present, as one narrative is shown to supersede another as a more substantive model of general experience. Hamlet, of course, is not a historiographer in the specialist sense of the term, nor indeed a systematically self-reflective historian, a task that falls to Horatio at the end of the play. He is, rather, a bearer of a history that is amenable to perpetual revision as it enters into the domain of personal and communal experience. He is also, however, a playwright who can recover earlier plays from his own memory, and who is capable of modifying fragments to fit contemporary circumstances. This is the point of intersection of agency and the communal life of the audience who are invited to share the dramatic character's perspective. This is a succinct example of 'the identity-forming character of memory', an initially oral faculty that avails itself of the technology of writing ('it did me yeoman's service', 5.2.36), and the 'learning' associated with the literate, ordered and educated memory of the historian proper. Each of these different facets of expression converge in the process of generating and recording of experience, of transforming it into a document.

As part of the historiographical operation of cultural memory, the case continues to be made for the textually derived authority of particular classical writers upon whom Shakespeare is thought to have relied. Hamlet's 'table-book' appears to echo Cicero, and/or bears a family resemblance to Erasmian proverbial utterances that identify and gloss particular experiences, raising them to a level of generality both as typical descriptions of actual human behaviour and as precautionary statements offered for moral, ethical and practical guidance. The criterion of association is similarity (usually supported by documentary – i.e. print – evidence) and this has been consistently used as the primary means to identify influence and, indeed, 'sources'. Indeed, this critical manoeuvre has been used consistently to align Shakespeare almost exclusively with literary sources. For example, in her recent *Greek Tragic Women on Shakespearean Stages* (2017) Tanya Pollard makes a very persuasive, though not entirely original, case for the acknowledgement of the influence on Shakespeare of Euripides, who had been recognised by Longinus to have absorbed 'the inspiration of Homer, Aeschylus, and Sophocles before him', and whose dramatic innovations, handed down to the sixteenth century through translation, led to borrowing and adaptation.[50] Pollard's claim is that Euripides 'attracted a striking degree of female interest' that subsequently spread to writers like Shakespeare, and that he was thereby endowed with cultural authority in spite of the fact that his texts were themselves anything but 'original'. Indeed, Jonathan Bate in his *How the Classics Made Shakespeare* (2019) invoked the historian Patrick Collinson's phrase 'republics of letters' to expand the purview of the multiform influence exerted upon early modern writers by 'the Church of England, grammar school, university, inns of court, literate citizenry, country gentry household, aristocratic circle, and court'. Bate extends an expanding range of textual pressures to include social institutions, although again his quarry is 'the classics' in a literary sense.[51] However, the general distinction between 'source' and 'influence' is often muddied by the porous boundary that separates the one from the other,[52] and from the more general pressures of culture, although as we have seen, the primary criterion of judgement always depends in the final analysis upon specifically verbal traces or textual forms shared by an antecedent text and its successor.

In an attempt to negotiate complex issues of this kind, John Kerrigan suggested that, 'Shakespeare does new things with, and adds extensively to what he draws from, pre-existing texts, but his originality is partly original-ity, a drawing upon originals.'[53] Except that in the case of a classical dramatist such as Euripides, or a composite text such as Holinshed's *Chronicles*, the issue of 'originality' as source hardly applies, while the practice of drawing explicitly upon precursor texts that may themselves be composites, does. And what do we make of Bate's 'exemplary force of Cicero', which he cannot resist tying to a textual echo in *Julius Caesar*?[54] In situations such as this, Lorna Hutson's 'circumstantial' rhetorical models that can be traced to the recognition of classical writers such as Cicero or Quintilian, who provided techniques for solving particular dramaturgical problems, would seem to apply:

> Techniques were required for representing all that is not showable – past or distant occurrences, implied motives, habitual actions – the whole inferred or virtual 'world' which apparently subtends the performance we watch, but which, as we know, is actually an effect of our trying to make sense of it.[55]

That 'we' should share such rhetorically based techniques with early modern audiences even as they were beginning to recede, or become subject to creative curtailment, is perhaps questionable, except in the sense that we attempt to reconstruct retrospectively those broad-based historical forces that we identify as constituent elements of the mindset of spectators and of the wider context within which the play is embedded. Such literary and 'forensic' forces – linked here very explicitly to the agency of the writer – may also have been noted by some members of Shakespeare's audience who might have recognised rhetorical models derived from classical antecedents. For others, vague awareness of such phenomena may have surreptitiously entered into a communal cultural unconscious where they became confected with other indigenous habits of the orally attuned early modern mind. It is we who assemble the textual links that, 'as we know, [are] actually an effect of trying to make sense of it [the play]'.

It would appear, then, that in the discussion of 'sources' what matters is almost always archival linkage and documentary verification. Indeed, the appearance of electronic search engines has helped to cement this connection, thereby expanding further the breadth and variety of echoes that may link Shakespeare directly with particular antecedent texts. A dramatist faced with a burgeoning print culture, and forced to adjust by the emergence of a new technology, might be expected to take advantage of what it had to offer, but what is more problematical is what remained of the surrounding oral culture, and in particular how these conflicting forces impacted upon Shakespeare's memory.

The rhetoric of source study

Some half-century after H.R.D. Andes's book appeared, and on the eve of the publication of the first volume of Geoffrey Bullough's *Narrative and Dramatic Sources of Shakespeare* (1957–75), Kenneth Muir published the first of two projected volumes, *Shakespeare's Sources* (1957), which effectively sealed the terms in which the discourse of 'source' and 'origin' has since been largely conducted. In the aftermath of Andes's book, Muir's claim that 'there has never been, so far as I can discover, a book devoted to his [Shakespeare's] sources' was a little less than accurate.[56] Indeed, nowhere did Muir, who had already edited *King Lear* in 1952, an edition that had appeared with numerous corrections in the Arden 2 series in 1964, mention Andes's compilation. He did, however, note that in relation to particular plays, the question of 'sources' had emerged in publications that spanned the entire twentieth century. He mentioned Charles Prouty on *Much Ado About Nothing*, Mary Lascelles on *Measure for Measure*, R.K. Presson on *Troilus and Cressida* and H.N. Paul on *Macbeth* as having 'all shown in different ways that detailed studies of the sources of individual plays may contribute to our understanding of Shakespeare as a dramatist'. He went on to argue that 'until someone has surveyed the whole field our knowledge must remain fragmentary, and our conclusions tentative'.[57] Muir appeared to have abandoned his two-volume project, but in 1977, some three years after Bullough's final volume in *The Narrative and Dramatic Sources of Shakespeare* series appeared, he published a more complete overview in his *The Sources of Shakespeare's Plays* (1977). After an initial excursion through what he thought was Shakespeare's *apparent* familiarity with a range of antecedent texts and translations, and suggesting a number of 'unconscious' as well as conscious echoes of other texts in his writing, Muir concluded that it was 'possible that Shakespeare read hundreds of books which have left no trace on his writings; but the most unlikely books did leave their traces', and 'we may suppose that, like Coleridge, he created much of his poetry from forgotten reading'.[58] The category of 'forgotten reading' seems here to have been invented as a panacea for the literary scholar's frustration at the failure to prove that Shakespeare had access to a large library of books: the library existed independently, but Shakespeare, it is asserted, frequently forgot what he had read. Either this curious suggestion carries some truth, or what Muir seems to be saying is that Shakespeare remembered details but conveniently forgot where he had read them. The mention of Coleridge highlights the contradiction within Muir's discourse between the demands of a scholarly methodology shaped by an emphasis upon various forms of history, and a commitment to the almost superhuman, a-historical figure of Shakespeare, the imaginative creator *ex nihilo*, fashioned by the Romantics.

Notwithstanding these perplexing claims, the kind of source study that Muir favoured was both empirical and speculative, although it depended upon a retrospective linear, and implicitly causal, historical linkage between text and antecedent. But behind the romantic image of Shakespeare as a writer that Muir continued in part to support, was that of the abstracted and abstracting research scholar whose aim was, and continues to be, the reassembly of the historical contours of Shakespeare's creative imagination in which 'source' and poetic inspiration are fused in some more or less mystical fashion. At the same time Muir was clearly aware of the pitfalls that might accompany any excursion into 'the intentional fallacy', even though his argument led him, almost inevitably, into it. Either Shakespeare intended the links that the literary scholar detects retrospectively in the plays, or Shakespeare was in some unspecified way not entirely in control of his material. Indeed, while we cannot label Muir a Freudian, his account of Shakespeare's sources shares a discourse that, in part, sounds very much like Freud's account of the initial stages of the investigation of the unconscious, in which 'the true beginnings of scientific activity consist rather in the description of phenomena, which are then grouped, classified, and brought into relation with each other'.[59] For Freud, the process involved an acceptance of an initial degree of 'indeterminacy' and a lack of clarity, until 'we reach a consensus about their meaning by repeated reference to the empirical material from which they derive, but which, in reality, is being subordinated to them'.[60] But, Freud continued:

> Only after a more thorough investigation of the relevant empirical field can we formulate its basic scientific concepts more precisely, progressively revising them to widen their applicability while keeping them completely free of contradictions. Then the time may also have come to try to pin them down in definitions. But the advance will brook no rigidity here. As the example of physics strikingly demonstrates, even those 'basic concepts' firmly established in the form of definitions are constantly being substantially revised.[61]

This description, with its empirical uncertainties, might easily fit the progress and development of source study, as scholars who extend their fields of enquiry beyond that of literary texts have discovered. In the case of Freud, 'sources' might well form material that has been repressed and that, one assumes, only comes to consciousness at moments of crisis through the act of writing. Richard Helgerson's mapping of the evolution of a national consciousness from the tension between different forms of chorographical and 'survey' accounts between 1579 and 1622 articulates the conflict as being between linearity and contiguity, influence and confluence.[62] He asks:

> How can an atlas and a lengthy poem be considered points on a single line – a line that also passes through an odd assortment of other texts, descriptive and antiquarian? Is it enough that they all

represent in their different ways the same land? Part of the answer is already before us. These books belong together because they refer so often and so conspicuously to one another. They are bound by a dense net of intertextual relations. Nor are the relations only between texts. They are between people. Though the group that supported *Poly-Olbion* in 1622 had little in common with the one that produced Saxton's atlas in 1579, the two are nevertheless linked by various intermediate figurations, most importantly the one that formed around Camden's *Britannia* in successive editions from 1586 to 1610.[63]

Helgerson's inclusive narrative of an emergent sense of Elizabethan and Jacobean nationhood is forced to acknowledge 'various intermediary social figurations' that circulate 'intertextually' and that challenge the linear, ostensibly literary map that he attempts to construct, but that keeps extending into areas beyond the strictly literary. His mapping of the resulting tensions offers a reminder of the fact that many literary commentators have held on to the linear concept of 'source', no matter how the term is qualified. In the case of Shakespeare, they have privileged the concept of 'authorship', despite advances since the 1970s of what a theatrical text comprises, or what authorship might mean in the early modern period. To this extent, historical study has shackled itself, sometimes unwittingly, to a theory of the unconscious and to an ideological commitment to shoring up the 'myth' of Shakespeare, by projecting its own methodological concerns onto its object of enquiry.

Nor is the position clarified by the ambiguous identity of 'dramatic' poesy during the period. For someone like Sir Philip Sidney, and indeed, sporadically throughout the seventeenth century, there appears to have been no clear distinction between plays and poetry, although his commitment to classical precepts places him in opposition to what Helgerson identifies as a 'gothic' strand whose 'mixture and its undoubted imaginative appeal called in question the commitment to absolute authority – aesthetic authority, religious authority, and political authority – on which neoclassicism was founded'.[64] Sidney's disapproval of elements of popular theatrical fashion that mingled 'kings and clowns by head and shoulders to play a part in majestical matters',[65] maintains a commitment to classical literary authority that impacted upon theatrical performance, restricting it to a particular segment of the social hierarchy, while appearing to constrain the evidence that he acknowledges of the kind of rhetorically over-determined unpredictability and popular novelty – a version of Hutson's 'circumstance'[66] – that was a feature of early modern public theatrical experience and of the kind of literary composition to which schoolboys of Shakespeare's generation would have been exposed. This is part of what Shakespeare would have learned although what he acquired in the way of knowledge from actual experience, as the example from *Hamlet* demonstrates, exceeds by some degree his formal learning.

We can, perhaps, gauge the measure of the literary enterprise by recording the growth to encyclopaedic proportions of the direct nature of the link between theatrical texts and the alleged bookish contours of Shakespeare's 'mind'. For example, Andes's 315-page book has metamorphosed into the monumental 528 pages of Stuart Gillespie's impressive *Shakespeare's Books: A Dictionary of Shakespeare's Sources* (2004), due to be revised, expanded and reissued in the early 2020s. In his 'Introduction', Gillespie records the contribution of previous generations of literary scholars but purports to offer something 'different' in the wake of what he detects as the emergence of studies concerned with 'new aspects of previously recognised Shakespearean sources'. Moreover, he continues, 'partly because understanding of the nature of a source has been changing to embrace intertextuality more loosely conceived, fresh texts have been brought into conjunction with Shakespeare's'.[67] Muir's hesitancy in 1957 translates into Gillespie's expansive caution especially in relation to terminology such as 'intertextuality', a relatively new term but one that that he concedes is 'loosely conceived'. How loosely conceived, and what the consequences of its looseness are, will be the subject of Chapter 4. Moreover, the 'discovery' of new sources, alongside the revision of the significance of 'previously recognised Shakespearean sources', indicates that such a dictionary has endless possibilities for expansion and revision as scholars recognise the congruence of their own reading with that which is assumed to be Shakespeare's. However, Gillespie concedes cautiously that not all of the 'knowledge' that went into Shakespeare's theatrical texts had 'been acquired through reading (he saw plays on stage, for example)'.[68] In practical terms this is almost certainly true, although it begs the question of whether Shakespeare *read* a performance in the same way as he might have read a book or, more problematically, whether Shakespeare 'read' in a way in which, for our primarily literary (and literate) culture, we can clearly envisage. Indeed, it is not entirely clear *how* Shakespeare himself responded to what was, at the time, a relatively new technology and the practices of reading that it stimulated.

Roger Ascham's *The Scholemaster* (1579) provides a contemporary insight into the practice of learning, and hints at a common process of reading. In his 'Preface to the Reader' Ascham notes, alarmingly, that 'the best Scholemaster of our time, was the greatest beater'.[69] In Chapter 1 he extends this observation in relation to the teaching of Latin and offers us a momentary insight into Jacques's portrait in Shakespeare's *As You Like It* of 'the whining schoolboy ... creeping like a snail / Unwillingly to school' (2.7.146–8):

> For the Scholer, is commonly beate for the making, when the Master were more worthy to be beat for the mending, or rather marring of the same; the Master many times, being as ignorant as the childe, what to say properly, and fitly to the matter.[70]

Elsewhere in the 'Preface', Ascham recalls an occasion of his reading Greek with the Queen, and in a manner that suggests that the act of reading itself was a communal, possibly oral, matter:

> After dinner I went vp to read with the Queenes Maiestie. We red together in the Greek tongue, as I well remember, that noble Oration of *Demosthenes* against *Aeschines*, for his false dealing in his Ambassage to King *Philip* of Macedonie.[71]

The imprinting of Demosthenes's speech on Ascham's memory establishes an important link that, as Andrew Hiscock has observed, may be traced back to the Socratic definition of memory.[72] The complex interconnection between a long, recognised and valued faculty and the relatively new technology of what Lucien Fevbre and Henri-Jean Martin describe as a process that depended upon the availability of financial capital,[73] raises significant questions about how a writer like Shakespeare may have read, and what access he had to entire texts. Hiscock invokes Deleuze and

Guattari's definition of the fragmentary nature of post-modern experience, and he argues that what they identify as a bygone quest for 'the primordial totality that once existed, or the final totality that awaits us at some future date',[74] was exactly the 'vexed question' that Spenser engaged with in Book 2 of *The Faerie Queene*.[75] However, the process of fragmentation that Deleuze and Guattari associate with the post-modern, may just as easily have been the *experience* of reading and remembering that formed an important and abiding part of the subjectivity of the schoolboy Shakespeare, and the adult dramatist.[76]

In the same year that Muir's *The Sources of Shakespeare's Plays* was published, and three years after Bullough, Emrys Jones's *The Origins of Shakespeare* (1977) sought to overhaul the prevailing emphasis upon the location and the identification of antecedent texts, and to complicate considerably the concept of 'origin', embedding it firmly in what Helgerson later identified as the 'gothic' elements of an emerging popular English culture. Jones began by revisiting the Romantic notion of 'genius' and by dispelling 'the Shakespeare myth' enshrined in 'over-imaginative' biographies,[77] thereby anticipating the critical practice of demythologisation that was shortly to become a central tenet of British cultural materialism.

Jones's objective was twofold: to establish a pre-history in the early sixteenth century that might challenge the claimed unhelpfulness of literary historians; and to counter 'the desire to impose manageable period-divisions [that] has put more stress on superficial discontinuity' – an emergent radical critical manoeuvre – 'than continuity at a deeper level'.[78] Following on from T.W. Baldwin's two-volume monumental study of the Elizabethan secondary education system in *Shakespere's Small Latine and Lesse Greeke* (1944), Jones sought to reinstate the figure of Erasmus whose 'ideals, values, and practices' were well established in Elizabethan grammar schools, and whose particular brand of 'northern humanism' must have filtered through to the adolescent schoolboy Shakespeare at Stratford.[79] More generally, Jones defines this ethos in the following manner:

> The entire temper of northern humanism was one of sober practicality, usefulness, and servicebleness; which explains why it achieved so

much. The humanist impulse quickly merged with religious, political and educational activity; it was never concerned to keep itself separate from everyday affairs. Its whole purpose was to improve the quality of lay life; its workings therefore rapidly become invisible and hard to trace.[80]

He identified textual echoes of Erasmus's *Adagia* and *Apophthegmata* in passages from *Hamlet* and *Antony and Cleopatra*,[81] the latter providing the occasion for a more plausible explanation for Cleopatra's 'His delights / Were dolphin-like' than Stephen Greenblatt's later engaging but wholly fanciful attempt to link the image to a hypothetical journey that the young Shakespeare might have made with his father to Kenilworth in 1575.[82] Jones was at his sloganising best when he concluded that, 'Without humanism, in short, there could have been no Elizabethan literature; without Erasmus, no Shakespeare.'[83] But he did not leave it there. Shakespeare was, like Erasmus, 'a transmitter – he lets others speak through him. He lacks egoism and self-assertiveness, *and is all the more original for seeming not to seek originality*' (my italics).[84] This is something much more sophisticated than the stock Romantic definition of 'genius', emphasising the pedagogic concept of 'imitation' that was 'something quite distinct from either reproduction or translation. It was', Jones insists, 'a principle of real assimilation.'[85] He went on to adduce Petrarch and Roger Ascham in support of the claim that: 'The best writers of the past were studied by making the student produce not a copy of the original but a work both similar and different. The difference, the element of novelty and originality, was vital.'[86] Writers of the past were 'authorities' who provided models, and if, as Jones, argued that '[i]t is often as if, at some deep level of his mind, Shakespeare thought and felt in quotations',[87] it was presumably because particular modes and forms of expression had been deeply imprinted on a mind that we might say was, by the time he came to write, already textualised. This surprisingly opportunistic angling in the Saussurean stream of what was in 1977 an emergent post-structuralism raises the question of how these quotations might have been preserved in the dramatist's 'mind'. This thought turns out to be less radical than it appears, since Jones thinks that like his contemporaries, and like Hamlet, 'Shakespeare *must have* kept copious literary notebooks which, under classified topics, would preserve an analytical summary of his reading' (my italics).[88] So, Shakespeare was a literary scholar after all, capable of making copious notes in table-books that he could recall when he came to compose his plays. Jones then goes on to examine Hamlet's soliloquy at 2.2.485ff.,[89] which he compares with the first monologue of Atreus in Seneca's *Thyestes*, and he concludes that:

> Examined in this way, Hamlet's soliloquy is seen to be a tissue of submerged and no doubt unconscious literary memories and quotations. It would be absurd to suppose that Shakespeare needed to consult Quintilian, Seneca, and perhaps others; it seems altogether likelier that he carried these scraps in his head, perhaps looking up a notebook, but knowing what their gist and shape and tone were and in what sort of context they could be put to work.[90]

For Jones, Shakespeare was, and was not, a bookish writer, relying on 'submerged and no doubt unconscious literary memories and quotations', a substrate of a literary mind, but he occasionally consulted an imaginary 'notebook', thereby aligning him with the oral poet *and* the studious researcher. Baldwin had cited the Erasmus of *Copia* on the function of memory, although he linked it with literary 'reading': 'nor is memory to be neglected, the storehouse of reading', alongside the larger process of memorisation that was dependent upon three conditions:

> thorough understanding of the subject, logical ordering of the contents, repetition to ourselves. Without these we can neither retain accurately nor reproduce promptly. Read, then, attentively, read over and over again, test your memory vigorously and minutely. Verbal memory may with advantage be aided by ocular impression.[91]

And his idea of Cicero and Terence as 'prime models of imitation'[92] provides the comparatively loose concept of the 'model' or authority that Jones resurrected in his suggestion that Suetonius's *Life of the Emperor Claudius* provided 'the Claudian model for Macbeth's tyrannical behaviour'.[93]

Of course, a systematic study of Shakespeare's memory would be difficult, even with the aid of computers, but the issues it raises underpin virtually every study of 'sources'. There are precious few

Introduction   27

accounts of the Elizabethan unconscious, much less about what its contents might have been and the gap between what can be surmised about Shakespeare's education. Moreover, what he retained in his memory that he could 'promptly' and 'accurately' recall, is virtually unbridgeable except by speculation, judicious or otherwise. Nor can we be totally accurate in our speculations of what circulated orally in the circles in which Shakespeare moved. For example, Richard Helgerson begins his chapter on 'Apocalyptics and apologetics' with a reference, first, to the treatment in Foxe's *Acts and Monuments* of the plight of that 'worthy martyr of Christ, Sir John Oldcastle, knight, Lord Cobham'. He then links it to the play commissioned by Philip Henslowe, *The first part of the true and honourable history, of the life of Sir John Oldcastle, the good Lord Cobham* (1599), and thence to Shakespeare's *1* and *2 Henry IV*.[94] Helgerson's claim is that Drayton, Hathaway, Munday and Wilson's play was a response to Shakespeare's mocking depiction of Sir John Oldcastle in the figure of Falstaff and that in his recollection of a 'language replete with the tell-tale phrases of Puritan spirituality, he must have thought of the martyr'.[95] This is also a speculation that Andrew Gurr has advanced in his suggestion that Henslowe's commission may have been 'a reprisal against the intruder company at their new playhouse', and that this hostile gesture 'would explain his "gefte" to the writers along with the play's explicit criticism of the neighbouring playhouse's Falstaff plays'.[96] It would not be difficult to produce a proto-capitalist account of the competition for audiences between the Chamberlain's and either the Admiral's or Worcester's Men that came to a head in 1599 with the appearance of *The first part of the true and honourable history* that was either stimulated by, or was co-existent with, the relevant three plays of Shakespeare's Second Tetralogy, extending to *Henry V*, which may have been the inaugural play chosen to open the new Globe Theatre. However, the knot of plays including *1* and *2 Henry IV*, *The first part of the true and honourable history* and *Henry V* that span the years 1597–99 hint at something more complicated than a 'source' would suggest. Indeed, the corrective to Shakespeare's mocking imagining of the dramatic character whose original name was Sir John Oldcastle provides an alternative characterisation that specifically and repeatedly emphasises an explicit religious affiliation that resurrects the substance of Foxe's account in his *Book of Martyrs*. Moreover, in addition to a cultural memory, and to the complexity of religious affiliation, it is not unreasonable to suppose that an experienced spectator might have been familiar with the long history of performance that stretched back to 1586 and to the anonymous *Famous Victories of Henry V*. Nor is it unreasonable to suppose that this cumulative and complex memory was shared by Shakespeare and by the collaborators who produced *The true and honourable history*.

However, in addition to these cultural confluences, there are moments in Shakespeare's texts where we catch the dramatist with what we suspect is an open page of Holinshed or Plutarch in front of him, and in the case of *Macbeth*, as we shall see, it is possible to identify a particular edition of Holinshed. But without succumbing to the extremes of deconstructive practice, we need to remind ourselves, as Annabel Patterson has observed, that Holinshed 'was only one of nearly a dozen persons who contributed to the project over two decades and in two quite different editions, the first appearing in 1577, the second, expanded version of 1587 largely produced after Holinshed's death'.[97] The point is, surely, that even where it is possible to identify origins they tend to be either plural, or, where no individual writers can be identified, they remain anonymous. In a similar vein to Emrys Jones, Colin Burrow argues that in Shakespeare's 'most "Greek" play, *Troilus and Cressida*', where he might have been expected to show an interest in Homer, the drama 'is steeped in parallel versions of the Troy story from different languages, from Chaucer and from Lydgate, and perhaps from Henryson, which all but blot out the lineaments of Homer'.[98] Burrow is forced to conclude that this apparent lack of an identifiable lineage confuses 'the sequence of texts which we regard as "primary" and "secondary"'.[99] But what in Jones is a rather more cautious approach to the contents and organisation of Shakespeare's mind that we can only reassemble retrospectively and speculatively, in Burrow turns into a rather more confident assessment of Shakespeare's reading intentions:

> Shakespeare read classical and contemporary works not just to plunder content (similes, *exempla*, phrases that could be out into

plays) or narrative ideas (plots, sub-plots, scenes gestures). He also read to learn a practice.[100]

None of this is to doubt Shakespeare's competence and consummate skill in reading, even though the difficulties in separating out the contents of a memory that frequently occludes 'origins' remains. If Gillespie's dictionary of Shakespeare's books describes a 'library' then we cannot but conclude that, cultural context notwithstanding, Shakespeare's memory was phenomenal by any standards. If we follow Jones and Burrow, then the sheer untidiness of Shakespeare's mind and its capacity to make connections without necessarily being aware of their origins is the true source of Shakespeare's originality and his genius.

There are many examples in Shakespeare's dramatic texts of the *failures* of memory, a sufficient number to indicate that loss of memory was culturally, politically and personally significant. Thus, the paradox of a writer possessed, we think, of a phenomenal memory, thinking seriously and in a way that audiences would recognise, about loss of memory. Indeed, in a play like *Hamlet*, preoccupied with 'remembering' and 'forgetting' the Machiavellian Polonius, 'dries' in the process of instructing his lackey Reynaldo how to spy on Laertes, calling forth a prompt from his interlocutor:

And then, sir, does 'a this, 'a does –
What was I about to say? By the mass, I was
About to say something. Where did I leave?
REYNALDO. At 'closes in the consequence'.
(2.1.48–51)

The Arden 3 editors, Ann Thompson and Neil Taylor, quoting Patricia Parker, link this and the later episode at 2.2.340–58, with 'the emergent world of statecraft contemporary with the play'.[101] This is not the place to explore the complex workings of memory and forgetting in *Hamlet*, except to say that its protagonist struggles to preserve the faculty of memory, and invokes practical aids to do so in the face of a political force whose capacity for the provision of fake news, misremembering and forgetting permeates the entire court of Denmark. A number of commentators on the play have claimed that the drama of remembering and forgetting has its roots in Shakespeare's own repressed, and then projected, domestic experience. We might also speculate that it is connected to his professional life as an actor and playwright, whose experience may have been even less methodical than a literary scholar such as Colin Burrow describes. Commenting on how Shakespeare's amalgamation of his 'training' and his 'profession' could derive from Ciceronian rhetoric, Burrow suggests the following scenario in which the methodological and the affective combine:

> This combination of his training and his profession means that Shakespeare can usefully be thought of as asking two questions of what he read. The schoolboy humanist in him might ask 'What can I learn from this text?' The playwright might wonder 'What are these words *doing* to their audience?' These questions lead to what is in two distinct senses a 'pragmatic' way of thinking about texts. A writer who asked them would have thought always about how he could use or or learn from his reading. He would have thought about how a particular remark or literary allusion might have performative force within a conversation between different people.[102]

This necessarily speculative account of the mental life of Shakespeare charged with reassembling and gluing together the shards of a much fuller textuality to produce a particular kind of order in which the act of remembrance is central, is deeply imbued with the modern perspective of the knowing and knowledgeable scholar. Moreover, a dramatist learning and mastering his craft, accumulating practical experience, would certainly have been exposed to what Louise George Clubb in her analysis of Italian drama has referred to as 'theatregrams' – 'permutation and declension by recombination with compatible units, whether of person, association, action or design'[103] – that were the building blocks of dramatic structure adapted to the early modern English professional theatre. Here the scholarly and aristocratic earlier perception of 'untidiness' that leaves Shakespeare always in full control of his writing, gives way in this formulation to a rhetorically informed 'pragmatism' – Hutson's 'circumstance' – and a conscious purpose that allows Shakespeare to retain partial control. What was conscious and what was internalised is always difficult to determine, and this is perhaps why scholars have been reduced to identifying the traces of Shakespeare's inspiration in 'books' to which he is assumed to have had regular access.

There is some evidence to suggest, however, that Shakespeare may not have been fully in control, or at least not in the systematic way that Burrow suggests. In addition to occasional appeals to Shakespeare's 'unconscious' as an explanatory tool, critics have generally regarded the occasional appearance of the names of actors such as Kempe and Cowley and the designation of the one as 'Andrew' and the other as 'Kempe' in Q1 *Much Ado About Nothing* (1600) as examples of 'foul papers',[104] detectable as moments of creative indecision. Claire McEachern, the Arden 3 editor of the play argues, plausibly, that these foul papers stand as witness to 'Shakespeare's compositional process, a kind of picture of his mind in action, making it up as he goes along, changing his mind as the story line emerged, and not necessarily backtracking to render his document internally consistent'.[105] At one level there is no inconsistency in these variations, but the 'picture' of Shakespeare's mind 'in action', as McEachern puts it, presupposes that a process of psychological internalisation has already taken place, and that the result is untidy. But what this example reveals is, on the surface, a tripartite fusion: the dramatist (implied) who is effectively the agency, the name of the actor(s), and the 'type' or role. If we subscribe to the image of Shakespeare as solitary 'writer' then we can conclude that when he was formulating the roles of Dogberry and Verges he had two actors skilled in comic roles 'in mind', and that in composing their lines he inadvertently alternated between actor, dramatic character and role at the moments of inscription. According to this explanation, Shakespeare was *imitating* – one might even say ventriloquising – the theatrical skills of two actors, Kempe and Cowley, whose voices he could 'hear' and reproduce; also, the process would be linear and pragmatic: identifying the necessary acting proficiency of members of the company, selecting and scripting parts for them and, at an early stage, recording that combination on paper.

A more complicated, but no less compelling explanation, might give much more agency to Kempe and Cowley in this process, almost to the point that we could claim that, without sinking into the morass of attribution studies, *they* wrote this portion of the playscript. At the moment of inscription, Kempe and Cowley at the very least *inhabited* Shakespeare's 'mind', although they may actually have been present at the moment of inscription. This raises some fundamental questions about the nature of composition that may even extend to the process of rehearsal. In her magisterial survey of *Rehearsal from Shakespeare to Sheridan* (2000), Tiffany Stern has insisted that 'actors in the professional and non-professional theatre alike, studied alone, away from their fellow players'.[106] Her case rests substantially on the weight she gives to the meaning of 'study' and she adduces a body of evidence to indicate that the actor was a solitary figure in relation to the process of learning his part, and that it 'contained his own lines and the one, two, three, or (occasionally) four words that preceded each of his speeches'.[107] The assumption upon which this is based is that it is only the dramatist who had a full conception of the total play. But the evidence from the text of Q1 *Much Ado About Nothing* points in a different direction. It is as likely that Kempe and Cowley already *knew* what was expected of them and that this was a knowledge and a theatrical skill that they shared with the dramatist. Here the process of composition was not linear but cyclical, moving between actor(s) and writer, to the point when it would be equally plausible to suggest that for this part of the play – and elsewhere in the action where Dogberry and Verges appear – the actors themselves 'wrote' Shakespeare. This does not entirely invalidate the process of rehearsal that Stern charts, although it complicates its dynamics significantly and raises new questions about the *contents* of those Shakespearean texts that are designated 'foul papers', and the various ways in which they can be read.

The predominantly linear arguments that have underpinned the study of sources, and that have led to dismissive allegations of pedantry have persisted despite a growing body of evidence to suggest that alternative approaches are both possible, and necessary. An all-too-common strategy has been to routinely identify texts, to establish a common identity with one or more of Shakespeare's plays and to then insist that the dramatist *must* have been aware of them, that they provided the comic models upon which he could depend, and was therefore in some basic way *influenced* by them. We have already seen how Emrys Jones could claim that 'Shakespeare thought and felt in quotations', a compositional practice that could extend to the sphere of influence of extant tradition of the Mystery Plays. Jones, like those who have followed him from within the purview of literary history, perceived non-literary influences as being intrinsic to the business of writing, but only secondary compared to literary and dramatic influences that continue to occupy a prominent position in the scholarly ranking of sources and origins. However, historians, whose preoccupations have been primarily historiographical rather than literary, have begun to propose alternative explanations of the relationship between the plays and the historical context within which they are embedded.

Influence versus confluence

In his detailed study of *How Shakespeare Put Politics on the Stage: Power and Succession in the History Plays* (2016) Peter Lake aims to replace a now familiar quasi-Foucauldian New Historicist formalist and 'broadly cultural' account of the subversion/containment debate, with a series of oppositional texts that, he argues, sought to frame 'the range of cultural expression, driving the political narrative and indeed determining the political and cultural outcome'.[108] Lake takes his cue from what he calls 'the outpourings of the exile Catholic press' that resisted containment and that he suggests 'can take us to parts of the Elizabethan political imaginary that other sources cannot reach; they give us access to something we might want to regard as the political unconscious of the Elizabethan *fin de siècle*'.[109] Lake prefaces his argument with a careful disclaimer. He does not want to enlist Shakespeare for the Catholic cause, but even more, he 'does not even want to claim that the author of these plays *must* have read these particular tracts. That remains a distinct (but entirely unprovable) possibility.'[110] The explicit claim that Lake makes is that 'what is at stake here is not so much *influence* but *confluence*' (my italics).[111] Thus, while not wanting to dispense entirely with the linear trajectory of source study, Lake opts for a historiographical excavation of texts that replicate, collide with, challenge or even undermine what we might perceive to be a dominant Protestant ideology, whose proximity to Shakespeare's History Plays served to expand their appeal and in a number of directions. He invokes Annabel Patterson on the dynamics of Elizabethan censorship, but wants to uncover, at a much less programmatic level, the dangers that these plays risked in performance:

> Even if we accept the existence of the sort of unwritten rules, the nexus of tacit assumptions, described by Annabel Patterson, and even if we emphasise the elements of plausible deniability, of interpretative flexibility and multivocality, built into both text and performance, it surely remains the case that there were very considerable risks that, I would argue, these plays took consistently, and just as consistently, got away with.[112]

It is the concept of 'confluence' that lays down a challenge to the linearity of a more traditional account of source study. This methodological adjustment was anticipated in 1985 by Francis Barker and Peter Hulme in their path-breaking essay 'Nymphs and reapers heavily vanish: the discursive con-texts of *The Tempest*'. The significance of the hyphenated 'con-texts', which will be considered in more detail in Chapter 5, is that it signals a refusal to arrange texts in a hierarchy that opposes 'foreground' to 'background', a process that not only separates the text from its history but that both recognises and abolishes the latter 'at one and the same time'.[113]

It is clear from the foregoing discussion that the time has come to rethink the concept of 'source' in relation to Shakespeare's text, and to revise substantially the categories that Geoffrey Bullough evolved in his *The Narrative and Dramatic Sources of Shakespeare* (1957–75). Barker and Hulme's 'con-texts', Lake's 'confluence', the inbuilt repetitions that were part and parcel of the culture of oracy and the number of occasions when Shakespeare himself returned to his own earlier texts as 'resources' all indicate that the simple nomenclature of 'source' is restrictive and ideologically inflected, as we shall see in Chapter 2. A better, and less tendentious, term that does not dispense entirely with a recognisable but limited commitment to linearity, or to the availability of texts of a literary and printed kind, would be 'resource'. This allows us to supplement a linear trajectory with a range of what, in the case of printed evidence, we might call conjunctural texts – texts that exert pressure on other texts and that are contemporary with them. It also allows for connections with what was available to Shakespeare from non-literary resources, narratives and techniques that circulated as part of a communal cultural memory beyond what Frances Yates identifies as 'the main line of descent from the scholastic tradition'.[114] What, of course, is open to question is how we might make connections between these very different kinds of resource, some explicitly textual and some not. However, what would amount to a substantial shift in customary emphasis, would serve to expose a number of hitherto obscured connections within the complex organisation of Elizabethan and early Jacobean society. The exposure of these various points of convergence that may take us closer to an understanding of the early modern political unconscious that now seems strange to us.

Notes

1 H.R.D. Andes, *Shakespeare's Books* (London, 1903), p. xvi.
2 *Ibid.*
3 Park Honan, *Shakespeare: A Life* (Oxford, 1998), p. 44.
4 *Ibid.*, p. 49.
5 *Ibid.*, pp. 54–5.
6 Emrys Jones, *The Origins of Shakespeare* (Oxford, 1977), p. 21.
7 *Ibid.*, p 33.
8 *Ibid.*, p. 47.
9 Colin Burrow, *Shakespeare and Classical Antiquity* (Oxford, 2013), pp. 37–8.
10 See James Notopoulos, 'Mnemosyne in oral literature', *Transactions and Proceedings of the American Philological Association*, 69 (1938), 474. At no point does Emrys Jones distinguish between this kind of memory and the primarily 'literary' recollection that informs Shakespeare's plays, although the identification of the Mystery Plays as an 'origin' implies just such a distinction.
11 Aristotle, 'On memory', *On the Soul and Other Psychological Works*, trans. Fred D. Miller Jnr. (Oxford, 2018), p. 98. See also Frances A. Yates, *The Art of Memory* (reprinted, London, 2010), pp. 114ff.
12 Aristotle, 'On memory', p. 95. Aristotle claimed that 'those who are slow have better memories, while those who are quick and learn easily are better at recollecting'. Cf. also the *Ad Herennium*, trans. Harry Caplan (Cambridge, MA, and London, 1959), p. 207 for the distinction between 'natural' and 'artificial' memory.
13 Adam Fox, *Oral and Literate Culture in England 1500–1700* (Oxford, 2000), p. 14.

14 *Ibid.*, p. 19.
15 *Ibid.*, p. 97.
16 William Shakespeare, *King Richard III*, ed. James R. Siemon, Arden 3 series (London, 2009). All citations from this play are from this edition.
17 Fox, *Oral and Literate Culture*, p. 132.
18 *Ibid.*, p. 270.
19 I borrow these provocative terms and their glosses from Aleida Assmann, *Cultural Memory and Western Civilization* (Cambridge, 2013), p. 6.
20 Friedrich Nietzsche, 'On the uses and disadvantages of history for life', *Untimely Meditations*, trans. R.J. Holingdale (reprinted, Cambridge, 1990), pp. 74–5.
21 *Ibid.*, p. 74.
22 Fox, *Oral and Literate Culture*, p. 215.
23 Cf. Annabel Patterson, *Shakespeare and the Popular Voice* (Cambridge, 1989), pp. 33–4. Patterson distinguishes between what she calls 'the "great" tradition' and 'fragments of a culture that has already been defined as primarily recreational', and she puts the matter a little differently by extending the frame of reference with her suggestion that 'the record is distorted by our necessary dependence on texts *selected* for wide dissemination, whether printed ballads, almanacs or chapbooks, or on the references to festival morris dances, May games etc., that can be painstakingly collated from other texts, usually in the dominant culture'. Her concern is to ask questions about 'the "little" culture (paradoxically that of the vast majority) primarily recreational, or at most at the convergence of recreation and religion' (p. 33). These popular cultural forms, replete with the ideology that held them in place, were also dependent upon language, or, more precisely, 'speech'. See especially, Terence Hawkes, *Shakespeare's Talking Animals: Language and Drama in Society* (London, 1973), pp. 41–3.
24 Bruce R. Smith, *The Acoustic World of Early Modern England: Attending to the O-factor* (Chicago and London, 1999), pp. 96ff.
25 See n. 23, and more especially, Hawkes, *Shakespeare's Talking Animals*, pp. 41–3.
26 Smith, *The Acoustic World*, p. 109.
27 Quintilian, *The Orator's Education*, ed. Donald A. Russell, Loeb Classical Library, 5 vols (Cambridge, MA, and London, 2001), vol. 5, book 11, ch. 3, pp. 85ff.
28 Yates, *The Art of Memory*, pp. 335ff.

29 Assmann, *Cultural Memory and Western Civilization*, p. 67.
30 *Ibid.*, pp. 70–1.
31 *Ibid.*, p. 74.
32 *Ibid.*, p. 122.
33 *Ibid.*
34 Mary Thomas Crane, *Shakespeare's Brain: Reading with Cognitive Theory* (Princeton and Oxford, 2001), p. 39.
35 *Ibid.*, p. 19.
36 Edmund Spenser, *The Faerie Queene*, ed. A.C. Hamilton (London and New York, 1977), p. 256. All references to Spenser's text are to this edition.
37 Joan Evans, *A History of the Society of Antiquaries* (London, 1956), p. 8. Cotton's library was used by Ben Jonson and in 1629 was closed as a result of a scandal involving a series of documents. See John Drakakis, 'The Plays of Shackerley Marmion (1603–39): A Critical Old-spelling Edition' (unpublished PhD thesis, University of Leeds, 1988), vol. 2, pp. 693–703.
38 Andrew Hiscock, *Reading Memory in Early Modern Literature* (Cambridge, 2011), p. 31.
39 *Ibid.*
40 Cf. *OED* entry for 'grogram' initially applied to a 'mixed' garment but later in the eighteenth century transferred to the mixed drink of rum and water consumed by sailors ('grog'). And 'gimmal' as a finger-ring divided into two or more parts (*OED*. 1).
41 Quintilian, *The Orator's Education*, vol. 5, bk 11, ch. 2, pp. 63ff.
42 Yates, *The Art of Memory*, p. 20.
43 Eric A. Havelock, *Preface to Plato* (Cambridge, MA, and London, 1963), p. 97.
44 *Ibid.*, p. 201.
45 *Ibid.*, p. 100.
46 Walter J. Ong, *Orality and Literacy: The Technologising of the Word* (London and New York, 1982), p. 9.
47 Paul Ricoeur, *Memory, History, Forgetting*, trans. Kathleen Blamey and David Pellauer (Chicago and London, 2004), p. 24. Ricoeur's account is a highly sophisticated phenomenological study that begins with the positioning of the function of memory, in a specific philosophical rather than cultural-anthropological context. He invokes Henri Bergson's *Matter and Memory* to distinguish between 'habit-memory', which is 'the one we employ when we recite the lesson without evoking one by one each of the successive readings of the period of learning' that 'is part of my present, exactly like my habit of walking or of

writing; it is lived and acted rather than represented', and memory that requires imagination. Quoting Bergson, he continues: 'To memory that repeats is opposed memory that imagines: "To call up the past in the form of an image, we must be able to withdraw ourselves from the action of the moment, we must have the power to value the useless, we must have the will to dream. Man alone is capable of such an effort"' (Ricoeur, *Memory, History, Forgetting*, p. 25).

48 Rhodri Lewis, *Hamlet and the Vision of Darkness* (Princeton and Oxford, 2017), pp. 102–3. See also Nicolas Grimalde, *Marcus Tullius Cicero: Three Bokes of Duties* (London, 1556), especially fol. 131: 'Doutlesse it is a parte not of a plaine, not of a simple, not of a gentlemanly, not of a iust, not of a good manne: but rather of a suttlewitted, close, wylie, deceitfull, gylefull, craftie, forlick, and a verie dubbler. These so manie, and other mo names of vices to enter into, is it not unprofitable: if they be dispraiseworthie, who haue helde their peas: what is to be thought of those, who haue used vannesse of talke?' See also fols 135–6: 'Is it then anie deceit, to pitche the toile, although you go not aboute to rouse nor chase the game? For the verie game lights upon it oftētimes, when nobody folowes them. So when you offer your house to sale: you sett up your bill, as a nett.'

49 William George Smith, *The Oxford Dictionary of English Proverbs*, revised by Sir Paul Harvey (Oxford, 1948), p. 687.

50 Tanya Pollard, *Greek Tragic Women on Shakespearean Stages* (Oxford, 2017), pp. 18–19.

51 Jonathan Bate, *How the Classics Made Shakespeare* (Princeton and Oxford, 2019), pp. 48–9. Bate's title has a familiar ring to it. Cf. Stephen Greenblatt, *Will in the World: How Shakespeare Became Shakespeare* (London, 2004).

52 See Bate, *How the Classics Made Shakespeare*, p. 12.

53 John Kerrigan, *Shakespeare's Originality* (Oxford, 2018), p. 2.

54 Bate, *How the Classics Made Shakespeare*, p. 12.

55 Lorna Hutson, *Circumstantial Shakespeare* (Oxford, 2015), p. 5. See also Lorna Hutson, *The Invention of Suspicion: Law and Mimesis in Shakespeare and Renaissance Drama* (Oxford, 2007), pp. 308 and 309–10, where she argues that 'the evidential and mimetic techniques which Shakespeare in earlier plays used to create the effects which Auerbach celebrated as enabling us to 'form an idea of [characters'] normal lives', have now (though not abandoned as mimetic techniques) become decisively associated, within the probable fiction of the play itself, with malevolence and with the imagination's credulous susceptibility'.

56 Kenneth Muir, *Shakespeare's Sources*, vol. 1 (London, 1957), p. vii.
57 *Ibid.*
58 Kenneth Muir, *The Sources of Shakespeare's Plays* (London, 1977), p. 7.
59 Sigmund Freud, *The Unconscious*, trans. Graham Frankland (Harmondsworth, 2005), p. 13.
60 *Ibid.*
61 *Ibid.*, pp. 13–14.
62 Richard Helgerson, *Forms of Nationhood: The Elizabethan Writing of England* (Chicago and London, 1994), pp. 107ff.
63 *Ibid.*, p. 131.
64 *Ibid.*, p. 47.
65 Sir Philip Sidney, 'An apology for poetry', *English Critical Essays XVI–XVIII Centuries* (London, 1961), p. 46.
66 Hutson, *Circumstantial Shakespeare*, pp. 2–3. Hutson notes issues of 'motive, time and place' that in the cases of Erasmus and Quintilian '(why, when and where) would be more or less indispensable to most form of composition involving human action' (p. 3).
67 Stuart Gillespie, *Shakespeare's Books: A Dictionary of Shakespeare's Sources* (London, 2004), p. 2.
68 *Ibid.*
69 Roger Ascham, *The Schoolmaster* (London, 1579), sig. B1^v.
70 *Ibid.*, sig. C1^r.
71 *Ibid.*, sig. B2^v.
72 Hiscock, *Reading Memory*, pp. 6–7.
73 Lucien Fevbre and Henri-Jean Martin, *The Coming of the Book*, trans. David Gerard (London, 1984), pp. 115–27.
74 Cited in Hiscock, *Reading Memory*, p. 30.
75 *Ibid.*
76 Cf. Hiscock, *Reading Memory*, p. 30, where Deleuze and Guattari are invoked to support a slightly different argument.
77 Jones, *The Origins of Shakespeare*, p. 1.
78 *Ibid.*, p. 7.
79 *Ibid.* See also Lewis, *Hamlet and the Vision of Darkness*, pp. 7–8, where it is argued that, *pace* Joel Altman, *Hamlet* marks 'the point at which many of its [Elizabethan humanism] governing assumptions can be said to have died'.
80 Jones, *The Origins of Shakespeare*, p. 10.
81 *Ibid.*, pp. 11–12. Cf. also Hutson, *Circumstantial Shakespeare*, pp. 2–3.
82 Greenblatt, *Will in the World*, pp. 46–7.

83 *Ibid.*, p. 13.
84 *Ibid.*, p. 18.
85 *Ibid.*, p. 19.
86 *Ibid.*
87 *Ibid.*, p. 21.
88 *Ibid.* Ben Elton's TV series *Upstart Crow* (BBC TV, 2018–19) offers a series of surprising comic insights into what in 1977 Jones regarded as a serious matter. Also, Jones's account of Hamlet's 'tables' here is a literary one that the example earlier seeks to revise.
89 The line reference is to *Hamlet*, ed. Ann Thompson and Neil Taylor, Arden 3 series, revised edn, 2 vols (London, 2016). All quotations from the play are from this edition.
90 Jones, *The Origins of Shakespeare*, p. 24.
91 T.W. Baldwin, *William Shakespere's Small Latine and Lesse Greeke* (Urbana, 1944), I.83.
92 *Ibid.*, I.440–1.
93 Jones, *The Origins of Shakespeare*, p. 28.
94 Helgerson, *Forms of Nationhood*, p. 249. The play that modern scholars refer to as *1 Sir John Oldcastle* was printed in quarto in 1600 but *2 Sir John Oldcastle* has been lost.
95 Helgerson, *Forms of Nationhood*, p. 249. See also *The Norton Shakespeare*, 2nd edn, ed. Stephen Greenblatt, Walter Cohen, Jean Howard and Catherine Maus (New York and London, 2008), p. 1183, and *William Shakespeare: The Complete Works*, ed. Stanley Wells and Gary Taylor (Oxford, 1986), pp. 509ff.
96 Andrew Gurr, *Shakespeare's Opposites: The Admiral's Company 1594–1625* (Cambridge, 2009), p. 101.
97 Annabel Patterson, *Reading Holinshed's Chronicles* (Chicago and London, 1994), p. 3. Patterson cites Stephen Booth's statement that 'we care about *Holinshed's Chronicles* because Shakespeare read them'.
98 Burrow, *Shakespeare and Classical Antiquity*, p. 37.
99 *Ibid.*, p. 38.
100 *Ibid.*, p. 52.
101 Cited in *Hamlet*, Arden 3 series, pp. 42–3.
102 Burrow, *Shakespeare and Classical Antiquity*, p. 52.
103 Louise George Clubb, *Italian Drama in Shakespeare's Time* (New Haven and London, 1989), p. 8.
104 See *Much Ado About Nothing*, ed. Claire McEachern, Arden 3 series (London, 2006), pp. 128–9.
105 *Ibid.*, p. 129.

106 Tiffany Stern, *Rehearsal from Shakespeare to Sheridan* (Oxford, 2000), p. 62. This could lead to considerable confusion, especially in those cases where the prompt words for different speeches were either identical, or in the case of passages such as that of the beginning of Act 3 Scene 1 of *1 Henry IV* in the exchange between Hotspur and Glendower where the dialogue is carefully choreographed for the purposes of a rather dangerous frivolity.
107 Stern, *Rehearsal from Shakespeare to Sheridan*, p. 61.
108 Peter Lake, *How Shakespeare Put Politics on the Stage* (New Haven and London, 2016), p. 62.
109 *Ibid.*
110 *Ibid.*, p. 60.
111 *Ibid.*
112 *Ibid.*, p. 66.
113 Francis Barker and Peter Hulme, 'Nymphs and reapers heavily vanish: the discursive con-texts of *The Tempest*', in John Drakakis, ed., *Alternative Shakespeares* (London, 1985), p. 191.
114 Yates, *The Art of Memory*, p. 114.

1

The legacy of Geoffrey Bullough

In the 'General Conclusion' that appears at the end of Volume 8 of *Narrative and Dramatic Sources of Shakespeare* (1974), Geoffrey Bullough inveighed against 'the cult of the Ph.D. thesis first in Germany and then in Anglo-Saxon countries' because it 'led to exaggerated claims for obscure and doubtful analogies; and the tendency to imagine that once a "source" had been unearthed and its parallels noted all that was necessary had been done, brought discredit on research'.[1] 'Obscure and doubtful analogies' of this sort continue to appear in Shakespeare Studies, although they are secondary to other concerns, and they usually appear as adjuncts to, rather than as 'a form of truancy from the proper study of the plays, an occupation only suitable for pedants, outside the scope of true criticism'.[2] Bullough invoked as support for his argument the Italian philosopher Benedetto Croce's notion of 'critical immediacy', that 'we make ourselves at home in the Renaissance',[3] and that we enter

> into the imagination of the poet, so to recreate the moment of vision and the process of composition as to apprehend the work of art in its totality.[4]

His choice of Croce as a support appears to have been maintained throughout the project, perhaps because from the outset the Italian philosopher emphasised an essential connection between 'history' and 'art'.[5] Bullough's 'narrative and dramatic sources' are themselves a kind of history in that they aim to demonstrate what the dramatist encountered, or may have encountered, at particular moments in the creation of his plays. The account of contingent 'truths' that he seeks to establish – hence the various categories of certainty or uncertainty: 'source', 'probable source', 'possible source', 'analogue', 'historical parallel' – presuppose the universal truths that are embedded in the Shakespeare *oeuvre* and that 'individual' and 'universal' truth are integral parts of the process of cognition and creation.[6] Bullough's own empirical pragmatism can thus proceed in the fullness of the philosophical and theoretical foundation that Croce provides, and that allowed him to gain entry into the poet's 'mind'.

This was a sufficiently important strategy for Bullough to reiterate a few pages later in his reaffirmation of the value of source study in relation to the History Plays and also to Comedies and Tragedies, that he narrows down to Shakespeare's 'reading'. He argued that entry into the poet's mind

> during the process of composition lets us see the difficulties he must have overcome when writing history plays based on Hall and Holinshed: the opportunities afforded him for dramatic scenes by Plutarch, Lodge or Cinthio; the skill with which he avoided the weaknesses of previous plays on the same subjects; the manner in which he interwove materials taken from different authorities (as in *Lear*); and how he changed the tone and purport of a story (as in *As You Like It* and *Othello*).[7]

The emphasis upon the comparative nature of the study of sources, Bullough suggests, 'often lets us glimpse the creative process in action as he [Shakespeare] took over, remade, rejected, adapted, and added to *chosen or given materials*' (my italics).[8] He leaves open the question of what is 'given' and what is 'chosen' to be resolved by his own selection and modulation of sources. Paraphrasing Hardin Craig's interpolation of Croce, he resists the temptation to explain 'the mystery of his artistic genius'; rather, it will at the very least provide an opportunity to perceive 'his constructive powers in operation, of seeing the ingenious collocations and associative energies which underlie the dynamic balance of the plays and which fuse plot, character, dialogue, and imagery into a poetic unity'.[9] In this Bullough is at one with the '[m]odern study of Shakespeare sources', although what he identifies as its 'twofold obligations' are only partly historical. These obligations are 'first to investigate the ambience of story, drama, ideas, beliefs, and current events which affected the dramatist from time to time', which initially assumes a certain kind of historical objectivity, and 'second, and even more important, to consider how he [Shakespeare] used this material as a poet and craftsman in the theatre so as to produce plays which were not only "for an age" but also "for all time"'.[10] Here the individual and the universal combine. The formal properties of the drama also assume precedence over the background of 'ideas, beliefs and current events' in what has since become a recognisable hierarchy. However, Bullough's evident conflation of what was locally practical and what has become of permanent value pulls the historically inclined investigator in two opposing directions. The combination of uncertainty and intellectual curiosity, and the emphasis upon the aesthetic properties of Shakespeare's texts, sometimes risks relegating their 'histories' to the status of what R.G. Collingwood labels 'chronicle', or 'the corpse of history'.[11] The elements of 'plot, character, dialogue and imagery' that comprise in part the assembly of theatregrams available to the practising dramatist can be independently identified as recurring elements in the plays' aesthetic structures, as indeed can the classical 'authorities' whose influences may be traced in them. But the task is made all the more confusing by Bullough's telling admission that 'Shakespeare was not academically learned',[12] while insisting that his plays are 'for all time'. Practice and posthumous reputation – two culturally related but distinct fields of enquiry – are here offered as the two sides of a single coin as Croce's philosophical rigour gives way to a familiar bardolatry.

Bullough and his contemporaries held on to the Drydenesque image of a writer who was 'naturally learn'd' and who 'needed not the spectacles of Books to read Nature'.[13] But he also insisted that the poet's fusion of the artisanal and the creative was supplemented by documented 'sources': Shakespeare 'the craftsman in his workshop' (that implied reading books as part of his craft) and Shakespeare the mysterious 'artistic genius'. This lacks the explicit extravagance of the Coleridgean claim that Shakespeare was 'the Spinozistic deity – an omnipresent creativity',[14] in whose 'various characters, we still feel ourselves communing with same human nature, which is everywhere present as the vegetable sap in the branches, sprays, leaves, buds, blossoms, and fruits, their shapes, tastes, and odours'.[15]

And it also minimises the temporal element of Bullough's identification of 'analogues' in the claim that 'so much of his source-material contains strong folk elements which anthropologists have traced in oral story and legend'.[16] But Bullough's aesthetic sense, that to some extent he shared with the Romantics and with Croce,[17] provides a structure for his thinking about elements of Shakespeare's dramaturgy. It also points to a confusion between what we may call the 'authority' of Shakespeare and the models and 'authorities' upon which, it is generally argued, Shakespeare may have relied in the process of remaking, rejecting, adapting and adding to material that has either been chosen or given. How these materials circulated, and in what forms, and how Shakespeare 'chose' them, or how they were 'given' to him, must always be the result of a retrospective critical and scholarly speculation, a narrative, so to speak, that cannot, no matter how hard it tries, make itself fully and unproblematically 'at home in the Renaissance',[18] even though its objective was to pinpoint the moment of artistic creation.

The problem for Bullough is that his own methodology conflates the discourse of the literary historian with that of the cultural and critical afterlife of the Shakespeare *oeuvre*. The brief glimpse that this offers of the augmented vocabulary and perspective that Bullough and his contemporaries inherited from Dryden and Coleridge, enlivened by the aesthetic philosophy of Croce and supplemented by their own ideological commitments, makes it impossible to treat the Renaissance simply, or indeed neutrally, as 'another country heard from'.[19] The contours of a source study that is primarily concerned with the one-way transmission of texts through time, is underpinned by a series of cumulative aesthetic judgements that emphasise organic structure and the abiding cultural value of 'Shakespeare'. Thus, two models of 'authority' are made to cohere: the authority of the models that can be traced in Shakespeare's texts, and that are, to some extent, predicated upon a rhetorical pedagogy based on the classical concept of 'imitation' and a philosophical linkage of the historian and the artist; and the cultural authority that is ascribed by successive generations of scholars and critics whose own formal education in the classics may have had some elements in common with that of Shakespeare himself. Of course, in the absence of firm documentation other than the printed texts themselves, the method for establishing evidence to support these claims in relation to Shakespeare is largely inferential. Exactly how complicated this is can be gauged from the following example from the beginning of the final act of Shakespeare's *The Merchant of Venice*. The 'narrative and dramatic sources' of the play appear in the volume that deals with *Early Comedies, Poems, Romeo and Juliet* (Volume 1); in the final volume of the series Bullough returned to the play as 'the finest example' of one of two methods of construction. These comprise 'either the movement in echelon of two plots involving different characters who are connected with one another at various points in the action', or the linear or serial movement of one stream of plot with a number of smaller tributaries which flow in and are assimilated by it. *The Merchant of Venice* is offered as an example of the second alternative, where

> Shakespeare took the basic theme of Antonio's friendship for Bassanio and traced its course and effects, plaiting together the the bond-story and Bassanio's winning of Portia and taking in Casket-story, Jessica's elopement, and Shylock's determination to have his pound of flesh as they emerged, placing the Casket-scene at the very centre of the play as that to which everything leads up and from which everything afterwards springs, including the resolution of the imbroglio by Portia.[20]

But at this early stage in the project the concept of 'source' proves to be less than stable, since what is, on reflection, 'the finest example' of one of two methods of construction started out in Volume 1 as a mixture of identifiable textual precursors and folk narratives. In Volume 1 Bullough begins the opening section on *The Comedy of Errors* with the category of 'probable sources' that proposes an almost certain connection between this play and its classical antecedents. In the case of *The Comedy of Errors* the matter seems to be straightforward: 'The play is based mainly on the *Menaechmi* of Plautus but it also draws on his *Amphitruo*.'[21] Shakespeare, he argues, 'doubtless knew enough Latin to read him in the original'. But what is then excerpted without comment, are the English translations by William Warner (1595) and Edward Sugden (1893).

The Merchant of Venice is the final section of Volume 1, and by this time Bullough had already begun to refine his categories. For example, in the case of *Love's Labour's Lost* he is forced to admit that for this play, 'The source-hunter has little to offer,'[22] although he manages two 'analogues', and two 'historical parallels'. In each category there is no certain linear connection between text and analogue or parallel, compared with the certainty of 'source' or the near certainty of 'probable source'. The category of 'historical parallel' has more in common with the category of 'confluence' referred to in the Introduction. For *The Merchant of Venice* Bullough gathers together some eight 'sources', four of which are designated 'probable', one 'possible source' and three 'analogues'.[23] The fullest 'probable source' is Ser Giovanni Fiorentino's *Il Pecorone*, an Italian narrative first published in 1558 and for which no known English translation existed during Shakespeare's lifetime. He speculates that a lost play, *The Jew*, mentioned in Stephen Gosson's *Schoole of Abuse* (1578) 'may have been Shakespeare's source',[24] and he invents a narrative that links the ballad 'Shewing the crueltie of *Gernutus* a Jew' with Robert Wilson's play *The Three Ladies of London* (1584) that he designates as an 'analogue'.[25] The 'pound of flesh' story is shown to have an international pedigree in that it 'probably begins in India, for the *Mahabharata* has a tale about King Usinara who saves a dove from a hawk by giving its weight from his own flesh instead',[26] an analogous narrative to that which is found in Alexander Silvayn's *The Orator* (1596),[27] while Anthony Munday's *Zelauto or The Fountain of Fame* (1580) is a 'possible source' for the trial scene.[28] Marlowe's *The Jew of Malta*, popular in the 1590s but not printed until 1633, is designated as a 'source' for the characterisation of Shakespeare's Jew, and for the relation between Shylock and his daughter Jessica, suggesting that Shakespeare must have seen it in performance, or knew about it from descriptions that were circulated orally. What might also have circulated orally was a narrative of the tension between a Jew and his family (especially his daughter) that might have provided a counterbalance to the relationship (and the tension) between Portia and her dead father.

The fourteenth story of Masuccio's *Il Novelino*, which remained untranslated from the Italian until 1895, is designated as a 'probable source', which raises the question of how Shakespeare may have come into contact with it. Wilson's and Marlowe's plays, the one an analogue and the other a source, require very little in the way of speculation. However, in the cases of the two untranslated Italian narratives, we are required to believe either that Shakespeare could read Italian, or that he knew of these *novellae* second-hand. It is also, of course, possible that the content of these stories circulated in London during the early 1590s, thereby demoting them from the status of 'probable source' subject to documentary verification, to 'analogue'. Stories about the behaviour of Jews and usurers (the two were not necessarily exclusively aligned) were part of the sort of common knowledge that would have attracted audiences to repeated performances of Marlowe's, and later, Shakespeare's play.[29] If this was indeed the case, then the linear model that Bullough implies as the mechanism for identifying the primacy of sources may be less convincing as an explanatory device. Rather, the principles of repetition and circularity that were characteristic features of a society still committed to an oral ethos, and that we can only identify by inference, may have helped to maintain the continued visibility of certain narratives whose collective resonance was sustained by larger current concerns and prejudices. However, this kind of repetition can be seen to overlap with the principle of 'imitation' that covered both representation and invention. For example, George Puttenham begins his *The Arte of English Poesie* (1589) with the following observation:

> a Poet may in some sort be said a follower or imitator, because he can express the true and liuely of every thing is set before him, and which he taketh in hand to describe: and so in that respect is both a maker and a counterfaitor: and Poesie an art not only of making but also of imitation. And this science in his perfection, can not grow, but by diuine instinct, the Platonicks call it *furor*: or by excellencie of nature and complexion: or by great subtiltie of the spirits & wit or by much experience and obseruation of the world and course of kinde, or peraduenture by all or most part of them.[30]

We need to bear in mind the issue of imitation both as a strategy for observing the world *and* as a yardstick for the provision of models that in the *Ad Herennium* accompanied theory and practice as means of perfecting the faculties of 'Invention, Arrangement, Style, Memory, and Delivery'.[31] It is worth noting, in passing, that what became an 'Erasmian concept of imitation' was still closely linked with speech, although the emphasis on 'daily intercourse' produced what Richard Halpern has called a reduction of 'a model based on the legal apparatuses of the state for one based on the practices of civil society'.[32] Halpern also notes that an early Latin primer, John Stanbridge's *Vulgaris* (*c*.1529) focused on 'English phrases drawn from everyday life at school and home', although he does not regard this as evidence of a tension between speech and the technologies of writing, but as part of a pedagogy that Erasmian humanism rejected 'because they inculcated an inelegant and sub-literary Latin'.[33] This is worth bearing in mind as we return to Shakespeare's play.

Bullough's account of the overall shape of the structure of *The Merchant of Venice*, continues to influence editors of the play, despite differences of opinion concerning particular details. But the dialogue between the newly married Jessica and Lorenzo as they await the arrival in Belmont of Portia introduces other kinds of stereotyping of a specific kind that might, in part, come under the heading of 'imitation'. It is night-time, and the moonlight and evening breeze stimulate thoughts of an explicitly 'literary', but implicitly cultural, nature. The situation in which the lovers find themselves prompts them to recall a series of analogues, established classical narratives that, taken together, represent what Alexander Kojève might call 'tradition', embodying at an archetypal level, 'the "cause" that has made of the contemporaries what they are'.[34] As such these analogues fulfil the function of a spiritual paternity in the face of whose 'authority' the lovers appear to offer no 'reaction', since to do so 'would be a reaction against oneself, a kind of suicide'.[35] If indeed Shakespeare is not thinking in quotations at this point, then his dramatic characters, insofar as they can 'think', certainly are, and they are aligned with models that will echo their own experience. In a play where the 'authority' of paternal figures is invoked, thematically explored and laid open to question, the allusions to a particular series of 'texts' from the literary and theatrical traditions that function as what David Quint, in another context, has called 'a series of outside authorities',[36] expands our awareness of the lovers' own situation. An episode from Homer's

Iliad, embroidered by Chaucer's *Troilus and Criseyde*, is offered by Lorenzo, and this prompts us to ask whether, and which parts of, the lovers' experience resemble the love-struck Troilus and the duplicitous Cressida. The specific contours of the literary reference might be lost on a 'non-literate' audience, but the depiction of female duplicity (for which Cressida was a type) recurs in Shakespeare's other Venetian play in 1604 where Brabantio inadvertently evokes the commonplace when he warns Othello that Desdemona 'has deceived her father, and may thee' (1.3.294).[37] Jessica invokes the episode of Pyramus and Thisbe that recalls both Chaucer's *Legend of Good Women* and its hilariously comic appropriation in the inept performance of the rude mechanicals in Shakespeare's earlier play, *A Midsummer Night's Dream* (c.1595); indeed, earlier in the volume Bullough had designated Ovid's *Metamorphoses* in Arthur Golding's translation as the 'source' of the Pyramus and Thisbe episode in that play.[38] At this point it is not certain which of the two versions audiences (and readers) would have been familiar with: Shakespeare's play, which his audiences would almost certainly have known, or Chaucer's text, possibly supplemented with Henryson's additions, with which few or any would have been familiar. Lorenzo responds with a reference to Dido, queen of Carthage, whom the Aeneas of Book 4 of Virgil's *The Aeneid* rejects in order to fulfil his destiny. Her story appears in Book 7 of Ovid's *Metamorphoses*, and in both Chaucer's *Legend of Good Women* and later Marlowe's play *Dido Queen of Carthage*, which was published in 1594 but performed much earlier during Marlowe's lifetime. Again, is the passage of this reference a linear, literary one, or does it come through the contemporaneous pressure exerted by Marlowe's play? In other words, has Shakespeare read what the more educated Marlowe read, or is he simply appropriating material that was already in public circulation and that he had seen in performance? Jessica retorts competitively with a more positive reference to Medea, arguing that, contrary to the Senecan emphasis on irrational, murderous jealousy, the poisoning of Medea's rival Creusa and her father, and her infanticide, involves an emphasis upon death and regeneration. This part of the narrative is omitted in Chaucer, but is told at length in Ovid and in Gower,[39] raising the question of precisely *how* Shakespeare came by these narratives.

Whether or not he had access to all of them in book form, there is clearly some circumstantial evidence of selection at work that involved the shaping of existing stories to what we might infer is a particular dramatic purpose. This is what Bullough refers to as 'watching Shakespeare the craftsman in his workshop'.[40] And there is more. Shakespeare 'was not academically learned', Bullough tells us, 'but vastly well-informed'. The dramatist drew from a very wide range of interests 'to vitalize his dialogue and imagery',[41] and some of this is evident in the Lorenzo–Jessica exchange, although the mixture is one that involves a combination of book learning, of the sort that Shakespeare's secondary education may have given him, knowledge that he gleaned from a variety of domains and popular dramatic stereotyping of the theatregrammatical kind.[42]

It is possible to argue that Lorenzo and Jessica are imprisoned in what Harold Bloom calls 'facticity' or 'the state of being caught up in a factuality or contingency which is an inescapable and unalterable context'.[43] Bloom goes on to claim that 'there is a brute contingency to all origins as such, and so the engendering of every tradition is absolutely arbitrary'.[44] From the reader or spectator's perspective, however, the apparently antithetical but connected categories of 'poetry and belief' lead to a negotiation between 'truth and meaning' that inaugurates what Bloom would call 'an excess, an overflow or emanation that we call originality'.[45] Indeed, he argues that it is because Shakespeare's principal resource and his originality lay in 'the presentation of persons', that '[w]e cannot see the originality of an originality that has become a contingency or facticity for us'.[46] This provides, it should be said in passing, a very different, much more pluralistic approach to 'meaning' from that of Hardin Craig's objective, which was to make 'manifest *what Shakespeare really means*' (my italics) since, for Craig especially, and for Bullough too, there is simply 'no doubt, in the minds of scholars at least, that Shakespeare's own meaning is the greatest of meanings and it is one the world needs'.[47] This sentiment, coming in the immediate aftermath of the Second World War, replicates the ideology of E.M.W. Tillyard's *The Elizabethan World Picture* (1943) and is part of the case to identify and emphasise the humanising influence of the Arts against the devastating consequences of a scientifically generated and devastating military technology.[48]

Bloom's terms 'contingency' and 'facticity' are part of a shared vocabulary with New Historicism,[49] and together they point towards a challenge to the alleged inertia generated from within what Greenblatt has called 'the conventional pieties of source study'.[50] It is difficult to determine, however, what Bloom means by the phrase 'brute contingency', since his Oedipal account of the struggle between 'strong poets' and their 'strong precursors' foregrounds 'anxieties of indebtedness' but says little about the more complex non-Freudian structures of desire, or indeed the pre-history of a Freudian symptomatic reading.[51] He proceeds, nevertheless, to except Shakespeare from his account on the grounds that he 'belongs to the giant age before the flood, before the anxiety of influence became central to poetic consciousness'.[52] It is important to emphasise that 'the giant age before the flood', to use Bloom's apocalyptic phrase, was not Freudian, but neither did the texts, narratives, proverbial utterances, and other elements of the long list that Bullough provides,[53] circulate in a neutral, or purely formal way. It would, of course, be possible to read Shakespeare's models and his 'authorities' such as Ovid, Plutarch, Seneca or Holinshed, for example, as strong poets or just strong writers, though not participants in an Oedipal struggle; but for Bullough, unlike Bloom, the artistic unconscious is instrumental rather than constitutive.[54] In addition, if indeed Shakespeare thought 'in quotations', then this iterability framed all aspects of artistic expression. It could be interpreted as something more than simple repetition, requiring investigation of the conditions of repeatability and the formal relations between what modern scholarship would identify as primary and secondary texts. But it could not, as Peter Lake and others have sought to show, be separated from the historical and social pressures that exerted themselves as shaping cultural and ideological forces upon the practising dramatist.

The Lorenzo–Jessica exchange from *The Merchant of Venice* traces a series of selected 'readings' that are, to be sure, collectively imbued with a dynamic and nuanced contingent force. They refer us to the characters' recent histories, but they also extend beyond this to a series of social issues and controversies, concerned with matters of miscegenation as well as with issues of desire and death. Taken together, this does provide us with glimpses of Shakespeare's creative imagination at work, but that imagination cannot be fully separated from the variable complex elements of the milieu that shaped it. This is exactly the point in relation to critical enquiry that Harold Bloom made ten years earlier when he sought, albeit tendentiously, to rescue 'origins' from critics who 'consign[ed] them disdainfully to those carrion-eaters of scholarship, the source hunters'.[55] Thus, far from being 'the elephant's graveyard of literary history',[56] what has been traditionally labelled 'source study' might offer a window into the activity (and possibly psychology) of the successful practising dramatist as he shapes, adapts and expands his frames of reference to generate new meanings, and is in turn shaped by them. To this extent, and notwithstanding its occasional expression in what is, for us, an outmoded critical vocabulary, Bullough was instinctively, perhaps even pragmatically, correct. Whether we can say categorically, with Bloom, that for the dramatist, 'the poet-in-a-poet is as desperately obsessed with poetic origins, generally despite himself, as the person-in-a-person at last becomes obsessed with personal origins',[57] is questionable, although both he and Greenblatt in their different ways attempt to breathe a kind of new life into the study of 'sources'. As is perhaps to be expected, Bullough does not theorise his position, but his instinctive pragmatism, which forces him to adjust his categories as he goes along, can be seen to jostle with a belief in authorial meaning that has since 1957 come under considerable strain.

Colin Burrow makes two important observations in this connection: firstly, that 'Shakespeare confused the sequence of texts that we have become accustomed to regard as "primary" and "secondary"', with the result being 'a creatively confused sense of literary chronology';[58] and secondly, that Shakespeare 'could make use of his classical reading because he did not have a dogmatic or programmatic attitude to it'.[59] It is possible to extend Burrow's second claim to cover the entire range of texts that in one form or another were circulating during Shakespeare's writing life. In a chapter contributed to a collection of essays entitled *Shakespeare and Authority* (2018), Burrow suggests that we should abandon the term 'source' whose usage he traces to Charlotte Lennox's eighteenth-century collections, *Shakespeare Illustrated, or the Novels and Histories on which the plays of Shakespeare are founded* (1753–54), in favour of 'authority', a term that has considerable added thematic and topographical power in a number of the plays.[60]

Burrow's usage of the term 'authority' relies on the gloss provided in *OED* 1: 'the power or right to enforce obedience; moral or legal supremacy; the right to command or give an ultimate decision'. This definition presupposes a qualitative judgement concerning the 'supremacy' of one or a series of texts over others, and suggests something much stronger than the term 'influence' that Burrow deploys in his book. For example, the chapter in his book on Ovid begins: 'Writers don't become influential by accident. They have to mean something to the people who read them and usually that results from affinities which they and their writings appear to have with their readers or with their interests.'[61] While this softens considerably the discourse that emanates from the determining concept of the 'source', 'influence' still assumes a predominantly literary hierarchy and reaffirms the quasi-political gloss on 'authority' that Kojève teased out. It is not unreasonable to suppose that the appearance of, say, classical texts in the late sixteenth century educational curriculum was 'authorised', insofar as they provided models to be imitated, but it is another matter altogether to suggest that this structure of 'authority' was carried over unquestioningly into Shakespeare's professional life, and into the theatre, and was sustained there. The problem lies in the semantic link between 'authority' and the 'author' that needs more radical revision if we are either to maintain it, or to dispense with the concept of the 'source' as a heuristic category altogether. It also requires us to produce a more convincing theoretical model of the circulation of texts. The question revolves initially around the *use* to which pre-existing narratives, dramatic and non-dramatic forms and styles could be put, and the ways in which they were internalised by writers straddling the differential impulses to produce allegory, or to negotiate in more complex, less obviously imitative ways the problematics of representation.

For over half a century, *The Narrative and Dramatic Sources of Shakespeare* (1957–75) has been the main authority documenting the texts upon which Shakespeare is generally thought to have depended in the process of constructing his plays and poems. Bullough's categorisations are shown to have evolved as the occasion demands, providing the models for continual expansion. The over-riding *telos* of the project seems to have been to trace Shakespeare's own texts back to their 'sources' or origins in order to locate and clarify the permanent, trans-historical 'truths' that they embody. The linkage between 'source' and 'truth' savours of a kind of textual theology, designed to return the texts, as we have already seen, to the moments of their creation. Implicit in Bullough's method was the recognition of a dynamic interaction between 'text' and 'source', and a linear, hierarchical arrangement whose over-determining 'authority' was, in purely empirical terms, variable. Moreover, his primary emphasis is on narrative *content* and 'plot', occasionally on theatrical texts, and only implicitly on cultural *context*, or what Lake calls 'congruence', as keys to what in traditional terms we would call 'influence', although it has to be said that the categorisations he evolved were extremely prescient. From the outset Bullough was aware of the possibility of 'multiple sources'.[62] But his adoption of the category of 'analogue' indicates unease with the more straightforward linear derivations that inform the categories of 'probable source', 'source' and 'possible source'. By the time he had published the final volume (8) in 1975, his practical methodology had become more flexible, although the abiding belief was that Shakespeare was always 'conscious' of his own creative decisions, no matter where individual details came from.[63] This image of an almost fully conscious and intentional creative artist, is somewhat at odds both with Muir's identification of a Shakespearean 'unconscious' and with Emrys Jones's suggestion that 'Shakespeare thought and felt in quotations',[64] and indeed with Bullough's own admission of the operation of the dramatist's mental faculties. The model of 'authority' that seems to have underpinned his critical discourse was, however, more complicated than that formulated by what Kojève, in another, more abstract philosophical context, describes as 'the purest case of the Authority of the Father considered as the "authority" of the "cause" over the effect'.[65] It is also significantly an advance on Harold Bloom's post-Enlightenment account of 'intra-poetic relationships as parallels of [Freudian] family romance',[66] where '[t]he profundities of poetic influence cannot be reduced to source study, to the history of ideas, to the patterning of images'.[67]

In his 'General conclusions', Bullough surveys the work of earlier editors and commentators, from Gerald Langbaine and John Dennis onwards, all of whom 'pointed out particular points of his [Shakespeare's] indebtedness to classical and Renaissance authors'.[68] He notes Richard Farmer (1767), 'who was the first to insist on the importance of minor Tudor writers for the elucidation of the text', and identifies a 'new school' that followed early editors of Shakespeare such as Rowe, Pope, Theobald, Hanmer and Johnson,

> whose acquaintance with what has been called 'black letter literature' was extensive enough to produce a decided revolution in Shakespearean commentary. Capell, Steevens, Malone, Reed, Douce, are the representatives of the later school. The first school [Rowe *et al.*] contained the most brilliant men; the second, the most painstaking commentators.[69]

Bullough then charts the rapid expansion of scholarly interest in 'historical and literary background' during the nineteenth and early twentieth centuries both in terms of making ancillary material more generally available and in extending enquiry into the European origins of some texts, as evidenced in Albert Cohn's raising of 'the spectre of the *Ur-Hamlet* in Germany' that incited 'inquiries into the origins of other pieces performed by the "English Comedians" in seventeenth-century Germany'.[70] What follows anticipates the denigration of traditional source study that, as we saw earlier, Bullough blames upon an expanding professionalisation of the field.[71] All readers of Shakespearean texts who pay attention to the wealth of historical, critical, literary and cultural material that surrounds them will immediately identify with Bullough's acknowledgement of the scholarly value to be derived from identifying 'sources'. But he is caught between what he calls 'the study of Shakespeare's literary origins [that] fell into disrepute',[72] and the claim that source study is the first step along the path of the journey to discover the dramatist's 'methods of composition'. In the light of comments by Muir and Jones, 'methods' may be misleading to the extent that, as we have seen, they presuppose a writer fully in control of his intentions. However, the dismissive comment that Bullough quotes from Walter Raleigh's *Shakespeare* that nominally challenges his own

The legacy of Geoffrey Bullough 57

claim that '[w]hat he added to the story was himself; and a comparison of what he found with what he left forces us to the conclusion that his choice of books *was largely accidental*' (my italics),[73] is not too far from his own estimation. Raleigh clearly chose a different aspect of the Romantic Shakespeare to emphasise, but in Plutarch he found one exception to his general rule. The 'more perceptive' T.S. Eliot was more to Bullough's liking, although his proviso that 'we must, *if* we go into the matter at all, inform ourselves of the exact proportion of invention, borrowing, and adaptation in the plot' (my italics).[74] Touchstone's '*if*' serves Eliot well here. But Bullough's paraphrase of an Italian Marxist philosopher, Benedetto Croce, reinforces the bold but not altogether novel quest for 'the moment of vision' (origin), 'the process of composition' (linear progression) and the ultimate perception of the apprehension of 'the work of art in its totality'.[75]

Some ten years after the completion of Bullough's project, David Quint embarked on a historicist analysis of what he called 'the topos of the *source*, the confluent origin of the rivers of the earth', which he believed to be both 'a literal geographic place and a symbolic commonplace'.[76] He contended that, historically, the Renaissance 'was seeking to re-examine – and represent – the source of its fictions' authority', and that a tension had emerged between 'non-historical transcendent truth which had been advanced for the text by traditional modes of allegorical reading and writing' and 'alternative allegorical and historicist readings of the text'.[77] Quint identifies a tendency during the Renaissance to acknowledge an underlying unity and coherence implied in the quasi-religious concept of 'source', while at the same time performing 'a critical examination of that culture's textual sources of authority that would ultimately challenge all forms of received truth'.[78] Under the pressures of humanism, what Quint describes as the new 'Renaissance appreciation of individual creativity' posed a serious challenge:

> For if the individual author was to be defined historically, his creation fell into the realm of historical contingency, at a remove from any timeless or fixed standard of truth. Historically de-limited, the meaning and authority of the text might be just as relative as its literary style.[79]

After a careful examination of a wide range of European literary texts – he omits any mention of Shakespeare – Quint draws the following conclusion:

> Seeking authorizing origins in the past, Renaissance culture encountered its own human historicity. The consequences of this discovery were felt with a special force in its literature, for it was in literature that the contest between individual innovation and the authority of tradition was recast as a struggle for independence from sacred authority, and it was in literature that Renaissance thought first achieved an autonomous, secular identity. But the very nature of this achievement may have obscured the extent to which it contributed to an intellectual revolution. By obtaining a cultural autonomy from systems of authorized truth, literature gave up its right to be authoritative.[80]

His concern is specifically with fiction and poetry, although the epistemological foundations that his study challenges still survive in the traditional usage of the term 'source' as a means of establishing a coherent account of the linear progression from origin to text and from one text to another. The struggle for 'cultural autonomy' that Quint maps out here bears something of a resemblance to Bloom's anxiety of influence, although it does offer an account of the rise of the concept of 'authorship' in the early seventeenth century.[81] If literature, firmly embedded in a technology of writing, could, in its acquisition of 'cultural autonomy', forfeit its claim to 'authority', then just imagine the pressure exerted upon authority by the mixed modes of representation that were a feature of the public theatre. Indeed, had Quint turned his attention to the English public theatre in the late sixteenth century, he would have found even more complicated examples of the very kind of historical contingency whose own complex pathways his study was at pains to excavate. It is this level of contingency that challenges the veracity of the term 'source'.

Bullough's impressive selection of the varying categories of 'source' texts that lay behind Shakespeare's plays, ranges across the gamut of literary and, to a lesser extent, cultural history. The difficulty is compounded by the growing reputation from the late seventeenth century onwards of 'Shakespeare' as a repository of 'truth'. Thus, in a sense not too far from Quint's position, the practical attempt to situate Shakespeare in a linear history of the cultural transmission of 'texts' does much to undermine the claims made on the dramatist's behalf of his unique access to transcendent truth. If Shakespeare is the 'authority' by which we measure creative achievement, then the examination of the semiotic and semantic foundations of that 'authority' threaten to undermine the force of its 'originality' and its cultural supremacy over time. Moreover, if he is, as Quint's historicist argument and others would imply, the 'origin' of his own meaning, then this anticipates the shift to an authorial sense of possession. This is, of course, something that it is difficult to pin on a Shakespeare who, unlike Jonson or Marston, appears to have had very little, if any, involvement in the printing or sale of his plays.

We know from the history of printing that during Shakespeare's lifetime written texts circulated widely, though not in large numbers, and we can speculate about which of them Shakespeare read, or even owned. But we need to liberate these texts from a limited and limiting linear structure that demands that they exert something that resembles a patriarchal power over writers and readers or indeed spectators. It is the case that these texts collide in the day-to-day practical transactions of writing and reception, although what has been missing, and what Bullough's linear account of transmission glosses over, is that the collision of technologies that emerges as 'writing' is transformed into 'speech' in the early modern theatre. A brief example of this collision appears in *Love's Labour's Lost*:

> HOLOFERNES. The deer was, as you know, *sanguis*, in blood, ripe as the pomewater, who now hangeth like a jewel in the ear of *caelo*, the sky, the welkin, the heaven, and anon falleth like a crab on the face of *terra*, the soil, the land, the earth.
> NATHANIEL. Truly, Master Holofernes, the epithets are sweetly varied, like a scholar at the least: but, sir, I assure ye it was a buck of the first head.
> HOLOFERNES. Sir Nathaniel, *haud credo*.
> DULL. 'Twas not an 'auld grey doe', twas a pricket.
> HOLOFERNES. Most barbarous intimation! Yet a kind of insinuation, as it were, replication, or rather *ostentare*, to show, as it were, his inclination, after his undressed, unpolished, uneducated,

    unpruned, untrained, or rather unlettered, or ratherest
    unconfirmed fashion, to insert again my *haut credo* for a deer.
DULL. I said the deer was not a 'auld grey doe', 'twas a Pricket.
HOLOFERNES. Twice-sod simplicity, *bis*. *Coctus*! O, thou monster
    Ignorance, how deformed dost thou look!
NATHANIEL. He hath not eat paper, as it were; he hath not drunk
    ink. His intellect is not replenished; he is only an animal, only
    sensible in the duller parts.

(4.2.3–27)

Here two modes of imitation, the literary and the vernacular, confront each other in a play that turns on the difference between the two, and the vibrancy of the latter. For all their rhetorical eloquence, Holofernes and Sir Nathaniel do not succeed in approaching Dull's blunt 'truth' as the world of 'writing', with its reliance on a very stilted form of imitation, is shown not to engage with everyday experience but to distort it. Here the clash of texts points to a clash of social positions that serves to underpin the comic tension of the exchange, to the point where we are not sure who is the butt of comedy.

In an attempt to correct some of the omissions that have been inherited from the traditional discourse of source study, a few commentators have ventured into the post-structuralist terrain of intertextuality as a means of loosening the linearity of Bullough's model. Stephen J. Lynch's *Shakespearean Intertextuality: Studies in Selected Sources and Plays* (1997) begins promisingly with the assertion that: 'Shakespeare's plays are no longer seen as being based on a few assorted borrowings, but are now seen as interventions in pre-existent fields of textuality. The old notion of particular and distinct sources has given way to new notion of boundless and heterogeneous intertextuality.'[82] At no point does he engage with the issues raised in *Love's Labour's Lost*, sticking only to plays such as *As You Like It*, *King Lear*, *Pericles* and *The Winter's Tale* that can be paired with earlier 'sources'. On the surface this seems like a subversive gesture, although Lynch overstates the freedom that the apparent liberation from source study offers. He goes some way to problematising the figure of 'the author' in plays such as *Pericles*,[83] but his account of intertextuality is, however, more indebted than he realises to the traditional vocabulary of 'sources'; for example, in his final chapter, revealingly entitled 'Source texts and contexts', he concludes:

> Consistently Shakespeare develops not merely new modes of perception, but multiple modes of perception. *Working within the limits and constraints of his source texts* and cultural contexts, Shakespeare demonstrated a slippery ability to move in a few directions at once, creating multiple dimensions of text within the same text – although, as revisionist, Shakespeare always enjoyed an edge, starting with rich and highly suggestive material, and reworking it into richer and more suggestive material.[84] (my italics)

Lynch's concept of 'multiple modes of perception' is appropriately pragmatic but the imposition of 'limits and constraints' begs an important question about precisely how such limitations were employed. The notion of Shakespeare as 'revisionist' reactivates the principle of intention, at the same time that it obscures, as we shall see, the 'unconscious' element of intertextuality. The result is an uncomfortable mixture of the traditional and the innovative, a repetition of Bullough's principles to which is added a general theory of the circulation of texts implied in a domestication of the term 'intertextuality'.

In another study that appropriates the same term, Murray J. Levith's *Shakespeare's Cues and Prompts* (2007) addresses directly, though in a limited fashion, the theory of intertextuality. He reasons from a small number of texts, only to collapse the discussion into the familiar practice of proposing 'new' sources and the meanings that they help to generate. This reversion to a familiar strategy, whereby 'new' sources are 'discovered' by the scholar and then aligned with an assertion that the dramatist *must* have been aware of them, is regressive considering Levith's post-structural emphasis on the composition and circulation of texts. Kristeva's account of intertextuality, which should be central to his argument, is breezily dismissed as positing 'a far-reaching complex of imbedded ideologies, sociologies and cultural nuances and complexities'.[85] Levith then proceeds to argue that 'Barthes distinguishes, as does Kristeva, between sources or influences and intertextuality', and he invokes Barthes's 'myth of filiation' within whose conceptual orbit Shakespeare 'would be diminished to a revisionary editor of inherited texts, cultural constructs and other multi-faceted cues and prompts *rather than an autonomous playwright and artist*' (my italics).[86] Levith's crass oversimplification omits the longstanding debate about Shakespeare's 'originality', and he seems to have failed to understand the contradiction between his invocation of post-structuralist principles and the insistence upon the figure of the 'autonomous playwright and artist'. Levith's selective deployment of post-structural theory, therefore, collides with a cherished mythology that owes much to the theory of the author as a free, autonomous subject, matched sporadically by the critic's capacity for identifying occasional indeterminacies of meaning. Of course, as we shall see shortly, the principles of intertextuality explode the myth of 'filiation' as well as challenge the autonomy (and by implication, the 'authority') of the playwright and artist. Intertextuality, then, is not a concept that can be easily co-opted into the existing hierarchical discourse of source study, nor can it be used to reduce the complex cultural and political status of the writer.

Indeed, this is the very point that Kristeva makes in her book *Revolution in Poetic Language* (1984), where she defines intertextuality in the following way:

> The term *inter-textuality* denotes this transposition of one (or several) sign system(s) into another; but since this term has often been understood in the banal sense of 'study of sources' we prefer the term *transposition* because it specifies that the passage from one signifying system to another demands a new articulation of the thetic – of enunciative and denotative positionality.[87]

This mobility of positionality that Kristeva traces to the semiotic *chora*, located at the centre of the female body, has come to stand for a more general account of the ways in which texts engage with each other, thereby disrupting the prospect of unitary meaning and endowing the hierarchical organisation of texts with a narrative that exposes more explicitly a patriarchal symbolic order.[88] Stripped of its feminist political objectives, the term intertextuality can be made to sit reasonably comfortably with the concept of authorship, thereby allowing the debate to slide back into the very familiar study of 'sources' and 'authorities' from which it claims to have escaped. Kristeva's account is a more gender-specific version

The legacy of Geoffrey Bullough

of Roland Barthes's absolute and implicitly class-inflected statement in 'The Death of the Author' of the destruction of authority in the very act of writing itself:

> Writing is the destruction of every voice, of every point of origin. Writing is that neutral, composite, oblique space where one subject slips away, the negative where all identity is lost, starting with the very identity of the body writing.[89]

Barthes's definition of 'the text' is that of 'a multi-dimensional space in which a variety of writings, none of them original, blend and clash'.[90] It is important to note here that he cannot be enlisted convincingly by those who wish to claim that Shakespeare's mind was full of quotations to which he had ready access, and that was identified as the source of his originality. Such domestications of intertextuality stop short of exploring the process of production of meanings and the consequences that follow from it.

Barthes presents a very real challenge to what Michel Foucault in his essay 'What Is an Author' asserts as the modern identity of the literary work 'dominated by the sovereignty of the author'.[91] Foucault's focus is upon a criticism that 'has been concerned for some time now with aspects of text not fully dependent on the notion of an individual creator'.[92] But more importantly, he relocates those elements of the individual writer's '"profundity" or "creative power", his intentions or the original inspiration manifested in writing' as 'projections, in terms always more or less psychological of our way of handling texts'.[93] The argument moves a little closer to Shakespeare with Foucault's claim that '[m]odern criticism, in its desire to "recover" the author from a work, employs devices strongly reminiscent of Christian exegesis when it wishes to prove the value of a text by ascertaining the holiness of its author'.[94] However, he does not wish to rule out completely some form of 'return'; indeed, he wishes to give the process 'its proper specificity', which, he argues,

> characterises the initiation of discursive practices. If we return, it is because of a basic and constructive omission, an omission that is not the result of accident or incomprehension. In effect the act of initiation is such, in its essence, that it is inevitably subjected to its own distortions; that which displays this act and derives from it is, at the same

time, the root of its divergencies and travesties. This non-accidental omission must be regulated by precise operations that can be situated, analysed, and reduced in a return to the act of initiation.[95]

For Foucault this always involves 'a return to a text in itself, specifically, to a primary and unadorned text with particular attention to those things registered in the interstices of the text, its gaps and absences'. But this is emphatically *not* a 'return' in the accepted sense of the term, where it fulfils the function of 'a historical supplement'; indeed – and this opens up the possibility for creative appropriation and innovation – 'it is an effective and necessary means of transforming discursive practice'.[96] Against Barthes's concern to do away with the figure of the 'author' altogether, Foucault wants to hold on to the category as a 'function' and to acknowledge some of the ways in which the 'return' tends 'to reinforce the enigmatic link between an author and his works'.[97] The theoretical work of Barthes and Foucault provides a critique of Bullough's persistent emphasis upon the centrality of the figure of the author despite his practical acknowledgement that the authorial subject is not quite as unified or organic as it appears to be. Viewed in this way it is easy to see how intertextuality can *appear* to be a logical consequence of identifying precursor texts embedded in primary texts.

In what is perhaps the most persistent application of the concept of intertextuality to Renaissance drama, Janet Clare has drawn attention to 'imitation, borrowing and competition in the ambience of Shakespeare's theatre', and she has sought to apply Stephen Greenblatt's principle of the 'circulation of social energy' to 'the exchange of theatrical energy ... as the matter and practice of plays were trafficked amongst playwrights and amongst communities of spectators'.[98] Clare offers 'invention' as a deliberate element in the process of 'converting and re-interpreting',[99] which, along with 'imitation' and 'borrowing', defines the practice of theatrical composition.[100] Clare cites the criticism, variously ascribed to Henry Chettle or Robert Greene, of the early Shakespeare as 'an upstart playwright who displays no colours of his own',[101] and her claim here is that Shakespeare was being accused of mere borrowing. This is not quite the view of 'imitation' with which Puttenham begins his analysis of poetry and poetic styles, or that modern

The legacy of Geoffrey Bullough

commentators favour; for Puttenham, the poet is 'both a maker, and a counterfaitor: and Poesie an art not only of making but also of imitation', where 'imitation' is an expression of 'the true and lively of every thing is set before him'.[102] Indeed, Thomas Nashe's praise of the figure of Talbot in *1 Henry VI* offers a much fuller gloss on the practice of mimesis with the following suggestion: 'How would it have joyed brave *Talbot* (the terror of the French) to thinke that after he had lyne two hundred yeares in his Tombe, he should triumphe againe on the Stage, and have his bones newe embalmed with the tears of ten thousand spectators at last (at severall times), who in the Tragedian that represents his person, imagine they behold him fresh bleeding.'[103] The act of making is clearly a conscious one, as indeed is the act of borrowing, but cast in Clare's discursive frame, intertextuality is hard to distinguish from allusion or quotation. The danger of treating the variety of intertexts that comprise a Shakespeare play as wholly the product of the dramatist's conscious choices, is to readmit the modern category of the 'author' by the back door, and to regard the assembly of texts as authoritative and determining sources from which the writer always makes a conscious choice. This is a long way from Kristeva's definition of intertextuality.

These distinctions are of particular value in seeking to differentiate between the identity of an 'author' such as Shakespeare and the discursive practices that we may be able to trace through his plays. It also raises the question of what we can attribute to conscious agency, and what might be the poet's 'unconscious', political or otherwise. To treat the 'author' function critically is not to diminish the dramatist's status, although it challenges many of the assumptions upon which that fabricated status rests, not the least of which involves challenging traditional assertions of 'authenticity' and 'originality'.[104] It also allows us to get closer to the distinction between the writer as a conscious agent, and the historically and culturally over-determined operations of the writerly unconscious. This is not a question of dismissing precursor texts whose presence critics have identified in Shakespeare's plays. Rather it is to see them in a context in which the competing technologies of orality and literacy jostle with each other in the process of producing meanings. Traditional source study tends to flatten out that tension when applied to a form embedded in oral culture, and to recuperate the figure of the author for an audience of readers for whom theatrical performance is a secondary activity.

This evisceration of the category of the 'author' does not, however, eliminate entirely the agency of the writer, the space where decisions are taken, where the limits of discursive propriety are transgressed and where the 'act of initiation', to use Foucault's phrase, involves 'distortions' and 'travesties'. We might see, in the example from *The Merchant of Venice* to which we referred earlier, the manner in which in a series of narratives, from Homer, Ovid, Chaucer and Gower, involving distortions and travesties, are crystallised in the problematical relationship between Jessica and Lorenzo. This would be to reduce this complex series of references to a single authorial meaning that as critics we can excavate. The result is an obscuring of our own constitutive role in the production of meaning and hence our role in what Terence Hawkes suggests is our appropriation of 'the words of which they [the plays] are made' as materials that 'we *use* ... in order to generate meaning'.[105]

The competitive listing of examples in *The Merchant of Venice* descends into a kind of literary game, and one that encourages a proliferation of meanings. But it is one that is not without risk, since it requires Lorenzo to finally rescue the situation, as it were ideologically, by invoking a cosmic order from whose orbit the post-lapsarian actors are distanced:

> Sit, Jessica. Look how the floor of heaven
> Is thick inlaid with patens of bright gold.
> There's not the smallest orb which thou behold'st
> But in his motion like an angel sings,
> Still choiring to the young-eyed cherubins.
> Such harmony is in immortal souls,
> But whilst this muddy vesture of decay
> Doth grossly close it in, we cannot hear it.
>
> (5.2.58–65)

Editors, of course, feel duty-bound to trace these references, and to gloss them, and critics read into this gesture a model of the play's aesthetic harmony. But in this, as in other cases, they form a palimpsest, or a series of textual layers that are symptomatic not only of the expanded formal layering of the text of *The Merchant of Venice* itself but also of our capacity to recover and recognise the literary analogues that the lovers invoke and that are here subsumed into a quasi-religious experience. The reference to 'patens', and from there to a moral universe governed by the 'harmony' that is the music of 'immortal souls' projects the lovers into roles that are adjuncts to a fuller literary aesthetic that the modern reader brings to the text. In the post-lapsarian world ('this muddy vesture of decay') it is a moral harmony that is beyond the reach of the lovers, a justification, perhaps, for the imperfect literary and theatrical liaisons that they invoke, and that hints critically at what early modern audiences might have recognised as indications of miscegeny. The layering that occurs at this point in the play resists the scholarly attempts to distribute sources into their respective compartments, nor will the 'origins' in and of themselves determine the meanings that this particular dramatic context can be made to generate.

The problem is what *we* make of this textual layering, and perhaps the most exhaustive study of the variety of the relationships between texts, and the meanings that are thereby generated is Gérard Genette's *Palimpsests: Literature in the Second Degree* (1997). His overarching categories are those of 'architextuality', which he describes as 'the entire set of general or transcendent categories – types of discourse, modes of enunciation, literary genres – from which emerges each singular text', and 'trans-textuality' defined as 'all that sets the text in a relationship, whether obvious or concealed, with other texts'.[106] In Genette's taxonomy, intertextuality is a sub-division of architextuality and is described as 'a relationship of co-presence between two texts or among several texts: that is to say eidetically and typically as the actual presence of one text within another'.[107] This is a less gender-inflected definition than that proposed by Kristeva. At one extreme Genette identifies 'plagiarism' or 'allusion', and he distinguishes these categories from 'paratextuality', which is the sum total of all that surrounds the printed text by way of subtitles, prefaces and other ancillary material.[108] At the other extreme is 'architextuality', which is not entirely deliberate but which signals 'a relationship that is completely silent' and that is of a 'purely taxonomic nature', involving matters that have to do with the classification of genres.[109] The taxonomic classification of texts involves the identification of their generic affiliations, such as whether a text is a comedy, a tragedy, a novel or a poem. This is important because 'generic perception is known to guide and determine to a considerable degree the readers' expectations, and thus their reception of the work'. A third and final category is labelled as 'hypertextuality', which he defines as 'any relationship uniting a text B (which I shall call the *hypertext*) to an earlier text A (I shall, of course, call it the *hypotext*) upon which it is grafted in a manner that is not that of a commentary'; he also speaks of an example of 'text B not speaking of text A at all, but being unable to exist, as such, without A, from which it originates through a process I shall provisionally call *transformation*'.[110] In some cases, the pressure of the hypotext exerts direct influence on its successor, but in others it is the pressure of the genre that requires to be recognised by both writer and (in this case) reader alike. Indeed, he insists that 'the less explicit the hypertextuality of a given work, the more does its analysis depend on constitutive judgement: that is, on the reader's interpretive decision', although he is also of the view that this relationship is not programmatic but 'more socialised, more openly contractual, and pertaining to a conscious and organised pragmatics'.[111]

In his essay 'The Slaughterhouse of Literature', Franco Moretti makes the point that the various elements of literary evolution (he uses the model of the tree and its various branches), are not generated by texts: 'the branches are the result of the twists and turns of a *device*, of a unit much *smaller* than the text. Conversely the branches are also part of something much *larger* than any text, which is the *genre*' (original italics).[112] Moretti then invokes Fernand Braudel's three modes of 'history' as an explanation of (a) the entwining of the text 'within contemporary events', (b) the much slower evolution of 'form' that he thinks is 'repeatable', and (c) those elements that survive over centuries. These three categories account for what is 'unique to a given text', what is 'repeatable' and what extends across '*the longue durée*'.[113] But it still remains caught in a net from which the comparatively neutral figure of the observer is excluded.

Genette's loosening of the links between the elements of a palimpsest is more radical than Moretti's wishing to cling on to the linear and hierarchical model of the tree-root as source. Genette's is a less extreme version of the layering of texts that we find in Deleuze and Guattari's *A Thousand Plateaus: Capitalism and Schizophrenia* (1987), where any traces of linearity and hierarchy in the arrangement of elements within a text are dispensed with altogether. The figure that Deleuze and Guattari adopt is the 'rhizome', which they define as a 'multiplicity [that] never allows itself to be over-coded, never has available a supplementary dimension over and above its number of lines'.[114] The challenge to unity that this presents exposes 'a power takeover in the multiplicity by the signifier',[115] and a politics implicit in the linear and hierarchical model.

The example from *The Merchant of Venice* – a text designed for the theatre and not the study – demonstrates a hypertextual connection between a series of imperfectly connected analogical texts that are more than simply allusions but that are not architexts. The burden here is placed upon 'the reader's interpretive decision' and upon 'a conscious and organised pragmatics' that is 'socialised' and 'more openly contractual', each of which spans the cultural *and* the professional domains. In Shakespeare's play the spectator is invited to make an investment in the dramatist's 'consciously organised pragmatics' and to share in them as part of an open communal contract. What the spectator does not know or recognise in the allusions can, to some extent, be compensated for by the contextual knowledge that the relationship between Lorenzo and Jessica remains problematical: an elopement has been legitimised in order to validate the Christian myth of the Jew's conversion.[116] Except that the examples chosen are never quite as analogical as a critical discourse predicated upon the principle of organic unity might suggest. Indeed, there is something quite unsettling about the analogues as they follow on from each other, to the extent that they approach what Deleuze and Guattari describe as 'a strangely polyvocal kind of writing' that is 'never a biunivocalised, linearized one'; it is a 'writing that ceaselessly composes and decomposes the chains into signs that have nothing that impels them to become signifying'. If, as Deleuze and Guattari suggest, 'the vocation of the sign is to produce desire',[117] then the exchange between Lorenzo and Jessica threatens to frustrate that vocation in its exposure of the possibility of chaos that threatens the marital harmony of the couple. While we may *read* for unity at this point, the result is disunity and disharmony.

To return to Genette, his primary concern is with the categories of 'parody' and 'travesty', both of which are dependent, in the main, upon prior knowledge of pre-existing hierarchically arranged texts. But within the context of the Renaissance public theatre, what is 'socialised' and what is 'more openly contractual' cannot simply be isolated as, or reduced to, a 'traffic' between plays or even between the parts of plays. Although trafficking is a necessary part of a much more complex (and for a modern reader, more speculative) activity of identifying social pressures, the limits of writerly agency and the psychological contours of a historically and politically over-determined unconscious also play an important role. For Kristeva, crucial to her definition of an intertext is the eruption of an unconscious, primarily feminine force that, in structural terms, the symbolic order can never manage to contain. The consequence is not, however, as Maria Margaroni has shown, a reductive, 'nostalgic return to an archaic maternal origin',[118] but a problematisation of the theoretical fiction of origin per se. This suggests that meaning(s) can never be fully and completely intentional, whether inherent in the text or whether supplied by the reader. Moreover, all texts inadvertently leave traces of sub-textual matter that is constitutive of the identification of male and female but that also generates new, less orderly possibilities. Read back into the political operations of patriarchy, this identification offers a key to an early modern unconscious that is not Freudian though it may appear to share some of the characteristics of Freud's analytical language, and it is not something that forms part of Bullough's own much looser conception of the 'unconscious'. Indeed, the emphasis on 'sources' points not to a multiplicity of narrative lines but to a hierarchy that supports the notion of the compiler's fantasy of deity. Or perhaps even more disturbing, the fantasy of being present at the moment of the text's conception, implying the idea of the source-hunter–patriarch as voyeur. The idea of 'resource' rather than 'source' does much to respond to the multiplicity *within* the text that unravels any gestures it may make through its adoption of a specific genre to an aesthetic teleology. It is worth recalling that *The Merchant of Venice* does not end unproblematically with 'concord of sweet sounds' (5.1.64), but with an imperative that accompanies the striking vision of 'the man that hath no music in himself', who

> Is fit for treasons, stratagems and spoils;
> The motions of his spirit are dull as night
> And his affections dark as Erebus.
> Let no such man be trusted. Mark the music.
>
> (5.1.85–88)

*

In much of the theory that has been invoked so far, the primary concern has been with literary texts and the various categories of trace that they leave in the hypertexts that are generated from them. *Hamlet* offers an intriguing and complex example of the various combinations that we have identified so far. Bullough nominates some fifteen texts that he divides into sources (one), probable sources (one), possible sources (three), analogues (seven), possible historical sources (one) and possible historical allusions (one). The genealogy of the *Hamlet* narrative stretches back to Saxo Grammaticus's *Historiae Danicae* (*c*.1208) that appeared as part of his *Danorum Regum heroumque Historiae*.[119] The *Danorum* was published in Latin in 1514 in Paris, in 1534 in Basle and in 1576 in Frankfurt. A translation from Latin into French by François de Belleforest as *Le Cinquiesme Tome Des Histoires Tragiques* ... appeared in editions in 1570, 1576, 1582 and 1601. It was from the 1582 Paris edition of *Le Cinquiesme Tome Des Histoires Tragiques* that Thomas Pavier produced *The Hystorie of Hamblet* in 1608.[120] It was not translated into English until 1894, but it appears as one of two sources in Sir Israel Gollancz's *The Sources of Hamlet* ([1926] 1967). Despite identifying it as a 'source', Bullough thinks that the lost play of *Hamlet* – the so-called *ur-Hamlet* that was known in 1589 and thought to be by Thomas Kyd – 'was based on the French *novella*, and I see no proof that either Shakespeare or his predecessor used Saxo Grammaticus at all'.[121] This raises a fundamental question concerning the conditions under which the *Hamlet* story was transmitted and the cultural filters through which it passed. Particularly puzzling is the connection between Q1 *Hamlet* (1603) and the German *Der bestrafte Brudermord* that was unprinted but that Bullough thinks was 'the degenerate version of an English play probably taken over to the Continent by English actors before 1626, when a *Tragoedia von Hamlet einen Prinz in Danemark* was performed in Dresden by Green's company of English players'.[122] The problems with timeline here are perplexing, particularly regarding the business of identifying the provenance of Q1 of Shakespeare's play. Did the German prose version of the play that emerged in 1626 reflect an earlier lost version that would thereby elevate it from the status of 'analogue' to that of 'source' in Bullough's lexicon? Or were these versions two of a number that circulated before the appearance of Q2 *Hamlet* in 1605? That the *Hamlet* story was popular, and that aspects of it were alluded to from the late 1580s onwards and long after Shakespeare's death is not in question. Elements of the narrative are dispersed across a range of texts, and they also appear in different combinations in the three texts attributed to Shakespeare. Bullough collects together texts that are both 'influential' and 'confluential' and what he labels 'Probable Historical Allusions' comprise a series of reports from the *Calendar of State Papers: Domestic* referring to the accession of Christian IV to the Danish throne (1588), to rumours of a Danish invasion (1598), to an engagement between Christian, his brother and some English sailors (1598–1600), and to a reference in a letter of 1597 from Robert Cecil to the Earl of Essex detailing the visit of a Polish ambassador that includes reference to an act of piracy by 'some of those in your companie that have robbed the Dantsickers and many other merchants'.[123] These historical and contextual elements, as they might have stimulated elements of *Hamlet*, depend for their relevance very much upon Shakespeare's intimate knowledge of matters of Elizabethan diplomacy, and they also assume a wide and detailed level of popular knowledge concerning the visit of Christian of Denmark to London in 1588. In the letter from John Petit to Peter Halms of 1598, reference is made to the secret agreement with James VI concerning the conditions of his possible accession to the English throne, to the King of Denmark's brother bringing troops to aid James and to the resurrection of 'a certain old payment which England was accustomed to give Denmark'.[124] These allusions furnish something of a historical context for the emphasis upon Denmark as a politically charged geographical location, but they extend beyond the tripartite categorisation of material that Moretti deploys from Braudel.

At a purely formal level we might, perhaps, allocate to Moretti/Braudel's category (a) Shakespeare's immediate theatrical environment and its historical context and pressures, the elements of which Janet Clare teases out thoroughly, although we would need to extend its parameters considerably to take in the wider cultural milieu. To category (b) we would allocate the generic features of 'revenge tragedy' with its set of theatregrams that would open up a proximate history but would also extend to the larger cultural environment within which the 'taste' for this genre emerged. And to category (c) we might allocate the centuries-long history of 'tragedy', revived particularly through Newton's 1581 translation of Seneca, and the archetypal narratives that were transmitted across large tracts of time and which provided the models for Elizabethan dramatists to repeat and adapt. A further sub-set of this category would also be the retrospective 'history' of the genre down to the present that provides a framework for modern interpretation. 'Repeatability', implied in Moretti's category (c), is, however, an inadequate term since, as Genette argues, 'to reproduce is nothing, and imitating supposes a more complex operation, the completion of which raises imitation above mere reproduction; it becomes a new production – that of another text in the same style, of another message in the same code'.[125] To this we might add a more expanded, and less generically specific, version of Gilles Deleuze's observation in relation to comedy that, *pace* Marx: 'Comic repetition works by means of some defect, in the mode of the past properly so called.'[126] As we will see below, this points us towards 'defects' in the history of the *Hamlet* narrative, and in the evolving revenge genre, replete with the theatregrams that the form developed over time, and that Shakespeare's innovative, and perhaps more mimetically authentic, version capitalised on.

As a 'revenge' play, *Hamlet* reproduces some of the stylistic elements of the genre that Shakespeare had utilised in earlier plays such as *Titus Andronicus*, and that contemporaries such as Thomas Kyd had helped to make popular. The classical models were, of course, primarily Sophocles and Seneca, especially the latter, whose plays had been translated by Thomas Newton and published in 1581.[127]

However, in *The Spanish Tragedy*, as T.S. Eliot noted, 'the greater number of horrors are such as Seneca himself would not have tolerated'.[128] Newton's 1581 'Preface to the reader' of *Oedipus* draws attention to the 'moral' of the play that, by the time Shakespeare came to write *Hamlet*, might well have become commonplace:

> Marke thou rather what is ment by the whole course of the History: and frame thy lyfe free from such mischiefes, wherewith the World and this present is universally overwhelmed, The wrathful vengeance of God provoked, the Body plagued, the mynde and Conscience in midst of deepe devouring daungers most terribly assaulted, In such sort that I abhorre to write; ... As in this present Tragedy, and so forth in the processe of the whole history, thou maist right well perceive. Wherein thou shalt see a very expresse and lively Image of the inconstant change of fickle Fortune in the person of a Prince of passing Fame and Renown, midst whole fluds of earthly blisse: by meagre misfortune (nay rather by the deepe hidden secret Judgements of God) piteously plunged in most extreame miseries.[129]

To this variety of precursor texts we may add all of those plays that comprise the stage 'traffic' of the revenge genre and that help to suggest a range of possible innovatory practices. But we may also add less obvious quasi-medical texts, such as Thomas Hill's *The Moste pleasaunte Arte of the Interpretation of Dreames* (1576) or Timothie Bright's more formally analytical *A Treatise on Melancholy* (1584) that provide a different kind of cultural context.

The texts by Hill and Bright are indicative of the growing sophistication of Elizabethan concerns with psychology, the world of dreams and with what we would now call clinical depression. These were issues of wider cultural significance that could impact in various ways upon art forms such as the theatre that were preoccupied with representing 'personae', or indeed, what we might call the life of the emerging human subject. For example, Hill reprises the long history of 'dream', details of which occur in writings stretching from Plato, Aristotle and Lucretius, and during the early modern period from Montaigne and Francis Bacon, to Robert Burton's *The Anatomy of Melancholy* (1621). Shakespeare's periodic engagement with the world of dreams, prevalent in plays such as *The Taming of the Shrew* (c.1594), *A Midsummer Night's Dream* (c.1595) and in a play like *Macbeth* (c.1606), allows him in plays like *Hamlet* (*c*.1600), to engage with issues that are more fully explored in Hill and Bright. Indeed, in *Hamlet* sophisticated engagements with the world of dream, and the issues of disturbed sleep and nightmare, are integral to the play's complex ideological framework. Hill's account of the physiologically disturbed psyche 'engendred of the burning and great heate of the blood' leading to the sufferer who seems 'to laughe withoute cause',[130] might be used to illuminate facets the behaviour of the fictional Hamlet, or before him Titus Andronicus.

That Shakespeare *knew about* Hill is one thing, but that he had *read* him is open to question. Nonetheless, that both play and prose analysis tap into a much wider resource seems certain. Nor does it end there. For example, Hill's account of 'sleep' anticipates Shakespeare's various dramatic deployments of its effects in plays like *Othello* (*c*.1604), and *Macbeth*:

> Sleepe is the reste of the spyrites, and the waking, the vehemente motion of theym, and the vayne dreame is a certayne tremblinge and unperfit motione of theym. Therefores al are vayne dreames caused through the spirites lightlye moued. Whereof whyles we soundly sleepe, we then dreame nothinge at all.[131]

Hill draws on the section 'On Dreams' from Aristotle's *Parva Naturalia*, sometimes paraphrasing some of what appears there, but he also 'gathers together' – as the title page of *The Moste pleasaunte Arte of the Interpretation of Dreames* indicates – examples of dreams that he has assembled himself. In other words, Hill's text is itself a palimpsest of both philosophy and folk wisdom that circulated in the late sixteenth century.[132] It would also be convenient to think that Shakespeare knew A. Nevil's Preface to Thomas Newton's translation of Seneca's *Oedipus*, and that he recalled its recognisably Calvinistic sentiments concerning a secret providence:

> The wrathful vengeaunce of God provoked, the Body plagued, the mynde and Conscience in the midst of deepe devouring danger most terribly assaulted ... Wherein thou shalt see, a very expresse and lively Image of the inconstant change of fickle Fortune in the person of a Prince of passing Fame and Renown, midst whole fluds of earthly blisse: by meare misfortune (nay rather by the deepe hidden secret Judgements of God) piteously plunged in most extreme miseries.[133]

But it is just as likely that Nevil is simply repeating what by 1581 had become an Elizabethan theological commonplace.[134]

The relationship between Hill's accounts and the appearance of dreams in early modern drama is not linear or indeed hierarchical, but circular in that these accounts are part of a larger reservoir of popular knowledge that was available to the alert writer, and to which he could return as occasion demanded. In the case of Hill, who 'gathered' his examples, his text is mixed, sometimes acknowledging authorities and at others appearing to derive his examples either from his own empirical investigations or from folk wisdom brought into alignment with an obviously derivative medical knowledge.

We might say the same of Timothie Bright's much more formally sustained scholarly account, *A Treatise on Melancholie* (1586), in which appear statements such as those describing the melancholy person's complexion, for example statements such as, 'Of colour they be black, according to the humour whereof they are nourished, and the skin always receauing the black vapors, which insensibly do passe from the inward parts, taketh die and stain thereof',[135] which strongly resemble Hamlet's 'But I have that within which passes show, / These but the trappings and the suits of woe' (1.2.85–6). Bright draws from a familiar reservoir of medical, philosophical and psychological material whose pedigree shared much with common knowledge that was in circulation at the end of the sixteenth century. Moreover, Shakespeare and many of his fellow dramatists were so steeped in it that they could move easily between the linearity that we associate with traditional source study, and the popular, more fragmentary, practice of reaching out, incorporating and embellishing material that had already been introjected via hearsay as much as by reading, or by echoing what was heard in other contemporary plays. In short, the oral and the literate could operate side by side as two modes of perception.

But what if the sheer multiplicity that a nominally unified text presents cannot be contained by the tendencies designed to shape its structure as part of a linear hierarchy? In his book *Hamlet and the Vision of Darkness* (2017), Rhodri Lewis poses just this question as he seeks to link the claim that 'Shakespeare had no ethical, political or philosophical system of his own' with the conclusion that 'Hamlet indicates that he came to find humanist moral philosophy deficient in the face of human experience as he observed it'.[136] Lewis's compelling but controversial reading of the play, replete with a scholarly apparatus of supporting texts, does not entirely shake itself free of the traditional discourse of the 'source'. He hints briefly at the uncertainties in *The Merchant of Venice* in his reference to Bassanio's choice of the leaden casket,[137] but does not pursue the matter further. Indeed, Bassanio's own suspicion of female beauty that precedes his choice of casket actually challenges what many have identified as the play's predominantly romantic ethos.

We have very little evidence to support what might have gone on by way of discussion within Shakespeare's theatre. He left no analytical account of his exchanges with his fellow actors, or of the ways in which the structures of particular plays developed. The various texts of *Hamlet* that have survived offer some indication of practical emendation, development of ideas and, even, alteration designed to provide additional explanation, or to respond to the changing tastes of audiences. They offer none of the certainties that we would normally expect documentary evidence to provide. But internalisation of what seem to us to be the potentially chaotic practices of what is still residually an oral culture depends upon the pressure exerted by continual circulation of current issues. This suggests a more fluid kind of social exchange that makes the theatre a conduit for a gallimaufry of ideas and topics for discussion that already had a wider, and at times popular, public circulation. Indeed, in the case of plays, print *followed* public performance, and public performance itself might easily have stimulated print. For example, it would seem to be more than a mere coincidence that following on from performances of *The Merchant of Venice* (1596–97), Lewis Lewkenor's translation of Gasparo Contarini's *The Commonwealth and Government of Venice* (1599) appeared, followed in 1600 by the publication of the first quarto of the play. But all that we can deduce from this is that 'Venice' and 'usury' were hot topics from 1597 onwards, and that in Shakespeare's case they had become familiar by 1604. In the case of *Othello* (c.1604) there were also other stimuli that Shakespeare shared with his audiences and that occasionally found their way into printed documents, royal declarations and what emanated from historically specific popular prejudices. One further element in this increasingly complex network was the adaptation of earlier plays where earlier versions (as in the case of works like the anonymously authored 1605 play *The True Chronicle Historie of King Leir*) were brought up to date and revised to address current concerns.

These practices need to be added to the more limited resources disclosed by textual transmission, translation and adaptation. In their Arden 3 edition of *Hamlet*, Thompson and Taylor resuscitate a familiar category that they label 'the origins of Shakespeare's conceptual thinking'. Hill's and Bright's texts might fit into this category, although, as with most editors, they remain within a linear model of influence and restrict their emphasis to the occurrence of verbal parallels with texts such as the essays of Montaigne.[138]

In terms of textual transmission, the matter is already complicated by the appearance in 1603 of a quarto of *Hamlet* printed probably by Valentine Simmes for Nicholas Ling and John Trundell, and now thought to be a 'performance' text rather than a memorial reconstruction. Of the many idiosyncrasies of this so-called 'bad' quarto, the name 'Corambis' for Polonius is similar to the name of the character in a German version of the story, *Der bestrafte Brudermord oder Prinz Hamlet aus Dännemark*, which, as we have seen, Bullough suggests was 'the degenerate version of an English play' performed in Dresden.[139] This quarto was succeeded by a longer text in 1605, 'Newly imprinted and enlarged to almost as much againe as it was, according to the true and perfect Coppie', and attributed to the printer James Roberts, who had printed the first quarto of *The Merchant of Venice* in 1600. Though Q2, like Q1, is attributed to 'William Shakespeare', the question of the provenance of the claim to be 'the true and perfect Coppie' remains. The 'author's' name appears on the title pages of both quartos, although it does not follow that the signature 'authorises' either quarto. Given that a number of Shakespeare quartos remain unsigned, we have no way of knowing for certain whether this signals Shakespeare's public reputation at the turn of the sixteenth century, or whether this paratextual indication is, as Genette would put it, a matter of 'legal responsibility rather than of factual authorship'.[140] We might invoke Janet Clare's argument regarding

The legacy of Geoffrey Bullough

'competition' by way of explanation, but some of the details of Q1 (1603) indicate a provenance for that text that is different from that of Q2, despite some of the similarities that both texts share. The link is 'intertextual' only insofar as that by 1604 the two texts were in public circulation. The element of competition certainly applies, and to the short list of competing plays that Clare provides,[141] we might add Henry Chettle's lost play, *A Danish Tragedy* (1602), and *Hoffman, or a Revenge for a Father* (1602), performed by the Admiral's Men but not published until 1631. The entanglements of performance dates, publication dates and the nature of the competition are not easy to unravel, and a simple linear explanation appears reductive in the circumstances.

On the other hand, a simple identification of cognate texts and an assumption of their intertextual connection – however one might define the principle of intertextuality – would seem to be insufficient to account for the interactive force of the various elements of a palimpsestic text. The textual collisions that occur and the meanings that they generate are always contingent upon wider social tensions that are not easy to separate from the investments of the enquiring scholar. Issues of power, political authority, gender, professional and domestic pressures, all contribute in various ways to understanding, while comprehension itself is not static. At any stage of interpretation, elements of the palimpsest are capable of rising to the surface, either as simple repetitions of past events or as allegorical formulations where direct reference might have been dangerous. The deposition scene in *Richard II* or Lear's division of the kingdom are examples that immediately come to mind in plays that combine history and tragedy. In Shakespearean comedy the domestic tensions involving parents and children are replayed in a variety of ways that more analytical texts such as Sir Thomas Smith's *De Republica Anglorum* or the sermons of Henry Smith figure in their accounts.

Be that as it may, the precise manner in which the content of something like the *Hamlet* narrative reached Shakespeare is uncertain, and editors are in general agreement that he had not read Saxo, and that he would not have read Belleforest in French, even though he may have known of it.[142] Moreover, the sheer variety of texts in which elements of style as well as content appear suggests something other than a hierarchical or linear evolution of the story. In fact, the content appears to exist only in the recreation of each version of the narrative, whereas the style owes much more to contemporary theatrical tastes and to those elements of the past that, as a result, have been exposed 'for examination'.[143] To explain this process as one of locating a 'source' or 'sources' is to organise the evidence in a particular way, and as Moretti points out: 'That's not history; that's theodicy.'[144] Rather, we need to acknowledge an endlessly expanding constellation of circulating and receding narratives that either the writer encounters in the process of composition, and that will include content (or 'information') and form, and elements of the story that are sedimented in the writer's unconscious surfacing only partly as the details are brought momentarily into focus as a result of both theatrical and extra-theatrical stimuli. Above all, we need to register that a writer like Shakespeare would have encountered all of these elements but not in conditions that were exclusively of his own making. Francis Barker and Peter Hulme make this point forcefully in the claim that, traditionally:

> The text is designated as the legitimate object of literary criticism, *over against* its contexts, whether they be arrived at through the literary-historical account of the development of particular traditions and genres, or, as more frequently happens with Shakespeare's plays, the study of 'sources'. In either case the text has been separated from a surrounding ambit of other texts over which it is given a special pre-eminence.[145]

They evolve a category of con-text that returns the text to its surrounding discourses in such a way that what is privileged is the process of interaction rather than the construction of a retrospectively reified hierarchy. It is the difference between 'source' and 'resource' whereby the conscious agency of the writer as reader is brought into alignment with the varied unconscious pressures emanating from contiguous existing discursive fields. The result is a series of layers or strands that can be shown to operate dynamically in encounters that encapsulate both the pressures of ideology and the innovative attempts to resolve the contradictions that surface from time to time to disrupt its normalising tendencies. Composition in these circumstances is thus not a creation *ex nihilo*,

The legacy of Geoffrey Bullough 81

nor is it either 'imitation' in the weak sense of repetition, nor is it an entirely arbitrary collocation of 'quotations'. The text becomes a palimpsest whose sedimented layers interact creatively as producers of meaning that alter as personal, professional, social and cultural pressures change.

The catalogue of details of the *Hamlet* narrative that Shakespeare adopted has been the concern of almost every scholarly editor of the play. As the evidence of the three printed editions of the play shows, what *Hamlet* as an evolving text adopted and adapted is what has contributed to the general claim that Shakespeare was innovative and original. Yet even here the tangle of detail may offer a clue about compositional practice. For example, in the earlier *Romeo and Juliet* (c.1594), the stimulus for the dramatic action is an unspecified 'ancient grudge' leading to a 'mutiny' where 'Civil blood makes civil hands unclean' (Prologue, ll. 3–4). In *Titus Andronicus* (c.1593) it is the secret crimes of Tamora, accommodated at the heart of the Rome that Titus himself helped build and defend, that stimulate a horrific Senecan revenge. In *Julius Caesar* (c.1599) it is the republican assassination of Caesar that provokes a 'revenge' that culminates in the inauguration of the Roman Empire. And in *Othello* a revenge is sought for an imaginary offence. Behind all of this is Kyd's *The Spanish Tragedy* in which Hieronimo, charged with dispensing justice, cannot secure it for the murder of his son Horatio. In the cases of both Hieronimo and Titus (and perhaps Othello), the 'madness' that is induced by the failure to secure justice is explicit, as well as speaking of a much more widespread social malaise and disorder. All of these examples can be brought within the aegis of theatregrams, stock patterns the details of which are evoked almost in the moment that they are deployed, and whose abiding presence furnishes the writer with the confidence to innovate.

In the light of these various extant strands of thought and experience, we can only surmise about what attracted Shakespeare to the *Hamlet* story. Moreover, the closer we look at the conceptual implications of the term 'sources' – as in part Bullough invites us to do – the more we uncover a complex network of intertexts and con-texts that challenges a rigidly hierarchical and linear organisation. In addition, the logic of the 'source' presupposes an originary moment of creation that, as we shall see in the next chapter, underpins a quasi-theological explanation of the moment of creation. Indeed, to deal with this phenomenon we need a more capacious, less tendentious term such as 'resources'. Shakespeare may have been initially attracted by the similarity of his eponymous hero's name to that of his dead son,[146] and this may have prompted him to fantasise on what in terms of his own personal history would have been an inversion of the norm. But there is a considerable distance from this wholly speculative personal stimulus, and the nuanced narratives that were in circulation, as well as the full-scale revision of the revenge genre in which new motivations for the revenger's delay were beginning to appear. All of this, coupled with an innovative gloss on the operations of a divinely sanctioned justice, as well as an engagement with the issues of memory and representation, comprised the active constituents of the Elizabethan culture of the *fin de siècle*, and for which the term 'source', with its hierarchical and theological implications, is now wholly unsuited. The sheer scope of the material to which Shakespeare would have had access, and the circumstances in which he utilised it, indicate firmly that terms like 'source' and 'authority' lean too firmly in one direction, and that a term such as 'resource', as the following chapters will show, is much more suited to describe the variety of elements that comprise Shakespeare's complex processes of composition.

Notes

1 Geoffrey Bullough, *Narrative and Dramatic Sources of Shakespeare*, 8 vols (London, 1957–75), vol. 8, p. 342.
2 *Ibid.*
3 See Hardin Craig, 'Trend of Shakespeare scholarship', *Shakespeare Survey*, 2 (1949), 110, which provided Bullough with a point of access to this argument.
4 Bullough, *Narrative and Dramatic Sources*, vol. 8, p. 343.
5 See Benedetto Croce, 'History', in *A Croce Reader: Aesthetics, Philosophy, History, Literary Criticism*, trans. and ed. Massimo Verdicchio (Toronto and London, 2017), p. 53: 'any serious historiography and any serious philosophy must be a historiography-philosophy "of occasion" just as Goethe used to say about genuine

poetry: one passionately and the other practically and morally motivated'.
6 Cf. R.G. Collingwood, *The Idea of History* (Oxford and London, 1961), pp. 191ff.
7 Bullough, *Narrative and Dramatic Sources*, vol. 8, p. 345.
8 *Ibid.*, p. 346.
9 *Ibid.*
10 *Ibid.*, p. 344.
11 Collingwood, *The Idea of History*, pp. 202–3.
12 *Ibid.*, p. 346.
13 Brian Vickers ed., *Shakespeare: The Critical Heritage, vol. 1: 1623–1692* (London, 1974), p. 138.
14 Jonathan Bate, ed., *The Romantics on Shakespeare* (Harmondsworth, 1992), p. 161.
15 *Ibid.*, pp. 159–60.
16 Bullough, *Narrative and Dramatic Sources*, 8.367.
17 Cf. Benedetto Croce, *Guide to Aesthetics*, trans. Patrick Romanell (Indianapolis, 1965), p. 56: 'Our thought is historical thought about an historical world, process of development about a development; and no sooner has the attribute of a reality been articulated than the attribute no longer holds because it has itself produced a new reality which awaits a new attribute. A new reality, which comprises the economic and moral life, transforms intellectual man into practical man – the man of politics, the saint, the man of industry, the hero – and elaborates the *logical a priori synthesis* into *practical a priori synthesis*. But this new reality is, somehow, always a new feeling, a new desiring, a new willing, a new passionateness, in which not even the spirit can rest, inasmuch as it solicits first of all, a new material, a new intuition, a new lyric, a new art.'
18 Craig, 'Trend of Shakespeare scholarship', 110.
19 This was the mantra of cultural anthropologist Clifford Geertz that influenced Greenblatt's New Historicism. The fact that Greenblatt's title was identical to that of a 1931 essay by Croce, 'The New Historicism', seems to have passed unnoticed.
20 Bullough, *Narrative and Dramatic Sources*, vol. 8, pp. 359–60.
21 *Ibid.*, vol. 1, p. 3.
22 *Ibid.*, p. 426.
23 *Ibid.*, pp. 463ff.
24 *Ibid.*, pp. 345–6.
25 *Ibid.*, pp. 449–50.
26 *Ibid.*, p. 446.

27 *Ibid.*, pp. 482ff.
28 *Ibid.*, pp. 486ff.
29 It is worth noting that in Marlowe's *The Jew of Malta* Barrabas's usurious activities are only part of a much larger empire: 'Then after that was I an usurer, / And with extorting, cozening, forfeiting, / And tricks belonging unto brokery, / I filled the jails with bankrupts in a year' (2.3.192–5).
30 George Puttenham, *The Arte of English Poesie* (London, 1589; Scholar Press facs. edn, Menston, 1989), pp. 1–2.
31 [Cicero] *Ad Herennium*, trans. Harry Caplan (reprinted, Cambridge, MA, and London, 1989), p. 7.
32 Richard Halpern, *The Poetics of Primitive Accumulation: English Renaissance Culture and the Genealogy of Capital* (Ithaca and London, 1991), p. 31. Halpern goes on to make the political point that: 'Imitation thus governs the mastery of prescribed social behaviours as well as the mastery of literary style. Conversely, humanist methods of teaching Latin style partake of a well-nigh global process for the ideological (imaginary) production of social subjects' (p. 33).
33 *Ibid.*, p. 31. Some of these issues have been resurrected in Lynn Enterline, *Shakespeare's Schoolroom: Rhetoric, Discipline, Emotion* (Philadelphia, 2012), pp. 33ff.
34 Alexander Kojève, *The Notion of Authority (A Brief Presentation)*, ed. François Terré, trans. Hager Weslati (London and New York, 2014), p. 28.
35 *Ibid.*
36 See David Quint, *Origin and Originality in Renaissance Literature* (New Haven, 1983), p. 117.
37 William Shakespeare, *Othello*, ed. E.A.J. Honigmann, Arden 3 series (Walton-on-Thames, 1997) p. 154.
38 Bullough, *Narrative and Dramatic Sources*, vol. 1, pp. 405ff.
39 Cf. Thomas Newton, *Seneca, His Tenne Tragedies*, ed. Charles Whibley, 2 vols (London, 1927), pp. 54–98. *Medea* ends with the following lines from Jason: 'Goe through the ample spaces wyde, infect the poisoned Ayre, / Beare witnesse, grace of God is none in place of thy repayre' (p. 98). Earlier in Act 4 both the Nutrix and Medea describe in detail the deadly concoction of poisonous herbs that she will administer to Creusa and her father (pp. 85–9).
40 Bullough, *Narrative and Dramatic Sources*, vol. 8, p. 346.
41 *Ibid.*, p. 347.
42 Cf. Bullough, *Narrative and Dramatic Sources*, vol. 8, p. 347. But also see Colin Burrow, *Shakespeare and Classical Antiquity* (Oxford,

2013), p. 30, who adopts an important pragmatic response with the suggestion that 'we should think of Shakespeare's knowledge of classical writing dynamically as a changing and theatrically inflected resource rather than simply a static body of learning which he acquired during his teens and then used throughout his career'.
43 Harold Bloom, *Ruin the Sacred Truths: Poetry and Belief from the Bible to the Present* (Cambridge, MA, and London, 1989), p. 7.
44 *Ibid.*
45 *Ibid.*, p. 12.
46 *Ibid.*, p. 53.
47 Craig, 'Trend of Shakespeare scholarship', 112.
48 Cf. E.M.W. Tillyard, *The Elizabethan World Picture* (London, 1943), p. 102, where 'the Elizabethan habit of mind' is pitted against 'certain trends of thought in central Europe, the ignoring of which by our scientifically minded intellectuals has helped not a little to bring the world into its present conflicts and distresses'.
49 Cf. Stephen Greenblatt, *Shakespearean Negotiations: The Circulation of Social Energy in Renaissance England* (Oxford, 1988), pp. 4–5.
50 *Ibid.*, p. 94.
51 Harold Bloom, *The Anxiety of Influence* (London, Oxford and New York, 1973), p. 5.
52 *Ibid.*, p. 11. Bloom's avowed concern is with what he calls '*the poet in a poet*, or the aboriginal poetic self'.
53 Bullough, *Narrative and Dramatic Sources*, vol. 8, pp. 346–7: 'He remembered the popular law of his country upbringing with regard to flowers, birds, animals, medicine and superstitions. He knew enough about sea-faring terms, warfare and the law to astonish modern enquirers into these subjects; he knew and could apply the terms of rhetoric seriously and with humour; he developed an interest in the ethical psychology of his day which profoundly affected his work; he knew the Bible, Prayer Book, and Homilies well. ... He seems to have forgotten nothing that he read or heard, or rather, his powers of associative memory were such that if he required a parallel or contrast for plot and incident or a poetic image, something relevant and vivid floated up from his unconscious.'
54 But see Harold Bloom's *The Anatomy of Influence: Literature as a Way of Life* (New Haven and London, 2011), p. 27, where he seems to revise this view of Shakespeare, who 'has to be the paradigm for self-influence', and in whose 'self-possession ... exhausted his precursors to unfold finally in relation to his own prior work' (p. 29).
55 Harold Bloom, *A Map of Misreading* (Oxford, 1975), p. 17.

56 Stephen Greenblatt, 'Shakespeare and the exorcists', in *Shakespearean Negotiations: The Circulation of Social Energy in Renaissance England* (Oxford, 1988), p. 101. See also Jonathan Goldberg, '*Macbeth* and source', in *Shakespeare Reproduced*, ed. Jean E. Howard and Marion F. O'Connor (New York and London, 1987).
57 Bloom, *A Map of Misreading*, pp. 17–18.
58 Burrow, *Shakespeare and Classical Antiquity*, p. 38.
59 *Ibid.*, p. 242.
60 Colin Burrow, 'Shakespeare's authorities', in Katie Halsey and Angus Vine, eds, *Shakespeare and Authority* (London, 2018), pp. 31–54.
61 Burrow, *Shakespeare and Classical Antiquity*, p. 92.
62 Bullough, *Narrative and Dramatic Sources*, vol. 1, p. xii. See also Kenneth Muir, *Shakespeare's Sources*, vol. 1 (London, 1957), pp. 16–17.
63 See Bullough, *Narrative and Dramatic Sources*, vol. 8, pp. 341ff., for a retrospective view of the entire project, in which, *pace* Benedetto Croce, Bullough aligns himself with the quest that 'it was the critic's task, by entering into the imagination of the poet, so to recreate the moment of vision and the process of composition as to apprehend the work of art in its totality' (p. 343). Bullough's concern, however is with 'Shakespeare's immediate literary milieu, the pressures both external and internal which affected the substance of his plays by causing him to incorporate allusions, attitudes, and ideas which he might otherwise have omitted' (p. 345). He goes on to say that source study 'often lets us glimpse the creative process in action as he took over, remade, rejected, adapted or added to chosen or given material' (p. 346). But see Muir, *Shakespeare's Sources*, p. 16, for the suggestion that some of Shakespeare's allusions appear 'to have been unconscious'.
64 Emrys Jones, *The Origins of Shakespeare* (Oxford, 1977), p. 21.
65 Kojève, *The Notion of Authority*, p. 28.
66 Bloom, *The Anxiety of Influence*, p. 8.
67 *Ibid.*, p. 7. This implies a direct challenge to Bullough's account of Shakespeare's 'imagery' in the conclusions to his final volume; see Bullough, *Narrative and Dramatic Sources*, vol. 8, pp. 379ff.
68 Bullough, *Narrative and Dramatic Sources*, vol. 8, p. 341.
69 *Ibid.*
70 *Ibid.*, p. 342.
71 *Ibid.*
72 *Ibid.*, p. 343.
73 *Ibid.*, pp. 76–7.

74 *Ibid.*
75 *Ibid.* 'Benedetto Croce's theory of critical immediacy was an influence in the right direction when he declared that it was the critic's task, by entering into the imagination of the poet, so to recreate the moment of vision and the process of composition as to apprehend the work of art in its totality.'
76 Quint, *Origin and Originality*, p. ix.
77 *Ibid.*, p. x.
78 *Ibid.*, p. xi.
79 *Ibid.*, p. 7.
80 *Ibid.*, p. 219.
81 Ben Jonson is a key figure here. See David Riggs, *Ben Jonson: A Life* (Cambridge, MA, and London, 1989), pp. 64–5: 'When Jonson sold his copy of *Every Man Out of His Humour* to Holme within a year of its successful debut, he was claiming, in effect that the author continued to own his own work after the players had purchased a copy of it' (p. 65). See also Shackerley Marmion, *A Fine Companion* (1633) where the Induction consists of a dialogue between 'the Author' and 'the Critick'.
82 Stephen J. Lynch, *Shakespearean Intertextuality: Studies in Selected Sources and Plays* (Connecticut and London, 1998), p. 1.
83 *Ibid.*, pp. 64ff.
84 *Ibid.*, p. 115. See also Jeffrey Masten, *Textual Intercourse: Collaboration, Authorship, and Sexualities in Renaissance Drama* (Cambridge, 1997), p. 4, for a roughly contemporaneous study that avoids explicit discussion of the principles of intertextuality, choosing instead to explore theatrical collaboration during a period that preceded 'post-Englightenment paradigms of individuality, authorship, and textual property'.
85 Murray J. Levith, *Shakespeare's Cues and Prompts* (London, 2007), p. 1.
86 *Ibid.*, p. 2.
87 Julia Kristeva, *Revolution in Poetic Language*, trans. Margaret Waller (New York, 1984), pp. 59–60. See also Toril Moi ed., *The Kristeva Reader* (Oxford, 1986), pp. 93–8.
88 Kristeva's notion of the 'semiotic *chora*' has a long philosophical pedigree that goes back to Plato's *Timaeus*. See also Maria Margaroni, '"The lost foundation": Kristeva's semiotic *chora* and its ambiguous legacy', *Hypatia*, 20:1 (Winter 2005), 79.
89 Roland Barthes, 'The Death of the Author', *Image, Music, Text*, ed. and trans. Stephen Heath (Glasgow, 1977), p. 142.

90 *Ibid.*, p. 146. We might add to this Foucault's account of the author in his essay 'What Is an Author', *Language, Counter-Memory, Practice: Selected Essays and Interviews*, trans. Donald Bouchard and Sherry Simon, ed. Donald Bouchard (Oxford, 1977), pp. 113–38; here Foucault argues that 'the name of the author is not precisely a proper name among others' (p. 122), and that 'Its presence is functional in that it serves as a means of classification' (p. 123). Foucault goes on to argue that the author's name 'characterises a particular manner of existence if discourse', and that 'it points to the existence of certain groups of discourse within a society and culture' (p. 123).
91 Foucault, 'What Is an Author?', p. 126.
92 *Ibid.*
93 *Ibid.*, p. 127.
94 *Ibid.*
95 *Ibid.*, p. 135.
96 *Ibid.*
97 *Ibid.*, p. 136.
98 Janet Clare, *Shakespeare's Stage Traffic: Imitation, Borrowing and Competition in Renaissance Theatre* (Cambridge, 2014), p. 1.
99 *Ibid.*, p. 5.
100 *Ibid.*, p. 9. Cf. Puttenham, *The Arte of English Poesie*, p. 1: 'A Poet may in some sort be said a follower or imitator, becaue he can express the true and lively of everything is set before him, and which he taketh in hand to describe: and so in that respect is both a maker and a counterfaitor: and Poesie an art not only of making, but also of imitation.'
101 Clare, *Shakespeare's Stage Traffic*, p. 11.
102 Puttenham, *The Arte of English Poesie*, p. 1.
103 William Shakespeare, *King Henry the Sixth Part 1*, ed. Edward Burns, Arden 3 series (London, 2000), p. 1.
104 Cf. Foucault, 'What Is an Author?', p. 138, where Foucault seeks to depart from 'tiresome repetitions' and formulates a series of five formal alternatives, in which subjectivity is subordinated to the demands of discourse and its capacity to determine the position of the human subject.
105 Terence Hawkes, *Meaning by Shakespeare* (London, 1992), p. 3.
106 Gérard Genette, *Palimpsests: Literature in the Second Degree*, trans. Channa Newman and Claude Doubinsky (Lincoln, NE, and London, 1997), p. 1.
107 *Ibid.*, pp. 1–2.
108 *Ibid.*, p. 3.
109 *Ibid.*, p. 4.

110 *Ibid.*, p. 5. Genette later goes on to note that 'the same hypertext may simultaneously transform a hypotext and imitate another' (p. 30). In the case of 'travesty', Genette notes that 'the crucial issue is to know who, the original poet, or the transposer, will be inscribed within the text as having authority over the narrative discourse and its commentary' (p. 62). However, what he calls 'the source' is 'a source not of the narrative, to be sure, but of the narrator's information' that is 'often invoked at times as an indisputable source' (p. 63).
111 *Ibid.*, p. 9.
112 Franco Moretti, *Distant Reading* (London and New York, 2013), pp. 76–7.
113 *Ibid.*, pp. 85–6.
114 Gilles Deleuze and Felix Guattari, *A Thousand Plateaus: Capitalism and Schizophrenia*, trans. Brian Massumi (London, 1987), p. 9. Also see p. 7: 'A rhizome ceaselessly establishes connections between semiotic chains, organisations of power, and circumstances relative to the arts, sciences, and social struggles.'
115 *Ibid.*, p. 8.
116 See John Drakakis, 'Jessica', in John W. Mahon and Ellen Macleod Mahon, eds, *The Merchant of Venice: New Critical Essays* (New York and London, 2002).
117 Gilles Deleuze and Felix Guattari, *Anti-Oedipus: Capitalism and Schizophrenia*, trans. Robert Hurley, Mark Seem and Helen R. Lane (London, 1983), p. 39.
118 Margaroni, '"The lost foundation"', p. 83. See also p. 87, where Margaroni notes that Kristeva's *chora* must be understood 'not as the forgotten past itself (whose status Kristeva warns us is that of a theoretical fiction), but as the force of this palintropic move thsat destabilises the subject and frustrates any effort to (im)pose an absolute origin'.
119 Bullough, *Narrative and Dramatic Sources*, vol. 7, p. 5.
120 See Stuart Gillespie, *Shakespeare's Books: A Dictionary of Shakespeare's Sources* (London, 2004), pp. 36–41, for the suggestion that if Shakespeare knew Belleforest then he must have encountered him in French (p. 39).
121 Bullough, *Narrative and Dramatic Sources*, vol. 7, p. 15.
122 *Ibid.*, p. 20.
123 *Ibid.*, p. 187.
124 *Ibid.*, p. 185.
125 Genette, *Palimpsests*, p. 84. Cf. also Gilles Deleuze, *Difference and Repetition*, trans. Paul Patton (London, 1994), p. 90: '*Repetition is*

a condition of action before it is a concept of reflection. We produce something new only on condition that we repeat – once in the mode which constitutes the past, and once more in the present of metamorphosis' (original italics).

126 Deleuze, *Difference and Repetition*, p. 92.
127 Cf. Newton, *Seneca*. This 1927 limited edition contains an Introduction by T.S. Eliot. But see also Tanya Pollard, *Greek Tragic Women on Shakespearean Stages* (Oxford, 2017), which makes the case for the influence of Euripides upon early modern English dramatists.
128 Newton, *Seneca*, vol. 1, pp. xxvi–xxvii.
129 *Ibid.*, p. 189.
130 Thomas Hill, *The Moste pleasaunte Arte of the Interpretation of Dreames* (London, 1576), sig. B5^r.
131 *Ibid.*, sig. D4^v.
132 *Ibid.* Cf. the following paraphrase of Aristotle: 'The causes of all dreames bee on this wyse, firste those which are caused of meates and drinkes, as in surfeytes are wont to be is the cause of the mocion whiche properlye is caused of the vapours breathing out of the soul' (sig. D4^v). Also see the following quotation that combines interpretation with folk wisdom: 'ther be foure kyndes of dreames, Now the new and bodelye causes are meate and drinke, lyke as the heades of Garlike, the Coleworts, the Onyones, the Beanes, and what soeuer ascend to the head, and especiallye those which engender melancholy' (sig. D6^v).
133 Newton, *Seneca*, vol. 1, p. 189.
134 Cf. Claire McEachern, *Believing in Shakespeare: Studies in Longing* (Cambridge, 2018), p. 37, which provides a large theological context for such statements: 'The school of Reformation historiography that emphasises theological continuities and commonalities would rightly point out that neither grace nor predestination are unprecedented ideas in Christian theology and that what we often view as a dramatic change from Catholicism to Protestantism might be more like a shift in weight from one theological foot to another (that the shift was disseminated through print may have been the real game-changer).' I am grateful to Professor Adrian Streete of the University of Glasgow for drawing my attention to McEachern's book.
135 Timothie Bright, *A Treatise of Melancholie* (London, 1586), pp. 118–19.
136 Rhodri Lewis, *Hamlet and the Vision of Darkness* (Princeton and Oxford, 2017), p. 26.
137 *Ibid.*, p. 86.

The legacy of Geoffrey Bullough   91

138 Ann Thompson and Neil Taylor, eds, in William Shakespeare, *Hamlet*, Arden 3 series, revised edn, 2 vols (London, 2016), vol. 1, p. 73.
139 Bullough, *Narrative and Dramatic Sources*, vol. 7, p. 20.
140 Gérard Genette, *Paratexts: Thresholds of Interpretation*, trans. Jane E. Lewin (Cambridge, 1997), p. 40.
141 Clare, *Shakespeare's Stage Traffic*, pp. 166–8.
142 See Harold Jenkins, ed., in William Shakespeare, *Hamlet*, Arden 2 series (London, 1982), pp. 85ff., and p. 89. See also the much more circumspect treatment of 'source' in Thompson and Taylor's Arden 3 edition of *Hamlet*, vol. 1, pp. 59–70.
143 Fernand Braudel, cited in Moretti, *Distant Reading*, p. 85.
144 Moretti, *Distant Reading*, p. 89.
145 Francis Barker and Peter Hulme, 'Nymphs and reapers heavily vanish: the discursive con-texts of *The Tempest*', in John Drakakis, ed., *Alternative Shakespeares* (London, 1985), p. 192.
146 Shakespeare elsewhere seems to have been attracted to the process of metathesis; for example, he was known to have acted in Ben Jonson's comedy *Every Man in His Humour* (1598) in which the jealous merchant Thorello appears. Hamnet/Hamlet and Thorello/Othello suggest a playful metathesis at work.

2

Myths of origin

In the account of language in his book *Marxism and Literature* (1977), the late Raymond Williams observed that Marx paid little attention to language as such, and that by the nineteenth century, 'language could be grasped only as physical – a set of physical properties – and not as material *activity*: in fact the ordinary scientistic dissociation of the abstracted faculty from its actual human use'.[1] Williams concedes the point that language must have appeared at a particular historical conjuncture in human evolution, but he then elaborates its history in such a way that casts doubt upon the question of the pursuit of its 'origins':

> Language of course developed at some point in evolutionary history, but it is not only that we have virtually no information about this; it is mainly that any human investigation of so constitutive an activity finds language already there in itself and in its presumed object of study. Language has then to be seen as a persistent kind of creation and recreation: a dynamic presence and a constant regenerative process.[2]

Although the matter would seem to be clearer in the case of the evolution of literary (and, perhaps all) texts, the question of origin, and the distinction between its diachronic and synchronic dimensions, appears at various historical moments to have preoccupied writers, and latterly literary historians. The question of origins has sometimes also led to enquiries concerning the originality of the writer. In the early modern period, and before writing had become an extension of the property of the writer, this became an important issue that subsumed into the category of 'origins' the agency of the writer and the source of his (usually his) creative talent.

Let us return for a moment to David Quint, who begins his study of *Origin and Originality in Renaissance Literature* (1983) by citing an observation from Vasari's *Proemio* to his *La Vite de Michelangelo* that emphasises a surprising relativism in matters of textual transmission that is reflected in Williams's critique of the quasi-metaphysical category of *langue* that had played so important a part in structuralist thinking about language since Saussure. Here, however, it appears as part of a critique of 'historical priority' that is the precursor to an acceptance of the link between 'individual greatness' and the concept of 'originality':

> The ancients themselves were preceded by even more ancient artists whose work and names are lost. The claim to historical priority is vitiated since no human work of art is absolutely prior, originating outside of history. Rather the artist's individual greatness confers upon him an originality which makes him *seem to transcend* history.[3] (my italics)

The issues of 'originality' and the text's transcendence of history are regarded from the outset by Quint, not as an intrinsic feature, but as 'the by-product of a historicist criticism which considers the work of art within its historical context *without necessarily assigning value to the context itself*' (my italics).[4]

This separation of 'art' and 'context', and the relegation of the latter to an inferior position in what is an aesthetic hierarchy, reinforces the Crocean distinction between the 'sources of inspiration' that formally belong to artistic creation, and the historical, social, cultural, economic and psychological pressures that stimulate the imagination of the artist. It is at the point of this conjuncture that logical explanation gives way to an appeal to 'mystery'. Croce tried to extricate himself from the problem by identifying 'the philosophy of spirit' with 'historical or historiographical thought' which involves perpetual growth upon itself, and of which every new act, since it includes its predecessors, comes together in 'the form of a dialectical unity'.[5] Here the creative artist subsumes into his own orbit the work of his 'predecessors': he imitates, he innovates, and in doing so produces something new. But for Croce the resource to which the artist has access includes, as we shall see in Chapter 7, his own earlier works that also contribute to an endlessly renewed, but individually distinct 'aesthetic coherence'.

This discourse, whether that of Bullough or the Marxist philosopher Croce, remains within a longstanding Christian framework, in which the process of 'creation' and the narrative of 'history' remained visibly interconnected in the face of pressures of a growing secularism visible during the early modern period. This long tradition finds its clearest expression in the frontispiece, and the accompanying poem of Sir Walter Raleigh's unfinished *The History of the World* (1614), which draws together an amalgam of classical and Christian motifs. Here the personified and feminised History is attended by an androgynous Experience ('Experientia') and a naked feminine Truth ('Veritas') carrying a torch. History tramples underfoot a skeletal Death and an androgynous Oblivion, and she raises the globe above her shoulders, flanked by two trumpeting angels: 'Fama Bona' and the speckled 'Fama Mala'. All this is under the watchful eye of Providence ('Providentia').[6] Raleigh's narrative of the Creation was shared by a number of his contemporaries, and begins with the Old Testament account of creation, before proceeding through large tracts of ancient Roman history. The biblical and the incipiently nationalistic are, however, aligned in such a way that suggests that the one is organically related to the other:

> For beginning with the Creation: I have proceded with the History of the World; and lastly purposed (some few sallies excepted) to confine my Discourse within this our renowned Iland of Greate Brittaine.[7]

For Raleigh the Creation inaugurates 'History', which orders 'Time', 'Antiquitie' (the past) and 'Memorie' (the faculty that keeps the past alive) that is also the gateway to 'Truth'. In his long Preface he describes the moment of creation and then proceeds to account for earthly variety:

> But such is the multiplying and extensiue virtue of dead Earth, and of the breath-giuing life which GOD hath cast upon Slime and Dust: as that among those that that were, of whom we read and heare, and among those that are whom we see and conuerse with; euery one hath receiued a seuerall picture of face, and euery one a divers picture of minde; euery one a forme apart and euery one a fancy

Myths of origin 95

and cogitation differing; there being nothing wherin Nature so much triumpheth as in dissimilitude. From whence it commeth that there is found so great diversity of opinions; so strong a contrariety of inclinations; so many naturall and vnnaturall; wise, foolish, manly and childish affections; and passions in mortall Men. For it is not the visible fashion and shape of the plants, and of reasonable Creatures that makes the difference, of working in the one, and of condition in the other; but the forme internall.[8]

God is both the *source* of life, but also of its 'dissimilitude' and its 'diversity', inscribing both categories in 'Nature' whose 'forme internall' inheres in each manifestation of what Erasmus, in an alternative account, identified as human 'folly'.[9] Both Erasmus and Raleigh share a humanist account of the ways of the world, and whether Shakespeare had or had not read 'The Praise of Folly', he certainly shared many of the topoi to be found there and that are important elements of Raleigh's much more serious concern. Raleigh identified 'GOD' as the source of creation, but the narrative that follows is an amalgam of 'myth' and historiography. Erasmus inverts and sexualises the myth of creation, urging the case that Folly is the assistant of the gods, whose own subversive femininity is instrumental in what is at root a sensuous and venereal act of creation:

> The wise man must send for me if he wants to be a father. But why not speak to you more openly, as I usually do? I ask whether the head, the face, the breast, the hand, or the ear – each an honourable part – creates gods and men? I think not, but instead the job is done by that foolish, even ridiculous part which cannot be named without laughter. This is the sacred fountain from which all things rise, more certainly than from the Pythagorean tetrad.[10]

In effect, Erasmus playfully desacrilises and demystifies creation, locating it not in the transcendental world of God, or the gods, but in the physical, tactile world of the flesh. For him, even the classical deity of Venus, whom Lucretius had identified as the source of creation in his *On the Nature of Things*, cannot, according to Dame Folly, 'deny that her work would be weak and inconclusive without my help'.[11]

Erasmus's playfully ironical account of both the source and the contribution that Dame Folly makes to the enrichment of earthly life is, by comparison with other treatments of folly, characterised as the norm of human experience. This is a very different account from that of, say, 'The Prologe of James Locher' that heralds Alexander Barclay's 1536 translation of Sebastian Brandt's fifteenth-century poem, the *Narrenschiff*, entitled *The Ship of Fools*. Locher begins with a musing 'of the sore confounded and vncertayne cours of mannys lyfe, and thinges therto belonginge', and proceeds to the following observation:

> at the last I haue by my vigilant meditacion found and noted many degrees of errours: wherby mankind wandreth from the way of trouth I haue also noted that many wyse men and wel lettred haue written right fruteful doctrines: wherby they haue heled these dyseses and intolerable perturbacions of the mynde: and the goostly woundes therof, moche better than Esculapius which was first Inuentour of Phesyke and amonge the Gentyles worshypped as a God.[12]

For Locher, folly is a disease, a type of psychological deviancy, 'intolerable perturbacions of the mynde' with its 'goostly woundes', from a singular 'truth'. However, Barclay's moralistic agenda is very different from Erasmus's much more tolerant, gently ironic approach to Folly, though both are concerned to identify a source of its energy. Barclay's collection of moralistic aphorisms is predicated upon a clear and persistent sense of a post-lapsarian world that looks back with regret to the paradise that it has lost.[13] His account of 'the Argument' of his translation situates it in both a historical and a moral context: it is a 'Satyr' that reflects sin as in a 'mirrour' and counsels a return to goodness. But like Raleigh, Barclay offers a universal history: 'this Boke is named the Shyp of foles of the worlde',[14] and his first example is the bibliophile who has no understanding of what he reads: 'what they mene I do nat vnderstonde'. He can clinch arguments merely by the display of his books, and while 'lernyd men' dispute and 'of my cunnynge shold make probacion',

> I kepe nat to fall in altercacion
> And whyle they common my bokes I turne and wynde
> For all is in them, and no thynge in my mynde.[15]

This hints at the idea that 'bokes' erode memory. There follows a gallery of 'fools' that is also a kind of history, ending with the 'unyuersall shyp for those that yet hath no charge',[16] but that visits and picks up passengers from Europe, Africa, Ireland and England. The assembled crew of wandering sailors are then caught in a Sysyphean dialectic of their own desires, but the striking image that Barclay deploys has, unfortunately, had some elements of modernity thrust upon it:

> About we wander in tempest and tourment
> What place is sure, where Foles may remayne
> And fyx theyr dwellynge sure and permanent
> None certainly: The cause theof is playne
> We wander in the se, for pleasour bydynge payne
> And though the haven of helth be in our sight
> Alas we fle from it with all our might.[17]

For each of these narratives, serious or not, religious or classical, satirical or moralistic, an identifiable source is postulated, one that either traces the material world to its divine origins in a transcendent 'mystery', or that more playfully supplements that mysterious causality by returning the act of creation to the secular world of human folly, where pleasure is to be derived from imitation, or is linked to perversion.[18] In an appeal that inverted Plato, and gestured, perhaps incidentally, to the function of art as an earthly process of creation, Erasmus praised the practicality of imitation and the pleasure that it was capable of generating. Here he makes the point anecdotally:

> I know a man by my name, a practical joker, who gave his new wife some imitation jewels and persuaded her that they were genuine and very valuable. Now what difference did it make to the girl? She was delighted with the glass trinkets and kept them locked in a secret place. In the meantime the husband had saved money, and enjoyed fooling his wife, and had won her devotion as well as he would have by a more expensive present.
> What difference do you see between the self-satisfied inhabitants of Plato's cave who contentedly admire the shadows of things, and the wise man who emerges from the cave and sees reality?[19]

Raleigh's ultimate creator, like that of Thomas Wilson, was 'GOD', and Lucretius's prime mover was 'nurturing Venus, who beneath the smooth-moving heavenly signs fill with yourself the sea full-laden with ships, the earth that bears the crops, since through you every kind of living thing is conceived and rising up looks on the light of the sun'.[20] For Erasmus, human behaviour had its source in pretence encouraged by Folly, although even here there remains a link with what Georg Lukács has called 'the transcendental home'.[21] If it was the Italian bibliophile Poggio Bracciolini whose discovery of the manuscript of Lucretius's *De Rerum Natura* that kick-started the Renaissance, and who, according to Stephen Greenblatt, became 'a midwife to modernity',[22] then it was Erasmus, a writer who himself composed in quotations, who emphasised the theatrical value of illusion compared with 'the wise man [who] takes refuge in the books of the ancients, and gains from them a merely verbal shrewdness'.[23] Dame Folly's dismissive account of the bookish labours of the wise man established her as the vital and constitutive 'other' of a relatively new technology – print culture – that was fast becoming the repository of 'memory'.

From Erasmus to Raleigh, writers challenged in different ways the modern obsession with 'sources' and 'origins' as reductively temporal phenomena, fabricating, in the wake of the humanist practice of historiographical writing, narratives that used classical texts as models. 'Origin' is defined in the *OED* as 'the act or fact of arising or springing from: derivation, rise; beginning of existence in reference to its source or cause' (1a) and 'the fact of springing from some particular ancestor or race descent, extraction, ancestry or parentage' (1b). Origin was frequently attributed to a divine source from whose plan and values humans deviated. In the case of Lucretius, Barclay and Wilson or Raleigh this process is taken seriously, but for Erasmus it was an object of derision. Each selects textual authorities to document and sustain their position, although in the case of Barclay even that selection can be perverted. Moreover, those texts that were elevated to the status of 'authorities' as a consequence of figuring as models in school and university curricula, could themselves, on closer examination, be indebted to antecedent, or indeed confluential, texts or events. To this extent, linearity and hierarchy, essential in the process of textual transmission and the construction of models of 'authority', might easily be complicated, or indeed undermined, by the entry and circulation of narratives into the popular domain. There in the material world, the vocabulary, the discourse and the ideology of 'source' and 'origin' might prove, on empirical grounds, to be inadequate or misleading. David Quint suggests that the 'new Renaissance appreciation of individual creativity and human differences' resulted in a historicising of 'the individual author' that in turn meant that 'his creation fell into the realm of historical contingency, at a remove from any fixed standard of truth'.[24] In his Epilogue, Quint uses the example of Milton who systematically '"corrects" the texts of his literary predecessors in order to reveal a true narrative of sacred history that lies embedded beneath layers of profane prose fiction'.[25] In effect this constitutes a 'desacralization of tradition [that] makes possible the appreciation of a purely literary originality'. Quint argues: 'So long as literary tradition is vested with sacred authority, the writer may find it difficult to valorize his own individuality and innovation.'[26] He resolves the problem in Milton's case by suggesting that while it is 'the originary Holy Spirit which dictates his own unpremeditated verse', he is able 'with one and the same gesture, to affirm both his unique authority and his authorial uniqueness'. This, however, leads to another problem:

> The individuality of spiritual experience which is part both of Milton's faith and of his claim to singular poetic authority may be difficult to distinguish from the larger Renaissance individualism against which his poem polemicizes in the figure of Satan.[27]

Here the individualising of 'spiritual experience' is shown to carry the risk of aligning 'singular poetic authority' not with a sacred source but with an individualism that the teleological thrust of *Paradise Lost* itself insists is fundamentally subversive.

Quint offers a specific instance of a textualised past, in which an authorised discursive field is imitated, replicated, memorialised and transformed. He is also concerned to chart the process whereby the 'author' might establish a domain of creative individuality in which originality could claim to be *sui generis*, independent of antecedent texts. However, it is not easy to make the claim of 'individuality' stick convincingly with a dramatist like Shakespeare who collaborated with others, who was involved in a communal enterprise and who was not 'literary' in this sense, despite the modest attempts by scholars such as Lukas Erne to claim that he was.[28]

Quint's historicisation has a specific objective: to lay bare a mythology and an ideology that continues to be upheld by those who insist upon the absolute integrity of the concepts of 'source' and 'origin'. But it is also the case that that certainty is sometimes open to challenge by categorisations that bring Bullough's classifications of 'probable sources', 'possible sources' and 'analogues' into question.[29] To be fair to Bullough, he confines his task to assembling 'narrative and dramatic sources', although his predominant concern is to posit a linear and historical connection between predominantly antecedent literary texts and the plays of Shakespeare. To this extent his behaviour shadows that of the professional historian concerned with distinguishing 'facts' from opinions, and who uses documentation ('primary' and 'secondary' texts) to verify conclusions.[30] However, embedded in the concepts of 'source' and 'origin' and implicit in appeals to Shakespeare's dramatic process, is, as we saw earlier, the quest for unitary 'truth'. For Raleigh, History, the figure upon whose shoulders the world is sustained, and who mediates between Death and Oblivion, is flanked by Experience, which is by its very nature disordered and contingent, and Truth that illuminates and shapes it. Indeed, the pivotal concept of unitary 'truth' opens up a much wider avenue of enquiry that takes us into the problems confronting language itself, its connection with veracity and its capacity for inversion and perversion. Indeed, if we are to remain within the sphere of textuality, it is in language that the various economic and social pressures converge and are mediated, and where questions of originality and individuality are exposed as symptoms of an ideology under threat from various forces that it becomes increasingly difficult to contain. To quote Walter Benjamin:

> all communication of mental meanings is language, communication in words being only a particular case of human language and of the justice, poetry, or whatever underlying it or founded on it. The existence of language, however, is not only co-extensive with with all the areas of human mental expression in which language is always in one sense or another inherent, but with absolutely everything.[31]

Shakespeare's *Hamlet* offers a succinct quasi-factual example of a dramatisation of this process. At the point in the play where Laertes returns to demand an explanation for the 'fact' of the death of Polonius, his entry is heralded by a Gentleman who confronts the mendacious Claudius with the political, and linguistic, effects of a possible popular rebellion that, contradictorily, articulates itself in monarchical terms:

> Save yourself, my lord.
> The ocean overpeering of his list
> Eats not the flats with more impiteous haste
> Than young Laertes in a riotous head
> O'erbears your officers. The rabble call him lord
> And as the world were now but to begin,
> Antiquity forgot, custom not known,
> The ratifiers and props of every word,
> They cry, 'Choose we: Laertes shall be king!' –
> Caps, hands and tongue, applaud it to the clouds –
> 'Laertes shall be king! Laertes king!'
> (4.5.98–108)

Here the variety and the vicissitudes of a nature out of control that would destabilise the operations of language to produce primeval chaos are pitted against 'antiquity' and 'custom' as authorities that guarantee order and that combine to 'ratify' and support 'every word'. Rebellion here is figured as an oceanic threat, a compression of a more familiar image of the rising of an underworld that is otherwise contained, and that would overwhelm its Christian counterpart of the life-giving sacred river as 'source'.[32] The irony of this scene lies in the fact that Claudius is emphatically *not* the yardstick by which 'truth' – divine or secular – can be measured since he is a player-king in every sense of the term, and a master of illusion. This confrontation risks a return to primal chaos, just as it hints at the dangers of theatrical representation itself. Indeed, Laertes, like Claudius, performs actions that effectively repeat the act of creation, although as Michel Jeanneret observes, the return to chaos is also a return at the human level to an imitation of God as the first creator:

> Once the creative impulse is set in motion, it doesn't stop propagating: Man the craftsman takes over from God the creator; the living produce more life. Of course, chaos is the opposite of all that, but it

is also the cradle. This will help us understand the fascination exerted on the sixteenth-century mind by the inaugural churning: It is the moment of all possibles and the beginning of the metamorphoses that carry the world forward.[33]

This certainly accounts for the impulse of the anonymous Gentleman who defines chaos in almost the same breath as he postulates a new political order. Laertes's revolution will produce a new hierarchy whose structure does not depart from the old, whose force imitates that of Claudius who proceeds to defend his own authority by having recourse to the ideology of divine right.

However, in this case, and in the face of radical challenge, the stability of language is the first casualty, and the image that both Claudius and Hamlet share is that of the 'harlot' whose aping of beauty in the former's case disguises a grotesque ugliness that opposes 'my deed to my most painted word' (3.1.50–3).[34] This echoes the evacuation of meaning from representation that both share as divided subjects, while at the same time gesturing towards the dangers of substituting for the creative power of the Divine, the metamorphic capacity for creation with which the 'fallen' human subject is endowed.

At issue here is the problematical articulation of meaning with 'truth', where the hermeneutic process of sense-making is part of a hierarchical structure that leads inwards to stable and fixed meaning. In historical terms, the relations between chaos, truth and order retain a degree of ambivalence that is not usually replicated in modern Shakespeare criticism.[35] E.M.W. Tillyard's *The Elizabethan World Picture* (1943) subscribed to this dictum, as indeed did Bullough and Hardin Craig who, as we saw earlier, appropriated Benedetto Croce's 'doctrine of critical immediacy' that gave the critic confronting 'earlier literature' a licence to restore 'within himself the thought and feeling of the author of that work' and to repeat 'the process of creation' and to comprehend 'immediately the work before him'.[36] Craig went on to suggest that 'no doubt, in the minds of scholars, at least, Shakespeare's own meaning is the greatest of meanings and it is one the world needs'.[37] The theoretical constraint that he imposes on meaning here is disquieting, although the context of this statement is the aftermath of the Second World War and its devastation that Tillyard, writing in the early years of the war, could attribute to the disregard of an earlier cultural formation:

> we shall err grievously if we do not take that seriousness into account or if we imagine that the Elizabethan habit of mind is done with once and for all. If we are sincere with ourselves we must know that we have that habit in our own bosoms somewhere, queer as it may seem. And, if we reflect on that habit, we may see that (in queerness though not in viciousness) it resembles certain trends of thought in central Europe, the ignoring of which by our scientifically minded intellectuals has helped not a little to bring the world into its present conflicts and distresses.[38]

Tillyard's 'queerness' that rejects 'viciousness' is part of a larger complex cultural narrative that seems intended to narrow down the parameters of a civilised and civilising discourse, while at the same time to counter an accusation of racism, as part of a strategy to reawaken the order of a carefully circumscribed past now threatened by war. Elsewhere, Walter Benjamin encapsulates what is here articulated as regret for the departure from the fantasy of origins by critically invoking 'the historical progress of mankind' that, he says, 'cannot be sundered from the concept of its progression through a homogeneous empty time'. That this 'progression must be the basis of any criticism of the concept of progress itself' appears to have escaped those who yearn for a fictionalised early modern past.[39]

Craig's assertion of a unitary meaning, also located in a cultural past, implies a singular 'truth' that has come under severe pressure from what Quint might identify as a different, more textually confined warfare that was a consequence of a historicising of the principles of 'source' and 'originality'. Indeed, and as a result of the renewed and intensified scrutiny of historical context, the ideological underpinnings of this deep-seated cultural shift are laid bare as fabricated narratives excavated by the literary historian as ways of negotiating the fissures in what Laurence Coupe has identified as a 'creation myth'.[40] For Craig and his contemporaries, the source of singular truth is the cultural icon, Shakespeare, while for Bullough it is possible to assent to a practical empirical procedure while at the same time positing speculatively particular narrative 'sources' and 'origins'. Thus, in one sense, the Shakespearean text becomes the comparatively stable focus of a narrative that is also the repository of truth. And yet in another sense the dramatist's originality is inscribed within a *tradition* that concedes that these texts habitually, if not systematically, utilise existing paradigms of thought and expression. The narratives that emerge are part of a multiple and complex pre-history that itself yields to the stimuli and the pressures of successive contemporary events and crises.[41] We may, of course, argue that the contours of Sir Walter Raleigh's unfinished 'history', which incorporates biblical and secular 'classical' narratives, subscribe to this creation myth. Moreover, the emerging Renaissance penchant for an emphasis on authorial individuality, when looked at retrospectively, offers a further example of nostalgia, loss and displacement. In this latter case the myth is internalised both as a desire to dispense with Benjamin's 'empty time' while simultaneously taking a necessary step on the long and tortuous road towards modernity. The fragmentary circulation in the early modern present of recognisable ancient classical myths through formal education, casual reading or simply through persistent oral repetition and circulation is accompanied in this instance by a regressive creation myth that acknowledges the ultimate source of culture *and* of texts.[42]

What does all this mean for the traditional discourse of source study that relies on a limited diachrony or, indeed, what might it mean for an editor glossing a Shakespeare text? Laurie Maguire and Emma Smith acknowledge the shortcomings of Bullough's approach, and they rightly point to the persistent influence that it has exerted on the study of relations between Shakespearean and other texts. They acknowledge candidly that; 'Source study, unlike its Edwardian scholarly contemporaries, has not substantively revisited its intellectual foundations during the course of the twentieth century.'[43] They are also critical of the few concluding comments that Bullough makes at the end of Volume 8 of *The Narrative and Dramatic Sources of Shakespeare*, and they take as a test case the relation between Marlowe's *Dido Queen of Carthage* and the appearance of elements of the narrative throughout the Shakespeare *oeuvre*, all of which leads them to conclude that 'the stand-alone word "source" has outlived its usefulness'.[44]

The issue they seek to resolve is whether Shakespeare was independently indebted to Virgil's *Aeneid* in *The Tempest*, or whether some form of mediation took place, or whether elements of both were involved. After rehearsing a number of revisions of Bullough's categories from mid-twentieth century scholarship onward, they conclude, that 'Shakespeare knew his Virgil and certainly he used Virgil in *The Tempest*',[45] although the links between Virgil, Marlowe and Shakespeare were various and in need of a more theoretically informed descriptive vocabulary. The links range from direct quotation to errors of memory and learning comprising a category of 'inspired misremembering and mislearning', all of which 'can be as much a response … as careful imitation and artful echoes'.[46] They rehearse a list of references and cite in detail the kind of critical squirming with the vocabulary of 'source' that their immediate predecessors and contemporaries have engaged in before striking out on their own revisionist quest: 'This, then, is an article not about what Shakespeare read (or saw) but about how he remembered (and what he could not forget).'[47]

The presence of Dido references and various parts of the Troy story throughout Shakespeare's plays are beyond dispute.[48] They include – although problematically in *The Merchant of Venice* – brief references to Troilus and Cressida, Pyramus and Thisbe, *and* Dido:

> In such a night
> Stood Dido with a willow in her hand
> Upon the wild sea banks and waft her love
> To come again to Carthage.
> (*The Merchant of Venice*, 5.1.9–12)

Unlike in the case of *The Tempest* where, despite other influences, Maguire and Smith are able to concentrate on the Virgil–Marlowe–Shakespeare trio, in *The Merchant of Venice* Ovid, Gower and Chaucer intervene, as we suggested earlier, making clear lines of descent in the process of constructing textual meaning difficult to determine.[49] Even so, the search for a clear diachrony seems always to collapse back into Bullough's categories no matter how problematical they have become. Indeed, Maguire and Smith's proposing of *Dido Queen of Carthage* as a 'source' for *The Tempest* retains elements of that discourse, no matter how sophisticated, from which they seek to release themselves.

Maguire and Smith are, of course, aware of this pitfall and seek to avoid it by proposing a different way of theorising 'source' in which Freudian and Derridean terms are employed to unlock a process rather than simply to identify particular attributions. They argue that in *Dido Queen of Carthage* and *The Tempest*, 'Trauma and the operations of memory are key to the construction of both plays', and taken together they are the constituent elements of a concept that is 'useful not as an attribute of characters but as one of plays: it is located textually rather than psychologically'.[50] In his *Introductory Lectures on Psychoanalysis* Freud offers the following definition:

> The term 'traumatic' has no other sense than an economic one. We apply it to an experience which within a short period of time presents the mind with an increase of stimulus too powerful to be dealt with or worked off in the normal way, and this must result in permanent disturbances of the manner in which energy operates.[51]

But Freud then proceeds to distinguish between 'a fixation to a particular phase in the past' and 'neurosis': 'Every neurosis includes a fixation of that kind, but not every fixation leads to a neurosis, coincides with a neurosis or arises owing to a neurosis.'[52] Maguire and Smith want to recast Shakespeare's 'writing career in terms of a trauma response' by replacing the word 'source' with the word 'stressor', and by looking for 'transformed, repressed, unbidden traces' of *Dido Queen of Carthage* in *The Tempest*.[53] They cannot free themselves entirely from character psychology, but they seek to equate Aeneas's recollection and reconstruction of 'the experience of Troy' and Prospero's 'narrative of his overthrow' with the play's 'attempts to process the trauma of Marlowe's doomed brilliance'.[54] It is indeed true that Prospero and Miranda are initially preoccupied with events in 'the dark backward and abysm of time' (1.2.50), and in Prospero's case the trauma relates immediately to the effects of the storm itself: 'O, I have suffered / With those that I saw suffer' (1.2.5–6). Moreover, the attempt to project the drama of the play's characters into a psychodrama in which Shakespeare is traumatised by the premature death of Marlowe stretches credulity insofar as it strays into the realm of over-determined biography. While we may extract from the plays evidence to support our own psychological theories of the way the human mind operates, projecting them onto the agency of the dramatist and then constructing a textual unconscious raises a number of historiographical problems, not the least of which is an a-historical conception of the way in which Shakespeare's brain may have worked. We have no idea if Shakespeare perceived Marlowe's truncated life in formally 'traumatic' terms, but as a popular dramatist who left behind him a body of work that those who survived him could access and use, we could say that Marlowe assumed the status of an 'authority'. Or, to put the matter a little more neutrally, Marlowe was a 'resource' for Shakespeare, elements of which he could access randomly, and could well have occupied a similar position as other accessible versions of the Troy story. But Maguire and Smith seem to show some awareness of the problem that the term 'trauma' poses. They go on to suggest that they 'employ the term in the way trauma theorists to refer simply to memories of "an originary event" where "something that has already happened acquires meaning after the fact"'.[55] The question here is, meaning for whom? Virtually all of Shakespeare's plays begin with some form of disruptive 'originary event' that the subsequent action proceeds to develop and then resolve. The drama that Freud proposes is rather different and the dilemma that Maguire and Smith seek to resolve is rooted in a post-Freudian world of complex symptomatology, the key to which resides in the reader.

The second term that Maguire and Smith deploy is 'hauntology'. Whereas for Marx and Engels it was 'the spectre of communism' that haunted nineteenth-century Europe, for Derrida his philosophy is 'haunted' by the spectre of Marx. They quote Derrida's definition from *Specters of Marx*: 'Hauntology supplants its near homonym ontology, replacing the priority of being and presence with the figure of the ghost as that which is neither present nor absent, neither dead nor alive.'[56] Derrida approaches his own brand of Marxism through the medium of Shakespeare's *Hamlet*, both of which are 'inheritances', and in the process he seeks to emphasise 'the radical and necessary *heterogeneity* of an inheritance, the difference without opposition that has to mark it, a "disparate" and a quasi-juxtaposition without dialectic (the very plural of what we will later call Marx's spirits)' (original italics).[57] Unsurprisingly, Maguire and Smith link Derrida's notion of the spectre to the Ghost of Old Hamlet which they say, '"appears"; it is not summoned'.[58] From this they jump to the curious claim that in *Hamlet* 'the source-spectre *Dido* comes unbidden and unexpectedly'.[59] Unexpected from the point of view of the modern reader, perhaps, but 'unbidden'?

Let us examine this claim a little more closely. Hamlet's first explicit 'classical' reference is at Act 1 Scene 2 where Gertrude following 'my poor father's body' is likened to 'Niobe, all tears' (1.2.148–9). The narrative of Niobe appears in Golding's translation of Book 6 of Ovid's *Metamorphoses*, where her overweening pride provokes the anger of the goddess Latona who kills her children. The proud Niobe ('tother Niobe' (6.343)) gives way to the grieving Niobe:

> Then down she sate
> Bereft of all hir children quite, and drawing to her fate,
> Among hir daughters and hir sonnes and husband newly dead.
> Hir cheeks waxt hard, the Ayre could stirre no haire upon hir head,
> The colour of hir face was dim and clearly void of blood,
> And sadly under open lids hir eyes unmoved stood.
> In all hir bodie was no life. For even hir verie tung
> And palat of hir mouth was hard, and eche to other clung.
> Hir Pulses ceased for to beate, hir necke did cease to bow,
> Hir armes to stir, hir feete to go, all power forwent as now.
> And into stone her verie wombe and bowels also bind.
> But yet she wept: and being hoyst by force of whirling wind
> Was carried into Phyrgie. There upon a mountains top
> She weepeth still in stone.
>
> (6.382–95)

The centrality of Ovid, partly through Golding's translation of the *Metamorphoses*, is universally accepted. But if Shakespeare is drawing on the passage just quoted, how much of the Niobe story is actually relevant to Hamlet's invocation? Whatever Niobe's faults (and they are sufficient to arouse the anger of a goddess, and to produce a cataclysmic retaliation), it is the fact that she is a model of 'weeping' that is important here, even when she is 'still in stone'. Ovid is not, in this case a 'source' so much as a model, one of a number available to Shakespeare for the expression of calamitous – one is almost tempted to say traumatic – grief. Here Golding's retelling of the 'plot' narrative is less important than what may have been a commonly recognised motif that by the time of *Hamlet* had become what Helen Cooper, in another context, has called a 'meme' with an 'ability to replicate and adapt' to changing situations.[60] Cooper goes on to suggest that within the larger framework, '[v]ariations on conventions happen not only synchronically, within time, as authors choose the particular angle on a motif that suits them, but diachronically, across time, as cultural, historical, and political change alter beliefs and expectations'.[61] Nor can we say that this is 'hauntology' in the Derridean sense of the term, so much as a handy resource that is part of the dramatist's laboratory of models on which he can draw.

Of course, it is not the only model available to Shakespeare in *Hamlet*. There is Hecuba, whose grief is motivated by a different stimulus from that of Niobe. Here the scene, and the context, shifts to Troy and to Pyrrhus's execution of Priam, and there is no lengthy back-story of the sort that there appears to be in the case of Niobe. But as in the earlier case, what is invoked is a model of grief, this time involving a king's death. If, on the other hand, Hamlet wishes to prick the conscience of his mother, then his attempt at dramaturgy fails initially, although it may communicate something to the theatre audience. The Niobe model is directed to Gertrude, whereas the Hecuba model is directed towards Hamlet's own inability to articulate clearly and to project outwardly his own grief at the death of his father. The availability of these models in Shakespeare's dramaturgical workshop testify to their synchronic existence, and, to some extent, to the dramatist's own agency. That Shakespeare should be 'haunted' by Ovid, or Golding, or Marlowe, represents an attempt to explain a psychology for which Freud (and Derrida) are themselves inadequate and historically anachronistic models. The question is also, how in a scholarly edition might we represent these models in such a way as to circumvent Bullough's hierarchy? It may simply be a case of noting them while resisting the temptation to make a judgement about which narrative assumes precedence over the others.

As we saw in Chapter 1, what appear to be 'references back' in a play such as *The Merchant of Venice* turn out to be fragments that challenge, or even undermine, the play's teleological trajectory. In *Hamlet* the choice of models also seems to depend almost entirely on context, and on where the model sits in the dramatist's memory. The dramatist here seems to be aping the logic that Hamlet later confronts in his exchange with the Gravedigger: both the register and references to immediate events are adjusted as occasion demands, and in a way that defeats grammatical logic and stable meaning.[62] It would be convenient to reach for Freud's chapter on 'Forgetting of proper names' in his *The Psychopathology of Everyday Life* to explain this, except that in Freud's case forgetting involves repression.[63] There is no evidence to suggest – either directly or through a symptomatic reading – that forgetfulness, partial remembering or even misremembering necessarily involve repression in Freud's sense of the term as a form of defence observable clinically in hysterical behaviour as part of a structured narrative of the unconscious.[64] Moreover, in the examples that we have been discussing the fragmentary references cannot easily be explained as traces of a fuller narrative in terms of Freudian psychopathology that reads the writer's unconscious *through* the psychology of the dramatic character.[65] They stand almost as isolated examples, each moving in slightly different directions, of various facets of grief, abstracted from larger narrative structures that in our attempts to make sense of we seek to appropriate into 'a centred or segmented higher unity'.[66] To this extent, they share some of the characteristics for which Deleuze and Guattari's anti-Freudian category of the 'rhizome' might offer a better explanation.

For Deleuze and Guattari the rhizome is a free-standing phenomenon that discloses evidence of a desire that is killed by being forced into a representational structure that obstructs its passage:

> You will be allowed to live and speak, but only after every outlet has been obstructed. Once a rhizome has been obstructed, arborified, it's all over, no desire stirs; for it is always by rhizome that desire moves and produces. Whenever desire climbs a tree internal repercussions trip it up and it falls to its death; the rhizome, on the other hand, acts on desire by external, productive outgrowths.[67]

In his *A Treatise on Monarchy* Fulke Greville registered a similar mobility of desire with the observation that 'when man beholds this boundles sea / Of will' he thinks that 'thoughts may saile every way / Till pow'rs contrary windes disperse these dreames'; it is these swirling instruments of power that 'make men see their freedome bound soe fast, / As it of noe forbidden fruite dare tast' (stanza 42).[68] He was candid in his assessment of the threat of desire since, if unchecked, humanity would return to the originary moment of Adam's transgression:

> Yet happily had man not thus bin bounded
> With humane wrests, as well as moulds divine;
> Hee in his passions must have bin confounded,
> Desire in him is such an endless Myne:
> *Eve* would have *Adam* bin, man kinge, kinges more;
> Till such destruction fall, as fell before.
>
> (stanza 43)

Neither Fulke Greville nor Shakespeare, we need to emphasise, were Freudians, nor were they living through an ethos of advanced capitalism where fragmentation might be considered the norm. Indeed, the pressures that Deleuze and Guattari ascribe to the fragmentary pressures that accompany the stages of advanced capitalism, and the explanations that are used to account for particular psychological states, cannot be uncritically applied to early modern writers. There are, however, as we shall see, occasions when the 'arborification' that Deleuze and Guattari deplore is evident in the close connection between isolated (or perhaps localised) elements of particular texts and pre-existing narratives. Their function is to enlarge, and complicate, plot structures and/or representations of dramatic character. But also, there are occasions when fragments generate a momentary impact for which no satisfactory larger narrative can be produced. On such occasions all we can do is note the instances of their circulation, but resist the temptation to fold them into a larger psychodrama; they are simply available, in circulation by a variety of means, and they appear from time to time in the dramatist's active memory as part of the emotional furniture of the mind. Here the expression of an emotion such as grief, or the possible disappointment following on from deposition, permit us to glimpse not only the rhizome as it exists and is experienced in the character's horizon of perception but also the investment that the fragment makes in the resistance to any form of 'arborification' and hierarchy. We are closer to explanations of textual disturbances if we resist folding them into a narrative that may have its roots in the psychology we invent for particular characters *or*, ultimately, in the narrative that traces the moment of the text's creation. It is for this reason, among others, that the term 'sources' is tainted, and it is why we need something more neutral, more flexible, such as 'resources', to account for this variety. In order to explain the link between Marlowe and Shakespeare, Maguire and Smith are forced to base their argument on a combination of Freudian and Derridean accounts of the way dramatic characters, plots and, ultimately, texts behave.

Nowhere more than in language itself were the myths of creation and of origins more keenly felt, especially around questions of order, authority, truth and conflicts of meaning, or the capacity of context to modify meaning. As we saw in *Hamlet*, 'custom' and 'antiquity' could be spontaneously pressed into the service of authorising language, while their withdrawal, for whatever reason, threatened the overwhelming of reason by desire, and a return to primeval chaos. Golding's translation of Ovid's *The Metamorphoses* runs together Christian and pagan myths of creation, and Book 1 charts the decline of humanity from a pre-lapsarian 'golden' age to an 'iron' one.[69] It is Shakespeare's *Hamlet* that provides language itself with a history that stretches back to a primal, one might almost say a Lucretian, chaos. Yet at the same time, and at a purely practical level, the constraints of what might be considered a textually rigorous authority were buttressed by the much more fluid orality of day-to-day communication.

One of the most adventurous of Shakespeare commentators, the late Terence Hawkes, asserted in the Introduction to *Shakespeare's Talking Animals* (1973): 'This is a book about Shakespeare, Language, and drama.'[70] He emphasised both the comparative scarcity of reading materials and the practical impediments to reading itself, in contrast to the fundamental orality that found its expression in the Elizabethan popular theatre:

The question is not how many people *could* read and write, but the extent to which they did in a society in which books, candles, privacy and motivation were variously in short supply and in which, perhaps even as a result, the most vivid and rewarding form of popular entertainment was provided by the oral art form of drama.[71]

In his separation in the book's first four chapters of 'Language as culture', 'Gesture as language', 'Drama as language' and 'Drama as culture', Hawkes proposed a complex system of representation in which signs could be read historically, but also re-read in modern contexts, with modern inflexions. While maintaining the link between Shakespeare and textuality, Hawkes brilliantly reversed the categories of 'source', 'imitation' and 'meaning' to suggest that what scholars had come to regard as a 'natural' link was, in fact, the product of a distorting glass of academic retrospection. In seeking to return Shakespeare to a historic 'popular' culture, and in suggesting that modern versions of the 'popular' were the most appropriate vehicles for the dissemination of Shakespeare, Hawkes implied that just as for Shakespeare, 'culture' in the broadest sense was a 'resource' accessible through a plethora of formulations and representations. In addition, and for us, Shakespeare himself was not a source but a 'resource' that could be endlessly recycled according to our own perspectives as a cultural vehicle through which our own meanings are generated. Indeed, Hawkes goes much further than that, laying down an absolute challenge to the traditional view that was advanced by Hardin Craig:

With the text's 'authority' and 'authenticity' so fundamentally questioned in this way, it has become more and more difficult to claim that *Hamlet* offers once-for-all revelations about what Shakespeare 'thought' and 'felt' with regard to the events and characters the play seems to deploy, or to assume that the 'meaning' of the play should be limited to or by whatever Shakespeare intended to say 'through' it. This not to say that the text known as *Hamlet* no longer materially exists. But it is to say that our way of describing, of accounting for, of establishing a productive purchase on that text must change. And the change will effectively serve to push the play's material existence into the foreground.[72]

In his use of the phrase 'material existence' Hawkes was doing something other than simply fetishising the textual or the performance object. Rather, he was laying down a challenge to the entire conceptual framework of 'authority' and 'authenticity'. He was also identifying a cultural form that is both initially innovative and endlessly renewable, and that depends for its meanings upon a demolition of the hierarchy in which 'text' is privileged over 'context'. This has serious ramifications, as we shall see, for the entire discourse involving concepts such as 'source' and 'originality', whose historical and ideological roots David Quint has done so much to expose.

Of course, we cannot reduce the 'language' to which Hawkes referred in *Shakespeare's Talking Animals* simply to written 'text', even though this may be the predominant form in which we receive and validate it. Indeed, he insisted that 'the structure of the "real world" is largely pre-determined by social forces', although he concedes that 'the most powerful of these is language'.[73] But, he continued: 'Man, this seems to suggest, is very firmly a creature of his distinctive feature of talking. Culture, or way of life, and language, or way of speaking, appear to be coterminous.'[74] We shall see later what the consequences of treating Shakespeare as a creature of 'language' in this radically extended sense of the term means for an analysis of the 'resources' available to him, and to us as we attempt to reassemble them in order to elucidate and illuminate his plays and his poetry.

In the same way that we cannot easily reduce Shakespeare's 'resources' to a series of books that comprise 'authorities', so we cannot reduce language to 'text' without considering its larger cultural implications. In his book *Shakespeare's Binding Language* (2016), John Kerrigan has assembled an impressive array of documentary evidence to indicate that the historical insistence upon performative, assertory and promissory language came under serious pressure during the early modern period. Indeed, and despite drawing attention to the plethora of moralising statements about what the integrity of language ought to be, Kerrigan observes that the plays of Shakespeare 'are far less often about truthful, assertory oaths and fulfilled promises than about broken vows, lying asseverations, and a bond for a pound of flesh'.[75] What was frequently in dispute were the ethical and moral dilemmas that arose

Myths of origin 115

from the breaking of oaths of various kinds, domestic and public, promises and treaties, where their validity was divinely sanctioned, and where the vernacular appeal to oaths did much to diminish their illocutionary force. While 'truth' might be found in the secular authority of books, its efficacy was paradoxically sustained by a theoretical appeal to a divine source and at the same time diminished by its incorporation into the vernacular process of 'swearing'. Kerrigan notes that the most challenging case was 'equivocation and mental reservation':

> those Jesuitical practices whereby the speaker worked with ambiguities to evade the apparent meaning of a given word, or swore something while qualifying or correcting it silently on the grounds that God would accept the truth of what was thought not what was said.[76]

Here the 'source' of truth, its origin and its authority can be traced back to God, a trajectory that Erasmus parodies in 'The Praise of Folly', when he has Folly trace her own ancestry back through the theatre of human affairs to her own divine origins:

> My father was neither Chaos, Orcus, Saturn, Japetus, nor any other of that obsolete and senile set of gods; on the contrary he was Plutus, the real father of men and gods, despite the opinion of Hesiod, Homer, and Jove himself. Now, as always, one nod from Plutus turns everything sacred upside down. By his decisions, wars, peace, empires, plans, judgements, assemblies, marriages, treaties, pacts, pires, plans, laws, arts, sports, solemnities (I am almost out of breath) – in short, all public and private affairs are governed. Without his help, all the poets' multitude of gods, even, I may boldly say, the chief ones, either would not exist or would have to live leanly at home. Not even Pallas can help the person who arouses Plutus' anger but with his favour one can laugh at Jove's thunderbolts. What a magnificent father![77]

Folly's carnivalesque inversion of authority and ancestry acknowledges the existence of a paternal God, but the phrase 'poets' multitude of gods' hints that even this genealogy may be the result of a human contribution to the process of creation and to history. Folly's genealogy is imbued with a linearity *and* a circularity, that taps into what David Quint, in a more specific context has identified as 'a model for the cyclical alternation between spirit and matter'.[78] Within that larger model, narratives and texts are arranged within hierarchies that are all underpinned by a validating godhead who authorises and legitimises every utterance.

The Gospel according to St John begins by identifying the plain source of all utterance: 'In the beginning was the Word, and the Word was with God and the Word was God.' This was of particular interest to the Protestant project of cleansing language from the Catholic rhetoric of icons, but, of course, that was not the only narrative of origins available to the early modern period. In his analysis of the opening of the 'Pantagruel' chapter of Rabelais's *Gargantua and Pantagruel*, Quint observes that the origin of sin is attributed to the fratricide of Cain, and the creation of Babel. He concludes: 'The violence which accompanies the genesis of the Rabelaisian books suggests the potential for any linguistic discourse to estrange itself from its audience, to become sufficient unto itself, nonsense to others.'[79] Clearly, the inversion of order, or the removal of a transcendent validating authority from language, has serious consequences for society at large; but more than that, it drives a wedge between an originating and authorising religious narrative, and those accounts of human behaviour rooted in historically over-determined contingency. Insofar as we can think of the contingent as being embedded in what Steven Mullaney identifies as 'modes of thinking as well as feeling that are inseparable from lived experience',[80] then contingency must be determined by larger cultural and political pressures that point to particular 'faultlines'.[81]

The problems that arise from submitting language itself and its various forms to the vicissitudes of contingency is precisely the subject matter of Shakespeare's *Love's Labour's Lost* (c.1595). The 1598 quarto is important since this is recognised to be one of the first published play-texts that identifies the author as 'W. *Shakespere*' on its title page.[82] It is also, as the play's Arden 3 editor, Henry Woudhuysen, observes, 'the earliest of Shakespeare's three plays for which no primary source is known'.[83] Clearly this causes the editor some anxiety, but it does not prevent him, however, from speculating; indeed, the question of 'source' is quickly transformed into one of 'influence', and from there into near certainty that 'a

Myths of origin 117

major influence on the play came through Shakespeare's reading of Sidney, but he is more by way of an influence on it than a source for it'.[84] Bullough himself cites *The Countess of Pembroke's Arcadia* (*c*.1580) as a 'source', but not for *Love's Labour's Lost*, whose sparse antecedents are divided into a very small number of 'analogues' and 'historical parallels'. Bullough cites *Arcadia* more fully in his section on *King Lear*,[85] but although his focus is on the storm scene in *Lear*, and significant aspects of the Gloucester sub-plot, he also identifies echoes of Sidney's text in *Othello*,[86] and more questionably in *Macbeth*.[87] He excerpts 'sources' from books 2 and 3 of Sidney's text, but he refrains from commenting on the ethos of 'The last book or Act' (Book 5) that is not too dissimilar in parts from the general political emphasis in *King Lear*.

In *King Lear*, Edmund's 'we make guilty of our disasters the sun, the moon and the stars, as if we were villains on necessity' (1.2.120–2) and Kent's 'It is the stars, / The stars above us govern our conditions' (4.3.33–4) draw on the same discourse as the comparison in Sidney's text between human destiny and tennis balls. This sentiment is embedded in a convoluted plot involving shifting gender identity, allegations of rape and patricide, and consequently trial according to the laws of Arcadia. In an indirect narrative, 'Timopyrus, despot of Lycia, and Palladius, prince of Caria' are made to consider their precarious positions in a strange country:

> The princes stood a while upon that, demanding leisure to give perfect knowledge of their greatness. But when they were answered that in the case of a prince's death the law of that country had ever been that immediate trial should be had, they were forced to yield, resolved that in those names they would as much as they could cover the shame of their royal parentage, and keep as long as might be (if evil were determined against them) the evil news from their careful kinsfolk. Wherein the chief man they considered was Euarchus, whom the strange and secret working of justice had brought to be the judge over them – in such a shadow or rather pit of darkness the warmish mankind lives that neither they know how to foresee nor what to fear, and and are like but tennis balls tossed by the racket of the higher power.[88]

This image of humans as the tennis balls of fate was still actively in circulation in Webster's *The Duchess of Malfi* (1614) in Bosola's observation: 'We are merely the stars' tennis-balls, struck and banded / Which way please them' (5.4.54–5). John Russell Brown traces the analogy to Sidney, Florio and ultimately to Plautus's *Captivi*.[89] How this image circulated is not easy to determine, and it might well be that Sidney, Shakespeare and Webster all drew on a common stock whose cultural vibrancy especially in relation to a possible revitalisation in the cause of Renaissance scepticism, cannot with certainty be reduced to a simple process of linear transmission. This kind of mental and emotional furniture distributed in various 'rooms' in the houses of memory, does not require, or indeed make it necessary to recall – as we saw earlier – full narratives. It is sufficient to note that they comprise a vocabulary of memes and theatregrams that are available to the practising dramatist. The available printed literature becomes a resource that can be absorbed into a theatre text sometimes shorn of its larger narrative context, as we saw earlier in the examples from *Hamlet* where different memes of grief might be deployed on different occasions. For non-literate members of Shakespeare's audience, these details are not reference points in a larger literary lexicon but simply punctual embodiments of emotional and/or mental states that do not require larger, narrative frameworks.

Shakespeare had access to a variety of resources for *Lear*, ranging from ancient Celtic narratives, through popular medieval stories, right down to anonymous contemporary dramas. *Love's Labour's Lost*, on the other hand, is embedded in a series of contemporary debates about language, rhetorical and artistic forms, as well as cultural stereotypes. Whereas for *King Lear*, and for other plays such as *Hamlet*, the History Plays, or the Roman Plays, and for some of the Comedies, we can establish a pattern of textual transmission that is identifiably linear (though not exclusively so), for a play like *Love's Labour's Lost* that begins in the library and ends with the seasons, the question of 'origin' seems at best secondary. The King of Navarre plans for himself and his three male courtiers a war against 'your own affections / And the huge army of the world's desires' (1.1.9–10), seeking 'fame' through converting the court into 'a little academe, / Still and contemplative in living art' (1.1.13–14). It is left to Berowne to put the anti-bookish case against Navarre's strategy:

> Small have continual plodders ever won,
> Save base authority from others' books.
> These earthly godfathers of heaven's lights,
> That give a name to every fixed star,
> Have no more profit of their shining nights
> Than those that walk and wot not what they are.
> Too much to know is to know naught but fame,
> And every godfather can give a name.
>
> (1.1.86–93)

Clearly, Berowne is on the side of the vibrancy of performance, and of those who would castigate source-hunters for rummaging in 'the elephant's graveyard' of literary studies. But what turns the debate between what is and is not 'realistic' into something that is politically and linguistically serious, is that each of the participants is expected to swear an oath. The comic obstacle that the play sets out to overcome involves a series of levels of representation that stretch from the discourse of the court, through that of the 'outsider', down to the representatives of a rural culture. The question here is not which of these discourses is the most authentic, or which of them best represents a discourse that we may trace back to a source in Shakespeare's own 'mind'. Indeed, as John Kerrigan forcefully demonstrates, the debate about language was a *public* one, and audiences would surely have recognised themselves, and others, in elements of the drama as it unfolded.

In invoking the example of *Love's Labour's Lost* my aim is not to trawl through the elements of its plot, or to tease out the various ways in which the initial 'oath' is countered, or violated, or indeed what these strategies contribute to the impossibility of a formal comic ending. This is a play that violates the expectation of a resolution; but it is also a play that opposes the creation of a narrative that will outlive the King of Navarre and his fellow aristocrats. As if to emphasise this tension, the play contains two of a series of sonnets that subsequently appeared in 1599 in a short collection set in octavo and published by William Jaggard entitled *The Passionate Pilgrim* that had already appeared in quarto a year before in *Love's Labour's Lost*, and probably in performance before that. This prompts us to enquire as to what happens when texts migrate from one context to another, and what meanings they accumulate as they do so. Two modern editors of *Shakespeare's Poems* speculate that Shakespeare had been displeased with Jaggard's publication and that this accounts for the fact that there were no further editions of *The Passionate Pilgrim* until the publisher's 'remarkably bold, even shameless re-launch' of the volume in 1612.[90] Another editor, Colin Burrow, observes that this short collection contains versions of sonnets 138 and 144, and proceeds to reconstruct speculatively the possible ways in which these, and other non-Shakespearean poems, came into the hands of the printer Jaggard. What frustrates Burrow is that: 'The origins of these and other texts included in the volume are, however, a mystery.'[91] The quarry in this case would be to seek to reaffirm the status of the author by tracing the poems back to a source in Shakespeare's imagination, to the moment of their composition, and thence to the process whereby particular versions are shown to differ from each other. Burrow is concerned with 'origins' rather than meanings, and to that extent he remains within the parameters of the discourse and its accompanying mythology that we have sought to investigate. In a play where letters go astray, sonnets are addressed to the wrong audiences, thereby making a mockery of a series of literary conventions and parodying the process of textual transmission. It is, of course, the theatrical circumstances in which the appropriation of a literary form appears that is important here rather than the extra-theatrical circumstances that a narrative of origins is designed to construct, and that are important in the process of producing meanings. Each context modifies the impact of these texts. Readers of *The Passionate Pilgrim* may have recognised the appearance of the sonnets in the play, whereas non-literate members of the audience may have concentrated on the *immediate* context in which the literary pretensions of Navarre's court are shown to be ridiculous.

As another example – although this involves the possibility of textual revision between the time of performance and its appearance in the First Folio – we might note the appearance of songs from Thomas Middleton's play *The Witch* in Shakespeare's *Macbeth*, the text of which one editor, Gary Taylor, ascribes to 'William Shakespeare, adapted by Thomas Middleton'.[92] These might be examples of what Jeffrey Masten calls 'a diachronic form of collaboration',[93] although Masten extends his remit considerably to suggest that

> The construction of meaning by a theatrical company was polyvocal – often beginning with a collaborative manuscript, which was then revised, cut, rearranged, and augmented by book-holders, copyists, and other writers, elaborated and improved by actors in performance, accompanied by music and songs that may or may not have originated in a completely different context.[94]

This 'diachronic form of collaboration' might be extended to include the psychological process undertaken by a single writer, who might adapt a text in one form or genre, thereby converting it into the very 'polyvocal' construction of meaning that is both necessary for, and part and parcel of, theatrical performance. But this does not quite exhaust the possibilities raised by the case of the sonnets that appeared in *Love's Labour's Lost* and reappeared in *The Passionate Pilgrim* after the play was performed and published. Indeed, the reverse might be true as these texts are displaced from their originary dramatic context and relocated in another, involving a different level of polyvocality as they collide with sonnets by other writers. Masten goes on to identify an important difference between viewing texts 'as literature in the library' and reading them 'primarily as written communications between writers and readers' on the one hand, and reading a play, say, in quarto form as 'a representation/recapitulation of a theatrical experience, a communication between actors and audience' on the other.[95] This is something that we need constantly to be reminded of as we arrange originary, analogous or parallel texts with a view to reconstructing a reductively linear hierarchical order of those theatrical working practices of composition in the early modern playhouse. We need a more capacious, less tendentious term to deal with the complexities of playwriting, especially in Shakespeare's case where different modes of articulation find their way into the scripts themselves.

The two poems from *The Passionate Pilgrim* as they first appeared in a performance of *Love's Labour's Lost* are separated from a particular literary context and accompanying cultural context in which they might normally be expected to be inscribed. The scene begins with Berowne in a quandary as he lurches from one extreme to another, concluding that 'I do nothing in the world but lie, and lie in my throat' (4.3.10–11). He then slips into the role of the stock Petrarchan lover, a melancholic rhyming poet who has written a sonnet to an unavailable mistress. His is the first of a series of situations in which the writer of a sonnet inadvertently performs it to hidden fellow (male) suitors. Each lover thinks that he has managed to get one over on the others, but the scene unravels as communications go awry; in fact, the final communication, that of Berowne to Rosaline, is revealed because a letter goes astray, with the result that the King and all of his companions are 'foresworn'. This exposes both the instability of written language and the aesthetic forms associated with aristocratic amorous discourse, as the play represents them, to merciless satire. Moreover, Navarre and his fellow suitors are forced to relinquish their commitment to a wholly artificial and unrealistic quest for fame in the world of books. They do so in the face of a devastating challenge from the unpredictable but politically contingent vicissitudes of language as it is forced to negotiate the varying and unpredictable pressures of the real world that only a respect for the veracity of 'oaths' can stabilise. Indeed, and in the face of the formal demands of comedy, the play ultimately opts for a language purged of its unworldly poetic and rhetorical extravagances, although as Berowne is forced to concede, this transformation cannot be effected fully and immediately:

> Henceforth my wooing shall be expressed
> In russet yeas and honest kersey noes.
> And to begin: wench, so God help men law!
> My love to thee is sound, *sans* crack or flaw.
> ROSALINE. Sans '*sans*' I pray you.
> BEROWNE.   Yet I have a trick
> Of the old rage.
>
> (5.2.412–16)

A little later, after the entry of Marcadé, Berowne is forced to reaffirm that 'Honest plain words best pierce the ear of grief' (5.2.747). This manifestly onanistic gesture is comically perverted by addressing the sonnet to concealed male auditors, just one of the examples of misdirected communication that occur throughout the play.

Myths of origin 123

The larger aesthetic question that these perversions raise is how to align the dilemma that the King and his lords have created with the formal requirements of a comic ending. And *Love's Labour's Lost* is one of the few plays in the Shakespeare canon that is forced to engineer an alternative, seasonal conclusion to an action that should end, as in the case of most Shakespearean Comedies, with a reaffirmation of the institution of marriage. Indeed, perhaps we need to think of this play in conjunction with *Romeo and Juliet*, which begins with a Prologue who speaks a sonnet, but where the subsequent action departs from a romantic idiom (replete with misdirected letters and frustrated love) to end in the frustration of love and tragedy;[96] and with *A Midsummer Night's Dream* in which the lovers miraculously overcome various obstacles so that at the end of the day 'Jack shall have Jill, / Nought shall go ill; / The man shall have his mare again, and all shall be well' (3.2.461–3).

The further we journey into comparative details such as these, the more we engage with cultural and aesthetic contexts for which explanations of 'origin' and 'source' cease to be of much help. To be sure, their theatrical effects depend upon particular perceptions of the distinction between 'literary' and theatrical forms, but these are memes that are available to the practising dramatist. Contemporary public debates about language, its authentication and legitimacy, and its stability in the face of challenges to its performative validity all figure here. The debates around marriage, the role of women in the Elizabethan household, the nature of different kinds of 'friendship', the intersection of politics and domestic life, and the distinctions between life and art are also elements of Elizabethan culture that impacted upon public and popular discourse. All of them put into question the reductive and constraining vocabulary of 'source' and 'origin' and the myths that underpin them. And it is important for us to make distinctions between those elements of texts that resonate with other texts, and fragments that cannot be easily pressed into the service of a narrative that privileges origins and their attendant myths. Indeed, the kind of orality capable of assimilating, recontextualising and revitalising details from an emerging book culture clearly eschews issues such as 'originality' and 'origin' in favour of practices of imitation, repetition, continuity and innovative bricolage, where fragments of those texts to which schoolboys in Shakespeare's situation were exposed, find their way into theatrical discourses that could, at the same time, be both imitative and critical as part of the corporate enterprise of theatrical activity. Our problem is to try to describe accurately how these elements cohere in a particular text, and what their relations might be with other contemporaneous texts. The overwhelming temptation is to establish a genealogy that depends upon hierarchical arrangement, except that the historical and fictional narratives in which particular incidents and events were embedded, might just as easily have survived through circulation in other, more oral, forms. In other words, the written form might just as easily have been later than an oral counterpart. But also, we need to acknowledge our own tendency as literary scholars to fabricate narratives as means of seeking connections between different categories of evidence. What we require is a little less attention to an ideologically over-determined diachrony in favour of a more careful synchronic approach. The dwelling upon matters of 'origin' preserves a hierarchy in which 'authorship' is primary, 'context' is always secondary, and in which an insistence upon the originary moment of the 'author's' conception of the text obscures a much more complex level of interactivity some of whose contours the following chapters will seek to explore.

Notes

1 Raymond Williams, *Marxism and Literature* (Oxford, 1977), p. 30.
2 *Ibid.*, p. 31.
3 David Quint, *Origin and Originality in Renaissance Literature* (New Haven, 1983), pp. 3–4.
4 *Ibid.*, p. 5.
5 Benedetto Croce, 'The concept of history as absolute historicism', *A Croce Reader: Aesthetics, Philosophy, History, Literary Criticism*, trans. and ed. Massimo Verdicchio. (Toronto and London, 2017), pp. 54, 56.
6 Sir Walter Raleigh, *The History of the World* (London, 1614). On the facing leaf of the frontispiece there is an explanatory poem 'THE MINDE OF / The FRONT'. The final couple sums up Raleigh's project: 'Times Witnesse, Herald of Antiquitie / The Light of Truth, and Life of Memorie.'

7 *Ibid.*, sig. A1ʳ.
8 *Ibid.*, sig. A1ᵛ.
9 Erasmus, 'The Praise of Folly', in *Essential Works of Erasmus*, ed. W.T.H. Jackson (New York and London, 1965), pp. 359ff. See especially pp. 366–7, where the source of human behaviour is not 'GOD' but the classical deity 'Plutus'.
10 *Ibid.*, p. 368.
11 *Ibid.*
12 Alexander Barclay, *The Ship of Fools*, 2 vols (New York, 1966), vol. 1, p. 5.
13 See Greg Walker, 'The Renaissance in Britain', in Patrick Collinson, ed., *The Sixteenth Century* (Oxford, 2002), p. 176, where the birth of 'the idea of a lost paradise' is linked to 'the destructive effects of Reformation discipline'.
14 *Ibid.*, p. 18.
15 *Ibid.*, p. 20.
16 Barclay, *The Ship of Fools*, vol. 2, pp. 306–12.
17 *Ibid.*, p. 311.
18 Cf. Thomas Wilson, *The Art of Rhetorique* (London, 1585), sig. A7ʳ, in which the origin of persuasive language is couched in the narrative of the Fall: 'even now when man was thus past all hope of amendment, God still tendering his owne workmanshippe, stirring up his faithfull and elect, to perswade with reason all men to societie. And gaue his appointed Ministers knowledge both to see the natures of men, and also graunted them the gift of utteraunce, that they might with ease win folke at their will, and frame them by reason to all good order.' See also Adrian Streete, *Protestantism and Drama in Early Modern England* (Cambridge, 2009), p. 129, and also *Apocalypse and Anti-Catholicism in Seventeenth-century English Drama* (Cambridge, 2017), p. 43.
19 Erasmus, 'The Praise of Folly', p. 397.
20 Lucretius, *De Rerum Natura*, trans. W.H.D. Rouse (Cambridge, MA, 1982), bk 1, p. 3.
21 Georg Lukács, *The Theory of the Novel*, trans. Anna Bostock (reprinted London, 2006), p. 122. Lukács distinguishes between 'epic' that 'has the blissful time-removed quality of the world of the gods' and the 'constitutive' time of the novel, which is 'the resistance of the organic – which possesses a mere semblance of life – to the present meaning, the will of life to remain within its own completely encliosed immanence'.
22 Stephen Greenblatt, *The Swerve: How the Renaissance Began* (London, 2011), p. 13.

23 Erasmus, 'The Praise of Folly', p. 381.
24 Quint, *Origin and Originality*, p. 7.
25 *Ibid.*, p. 213.
26 *Ibid.*, pp. 213–14.
27 *Ibid.*, p. 214.
28 See Lukas Erne, *Shakespeare as Literary Dramatist* (Cambridge, 2003), pp. 131–73.
29 Cf. Laurie Maguire and Emma Smith, 'What is a source? Or, how Shakespeare read his Marlowe', *Shakespeare Survey*, 68 (2015), 23–4.
30 See Richard J. Evans, *In Defence of History* (reprinted, London, 2018), pp. 109–11. Evans is hostile to much post-structuralist thinking in comments such as: 'Discourse does not construct the past itself; the most that it is possible to argue is that it constructs our attempts to represent it' (p. 109).
31 Walter Benjamin, 'On language as such and on the language of Man', *Reflections: Essays, Aphorisms, Autobiographical Writings*, trans. Edmund Jephcott (New York, 1978), p. 315.
32 Cf. Quint, *Origin and Originality*, p. 198. But see also Michel Jeanneret, *Perpetual Motion: Transforming Shapes in the Renaissance from da Vinci to Montaigne*, trans. Nidra Poller (Baltimore and London, 2001), pp. 86–7.
33 Jeanneret, *Perpetual Motion*, p. 86.
34 Cf. Hamlet's comment at 2.2.518–21 that anticipates Claudius's aside later: 'That I, the son of a dear murdered, / Prompted to my revenge by heaven and hell, / Must like a whore unpack my heart with words / And fall a-cursing like a very drab.'
35 See Jeanneret, *Perpetual Motion*, pp. 104ff. See also Rhodri Lewis, *Hamlet and the Vision of Darkness* (Princeton and Oxford, 2017) for a reading of *Hamlet* that emphasises its investment in the grotesque: 'there is a sense in which all those constrained to exist within the moral economy of *Hamlet* are interchangeable. All are bluffing their way through the dark' (p. 9).
36 Hardin Craig, 'Trend of Shakespeare scholarship', *Shakespeare Survey*, 2 (1949), 111.
37 *Ibid.*
38 E.M.W. Tillyard, *The Elizabethan World Picture* (London, 1943), pp. 101–2.
39 Walter Benjamin, 'Theses on the philosophy of history', *Illuminations*, trans. Harry Zohn (Glasgow, 1970), p. 263.
40 See Laurence Coupe, *Myth*, 2nd edn (London, 2009), p. 2.

41 *Ibid.*, p. 31. Here Coupe glosses 'myth' in relation to T.S. Eliot's understanding of the manner in which Joyce used an 'ancient paradigm' in his novel *Ulysses*.
42 See Steven Mullaney, *The Reformation of Emotions in the Age of Shakespeare* (Chicago and London, 2015), pp. 14–15, and especially the definition of the 'collective self' defined as 'at least in part by its flaws and fractures' (p. 15), suggesting disruption of narrative rather than reaffirmation.
43 Maguire and Smith, 'What is a source?', 16.
44 *Ibid.*
45 *Ibid.*, 20.
46 *Ibid.*, 17.
47 *Ibid.*, 19.
48 For a full and politically astute account of early modern investments in the Troy legend, see Heather James, *Shakespeare's Troy:Drama, Politics and the Translation of Empire* (Cambridge, 1997).
49 See William Shakespeare, *The Merchant of Venice*, ed. John Drakakis, Arden 3 series (London, 2010), pp. 367–8, and the glosses to ll. 1, 4–5, 7–13.
50 Maguire and Smith, 'What is a source?', 24.
51 Sigmund Freud, *Introductory Lectures on Psychoanalysis*, vol. 1, ed. James Strachey and Angela Richards, Pelican Freud Library (reprinted, Harmondsworth, 1978), p. 315.
52 *Ibid.*, p. 316.
53 Maguire and Smith, 'What is a source?', 24.
54 *Ibid.*, 24–5.
55 *Ibid.*, 26.
56 *Ibid.*
57 Jacques Derrida, *Specters of Marx*, trans. Peggy Kamuf (New York and London, 1994), p. 16.
58 Maguire and Smith, 'What is a source?', 26.
59 *Ibid.*, 27. They invoke Stuart Gillespie, *Shakespeare's Books: A Dictionary of Shakespeare's Sources* (London, 2004), p. 327, which notes 'the reminiscences of *Dido Queen of Carthage* in the tale of Troy as retold in *Hamlet* (2.2.440–2)'.
60 Helen Cooper, *The English Romance: Transforming Motifs from Geoffrey of Monmouth to the Death of Shakespeare* (Oxford, 2004), p. 13.
61 *Ibid.*, p. 22.
62 An even more extreme example occurs in the language of Dogberry in *Much Ado About Nothing*.

63 Sigmund Freud, *The Psychopathology of Everyday Life*, vol. 5, trans. Alan Tyson, Pelican Freud Library (reprinted, Harmondsworth, 1978), pp. 40–1.
64 Cf. also J. Laplanche and J.-P. Pontalis, *The Language of Psychoanalysis*, trans. Donald Nicol-Smith (London, 1985), pp. 390–94.
65 See Jonathan Bate, *Shakespeare and Ovid* (Oxford, 1993), p. 181, where he suggests that 'direct allusions to Ovidian mythological material became less frequent in Shakespeare's Jacobean Tragedies, perhaps because he no longer felt it necessary to display his literacy'.
66 Gilles Deleuze and Felix Guattari, *A Thousand Plateaus: Capitalism and Schizophrenia*, trans. Brian Massumi (London, 1987), p. 16.
67 *Ibid.*, p. 14.
68 Fulke Greville, Lord Brooke, 'A Treatise on Monarchy', *The Remaines Being Poems of Monarchy and Religion*, ed. G.A. Wilkes (Oxford, 1965), p. 45. See also an extension of this in the writing of Fulke Greville in Streete, *Protestantism and Drama*, p. 93.
69 Ovid, *The Metamorphoses*, trans. Arthur Golding, ed. John Frederick Nimms (New York, 1965), pp. 6–7. All citations to this text are from this edition.
70 Terence Hawkes, *Shakespeare's Talking Animals: Language and Drama in Society* (London, 1973), p. 1.
71 *Ibid.*, p. 3. See also Adam Fox, *Oral and Literate Culture in England 1500–1700* (Oxford, 2000), especially pp. 112ff., where Fox discusses the dissemination of 'proverbial wisdom', although his emphasis is upon the education system as a means of circulating proverbs (pp. 122–3).
72 Hawkes refined this view some twenty years later in his *Meaning by Shakespeare* (London, 1992), p. 6.
73 *Ibid.*, p. 10.
74 *Ibid.*, p. 11.
75 John Kerrigan, *Shakespeare's Binding Language* (Oxford, 2016), p. 15.
76 *Ibid.*, p. 18.
77 Erasmus, 'The Praise of Folly', p. 366.
78 Quint, *Origin and Originality*, p. 138.
79 *Ibid.*, p. 178.
80 Mullaney, *The Reformation of Emotions*, p. 41.
81 See Alan Sinfield, *Faultlines: Cultural Materialism and the Politics of Dissident Reading* (Los Angeles and Oxford, 1992), pp. 46ff. 'When a part of our worldview threatens disruption by manifestly failing to cohere with the rest, then we reorganise and retell its story, trying to get it into shape – back into the old shape if we are conservative-minded, or into a new shape if we are more adventurous' (p. 46).

82 H. Woudhuysen, 'Appendix 1', in William Shakespeare, *Love's Labour's Lost*, ed. Henry Woudhuysen, Arden 3 series (London, 1998), pp. 298–300. See also Colin Burrow, ed., *The Oxford Shakespeare: The Complete Sonnets and Poems* (Oxford, 2002), p. 84, which states that the quarto of *Richard II* is the first to identify Shakespeare as dramatist.
83 Woudhuysen, 'Sources and contexts', in *Hamlet*, p. 61.
84 *Ibid.*, p. 62.
85 Geoffrey Bullough, *Narrative and Dramatic Sources of Shakespeare*, 8 vols (London, 1957–75), vol. 7, pp. 402ff.
86 *Ibid.*, p. 409 n. 1.
87 *Ibid.*, p. 412 n. 2.
88 Sir Philip Sidney, *The Old Arcadia*, ed. Katherine Duncan-Jones (Oxford, 1985), p. 333.
89 John Webster, *The Duchess of Malfi*, ed. John Russell Brown (London, 1964), p. 164 nn. 54–5.
90 Katherine Duncan-Jones and H.R. Woudhuysen, eds, *Shakespeare's Poems*, Arden 3 series (London, 2007), p. 84.
91 Burrow, *The Oxford Shakespeare*, p. 76.
92 Gary Taylor and John Lavagnino, eds, *Thomas Middleton: The Collected Works* (Oxford, 2010), p. 1170.
93 Jeffrey Masten, *Textual Intercourse: Collaboration, Authorship, and Sexualities in Renaissance Drama* (Cambridge, 1997), p. 14.
94 *Ibid.*
95 *Ibid.*, p. 16.
96 See Bullough, *Narrative and Dramatic Sources*, vol. 1, pp. 269ff., which situates *Romeo and Juliet* in the volume on 'Early Comedies/Poems/Romeo and Juliet'.

3

Textual economies

In the Acknowledgements that appear at the end of Colm Tóibín's novel *House of Names* (2017) the novelist states:

> Much of this novel is based on imagination and does not have a source in any text. Indeed, some characters and many events in *House of Names* do not appear at all in earlier versions of this story. But the main Protagonists – Clytemnestra, Agamemnon, Iphigenia, Electra and Orestes – and the shape of the narrative are taken from Aeschylus's *The Oresteia*, Sophocles' *Electra* and Euripides' *Electra*, *Orestes* and *Iphigenia at Aulis*.[1]

A year later, and without an explicit authorial intervention, Pat Barker's *The Silence of The Girls* (2018) infers a source narrative and invests it with otherwise silenced female voices.[2] Both Tóibín and Barker write for an audience of individual readers. They *invent* modern narratives whose historical origins are clear, although Barker's engagement with the *Iliad* is political insofar as it is designed specifically to recover from Homer's poetry female voices that pose a challenge to a distant, primarily masculine, discourse. Tóibín, himself a reader, explicitly addressing other readers, makes a pitch for his own originality, while at the same time revealing a genealogy of textual authorities whose plays are the sources of a novelistic narrative whose contours have become deeply embedded in Western culture. His explicit claim appears on the surface to be disingenuous. If we strip away the post-modern scaffolding of his own narrative, and rearrange the events of his novel in a chronological order, what is dispersed across the plays of the three Greek dramatists that he nominates becomes clearer. Nor should we assume that this collection of classical writers represents what Derrida might have labelled 'an original plenitude'.[3] Indeed, what was an 'original plenitude' now provides in Tóibín's novel a solid structural framework for a series of imaginary forays into the extra-dramatic lives of the central characters of *The Oresteia*. The novel is divided between the narratives of Clytemnestra, Orestes and Electra, and each contributes a strand. In the first section we hear Clytemnestra speak, although it is not from a position of enforced silence. Indeed, the narrator simply *imagines* her and her lover's strategic responses to the return of Agamemnon:

> I held Aegisthus in my arms then, still worried that something might happen in those first hours when my husband came that that would spark suspicion. It must be open welcome, I thought, it must be all festive. Neither Aegisthus himself nor any of his followers must appear. Thus it would be up to me to make the returning warrior feel that everything was as it should be.
>
> Having charted a great choreography of welcome and good cheer, we made love ferociously, aware of the risks that we were taking, but aware too of the gains, the spoils.[4]

Barker's novel is explicitly political insofar as it seeks to reinstate hitherto occluded, and therefore invented, female voices of a series of episodes of the *Iliad*. Tóibín is, however, not entirely accurate in claiming that his own narrative is based on an apparently source-less 'imagination', since the interiority of his characters can be traced initially to an established structure of events that lie behind a modern perception of plausible adulterous human behaviour. The novelist's 'imagination' inheres in his unique fusion of an already known series of overlapping narratives with an affective psychological apparatus, and in the process the originary structure ossifies the dynamic role of the 'first reader' as a historical producer of dramatic writing. In this connection Derrida goes on to make an important observation:

> We would search the 'public' in vain for the first reader: i.e. the first author of a work. And the 'sociology of literature' is blind to the war and the ruses perpetuated by the author who reads and by the first reader who dictates, for at stake here is the origin of the work itself. The *sociality* of writing as *drama* requires an entirely different discipline.[5]

Tóibín's task, unlike that of Barker, is that of the adapter, of shifting narratives from one genre (classical tragedy) to another (the modern novel), engaging in what Julie Sanders describes as 'a transpositional practice, casting a specific genre into another generic mode, an act of re-vision in itself'.[6] Tóibín clearly shares with the literate reader a recognition of the genealogy of his own narrative, but by positioning the Acknowledgements at the *end* of the novel he encourages the playing of a game that involves the invoking of a series of embedded foundational myths that occupy a position somewhere between fiction and history. Thus, at one level the names in his own text indicate, to quote Sanders again, 'a relationship with an informing source text either through its title or through more embedded references'.[7] But his claim of originality and the privileging of his imagination points in the direction of what we might call appropriation, a practice whereby the text does not (or not regularly) make its 'founding relationships and inter-relationships explicit', especially if we were to ask basic questions about *how* the novelist negotiates between the narratives of Aeschylus, Sophocles and Euripides.

Tóibín invokes in his novel a particular kind of textual economy that requires both suppression and revision: a selective recall of the historical material and the contexts within which the plays of Aeschylus, Sophocles and Euripides were produced, and an updating of their concerns in the interests of a knowledge of human relationships with which modern (and post-modern) readers can identify. *House of Names* goes out of its way to efface its historical genealogy, but it allows us only a limited speculation about the text's production as part of the novelist's 'imagination'.

In contrast, in the sixteenth century those dramatists who were becoming conscious of their identity as writers openly constructed literary genealogies for themselves or for others, but they did so because the identification of 'authorities' was less rigidly prescriptive than we would be inclined to acknowledge. Moreover, play-texts were not the exclusive property of writers, and questions of ownership, borrowing and plagiarism did not become important until the eighteenth century. Ben Jonson was, perhaps, one of the most outspoken early modern aspirants to the status of proprietorial 'author', but even so, his reciting of the genealogies of writing was commonplace at the time. For example, his poem 'To the memory of my beloued, / The AVTHOR / Mr. WILLIAM SHAKESPEARE: / And / what he hath left vs' asserts that 'Thou art a Moniment, without a tombe, / And art alive still, while thy Booke doth liue, / And we haue wits to read, and praise to giue.'[8] He then proceeds to situate Shakespeare both among his contemporaries *and* among what we have become accustomed to call 'authorities', and in a manner that expands Tóibín's more limited pantheon:

> For, if I thought my judgement were of yeeres,
> I should commit thee surely with thy peeres,
> And tell, how farre thou didst our *Lily* out-shine,
> Or sporting *Kid*, or *Marlowes* mighty line.
> And though thou hadst small *Latine*, and lesse *Greeke*,
> From thence to honour thee, I would not seeke
> For names, but call forth thund'ring *Aeschilus*,
> *Euripides*, and *Sophocles* to us,
> *Paccuuius*, *Accius*, him of *Cordoua* dead,
> To life again, to heare thy Buskin tread,
> And shake a stage:[9]

Contemporaries and classical authorities are brought together here, but then the latter are dismissed ('Of all, that insolent *Greece* or haughtie *Rome* sent forth'), to be supplanted by an explicitly nationalistic claim that it is the 'British' Shakespeare, 'To whom all scenes of *Europe* homage owe'.[10] Some five years after the publication of the First Folio, the minor poet Thomas Randolph provided a slightly different genealogy for Ben Jonson in his poem 'A gratulatory to Mr. Ben Iohnson for his adopting of him to be his Son', where the debt to the dramatist's Greco-Roman heritage is articulated in a much more reverential manner:

> Orpheus, Musaeus, Homer too; beside
> Thy Brothers by the Roman Mothers side;
> As Ovid, Virgil, and the Latine Lyre,
> That is so like thy Horace; the whole quire
> Of Poets are by thy Adoption, all
> My uncles; thou hast given me pow'r to call
> Phoebus himselfe my grandsire; by this graunt
> Each Sister of the nine is made my Aunt.[11]

The combination of terrestrial *and* celestial authorities is characteristic of this kind of praise, but it is the mixture of association with, and difference from, antecedent writers, while at the same time claiming inspiration from classical deities, such as Mercury, Apollo, Orpheus or the Nine Muses, which seeks to establish not so much a 'source' or an 'origin' as a pedigree and a genealogy. So far as I am aware, Shakespeare himself did not construct a classical genealogy for his own or for any other writer. He deployed classical references as integral parts of his play-scripts, but he showed no interest either in attaching prefatory explanatory or dedicatory material to the printed versions of his plays or, indeed, engaging in explicit critical debate about them or their reception. Rather, his focus was on *performance* in the broadest sense of the term.

Stephen Orgel suggested in a discussion of plagiarism that the Renaissance writers who confined themselves to one single source or model revealed a mental incapacity, since they had 'no *copia* (supply, storehouse) on which to draw'.[12] The currency of theatrical writing still involved a deployment of resources in the form of exchanges of texts, of ideas and of forms, and a situating of all writing within the performative context of imitation at a time when theatre scripts were beginning to establish for their producers a degree of acceptance and respectability.[13] While on the one hand 'dramatic poesy' was regarded as a particular form of writing, the boundary between it and what we would now think of as 'poetry' was blurred. Clearly Ben Jonson regarded himself as an 'author', but his association of Shakespeare with the 'living' book implies something more dynamic and dialogic than the activity of a passive reading, or indeed that the consumption of the contents of a material text might suggest. András Kiséry has observed that a reference to Shakespeare's *Hamlet* is embedded in an annotation by Gabriel Harvey in his copy of *The Workes of our Antient and Lerned English Poet Geoffrey Chaucer* (1598) and that the note refers to a whole range of contemporary writers of prose, poetry and chronicles. However, Kiséry is not content simply to accept the view that the printing of *Hamlet* with its typographical indication of sententiae heightened its '(presumably low) cultural prestige' by associating the book of the play with 'scholarly reading' that involved the consumption of its contents.[14] Indeed, he seeks to excavate a dynamic, interactive context for the play, and to

> identify the wisdom of the play as political, as distinct from philosophical or literary in some general sense – ultimately as the wisdom that can inform political activity (which may not be independent political *action* in the strong sense) and can entitle one to such activity: to service, advising, analysis. The distinction of *Hamlet* and *Lucrece* depends not on their literariness as such, but on the pragmatic, political utility of specific formal qualities we identify as literary.[15]

Kiséry's analysis takes us into another kind of context that will require some further consideration, which will be the subject of Chapter 6. His concern here is with the play-text as an intervention or as a model for action in the public sphere, and/or a source of political wisdom. In this formulation the play becomes a repository of living wisdom, what in another much larger philosophical context Seán Burke labels 'a dominant educational resource' in which performance, recitation and repetition could serve 'simultaneously as theatre, festival and library'.[16] What Burke firmly locates in the Platonic oracy/literacy debates of Ancient Greece assumes a particular significance if it is applied to the tension between literature and theatre in the early modern period. Indeed, Jonson's reference to the First Folio as a 'living book' must surely be pejorative insofar as Shakespeare's skill resided in his ability to continually bring the past to life, to bring its concerns into the present and to make its concerns part of a living memory. However, whether the text is a model or an active resource is an indication of its abiding utility for a reader such as Harvey, whereas the text's production, susceptible to a pragmatics of composition in the moment of its emergence as a theatre script, will utilise textual material that it can both recall from the past and bring into alignment with its audiences' present concerns.

Commenting on the development of print technology during the sixteenth century, the historian Patrick Collinson notes how print infiltrated the oral tradition so that 'something as apparently oral and traditional as the legend of Robin Hood would be fed back into the orality of folk tales from printed ballad texts'.[17] We can get some idea of the flexibility of the Robin Hood motif from Shakespeare's deployment of it from an early play, *The Two Gentlemen of Verona* (*c*.1593), through *2 Henry IV* (1597) and *As You Like It* (*c*.1598) to the collaborative play *The Two Noble Kinsmen* (*c*.1613). In the first, the Third Outlaw's oath 'By the bare scalp of Robin Hood's fat friar' (4.1.36) invokes an element of the popular myth and is of a piece with the linking of outlawry with forest dwelling. In *2 Henry IV* Justice Silence interrupts Pistol's announcement of Falstaff's apparent elevation to a position of power with a line from the popular ballad 'And Robin Hood, Scarlet and John' (5.3.103) that suggests, ironically, a conflict of interest in the continued association between Falstaff and outlawry. The quotation itself is entwined with biblical, and classical references to the 'Assyrians' and to 'King Cophetua'. *As You Like It* offers a fuller reference in the description by Charles the Wrestler of the displaced Old Duke's dwelling:

> They say he is already in the forest of Arden and a many merry men with him, and there they live like the old Robin Hood of England. They say many young gentlemen flock to him every day and fleet the time carelessly as they did in the golden world.
>
> (1.1.109–13)

Here elements of a creation myth are utilised to suggest a return to 'the golden world' of an originary paradise, presided over by a secular authority, but the attraction of 'young gentlemen' to Duke Senior's cause also poses a veiled political threat to his usurping brother.

In what is perhaps the most 'literary' context, the Prologue of *The Two Noble Kinsmen* acknowledges the superiority of Chaucer, who 'of all admired, the story gives' (Prologue, l. 13) and whose 'cry from under ground' is quoted:

> Oh, fan
> From me the witless chaff of such a writer
> That blasts my bays and my famed works makes lighter
> Than Robin Hood!
>
> (Prologue, ll. 18–21)

In this comparison the tale rather than the figure of Robin Hood has a 'lighter' reputation, embedded, as it is, in what is essentially a literary comparison. Each deployment of a popular oral narrative indicates a slightly different inflexion: the first invokes in a descriptive sense the link between outlawry and Robin Hood, while in Silence's quotation the effect is ironic and suggestive. By the time we come to *The Two Noble Kinsmen*, where the issue is collaboration, a distinction is made between the 'source' of the story of the play in the reputable poet Chaucer, and the comparatively superficial popular myth of Robin Hood. Here a critical perspective is folded neatly into the Prologue's appeal to an audience as he apologises for threatening to disturb the eternal sleep of the established poet: 'You shall hear / Scenes, though below his art, may yet appear / Worth two hours' travel. To his bones sweet sleep; / Content to you' (Prologue, ll. 27–30). Throughout, both the written and oral versions of the Robin Hood narrative interact to the point where it is difficult to be certain which of them is active. In *The Two Noble Kinsmen* the oral version is downgraded, whereas earlier the popular ballad and the narrative are culturally active and carry with them an explicit political rather than a literary charge.

Of course, in comparing the intrinsic literary qualities of writers 'aunciet & moderne', Harvey's note in his Chaucer anthology makes no distinction between literary forms, and hence it pays no attention to the various levels of collaboration and co-operation necessary in the production of the text *and* the performance of an early modern play. It is this shuttling between the oral and the literary as discursive regimes that requires us to adjust our approach to composition, playwriting and performance during this period. Far too often scholars have sought to reduce the debate to questions of literariness and its force in determining the linear transmission of texts. The moment of print is always identified as the 'source' and the 'origin', whereas the reality is a negotiation between texts as part of an economy that shapes their evaluation in accordance with the pressures exerted upon them by a particular context.

In a fascinating essay, Barbara Mowat has attempted to align the literary with the theatrical in her account of the fortunes of *Pericles*. Her claim is that the play 'stands as an extreme example of the complex radical(s) of presentation of early modern drama'.[18] Mowat argues that the play 'exemplifies as well – perhaps more obtrusively than any other play of the period – the clear dependence of early modern theatre on literary culture, on the book as source of the play's dramatic fiction, as authority, as that which, already disseminated in manuscript codex and in print, was brought to life (as they say) on the stage'.[19] This is certainly one way of interpreting the frequently observed liveliness of dramatic characters as they are transformed from an antecedent printed narrative into a stage presence. In a well-known excerpt from *Piers Penniless his Supplication to the Devil* (1592), describing a performance of *1 Henry VI*, Thomas Nashe describes the dramatist's 'subject' as having been 'borrowed out of our English chronicles, wherein our forefathers valiant acts (that have line long buried in rustie brasse and worme-eaten bookes) are revived, and they themselves raised from the Grave of Oblivion, and brought to pleade their aged Honours in open presence'.[20] Similarly, although the genealogy of the much later *Pericles* remains speculative,[21] Mowat's aim is to evolve a precedent literary authority for the play and to assert it as a paradigm case for the primarily linear trajectory of the text as it has come down to us. This is not to challenge the claim that, as the Nashe example indicates, texts frequently evolve by means of adaptation and/or appropriation, from precedent texts, and in the case of *Pericles* the Chorus of Gower indicates a conscious strategy of seeking to revitalise 'a song that old was sung' (Chorus, l. 1). But from the outset, a distinction is made between performance and reading, outlining the different ways in which the narrative core of the play was circulated, to the point where we can claim for it a dual identity:

> It hath been sung at festivals,
> On ember eves and holy ales,
> And lords and ladies in their lives
> Have read it for restoratives.
>
> (Chorus, ll. 5–7)

If we are to take the Chorus at his word then the play's dual identity acts as a challenge to the precedence of its literary existence and emphasises a popular preference for performance, for the 'song', during religious and other festive occasions.[22] The Chorus's 'it' suggests something different from a printed text, something closer to performance that existed alongside a printed version of the story, and that remained alive in and through performance. Here the performance at 'ember eves and holy ales' is a testimony to the continued circulation of a narrative that has a parallel life, accessible to those who are not literary minded, and that is constantly repeated in and through performance. It is aristocratic readers ('lords and ladies') who have accessed the story through the medium of print, who have 'read it for restoratives' and therefore derived pleasure from reading, and it is also, of course, literary scholars who seek to construct a reductively linear passageway down which the historical transmission of the text can travel. The desire to establish an ancestry for the text, rather than to focus upon an exploration of the text's existence as part of an economy of textual practice, risks limiting the enquiry, at the same time that it reinforces an ideological commitment to a distinctly patriarchal account of textual transmission, and to a privileging of the literary existence of a narrative that by the Chorus's own admission continued to circulate in a number of versions. The difficulty with Mowat's argument is that this important variation is downplayed in favour of a linear account that inadvertently draws on the patriarchal language and assumptions of traditional source study, and that assumes a particular kind of agency of the dramatist which makes no categorical distinction between the different kinds of contemporaneous circulation of particular narratives. We need to remind ourselves in such circumstances that print is not *sui generis* and that the circulating power of stories endowed with cultural significance may also testify to their continued existence in the popular memory, of which the book becomes the written record of an extant and parallel *oral* narrative. We should, however, also remember that 'reading' in this context may well have been, in part, a communal rather than a solitary activity, thereby occasionally blurring the distinction between the oral and the literary. Be that as it may, the fact that the relatively new institution of the public theatre should seek to align itself with the operations and the practices of popular memory is a testament to its own advertising strategies, something that Heminge and Condell appear to have been aware of in their appeal to potential readers of the First Folio to buy the book as a record of performance.

One scholar who has firmly resisted this general tendency to align Shakespeare with literary reading is Jeffrey Masten, whose book

Textual Intercourse (1997) sets out to challenge the assumptions surrounding the concept of authorship as they have been applied to early modern drama texts. Masten begins by arguing that unlike the model provided by texts such as Brontë's *Wuthering Heights* whose readers are 'trained to see post-mortem sexual union as the height of romantic attachment', the early modern world was 'an everyday world suffused with, structured by, collaborative textual practice'.[23] This was particularly true of the early modern theatre and of the scripts that it produced, and that have now been assimilated into the critical purview of what Masten calls 'authorial univocality'; indeed, he insists:

> Viewing these texts as literature in the library rather than as working documents in the playhouse, criticism has read them primarily as written communications between writers and readers. Such an approach privileges 'writer' and 'reader' according to their value in modern literate literary culture and elides both the prior textual exchange(s) among writers and actors *and* the oral/aural transaction between actors and audience, the more prominent participants in the initial and most prolific form of these texts' public/ation.[24]

Masten is concerned to point out that if we challenge the primacy of the concept of 'literature' as 'original, as creative, as individual, as unique', then 'other traditional critical categories policing the circulation of language become problematical as well – for example "plagiarism", "borrowing", "influence" (and its "anxieties"), "source", "originality", "imagination", "genius" and "complete works"'.[25] This is, of course, the complex, theoretically difficult world in which modern writers such as Tóibín and Barker intervene. Masten invites us to consider this problematisation of terms that have become accepted features of critical discourse in relation to what he calls 'the inextricability of the question of authorship from patriarchy's interest in the identity of the father'; indeed, he wants to push this further to problematise 'the author's birth' since it 'naturalises and makes inevitable an event – or rather a complicated set of events – that were contingent and by no means biological, transcultural, or even uniformly distributed across discourses and genres within a given culture'.[26] He acknowledges a version of linear process in the, perhaps, rather obvious suggestion that textual revision was 'itself

Textual economies 141

a diachronic form of collaboration',[27] but his argument implies very strongly that the practice of imitation more generally falls into this category. Indeed, although he does not use the term 'synchronic collaboration', he proceeds to describe its contours:

> The construction of meaning by a theatrical company was polyvocal – often beginning with a collaborative manuscript which was then revised, cut, re-arranged, and augmented by book-holders, copyists, and others, elaborated and improved by actors in performance, accompanied by music and songs that may or may not have originated in a completely different context.

The phrase 'collaborative manuscript' suggests two or more writers combining their efforts, although the importation into a text of quotations of all kinds from other writings, including the classics, suggests that in this environment the playwright never composed in isolation, and that even when writing with another who brought his own 'copious' resources to the task, the resulting collaboration always exceeded the boundaries of what Foucault identifies as the 'proper name' of the author.[28] It is perhaps indicative that attempts to establish an implicitly limited form of 'collaboration' should content themselves with an insistence upon co-authorship, where the name of the author remains sacrosanct, thus providing a safeguard against the cultural fear of the disintegration of the text. What for some scholars has been the shrill articulation of an anxiety generated by the possibility that the individualised Shakespeare may not be individual at all in the modern sense of the term, is welcomed by Masten for whom this feared instability actually signals 'the intersections of acting company and audience in the language of a collaborative commerce'.[29]

Masten's primary concern, however, is with the dynamics of an exemplary formal collaboration in the production of play-texts, and so he narrows his attention to the collaboration of Beaumont and Fletcher, in which it is possible to tease out both the homoeroticism and the 'friendship' that is implicated in the act of collaboration. This certainly raises questions that impinge upon matters of 'source' or 'originality', but it does not engage fully with the complex issue of how a theatrical text is put together. Nor does it venture beyond the sexual dynamics of collaboration to suggest other ways of fashioning such narratives that, while they might draw on the protocols of homoerotic or homosexual discourse, cannot satisfactorily be reduced to them.

It is here that the question of 'authentication' begins to exert a pressure on the argument to the extent that exposure of the strands of resource would, on the one hand, take us further into a textual economy, while on the other would allow us to glimpse what Foucault regarded as a 'privileged moment of individualisation in the history of ideas, knowledge, and literature' that signalled the emergence of the category of 'the author'.[30] Here Derrida's 'sociality of writing as drama' begins to take on a new, but distinctly non-Freudian, significance in that the act of writing itself becomes, historically, the point of convergence of diachronic and synchronic pressures in its assimilation of different kinds of material. The issue of 'authenticity' raised discursively by Stephen Orgel in an essay that first appeared in 1988, and that has since been republished,[31] focuses on what is, and is not *authentically* Shakespearean, which is to enquire: how can we identify and authenticate what Shakespeare did or did not write? Orgel is, of course, aware of the demands of theatre, but he insists that the claims of authenticity are dependent upon manuscript provenance.[32] He insists, correctly, upon the difference between Shakespeare and Ben Jonson on the matter of the importance that the latter accorded to the issue of his own authorship of texts.[33] For Shakespeare, by contrast, he states that 'the authentic text ... is the acting text, at least if we are going to take Shakespeare's intentions into account', but he identifies 'source' in the following way:

> The autograph manuscript was where Shakespeare started, not where he ended, the first step, not the final version. This is a respect in which an authentic Shakespeare text would differ from an authentic Ben Jonson text: Jonson rewrote his plays for publication.[34]

At a purely practical level this claim is uncontroversial, although this does not seem to have deterred those committed to the view that Shakespeare was primarily a 'literary' writer from asserting the contrary. However, a critical enquiry into matters of 'source' and 'origin' raises questions concerning the level of authenticity that it is possible to claim for any Shakespearean text for which no convincingly proven manuscript exists. Orgel is ambiguous on the question of 'authority', tending towards an elision of this term with the business of authentication, and he expresses a desire (and a fantasy) that almost all Shakespeare scholars can identify with: the desire to discover an autographed manuscript that will tell us what Shakespeare actually wrote, so that as editors we can dispense with the informed guesswork generated by the printed texts that have come down to us. Although Orgel aims to demystify many of the assumptions that have bedevilled Shakespeare scholarship, and he does so with an appropriate level of civilised irony, having expelled the author through the front entrance he allows him to creep back in through a side window. Authentification still requires, in the words of Foucault, 'reference to the individual', and to the role of the author as 'an index of truthfulness',[35] *copia* notwithstanding.

Foucault offers the case of the eighteenth-century Gothic novelist Ann Radcliffe, whom he credits with the achievement of making possible 'the appearance of Gothic Romances'. He observes:

> The novels of Ann Radcliffe put into circulation a certain number of resemblances and analogies patterned on her work – various characteristic signs, figures, relationships, and structures that could be integrated into other books.[36]

The name Ann Radcliffe is the point of convergence of a series of novelistic discourses, and a cursory glance at *The Mysteries of Udolpho* (1794) reveals that the narrative contains embedded texts by Thomson, Shakespeare, Gray, Goldsmith and many others, to the extent that a modern annotator can declare with confidence that the novel was 'the high point of Thomson's influence on Radcliffe. Shakespeare, however, is to be found everywhere in her novels, not only with allusions drawn from the whole range of his work but in a number of scenes which recall memorable incidents in the plays.'[37] Had Foucault gone back to 1765 he could have said the same about Horace Walpole's *The Castle of Otranto*, advertised on its title page as 'A STORY / Translated by / WILLIAM MARSHAL, Gent. / From the Original ITALIAN of / ONUPHRIO MURALTO, / SANON of the Church of St. NICHOLAS / at OTRANTO'. At a time when authorship was beginning to assume a legal status, the figure of the author disappears in a series of fictions, while the text itself is a repetition in many respects of Shakespeare's *Hamlet*.[38] We will pay closer attention to the issue of repetition later, but for the moment we shall remain with Foucault's dislodging of the figure of 'the author' from the centre of textual production, and his re-designation of the position as an 'author function'.[39]

It was Foucault's contention – and he uses a version of the familiar Shakespeare/Bacon controversy to make his point – that 'the name of an author is not precisely a proper name among others'.[40] Biographers of Shakespeare have deployed considerable ingenuity in their attempts to establish connections between Shakespeare's texts and the writings attributed to him, to inscribe 'Shakespeare' as what Foucault calls 'a proper name, which moves from the interior of a discourse to the real person outside who produced it'. Except that in the case of Shakespeare, those 'relationships of homogeneity, filiation, reciprocal explanation, authentification', all of which are associated with his name that characterises 'a particular manner of existence of discourse',[41] are exceeded by what in terms of English culture generally, and the interpretative strategies of academic criticism in particular, 'Shakespeare' has become. Foucault's insistence upon the discontinuities of discourse is given a historical support once we seek to separate out those discourses (classical 'authorities', fragmentary narratives, aphorisms) that contribute to the making of a Shakespearean play-text.

Viewed through the prism of Foucault's reformulation of the concept of authorship, Marjorie Garber's question of 'Who is the author of Shakespeare's plays?' takes on a different emphasis from that with which modern criticism had been familiar.[42] What Garber does is to project concerns about 'authority, legitimacy, usurpation, authorship and interpretation' back into the plays themselves so that she can pose two further questions: 'Can the "Shakespeare Question" be situated within the text itself?', and 'Is the authorship controversy in part a textual effect?' Garber's theoretical model is provided by Freud, and depends upon a particular understanding of 'the compulsion to repeat'.[43] Moreover, she suggests that 'the ghost function' in Shakespeare's plays conforms to the Derridean account of 'the logic of the supplement', indicating 'an embodiment of the disembodied, a re-membering of the dismembered, an articulation of the disarticulated and inarticulate'.[44] The centrality of Freud in Garber's argument presupposes a particular transhistorical account of the unconscious that does not fully account for some of the details in particular Shakespearean texts. At a historical juncture when the modern subject has yet to come fully and clearly into view, it is questionable whether 'subject' and 'object' could be quite so clearly differentiated from each other. Moreover, Garber's symptomatic reading of Shakespeare's texts is elided with the dramatist's own symptomatic reading of the issues raised in plays such as *Hamlet*. This is clearly not an immersion of the critic in the text that is the object of enquiry; rather, it is a projection onto the text of a particular exegetical method of interpretation. It is here that Seán Burke's, albeit somewhat stark, description of oral tradition is important in terms of adjusting our approach to possible textual 'effect':

> Performers and audience alike simply immersed themselves within the tale and its telling – a species of identification quite the reverse of literary criticism which involves the standing back from the work, assessing it as an object of study rather than of direct experience.[45]

This distinction mirrors the difference between the two modes of reception identified by the Chorus in *Pericles*. But what Burke does not fully account for is the anxiety that the transition from one *episteme* to another might produce, an anxiety that involves cultural questions of loss and uncertainty (that *As You Like It* invokes with what seem to us its sentimental references to the 'golden' world) as early modern culture sought to cope with the gradual paradigm shift from the discursive demands of a receding oral culture in the face of an emergent literate culture. The model here is, as Collinson judiciously observed, a circular rather than a linear one, reactivating traditional practices while at the same time folding in and assimilating contemporary rearticulations of those practices as the influence of print began to exert itself. As far as the theatre as a relatively new commercial institution was concerned, this transition inaugurated a new self-consciousness that fed into the process of mapping out an identity for itself. It would, of course, be surprising if these concerns did not appear in some form or another in the plays, and the examples of *Henry V* and *Julius Caesar*, both of which are preoccupied with the business of theatrical representation and with scripting, are in some ways indicative of a new enterprise: the opening of the Globe Theatre. The issue surfaces at a particular moment in *Hamlet*, a play that might have been one of the earliest performed in the new playhouse.[46] It occurs after Hamlet's encounter with Rosencrantz and Guildenstern, and after he is told that a troop of players has arrived in Elsinore. In a soliloquy (the form is indicative of an emergent but not entirely clear interiority), Hamlet speculates on the affective power of the theatrical experience:

> Hum. I have heard
> That guilty creatures sitting at a play
> Have by the very cunning of the scene
> Been struck so to the soul that presently
> They have proclaimed their malefactions.
> For murder, though it have no tongue, will speak
> With most miraculous organ. I'll have these players
> Play something like the murder of my father
> Before mine uncle. I'll observe his looks,
> I'll tent him to the quick. If 'a do blench
> I know my course.
>
> (2.2.523–33)

In terms of repetition, this admission enacts a familiar popular aphorism at the same time that it deploys the strategy of representing in the form of a repetition, the murder of Old Hamlet. At issue here is the confidence that Hamlet has in the affective power of theatrical performance: 'The play's the thing / Wherein I'll catch the conscience of the king' (2.2.539–40). Garber's observation that the enactment of Claudius's crime 'can produce pleasure when it is received as a repetition',[47] may indeed be accurate for a modern audience whose emotional investment in performance might be to experience a suitably vicarious pleasurable return of the repressed, but it does not compare with the ethical urgency ascribed to an art form in which the act of representation is coterminous with an involuntary admission of guilt. In any case, Hamlet's theory only produces a clear result for himself and Horatio, since it is not until three scenes later that we are allowed to observe the play-within-the-play's effect on Claudius, although this has nothing to do with Freudian repression. Hamlet's intention is to harness the affective power of theatre in order to bring into the public domain

Claudius's guilt and to force the criminal to admit it. Gertrude's distant response is, at one level, 'aristocratic' as defined by the Chorus in *Pericles*, and it is wholly devoid of the tension that the theatre audience is expected to feel at what is clearly an act of damaging forgetfulness that in Hamlet's later encounter with her he seeks to rectify. The theatre audience, however, will have garnered clues that will enable it to interpret the ambivalence of Claudius's response along the lines of Hamlet's instructions to Horatio.

This is a complicated example of the interaction between dramatist, actors and audience that contributes to a larger dramatisation of the distinction between an 'oral' mindset that is required to memorialise the past as an extension of the continuous present, and a 'literate' mindset steeped in a pathological form of forgetfulness. Leaving aside the linear trajectory of a narrative that by 1601 was still active in the popular imagination, and for which the play itself became a substitute in the early decades of the seventeenth century, *Hamlet* gives us some idea of a larger debate about the nature of reading and theatrical representation that Shakespeare's dramatisation fed off. But nor was the narrative a stable one. Indeed, the existence of three early texts testifies to different theatrical versions, all of which must have been, and continue to be, eminently performable. The extent to which they were cut (Q1: 1603), expanded and augmented (Q2: 1605), or revised (Folio: 1623) indicates the continually responsive nature of the theatrical text that printing has fixed in what is, to some extent, a false linearity. Here, as elsewhere in relation to Shakespearean texts, the preoccupation with questions of 'authority' and 'authentification' have done much to obscure the dynamic demands and the cultural responsiveness of plays, and the justifications for their continual circulation in and through performance.

The matter of authority and authentification, has been reformulated in a way that is directly relevant to questions of 'source' and 'origin' in Stephen Orgel's essay 'Plagiarism Revisited',[48] where Sir Thomas Browne's *Pseudodoxia Epidemica* is cited to support the view that the authority associated with ancient texts is based upon a fraudulent claim to originality.[49] Orgel does not follow Quint in explicitly teasing out the theological and ideological implications of this view, rather he chooses to emphasise that: 'Plagiarism is the symptom, not the disease: the attack on plagiarism becomes almost at once an attack on Virgil, Ovid, Aristotle. That is the disease: literature, culture, the classics, are precisely the problem.'[50] The question for us – and this is of vital importance to the whole notion of 'source' and 'origin' – is where you start from. The problem for Sir Thomas Browne, who was evidently no advocate of the act of plagiarism even though he thought that ancient authors depended on earlier 'texts', is that it is the institutionalisation of literature, culture (in the limited sense) and the classics that represent 'the stronghold of the pernicious adherence to authority, the enemy of experience and empirical science'.[51] We might add that including Shakespeare in the canon contributes further to the problem and exerts a distorting influence that has encouraged modern scholarship to satisfy the desire to exercise 'the kind of moral superiority we have wanted to assert, over the material we work on'.[52] At the risk of re-stating an obvious point, we need to bear in mind that Shakespeare did not begin by exerting his own authority over the texts attributed to him by having his name added to them when they were printed. Indeed, even in those cases where his name appeared on title pages, it did so generally to support the commercial enterprise of printing and selling them, rather than as a statement of authorship. Indeed, nearly half of the total *oeuvre* only appeared for the first time some seven years after his death, and the full provenance of some of those that only appeared in 1623 raises a number of questions that continue to exercise Shakespeare textual scholars. We have become used to the critical commonplace that Shakespeare was not interested in publication, allegations of the primarily 'literary' preoccupations that some texts apparently reveal notwithstanding. Perhaps we should reformulate this misleading commonplace to which scholarship has attached itself by entertaining the possibility that with one foot in popular oral culture, and given the relative novelty of print, especially for theatre texts, this would not have been the first thought in Shakespeare's mind. Even the information contained on the title page of Q2 *Hamlet* (1605) – that it was 'Newly imprinted and enlarged to almost as much / againe as it was, according to the true and perfect / Coppie' – regards the originary text as a 'copy'. Editors have been careful to sidestep the issue of who authorised the 'copy' of Q2, although Thompson and Taylor rehearse one of the commonly held suggestions that Q1 may either be 'Shakespeare's adaptation of a play by another playwright (Thomas Kyd, perhaps) or Shakespeare's first draft of an original play [sic] which he went on to expand and rewrite almost in its entirety'.[53] By contrast, Q2 has generally been accorded more 'authority' although initially they resist the temptation to collapse 'authority' into the epithet 'authorial'; they observe that Q2 may be 'based on a different kind of manuscript [compared to Q1] and one which is designed for a quite different purpose'.[54] It is in the hypothetical relationship between Q2 and Folio that the importance of an authorial manuscript emerges, with the suggestion supported by modern editors of the play that the Folio was printed from a partially annotated copy of Q2, although for different reasons. Thompson and Taylor argue that Harold Jenkins (the editor of the Arden 2 series *Hamlet*) and Gary Taylor (one of the editors of the *Oxford Shakespeare* edition) concur in regarding Q2 as 'authoritative', because

> it derives more directly than any other printed text from Shakespeare's foul papers. But they represent alternative theories of F, one regarding it as a debasement of the authorial text which lies behind Q2, the other regarding it as deriving from a second later authorial text.[55]

In their printing of both the Q1 text and a conflation of the Q2-F texts Thompson and Taylor withhold judgement on the matter of the absolute 'authority' of one of the *Hamlet* texts. Rather, they collapse the issue into the problematical question of the alleged 'literary' provenance of both Q2 and F, with the latter constituting 'a preliminary abridgement rather than an acting text'.[56]

It is only in 1623 in Heminge and Condell's hyperbolic claim that the issue of 'origin' is raised as part of an explicit sales pitch directed specifically at readers:

> To have publish'd them, as where (before) you were abus'd with diverse stolne, and surreptitious copies, maimed, and deformed by the frauds and stealthes of injurious imposters, that expos'd even those, are now offer'd to your view cur'd, and perfect of their limbes; and all the rest, absolute in their numbers, as he conceiv'd them. Whom as he was a happie imitator of Nature, was a most gentle expresser of it. His mind and hand went together: And what he

thought, he uttered with that easinesse, that we have scarce received from him a blot in his papers.⁵⁷

We should be very careful not to project this claim back into earlier printed texts that emerged during Shakespeare's working lifetime. What Shakespeare's agency was in the emergence of the various *Hamlet* texts is not clear, and the manifest absence of authorial visibility does little to clarify the matter. What is tantamount to an obsession with the figure of the author, at a time when the category itself had yet to be firmly established, asserts a proprietorial relation between the author and text that flies directly in the face of the manner in which, and the methods whereby, texts may have been composed in and for the theatre. If the passage of narratives as they found their ways into theatre texts was not always or exclusively linear, then the limited empirical logic that editors have used to establish the pathways of transmission may also be defective. The textual economies within whose complex aegis theatre texts came into existence, and remained current for successive audiences, serves to demote the author as represented by the Romantic imagination, to a kind of *bricoleur* whose syntheses, repetitions, innovations, and borrowings from extant printed texts and from orally circulated narratives, require us to deploy a different kind of aesthetic judgement from that which privileges the category of the 'literary'. It is this *difference* that the traditional study of 'sources' and 'origins' has sought to obscure in the interests of establishing a particular set of criteria to account for Shakespeare's 'genius'.

Reflecting the 'language and incidents from other books' is how Barbara Mowat perceives the web of textual connections between the different versions of the narrative and Shakespeare's 'dramatisation' of *Romeo and Juliet*.⁵⁸ We read Shakespeare's text for such signs of origin, but also for what Seán Burke has called 'marks of design, signs of purpose'; Burke goes on to note: 'Where there is design there must be a designer, where there is the appearance of meaning there must be intention.'⁵⁹ This principle of literary causality has allowed scholars to read Shakespeare's texts back to their 'sources' in an attempt to locate moments of creative appropriation that will bring us closer to the dramatist's 'mind' and to its operations. More so than with any other of his contemporaries, and partly because of the paucity of ancillary documentary information, we perpetually read Shakespeare's texts in order to reconstruct the figure of the author, whose authority is then folded back into our own conceptions of the authorial subject. In Shakespeare's case the issue has been complicated by attempts to link 'authoritative reading', to appropriate Burke's phrase,[60] to various kinds of partisan reading that can be teased out of the text. These generally have very little to do with matters of intention, but they do tend to blur the boundary between authorial agency, textual authenticity and cultural authority. The debate about Shakespeare's 'resources' sits astride these different reading practices, and frequently these readings are projected onto the texts themselves.

What we cannot do – because it would be anachronistic to do so – is to impose upon the Shakespearean text a post-structuralist '*jouissant*' affirmation of indeterminacy, a dance of the pen, a Dionysian threshing floor', as Burke would have it.[61] Again, this is not to deny elements of ambiguity and instability that are part of a dynamic language that encourages multiple or alternative meanings. Some of these issues emerged, as we saw earlier in Chapter 2, in John Kerrigan's encyclopaedic account, *Shakespeare's Binding Language* (2016), in which he argues:

> During Shakespeare's lifetime the cluster of words around *bind*, *bound*, and *bond* was used of so many kinds of connection – bonds of kin, allegiance to a monarch, material threads and cords, being bound by goodwill or service, not to mention the power of the clergy (for some) to bind and loose from sin – that usage was coloured with implications that allow binding as act and description to draw fields of meaning together.[62]

Kerrigan's concern is not just with promissory or asseverative language (including 'swearing' at both the extremes of the juridical and the profane) but ultimately with the ways in which these kinds of language are represented in Shakespeare's plays and his poetry, as indices of a crisis within the culture of the period.

One of the examples that Kerrigan's otherwise impressively thorough analysis does not take full advantage of occurs in *Hamlet*. The encounter with the Gravedigger takes place immediately on Hamlet's return from England and it lays bare a context-specific respect for particular meanings that change as the situation changes. Hamlet's question, 'Whose grave is this, sirrah?', initiates the following exchange:

> GRAVEDIGGER. Mine sir.
> [*Sings.*]
> O, a pit of clay for to be made –
> HAMLET. I think it be thine, indeed, for thou liest in't.
> GRAVEDIGGER. You lie out on't, sir, and therefore 'tis not yours. For my part I do not lie in't, yet it is mine.
> HAMLET. Thou dost lie in't, to be in't and say it is thine. 'Tis for the dead, not for the quick. Therefore thou liest.
> GRAVEDIGGER. 'Tis a quick lie, sir, 'twill away again from me to you.
> HAMLET. What man dost thou dig it for?
> GRAVEDIGGER. For no man, sir
> HAMLET. What woman then?
> GRAVEDIGGER. For none, neither.
> HAMLET. Who is to be buried in't?
> GRAVEDIGGER. One that was a woman, sir, but rest her soul she's dead.
> HAMLET. [*to Horatio*] How absolute this knave is! We must speak by the card or equivocation will undo us. By the Lord, Horatio, this three years I have took note of it, the age is grown so picked that the toe of the peasant comes so near the heel of the courtier he galls his kibe.
>
> (5.1.110–33)

At the root of this exchange is an opposition between truth and lies, and the question is to what extent the Gravedigger possesses the grave he has been digging and the extent to which Hamlet himself is laid open to the accusation of lying. If this were not an obviously witty exchange – say, the serious confrontation between Bolingbroke and Mowbray at the beginning of *The Tragedy of Richard II* – it would provoke a bellicose response. Instead, it elicits from Hamlet an imperative to speak even more precisely than the 'absolute' Gravedigger whose oral dexterity will allow him to exploit meanings that are themselves bound by the specific contexts in which they are deployed. In this exchange Hamlet has the last

Textual economies 153

word, but he does so only by invoking his superior status, while at the same time lamenting the collapse of the social hierarchy. In the context of Shakespeare's play, populism is anything but a demagogic manipulation of proletarian emotion; indeed, it is a political challenge to an order in which the 'courtier' is shown to be at a clear linguistic disadvantage. Hamlet's 'card' is both a 'ship's compass' and a 'book',[63] whereas the Gravedigger's language derives its force from the immediacy of his situation and his lived experience. This, in miniature, encapsulates the crisis of language that the play (and Hamlet in particular) wrestles with.

We might say, of course, that in the absence of any comparable narrative, this episode is the product of the dramatist's 'imagination'. But the oral culture from which the Gravedigger's language springs, and the deft shifts of meaning that confuse his aristocratic interlocutor, expose two kinds of cultural authority: that of the representative of a court culture that is literate, and that of one who represents a non-literate demotic culture. This exchange exposes a tension between one form of language that points in the direction of one kind of cultural authority that privileges quasi-authorial political agency, on the one hand, and another whose cultural authority derived its energy from a different but no less powerful way of articulating reality. Indeed, as Robert Weimann astutely points out, 'The Elizabethan theatre offered a location where authority could not be of an exclusively literary provenance', but where text and performance 'together served as a new and newly effective form of cultural authority that henceforth could both jar with or complement the powerful regime of an enforceable authority in politics, jurisdiction, and government'.[64]

Weimann is not only concerned, however, with struggles that are represented *within* the text; he is also aware of the gulf between 'potentially historicising and actually editing the Shakespearean text'. Indeed, he offers a more historically accurate account of an empirically located textual instability:

> To a considerable extent, the instability of the Elizabethan play text participates in the precarious, unstable circumstances of theatrical production itself. And these, of course, tend to resist fixation by editorial inscription. The problem, then, as we have learned from the

editors themselves, is how to wrest a textual end-product from an extremely fluid, largely unrecorded, partially oral process of working, writing, rehearsing, and of course playing in the theatre.[65]

Another example of this process at work can be seen in the quarto *Much Ado About Nothing* (1600). The constable Dogberry, whose own persona as represented in the text is radically unstable, is questioned by Leonato (Hero's father) and he begins by excusing his partner Verges's initial account:

> A good old man, sir, he will be talking. As they say, 'When the age is in, the wit is out.' God help us, it is a world to see! Well said, I'faith, neighbour Verges. Well, God's a good man. And two men ride of a horse, one must ride behind. An honest soul, I'faith, sir, by my troth, he is, as ever broke bread. But, God is To be worshipped, all men are not alike. Alas, good neighbour!
>
> (3.5.32–9)

The direction of Dogberry's speech is not clear, and what begins as an apology for his colleague veers off into other matters, articulated through an accumulating series of proverbs.[66] What lends vitality to these proverbs is that, despite their repetition, they converge on the present figure of Verges. He is simultaneously in and out of focus, and at the mercy of Dogberry's oral meanderings, while Leonato gives him short shrift: 'Indeed, neighbour, he comes too short of you', and 'I must leave you' (3.5.40 and 42). When Dogberry and Verges later appear, it is to arraign Conrade and Borachio for what will emerge is their part in Don John's plot to discredit Hero. In the later scene, Dogberry conducts the interrogation and he dictates what the Sexton should record. However, as the dialogue develops it becomes clear that there is a serious tension between the grammar of writing and Dogberry's understanding of social (and religious) hierarchy. When Conrade asserts that he is a 'gentleman', Dogberry's response is:

> DOGBERRY. Write down 'master gentleman Conrade.'
> Masters, do you serve God?
> CONRADE, BORACHIO. Yes sir, we hope.
> DOGBERRY. Write down, that they hope they serve God; and write God first, for God defend but God should go before such villains. Masters, it is proved already that you are little better than false

knaves, and it will near to be thought so shortly. How answer you for yourselves?

(4.2.17–25)

This assault on the basic grammar of writing is made more complicated by the fact that, as we observed in Chapter 1, 'Dogberry' is represented in the printed text first as 'Andrew' and then as 'Kempe', while Verges is designated as 'Couly'. The textual instability manifest at these points in *Much Ado About Nothing* testifies both to the oral style of a 'clown' figure who can improvise dialogue, at the same time as the printed text can disclose a radical instability in the representation of roles. Behind the personae of Dogberry and Verges are the actors 'Kempe' and 'Couly', who may themselves as actors be behind the dramatist Shakespeare. In a very rare moment we glimpse the traces of an economic exchange as the voices and the skills of two of the company's actors are laid bare for an early reader who may have been less agitated at what from the modern reader's point of view might be regarded as a violation of the editorial principle of normalisation of speech prefixes.

The process of working and writing, by its very nature, involved imitation and the marshalling and appropriation of *copia* in acts of creative repetition as well as adaptation. On the larger question of repetition, given a very specific oral context in the episode from *Much Ado About Nothing*, it is easy to detect the duplication of scenes, situations and dramatic characters across the range of Shakespearean texts – in short, the memes – that serve to expand meaning and stimulate the audience's active theatrical memory. The accumulation of proverbial speech is in this sense memetic, but the larger duplication and triplication of dramatic characters in *Hamlet* provide a network for purposes of comparison and contrast, and include the following memes: the mobility of the topos of madness and its movement across the gender divide from Hamlet to Ophelia; the duplication of names (Hamlet and Fortinbras); the triplication (quadruplication, if we include Priam) of fathers; the triplication of sons. All of these repetitions serve to suggest alternative meanings, and all have the effect of syncopating, and improvising on, a series of mutually connected events and situations. We might call this a 'style' and it has been a critical commonplace to trace it to an authorial origin, but as the example from *Much Ado About Nothing* reveals, the origin may not be quite what it seems. Moreover, the late Pierre Bourdieu offers a definition of style that effectively describes the complex textual economy in which the writer or the artist is necessarily enmeshed:

> The ultimate truth of the style of a period, a school or an author is not contained as a seed in an original inspiration, but is defined and redefined continuously as a signification in a state of flux which constructs itself in accordance with itself and in reaction against itself; it is the continued exchange between questions which exist only for and through a mind armed with schemes of a specific type and more or less innovative solutions, obtained through the application of the same schemes, but capable of transforming the initial scheme, that this unity of style and meaning emerges which, at least after the event, may appear to have preceded the works heralding the final outcome and which transforms, retrospectively the different moments of the temporal series into simple preparatory outlines.[67]

This important observation presupposes both an awareness on the part of the artist of those 'schemes of a specific type' that comprise the 'rules' of the particular art form, and the capacity of the reader or spectator to recognise them and to appreciate retrospectively those 'more or less innovative solutions' proffered by a particular work. To this extent, a style is a *parole* – that is to say, a selection and combination of particular elements that contribute towards the specific texture of the work, and that derive their artistic strength from a *langue* consisting of the totality of those elements, narrative, formal, cultural and textual from which the writer as active agent selects. Bourdieu adds an explicitly sociological element since a recognition of the formal properties of a work depends upon the dynamic support of institutions of culture and politics, and, of course, history. Embedded in this economy is a principle of repetition that is something more than simply the echoing of incidents or situations, or dramatic characters. In his book *Difference and Repetition* (1994) the French philosopher Gilles Deleuze has this to say about the principle of repetition that clarifies the activity of the writer confronted with a plethora of resources:

Historians sometimes look for empirical correspondences between the present and the past, but however rich it may be, this network of historical correspondences involves repetition only by analogy or similitude. In truth the past is in itself repetition, as is the present, but they are repetition in two different modes which repeat each other. Repetition is never a historical fact, but rather the historical condition under which something new is effectively produced.[68]

Both Bourdieu and Deleuze make important statements about artistic structures that have serious implications for the study of Shakespeare's resources. Indeed, Deleuze adds to this the axiom that 'repetition is a condition of action before it is a concept of reflection'.[69] Although his concern is primarily with novels, J. Hillis Miller distinguishes between what he calls, 'Platonic' repetition, which he suggests 'is grounded in a solid archetypal model which is untouched by the effects of repetition' and that guarantees that 'the validity of the mimetic copy is established by the truth of its correspondence to what it copies', and what he calls a 'Nietzschean mode of repetition [that] posits a world based on difference'. He calls such 'simulacra' or 'phantasms' 'ungrounded doublings which arise from differential interrelations among elements which are all on the same plane'. The fact that this latter category is not grounded 'in some paradigm or archetype means that there is something ghostly about the effects of this second kind of repetition'.[70] Of course, we can apply this to the tropological structure of plays like *Hamlet*, *Othello*, *Macbeth* or *King Lear* to cite just a few examples, and this is the formalistic line that, as we saw earlier, Marjorie Garber takes. In a play such as *Hamlet* there is a ghost *in* the play but the play is the product of other 'ghosts', narratives whose contents are innovatively brought into creative alignment with each other and with the play's structure through Shakespeare's own agency as playwright. In other words, the principle of repetition allows the dramatist to embed his own distinctive narrative in a wider network that exerts its own variable pressures – sometimes even unconscious pressures – on the eventual outcome.

The categories that Bullough used to classify elements of this network – 'probable source', 'possible source', 'analogue', all within the framework of 'narrative and dramatic sources' – offer a reduced version of the textual economies that are embodied in each dramatic text. It is difficult to separate the formal properties of these texts from the full variety of forms and narratives that comprise this network, or, in the case of Shakespeare, to do more than assign them speculatively to particular discursive regimes. In the case of *Hamlet*, critics have isolated elements of the play whose function is both 'mimetic' in the Platonic sense, *and* Nietzschean in their emphasis on constitutive difference as identified by Hillis Miller. To take one brief example, John Dover Wilson, evidently basing his conclusions on the Q2-F reading of the play, argues that Laertes's return in Act 4 Scene 5 furnishes 'an exact parallel' of Hamlet's situation.[71] In contrast, Harold Jenkins, the Arden 2 editor, argues that Laertes 'appears to have been conceived to exhibit, even to the verge of caricature all that Hamlet as revenger might have been'.[72] Implied in Jenkins's comment is something akin to Deleuze's theory of repetition where events within the play are repeated but in different registers, with the difference itself generating meaning. Also, so far as we know, Laertes does not figure in the existing narratives of the story, which prompts the question why Shakespeare would have used the name of the father of Odysseus from Homer's *The Odyssey*. The name emerges in a different context much earlier in *Titus Andronicus*, in which 'wise Laertes' son' (Ulysses) (1.1.385) is mentioned. Jonathan Bate, the Arden 3 editor of the play, notes that the incident of the Trojan wars referred to here may have come to Shakespeare 'from a school commentary on Horace'.[73] In *Hamlet* the name of the father becomes that of an intemperate son, while the father, Polonius, is the feckless courtier whose 'accidental' death is the trigger for the events leading to the play's tragic denouement. What emerges from this brief example are the different categories of repetition that serve to generate a range of variable meanings that the text(s) of *Hamlet* suture together to produce subtly different effects.

As these details accumulate, so within the purview of the Shakespearean theatre as an enterprise they become part of a textual economy. Aristotle's *Oeconomica* differentiates between the different ways of balancing revenues and expenditure within different types of society.[74] The theatre, which was a kind of society within a society, was also central to Shakespeare's role in a commercial enterprise, and was committed to generating revenue; and, of course, the materials used to generate revenue were the textual economies that provided the dramatist, the actors and the theatre with the means of attracting audiences. Here the dramatic text was one of a number of resources, with its own species of economy that could be converted into performance and into the 'book' as a means of generating income. Plays were only relevant insofar as they were and continued to be popular and to generate audiences. This dynamic and dialogic activity is obvious, but what is not so obvious is a different category of 'economic' activity, of running the theatrical household, which involved various forms of textual exchange. It is to some of these exchanges that we will now turn.

Notes

1 Colm Tóibín, *House of Names* (London, 2017), p. 263.
2 Pat Barker, *The Silence of The Girls* (London, 2018). In her earlier novel *Life Class* (2007), set during the First World War, Barker announces what will become her rewriting of Homer's *Iliad*: 'The women have gone very quiet. It's like the *Iliad*, you know, when Achilles insults Agamemnon and Agamemnon says he's got to have Achilles' girl and Achilles goes off and sulks by the long ships and the girls they're quarrelling over say nothing, not a word, it's a bit like that. I don't suppose men ever hear that silence' (p. 111).
3 Jacques Derrida, 'Freud and the scene of writing', *Writing and Difference*, trans. Alan Bass (London, 1978), p. 203.
4 Tóibín, *House of Names*, p. 56.
5 Ibid., p. 227.
6 Julie Sanders, *Adaptation and Appropriation*, 2nd edn (London, 2016), p. 22.
7 Ibid., p. 35.
8 Charlton Hinman, ed., *The Norton Facsimile of The First Folio of Shakespeare*, 2nd edn, with a new Introduction by Peter W.M. Blaney (New York, 1996), p. 9.
9 Ibid.
10 Ibid., p. 10.

11 C.H. Herford, P. Simpson and E. Simpson, eds, *Ben Jonson*, 11 vols (Oxford, 1963), vol. 11, p. 390.
12 Stephen Orgel, 'The Renaissance poet as plagiarist', *The Authentic Shakespeare and Other Problems of the Early Modern Stage* (London, 2002), p. 105.
13 Cf. András Kiséry, *Hamlet's Moment: Drama and Political Knowledge in Early Modern England* (Oxford, 2016), p. 41.
14 *Ibid.*
15 *Ibid.*, pp. 41–2.
16 Seán Burke, *The Ethics of Writing: Authorship and Legacy in Plato and Nietzsche* (Edinburgh, 2008), p. 26.
17 Patrick Collinson, *The Reformation* (London, 2005), p. 35.
18 Barbara A. Mowat, 'The theater and literary culture', in John D. Cox and David Scott Kastan, eds, *A New History of English Drama* (New York, 1997), p. 220.
19 *Ibid.*
20 Cited in Edward Burns, '"HAREY THE VJ" ON STAGE AT THE ROSE', in William Shakespeare, *King Henry the Sixth Part 1*, ed. Edward Burns, Arden 3 Series (London, 2000), pp. 1–2.
21 See Kenneth Muir, *Shakespeare's Sources*, vol. 1 (London, 1957), pp. 225–31, and *The Sources of Shakespeare's Plays* (London, 1977), pp. 253–8. See also Suzanne Gossett, '"From ashes Gowwer is come": sources of *Pericles*', in William Shakespeare, *Pericles*, ed. Suzanne Gossett, Arden 3 series (London, 2004), pp. 70–6, for a digest of the issues involved in the antecedents of the play. All citations to *Pericles* are from this edition unless otherwise stated.
22 Cf. also, the final line of the 1600 quarto of *Love's Labour's Lost* where 'The words of Mercury are harsh after the songs of Apollo' (5.2.918–19). This line is printed in different type from the body of the play, but in the Folio text the line is incorporated into the dialogue and ascribed to Armado. See Terence Hawkes, *Shakespeare's Talking Animals: Language and Drama in Society* (London, 1973), pp. 69ff., which argues that 'the words of Mercury' refers to the play 'in written form', whereas Apollo is associated with the play's 'oral form, and its tonal aspects' (p. 70).
23 Jeffrey Masten, *Textual Intercourse: Collaboration, Authorship and Sexualities in Renaissance Drama* (Cambridge, 1997), p. 3.
24 *Ibid.*, p. 15.
25 *Ibid.*, p. 20.
26 *Ibid.*, p. 13.
27 *Ibid.*, p. 14.

28 Michel Foucault, *Language, Counter-memory, Practice: Selected Essays and Interviews*, trans. Donald Bouchard and Sherry Simon, ed. Donald Bouchard (Oxford, 1977), p. 123.
29 *Ibid.*, p. 115.
30 *Ibid.*
31 Cf. Stephen Orgel, 'The authentic Shakespeare', *The Authentic Shakespeare*, pp. 231–56.
32 *Ibid.*, p. 232.
33 *Ibid.*, p. 236.
34 *Ibid.*, p. 237.
35 Foucault, *Language, Counter-memory, Practice*, p. 126.
36 *Ibid.*, p. 132.
37 Ann Radcliffe, *The Mysteries of Udolpho*, ed. Bonamy Dobrée, with an Introduction and Notes by Terry Castle (Oxford, 1988), p. 674.
38 Cf. Dale Townshend, 'Gothic and the ghost of *Hamlet*', in John Drakakis and Dale Townshend, eds, *Gothic Shakespeares* (London, 2008), pp. 68ff.
39 Foucault, *Language, Counter-memory, Practice*, p. 137.
40 *Ibid.*, p. 122.
41 *Ibid.*, p. 123.
42 Marjorie Garber, *Shakespeare's Ghost Writers: Literature as Uncanny Causality* (New York and London, 1987), p. 13.
43 *Ibid.*
44 *Ibid.*, pp. 14–15.
45 Burke, *The Ethics of Writing*, p. 26.
46 Ann Thompson and Neil Taylor, '*Hamlet* at the turn of the century', in William Shakespeare, *Hamlet*, ed. Ann Thompson and Neil Taylor, Arden 3 series, revised edn, 2 vols (London, 2016), pp. 37–9. Thompson and Taylor date the play around 1601 (p. 37) and they comment: 'Certainly *Hamlet* has been read as a *fin de siècle* text in a number of ways' (p. 39).
47 Garber, *Shakespeare's Ghost Writers*, p. 161.
48 Stephen Orgel, 'Plagiarism revisited', in *Spectacular Performances: Essays on Theater, Imagery, Books and Selves in Early Modern England* (Manchester, 2011), pp. 211–28.
49 *Ibid.*, p. 220.
50 *Ibid.*, p. 222.
51 *Ibid.*
52 *Ibid.*, p. 227.
53 Thompson and Taylor, 'The relationship of F to Q2', in *Hamlet*, p. 80.
54 *Ibid.*, p. 84.

55 *Ibid.*, p. 85.
56 *Ibid.*, p. 86. Here they cite Lukas Erne, *Shakespeare as Literary Dramatist* (Cambridge, 2003), who correctly identifies the texts gathered together in Folio as 'conflations of theatrical scripts and reading texts' (p. 26) but who in the case of *Hamlet* thinks that both Q2 and Folio operate in accordance with a literary logic that 'correspond[s] to what an emergent dramatic author wrote for readers in an attempt to raise the literary respectability of play texts' (p. 220).
57 John Heminge and Hendy Condell, 'To the great variety of readers', in the 1623 Folio, sig. A3ʳ.
58 Mowat, 'The theater and literary culture', p. 223.
59 Seán Burke, *The Death and Return of the Author: Criticism and Subjectivity in Barthes, Foucault and Derrida* (1992; reprinted, Edinburgh, 1999), p. 23.
60 *Ibid.*, p. 24.
61 *Ibid.*
62 John Kerrigan, *Shakespeare's Binding Language* (Oxford, 2016), pp. 10–11.
63 See Thompson and Taylor, *Hamlet*, pp. 418–19, for glosses.
64 Robert Weimann, *Author's Pen and Actor's Voice: Playing and Writing in Shakespeare's Theatre* (Cambridge, 2000), pp. 30–1.
65 *Ibid.*, p. 37.
66 Cf. footnotes by Claire McEachern, ed., in William Shakespeare, *Much Ado About Nothing*, Arden 3 series (London, 2006), p. 254 nn. 33–7.
67 Pierre Bourdieu, *The Field of Cultural Production*, ed. Randall Johnson (Cambridge, 1993), p. 229.
68 Gilles Deleuze, *Difference and Repetition*, trans. Paul Patton (London, 1994), p. 90.
69 *Ibid.*
70 J. Hillis Miller, *Fiction and Repetition: Seven English Novels* (Cambridge, MA, 1982), p. 6.
71 John Dover Wilson, *What Happens in Hamlet* (Cambridge, 1935), p. 263. Q1 makes an important distinction between the two characters in that Hamlet says 'Beleeue mee, it greeues me much Horatio, / That to Laertes I forgot my selfe: / For by my selfe me thinkes I feele his griefe, / Though there is a difference in each other's wrong' (5.2. (sig, I2ʳ)). This is absent from Q2 and Folio.
72 Harold Jenkins, 'The second revenge', in William Shakespeare, *Hamlet*, ed. Harold Jenkins, Arden 2 series (London, 1982), p. 142. In their edition of *Hamlet: The Texts of 1603 and 1623* (London, 2007), Ann Thompson and Neil Taylor simply register the fact that Laertes's and

Hamlet's 'circumstances differ' and they note 'a slight difference' from Folio 'where Hamlet sees Laertes' cause as mirroring his own' (p. 164 n. 4).
73 William Shakespeare, *Titus Andronicus*, ed. Jonathan Bate, Arden 3 series (London, 1995), p. 152 nn. 384–6.
74 Aristotle, *Metaphysics Books 1–14: Oeconomica: Magna Moralia*, trans. G. Cyril Armstrong (Cambridge, MA, 1935), pp. 347–9.

4

Trafficking in intertextuality

It has long been accepted that an early modern theatrical text is a fundamentally unstable phenomenon. Quoting Stephen Orgel, Robert Weimann observes that 'the basic instability of texts' in the Elizabethan theatre is inseparable from 'a fluidity that is built in' so as to accommodate changing circumstances of performance. In such cases, 'the printed text is simply one stage in a continuous process, with no particular authority over any of the other stages in the process'.[1] Weimann's concern at this point in his argument, as we have seen, is with the fluidity of performance and its necessary 'collaborative economies',[2] in contrast to the authority of the printed and edited text. Indeed, he goes on to add that the realisation of the text in performance 'is no less than a transmutation that thrives on "surplus value," the semantic and semiotic overcharge, that results when a verbally composed representation submits to material (voiced, corporeal, and other audible and visual) articulations'.[3] Much later in his argument, Weimann goes on to insist that:

> Once written language was articulated orally, in the form of dramatic speech, and once performers' voices and bodies were sustained by prescribed roles, neither pen nor voice remained an isolated, univocal source of authority in the projection of theatrical space. Since this space was larger and more complex than either the writing of characters or the delivery of performers could occupy, only the given conjuncture of pen and voice could in each case decide on what grounds the place and time 'which speaks' might be larger than or otherwise different from the place and time which 'is spoken.'[4]

At no point in his discussion does Weimann deploy the vocabulary of 'trafficking' or 'intertextuality', although from the very outset he is preoccupied with the 'interaction of diverse modes of playing', whose intricacies commingle 'with the representation of character'.[5] What drives Weimann's complex argument is the distinction between 'literacy' and 'orality', between the demands upon the actor's 'voice' and his body in performance, and the authentication of the 'text' in print where the latter is a reductive mode or articulation compared with the fullness of the realisation of language in and through material representation that is embodied in performance.

Literary scholars have traditionally been preoccupied with the genesis of theatrical texts: where they have come from, how they have been compiled, the influences that have shaped them and the extent to which they imitate, paraphrase, adapt and/or appropriate the linguistic materials that dramatists encounter individually and collectively in the process of generating scripts. Janet Clare, as we saw earlier, begins her account in *Shakespeare's Stage Traffic* (2014) by emphasising a version of Greenblatt's appropriation of the classical term *enargia* in order to explain the 'trafficking' of texts between playwrights and audiences.[6] In his Arden 3 edition of *Romeo and Juliet*, René Weis glosses the Prologue's use of the word 'traffic' simply as 'business' and cites the *OED* as support.[7] In the interests of incorporating Shakespeare fully into the commercial world with which we are familiar, scholars have been content to assume that words such as 'traffic' and 'business' (alongside 'competition') adequately depict what are assumed to be the energies, competitive and otherwise, that generated plays.

For us the word 'traffic' has taken on far darker meanings, often associated with the illegal movement and sale of people. That the personnel of Elizabethan theatres hired out their skills, or in Shakespeare's case received a share of the income generated from performances, is not in question. Actors and writers made their living selling their texts and their thespian talents, and Shakespeare, through the company of which he was a part, could do both. That the process was still regarded as dubious is indicated initially by the customary acknowledgement of the geographical positioning of the public theatres outside the jurisdiction of the city authorities. The implication of Clare's title is that the circulation of social energy derived its power from the rivalry between theatre companies, and that it was this competition that fuelled the appetite for plays in much the same way as commodities circulate in modern market conditions. The 'traffic' that Clare isolates refers to the passage of plays across the early modern stage, and the manner in which they transported ancillary texts either through imitation, or adaptation and appropriation ('borrowing'). The 'business' to which she refers is very different from that which preoccupies Weimann, since Clare is concerned with the process of creative transportation of texts as they emerge into view under the variable pressures of playhouse practice. Clare is also concerned to explore what we would call the 'dialogue' between dramatists: Shakespeare's *Richard II* is in some sort of dialogue with Marlowe's *Edward II*; there is also the dialogue between Shakespeare's *The Merchant of Venice* and Marlowe's *The Jew of Malta*, although Clare does not explore it in any depth. Of course, in the last two cases the dialogue is one-sided, since Marlowe was long dead by the time Shakespeare came to write *Richard II* and *The Merchant of Venice*; or to put the matter a little differently, the dialogue, such as it was, operated at two levels: the one involving Shakespeare's own creative encounter with plays that he clearly knew, and the other involving audiences whose own history of theatregoing allowed them to construct an experiential library of references that enabled them to recognise events, structures (memes), phrases, lines and in some cases whole speeches as they shuffled between one theatrical experience and another. There is some slight evidence to suggest that these linkages extended beyond the theatre to permeate other formal occasions involving some sort of performance. For example, the spontaneous outbreak of anti-Semitic ridicule at the execution of Queen Elizabeth's Portuguese physician, Dr Roderigo Lopez, may have been provoked by elements in his speech on the scaffold that spectators associated with Marlowe's Barabas from *The Jew of Malta*,[8] even though little evidence survives to suggest that, beyond his Portuguese descent, Lopez was Jewish.

That there was a great deal of imitation, borrowing, innovating and experimentation, as well as competition for audiences, going on in the Elizabethan public theatre is not a matter of doubt. For example, in Q1 *Hamlet* (1603) Guyldensterne accounts for the players travelling by observing the competition emanating to some extent from a change in both audience composition and audience tastes:

> I' faith, my lord, novelty carries it away. For the principal public audience that came to them are turned to private plays, and to the humour of children.
>
> (7.271–3)[9]

Thompson and Taylor explain the inclusion in Q1 of the reference as a consequence of the so-called 'war of the theatres' that was current in 1600 but no longer topical in 1604–5 when Q2 was printed; or that with the transfer of patronage of the Children of the Chapel to Queen Anne, the excision was 'diplomatic'. It is uncertain whether the expanded version of the passage in the Folio (1623) is explanatory, or thematic.[10] We may of course see this as part of the process of 'trafficking', of the adjustments that companies made as responses to the varying behaviour of audiences. Equally, in *Hamlet* we might note that all three texts of the play contain a reference to Corambis/Polonius's thespian exploit: 'I did act (Q1)/enact (Q2-F) Julius Caesar. I was killed in the Capitol. Brutus killed me.' It is generally thought that the reference here is to the actor John Heminge, who probably played Caesar in *Julius Caesar* and is now playing Polonius, and to Richard Burbage, who previously played Brutus and is now playing Hamlet (who will, of course, go on to kill Polonius), something that an audience might well be expected to recognise, and in the case of the later play, to register.

'Traffic' is a way of describing the business of what passes across the stage in performance, and by implication what passes through the script in the process of composition. Even then, the example from *Much Ado About Nothing* that was discussed in Chapter 3, complicates the process of composition considerably. The process becomes ideological when it is linked to the legal issue of authorship, to the implicitly bourgeois urge to individualise the writer and to the question of ownership. Foucault's designation of the figure of 'the author', as we have already seen, is important for an understanding of what is implied in the process of 'trafficking':

> unlike a proper name, which moves from the interior of a discourse to the real person outside who produced it, the name of the author

remains at the contours of texts – separating one from the other, defining their form, and characterizing their mode of existence. It points to the existence of certain groups of discourse and refers to the status of this discourse within a society and a culture. The author's name is not a function of a man's civil status, nor is it fictional; it is situated in the breach, among the discontinuities, which give rise to new groups of discourse and their singular mode of existence.[11]

Donald Bouchard and Sherry Simon, Foucault's translators, gloss this passage by observing that the fundamental discontinuities of discourse are resolved traditionally either 'by reference to an originating subject, or to a language conceived as plenitude, which supports the activities of commentary and interpretation'.[12] For our purposes the issue is how we identify and categorise these fundamental discontinuities, and how in the process of their persistent collision they generate meanings. This is not simply a matter of *interpreting* an otherwise stable text, or performance, or indeed, the operations of the dramatist's 'mind',[13] rather it is a question of how those discursive elements enter the text, and the representational work that they perform and the meanings they generate *in the process of trafficking*. Janet Clare has done admirable service in bringing texts together, and in revealing many of the contents that are trafficked. What she does not do is proceed to an analysis of the more difficult task of identifying the meanings that are thereby produced beyond suggesting that the isolation of content provides a convincing pathway back to the writer's (or writers' in the case of multiple authorship) creative imagination. For Clare, 'trafficking' identifies texts and explores their influence on Shakespeare, but she is content to accept that 'traffic' and 'intertextuality' – the convergence of multiple texts within the dynamic organism of one text – are effectively synonymous terms used to describe a single process.

One way of problematising this assumption is to consider a specific example of the movement of one line in Thomas Kyd's play that was first published as *The Spanish Tragedie* in 1592, to Shakespeare's *Much Ado About Nothing* (1600). The moment occurs in Kyd's play at Act 2 Scene 1 after Balthazar, the nephew of the King of Portugal feels that he has been rejected by Bel-Imperia, the daughter of the Duke of Castile and sister to Lorenzo. She is the mistress of the dead Don Andrea who is now attended by Horatio, the son of Hieronimo and the person responsible for having shared in the capture of Balthazar in a recent war between Spain and Portugal. At the beginning of Act 2, Lorenzo and Balthazar discuss the latter's predicament:

> LORENZO: My Lord, though *Bel-imperia* seeme thus coy,
> Let reason hold you in your wonted joy:
> In time the sauage Bull sustaines the yoake,
> In time all haggard Hawkes will stoope to lure,
> In time small wedges cleaue the hardest Oake,
> In time the flint is pearst with softest shower,
> And she in time will fall from her disdaine,
> And rue the sufferance of your friendly paine.[14]

This collection of aphorisms from different discourses is cast in proverbial form, from which each element derives a cumulative rhetorical power. At one level these fragments are recalled to mind in what appears to be 'an art of compilation',[15] and they are assimilated into a very formal speech designed to give hope to the despairing Balthazar, who is less optimistic of success than his interlocutor.[16] In short, it is an accumulation of tropes that in this instance 'describe the structure of thought' of the dramatic character.[17] But while Kyd's text has a particular dramatic and literary focus, on closer inspection it is not a point of origin even though Shakespeare may well have been familiar with the play, and possibly with the printed text. Also, like Kyd, Shakespeare would, no doubt, have been very familiar with the proverbs that here function as memes. Kyd's ostensible purpose in these lines is to provide the dramatic character with an accumulation of textual evidence designed to provide reassurance in the face of female resistance. The resistant woman is at once a 'bull', a 'haggard hawk', a 'hardest oak' and finally a flinty rock: none of these images particularly complementary, or indeed consistent. This collocation is, however, a resource, and Shakespeare makes use of it in more than one play. For example, one of the aphorisms contained in this passage, a fragment carefully augmented and expanded, reappears in *The Taming of the Shrew* (*c*.1594), at the point where the newly wed Petrucchio reviews his strategy for taming his headstrong bride:

> My falcon now is sharp and passing empty,
> And till she stoop she must not be full-gorged,
> For then she never looks upon her lure.
> Another way I have to man my haggard,
> To make her come and know her keeper's call:
> That is, to watch her, as we watch these kites
> That bate, and beat, and will not be obedient.
>
> (4.1.179–85)[18]

What in Kyd gathers a cumulative, though not always coherent, rhetorical force, as Balthazar takes up Lorenzo's cue and embarks on a self-pitying diatribe, is contained in Petrucchio's soliloquy, although what is preserved is the focus on masculine control; what is still at the stage of wishful thinking in Kyd is, in Shakespeare's play, the beginning of a successful campaign, irrespective of whether we are expected to interpret this display of patriarchal force as fantasy. Here what is adapted from a general stock of images is pared down and paraphrased to serve a particular dramatic purpose albeit within a discourse that has much in common with the ways in which these images have already been customarily deployed. Shakespeare's quotation of a sentiment that is both proverbial *and* specific suggests a process of textual editing and literary fashioning that, compared with Kyd, is contained.

Even more specific, but also more controversial, is the one line in the series from Kyd's play that reappears verbatim in the later *Much Ado About Nothing* (1600), and in a context that has a transformative effect while still remaining nominally within the literary discourse of courtship:

> BENEDICK. If I do, hang me in a bottle like a cat and shoot at me, and he that hits me, let him be clapped on the shoulder and called Adam.
> DON PEDRO. Well, as time shall try. 'In time the savage bull doth bear the yoke.'
> BENEDICK. The savage bull may, but if ever the sensible Benedick bear it, pluck off the bull's horns and set them in my forehead;
>
> (1.1.239–46)[19]

Editors agree that the text from which Kyd adapted his lines, almost verbatim, was sonnet XLVII of Thomas Watson's *Hecatompathia* or *Passionate Centurie of Loue* (1582), the first two lines of which Watson admits are 'an imitation of *Seraphone, Sonnetto 103*':

> In time the Bull is brought to wear the yoake;
> In time the haggred Haukes will stoope to Lures;
> In time small wedge will cleaue the sturdiest Oake;
> In time the Marble weares with weakest shewres:
> More fierce is my sweete loue, more hard withal,
> Then Beast, or Birde, then Tree, or Stony wall.[20]

Philip Edwards, the Revels editor of *The Spanish Tragedy*, cites other parallel texts and notes that 'the images were extremely popular'.[21] Barbara Hodgdon, the Arden 3 editor of *The Taming of the Shrew*, does not cite an analogue for Petrucchio's speech, but Claire McEachern observes a proverbial source for the line 'In time the savage bull doth bear the yoke' in Dent (T303), and traces the sentiment back through Kyd and Watson to Ovid's *Tristia* and *Ars Amatoria*.[22] After initiating a series of contrasts between proverbial knowledge and the strong-willed mistress, Watson's poem goes on to reinforce her resistance, and the speaker invokes the assistance of the '*Heavenly Boy*' Cupid to 'frame her will to right, that pride be spent'. This is the sentiment, and indeed, the situation, that Kyd's lines evoke, although the context there proves to be much more sinister, since it is the first stage of a plot to murder Hieronimo's son Horatio. The initial movement from lyric poem to potentially tragic scenario involves a shift of genres, but Shakespeare effects a further adjustment within the more general discourse of romantic love by isolating one line, and applying it *not* to the wilful disdaining mistress, but to the obstinate bachelor, Benedick. Furthermore, the repetition is not verbatim, which suggests a process of 'remembering' rather than a more rigorous formal process of 'memorisation.'[23]

Reversing the gender relations with which this line has customarily been associated, a more complex sexual politics emerges. Shakespeare's 'In time the savage bull doth bear the yoke' preserves the iambic structure of the line, while at the same time offering a proleptic glimpse of one of the play's most important themes: the poetic link between romantic discourse, the turbulent emotions that it is capable of generating and the subterfuges that it encourages as the participants negotiate the obstacles that it throws up. As the play's title suggests, the 'nothing' about which there is 'much ado' turns out to be a determinate absence that is at the heart of the play, which is filled with cultural meaning. Don Pedro's iambic line initiates a discursive strain that Benedick picks up after he has been duped into thinking that Beatrice is in love with him: 'Fair Beatrice I thank you for your pains' (2.3.240). Ironically, the device that dupes Benedick and Beatrice is the same as the one that the villain Don John uses to drive a wedge between Claudio and Hero, thereby indicating a radical and dangerous instability that resides at the heart of patriarchal power that gets it wrong in this play as often as it gets it right. Thus, in Shakespeare's play the semantic and semiotic work that this one line performs is far in excess of what we might call quotation or citation, or, indeed, simply the result of compilation.

The shifts of tone that these aphoristic lines undergo as they migrate in whole or in part from one genre to another indicate a process much more complex than that of mere 'imitation'. In Watson's self-consciously imitative enterprise, prefaced by a brief account of the poem's rhetorical strategy for increasing the reader's pleasure, the invocation of Cupid's power is designed to serve the speaker's own patriarchal power, temporarily disabled by the disdain of a mistress. The repetition of elements of this collocation testifies obviously to the popularity of the sentiments they articulate, but the shift from one context to another involves transformations of meaning, as well as lacunae of memory, that pose a challenge to anything approaching the kind of neutrality that mechanical repetition might suggest. In teasing these transformations out we are approaching the realm of intertextuality where the collision of texts – regarded casually as the activity of mere 'trafficking' – takes on a different, more anxious, significance.

Indeed, the term 'intertextuality' has been thoroughly domesticated since its importation from French literary theory of the 1970s, and its re-exportation in a suitably domesticated form from the Anglo-American academy since then. The term came into existence in 1974 in Julia Kristeva's *La Revolution de Language Poétique*, later translated in English as *Revolution in Poetic Language*, and was designed to augment the processes of 'displacement' and 'condensation' familiar to Freudian analysis of the operation of the unconscious, but deployed in early structural linguistics by Roman Jacobson and others to describe the processes of 'metonymy' and 'metaphor' as they appear in literary texts.[24] Kristeva adds 'a third "process" – the *passage from one sign system to another*' (original italics) that she defines in the following manner:

> To be sure, this process comes about through a combination of displacement and condensation, but this does not account for its total operation. It also involves an altering of the thetic *position* – the destruction of the old position and the formation of a new one. The new signifying system may be produced with the same signifying material; in language, for example, the passage may be made from narrative to text. Or it may be borrowed from different signifying materials. The transposition from a carnival scene to the written text, for instance. In this connection we examine the formation of a specific signifying system – the novel – as the result of a redistribution of several different sign systems: carnival, courtly poetry, scholastic discourse. The term *inter-textuality* denotes this transposition of one (or several) sign system(s) into another, but since the term has often been misunderstood in the banal sense of 'study of sources,' we prefer the term *transposition* because it specifies that the passage from one signifying system to another demands a new articulation of the thetic – of enunciative and denotative positionality.[25]

This describes with uncanny exactitude the shift from Watson's to Kyd's usages, and from there to Shakespeare's of one or more lines in a particular discursive declension. Kristeva's rejection of terms such as 'source' and 'originality' is part of a fundamentally political project designed to open up to examination the process whereby what she labels the 'thetic' or 'enunciative positionality' is formed. She pulls together elements of Freud and Bakhtin, to define an inchoate 'semiotic *chora*' as a pre-Oedipal state in which the distinctions between masculine and feminine have yet to emerge. And Kristeva proceeds to distinguish it from the post-Oedipal symbolic order that establishes a range of distinctions in a hierarchy that habitually repress this disruptive and potentially revolutionary energy that remains beneath the level of an imposed semiotic and semantic order. In her reading of Bakhtin, Kristeva identifies 'the *status of the word* as a minimal structural unit' that allows him to 'situate the text within history and society, which are then seen as texts read by the writer, into which he inserts himself by rewriting them'.[26]

While this deprives the writer of absolute autonomy, just as it pluralises the possibilities of meaning, it emphatically does not eliminate agency; rather it aims to chart a transgressive movement from an existing stable diachrony into a more dynamic 'synchrony' replete with verbal imperfections that are the result of fragmentary recall. Kristeva narrows this process down in order to sharpen the distinction between diachrony and synchrony, but her invocation of the 'carnivalesque' as a transgressive discourse points to a fundamental (she would say infrastructural) instability that in her residually Freudian discourse points to the operations of the unconscious:

> Diachrony is transformed into synchrony, and in the light of this transformation, *linear* history appears as abstraction. The only way a writer can participate in history is by transgressing this abstraction through a process of reading–writing: that is through the practice of a signifying structure in relation and opposition to another structure. History and morality are written and read within the infrastructure of texts. The poetic word, polyvalent and multi-determined, adheres to a logic exceeding that of codified discourse and fully comes into being only in the margins of recognised culture. Bakhtin was the first to study this logic, and he looked for its roots in *carnival*. Carnivalesque discourse breaks through the laws of a language censored by grammar and semantics and, at the same time, is a social and political protest. There is no equivalence, but rather, identity between challenging official linguistic codes and challenging official law.[27]

Kristeva notes that 'Bakhtinian dialogism identifies writing as both subjectivity and communication, or better, as intertextuality',[28] which adds a further gloss to Bakhtin's own account of 'dialogism' as he defines it in his *Problems of Dostoevsky's Poetics*:

> Dialogic relationships are reducible neither to logical nor to relationships orientated semantically toward their referential object, relations *in and of themselves* devoid of any dialogic element. They must clothe themselves in in discourse, become utterances, become the positions of various subjects expressed in discourse, in order that dialogic relationships might arise among them.[29]

Bakhtin goes on to argue: 'Dialogic relationships are absolutely impossible without logical relationships or relationships oriented toward a referential object, but they are not reducible to them, and they have their own specific character.'[30] He also insists that: 'Dialogic relationships in the broad sense are also possible among different intelligent phenomena, provided that these phenomena are expressed in some *semiotic* material. Dialogic relationships are possible, for example, among images belonging to different art forms.'[31]

For Bakhtin, and also for Kristeva, in order for dialogism to function it needs to be embedded in language. But the relationships it calls into being are in fundamental tension with each other, arising not from their identity with each other but from their *difference*. Moreover, that tension is not primarily a stimulus to pleasure derived from a recognition of their origins – one of the sentiments aroused by source study – but the locus of a *political* tension, whether its roots lie in gender formation, or more generally in the division of society into particular hierarchies.

This represents a significant departure from the traditional discourse invoked in Shakespeare Studies by Hardin Craig in 1949, and that J.M. Coetzee's fictional post-colonial author Elizabeth Costello dismisses with heavy irony at the beginning of a lecture designed to tease out the consequences of the writer's engagement with 'the problem of evil':

> The first part of the lecture is routine, covering familiar ground: authorship and authority, claims made by poets over the ages to speak a higher truth, a truth whose authority lies in revelation, and their further claim, in Romantic times, which happen to have been times of unparalleled geographical exploration, of a right to venture into forbidden or tabooed places.[32]

Of course, what Coetzee is pinpointing and paraphrasing here is the traditional reading practice of extracting not *a* meaning but *the* meaning from a text, whereas the Kristevan alternative is to chart the process whereby the writer *produces* meaning by selecting and combining existing elements in the language.

The transposition of lines from poem to play that we have noted does more than simply actualise instances of a tradition. These shifts of texts from one genre to another are more complex than the process suggested by Michael Riffaterre in his overarching phrase: 'by reference to usage and to standard narratives'.[33] Shakespeare's deployment of the line that appears in one form or another in Watson and Kyd introduces an 'ungrammaticality' that is at variance with the lovers' discourse even as it is embedded in it. The resultant semiotic disturbance exposes the very problem, the 'much ado' that comic form seeks (and fails) to fully resolve. Leonato's 'Peace! [*to Beatrice*] I will stop your mouth' (*Much Ado About Nothing*, 5.4.97), that appears in both Quarto and Folio texts, but that after Theobald's edition of the play in 1733 is given to Benedick,[34] exposes the ideological baggage of patriarchy, at the same time that it reveals a revolutionary female loquacity that can only be subjugated by force. This is emphatically *not* the citation of an already canonised or authorised text, but one whose passage from the realm of the anonymously proverbial into the category of the dramatic or the literary allows it to accrue additional cultural power. Shakespeare's citation is intertextual because, to utilise a general formulation initiated by Ross Chambers, it 'distinguishes itself as a negativity with respect to the canon, and in so doing distances itself from the socially marked discourses that, nevertheless, necessarily traverse it'.[35] It is also worth remarking that this engagement cannot be reduced to the level of Bloomian intersubjectivity in which one writer, fully conscious of the need to overcome a patriarchal precursor, *creates*, thereby establishing origin and assuming ownership of, a fully individualised text. Indeed, by the end of *Much Ado About Nothing* the positions of man and woman are both reaffirmed and subject to ironic review. The ideologically orthodox position is occupied by Hero and Claudio, where Hero is now Leonato's 'brother's daughter' (5.4.37), and the revisionist position is occupied by Beatrice and Benedick. But there is also an accusative position occupied by the forgotten Innogen, wife of Leonato and mother of Hero, whose apparent invisibility provides the ultimate critical gloss on the determining power of patriarchy. The level of position-shifting at the end of the play is reinforced by means of another intertext that is not, this time, proverbial (as we shall see), but canonical.

Who, then, does the figure of 'the savage bull' properly represent at the end of the play? As Claudio is preparing to marry a wife of

Leonato's choosing, he comments on Benedick's 'February face, / So full of frost, of storm and cloudiness' (5.4.41–2). The imagery here is, possibly, commonplace, but it resembles a description of winter that appears in Book 2 of Arthur Golding's 1567 translation of Ovid's *Metamorphoses*:

> And lastly quaking for the colde, stood Winter al forlorne,
> With rugged head as white as Dove, and garments all to torne,
> Forladen with the Isycles that dangled up and downe
> Upon his gray and hoarie beard and snowie frozen crowne.[36]

Book 2 of the *Metamorphoses* concentrates specifically on Jupiter's infidelity with Europa in the form of a bull,[37] and in *Much Ado About Nothing* it is this familiar episode that now provides for Claudio both a reference back to, and an opportunistic extension of, Don Pedro's earlier aphoristic utterance:

> I think he thinks upon the savage bull.
> Tush, fear not man: we'll tip thy horns with gold,
> And all Europa shall rejoice at thee,
> As once Europa did at lusty Jove
> When he would play the noblest beast in love.
>   (5.4.43–7)

It seems appropriate that it should be Claudio, who was earlier deceived into thinking that he had been cuckolded by Hero's alleged infidelity, who should now be the interpolator of this confusing utterance. Benedick is transformed from 'savage bull' to 'the noblest beast in love' *and* a rapist, whose amorous activity will now become the subject of general rejoicing. Given Beatrice's behaviour up to this point it is unlikely that she will take on the role of Europa, and if, as McEachern suggests, 'Claudio's jest attempts to mock the prospect of being horned (or cuckolded) by promising that Benedick, like the golden calf, will become the glorious idol of a sacrilegious and widespread cult',[38] then this reinforces a destructive danger that is embedded at the heart of marriage itself. But Claudio's comment raises further questions.

Is it Benedick who, like Beatrice, now occupies a curiously doubled position – 'Here's our own hands against our hearts' (5.4.91–2) – as he becomes 'the married man' (5.4.98)? Or is it

Beatrice and Hero – male actors impersonating females – whose subjugation allows us to glimpse the boundary that patriarchy is charged with policing? Of course, there is, as we have seen, a police force in the play, the inept Watch, whose ungrammatical, but impeccably hierarchical, attempts to bring the bastard Don John to justice prove to be more efficient that Hero's accusers whose jealousies spur them on to engage in an alarmingly illiterate assertion of Hero's alleged pre-marital infidelity. What the 'much ado' of the play opens up briefly, and what the ambiguity of the mobile identity of the 'savage bull' reinforces, is a space in which masculinity and femininity are momentarily dissolved, thereby representing a threat that, in accordance with a now precarious dominant ideology, only the institution of marriage can avert. The shifts in what in another context Toril Moi has called 'positionality',[39] if we are to take the anxiety behind Claudio's jest seriously, now seem to affect the identities of both masculine and feminine. Indeed, the intertextual force of this citation raises a question about what exactly is marginal and what is central in Messina. Benedick's enforced transformation betrays an irrational impulse at the heart of masculinity: 'man is a giddy thing, and this is my conclusion' (5.4.106–7). Moreover, the identities of the masked women (Beatrice and Hero) only become clear once they answer to their names. Hero is revitalised: 'One Hero died defiled, but I do live, / And surely as I live, I am a maid' (5.4.63–4) and Beatrice removes her mask when, in answer to her husband's question, she is named:

> BENEDICK. Soft and fair, Friar. [*to Antonio*] Which is Beatrice?
> BEATRICE. I answer to that name. What is your will?
>
> (5.4.72–3)

What this comedy is designed to avert is a return to some kind of pre-Oedipal dissolution of subject positions that the distillation of the episode from the *Metamorphoses* threatens. Here intertextuality fulfils a much more dramatically effective function than stimulating the recognition of one text inside another. At this point in the play there are two, possibly three, wives onstage, each representing particular facets of the marriage state: Hero (who still occupies the stereotype romantic female), Beatrice (who is submissive but much more knowing) and Innogen (the silent wife of the patriarch

Leonato). The play gestures towards the precariousness of all these positions, and it reaches back into the *Metamorphoses* almost as a means of exposing the mythological, social and intersubjective means whereby society orders itself. Beatrice and Hero (and Innogen) represent different stages of identification of woman within the symbolic order of patriarchy, but the unstable nature of that order, embodied in the figure of the bastard Don John, coupled with the prejudices that are embedded within the play's masculine culture, are offered no more than a provisional resolution within the play's aesthetic structure. The mischievous Don John has been arraigned, but could escape again, and Messina could return to a primal chaos that only the ungrammatical – one might almost say anti-grammatical – procedures of the Watch might be able to unravel.

In *Much Ado About Nothing* a series of texts are 'trafficked' across the stage, but their interactions with each other are dynamic, and critical. Whether Shakespeare was fully conscious of all of the effects of their collisions is not of primary importance, unless we wish to sustain a post-Romantic image of the fully conscious creative writer and the bardolatry that usually accompanies it. That the play worries at the anxieties surrounding marital relations seems obvious, but it is the dramatist's agency in selecting points of reference in other texts and embedding them in the play that triggers the intertextual work that they then perform. Of course, it requires the reader or spectator to tease out the meanings that these texts produce, and here too the processes of recollection might well be partial, if not imperfect.

Intertextuality as a process has slowly been systematically drained of its political significance. At one extreme it is used to shore up a Derridian commitment to the deferral of meaning; for example, in his book *Intertextuality and Romance in Renaissance Drama: The Staging of Nostalgia* (1992), Richard Hillman notes in a stringently formalist manner that intertextuality entails 'the infinite postponement of significance', and he suggests that,

> No matter how two (or more) given texts play off one another, they must fail to exhaust the meanings they excite, simply because the very condition of those meanings is their difference.[40]

Hillman's objective is to allow 'a free interplay among texts, including the texts of historical reality (sometimes distinguished as "contexts")'.[41] And he defends 'the interplay of signifiers either within or among texts' against what he takes to be the New Historicist and Cultural Materialist – he thinks of the two projects as being roughly identical – 'collapsing of the mimetic gap' between 'history' and its representations.[42] He argues that in a play like Beaumont and Fletcher's *Philaster*:

> nostalgia becomes as politically charged as in *Henry V*. Yet, as in Shakespeare's historical romance, the implications are not readily reducible to a single (or even double) political statement – the less so because of the genre's repudiation of realism (if not reality).[43]

Hillman's desire to avoid reducing the text's manifest textuality to a single political statement that reflects a historical materiality drives him into a formal pluralism that risks obscuring the political work that the intertexts he identifies are doing. His emphasis on 'difference', formally appropriate though it may be, risks dragging him into another kind of politics that serves to shore up a subjectivism that his methodology seeks to problematise.

It is surprising that the term 'intertextuality' has not attracted more critical attention in Shakespeare Studies than it has, particularly in relation to some of the implications that it has for a study of 'sources'. In the aftermath of the flurry of theoretically informed literary criticism, Stephen Lynch recognised this in his book *Shakespearean Intertextuality: Studies in Selected Sources and Plays* (1998). From the outset Lynch set his face against the traditional view of 'sources as static building blocks that Shakespeare picked over, re-arranged, and artfully improved', which can now be 're-examined as products of intertextuality – endlessly complex, multi-layered fields of interpretation that Shakespeare refashioned and reconfigured into alternative fields of interpretation'.[44]

Lynch seeks to effect a rapprochement between the traditional view of the author and the challenge to his autonomy posed by the identification of intertexts. With what in professional literary critical circles is an unusual candour, Lynch acknowledges:

> My approach may suggest a basic contradiction in that I am invoking the amorphous power of intertextuality while claiming the

revisionary skill of a particular author. My attempt, however, is to bridge the gap between traditional assumptions about authorial power and control and post-structuralist claims that authors neither create nor control texts but are themselves products of pre-existent cultural discourses.[45]

In launching the idea of Shakespeare the revisionist, Lynch wants to identify a range of pressures that 'would have come into interactive play in Shakespeare's refashioning of his source materials', which he thinks may lead to the allegation that he 'may be placing Shakespeare the author back on stage – but not alone and not always at the center'.[46] Lynch understandably regards Shakespeare's revisionary activity as a 'skill', and that in his 'rewriting of his sources, the source texts are not simply used and discarded but linger in the margins of the plays – hypertexts, if you will, of alternative textual possibilities'.[47] But the rhetorical force of this argument is in inverse proportion to the complications that arise when the fragmentary operations of memory, and the pressures generated by the contexts of theatre and society, are all brought to bear on the issue.

Lynch is not unaware of the political content that results from the collision of non-Shakespearean texts with their revisionary author. Indeed, he notes that the masculinity of the disguised Rosalynd in *As You Like It* as represented in Lodge's *Rosalynde* becomes, after revision, a means of achieving a 'balanced indeterminacy', thereby enabling the play to swing 'both ways: exposing conventional gender differences as mere artifice, while affirming at least some level of innate and natural gender differences'.[48] Of course, the prising open of plural meanings is one thing, but the process whereby a politics is enacted in the text – in other words, the work that is undertaken in the moments of collision – is a different matter altogether. The author as over-determined agency, a conception with which Lynch seems to begin, is gradually replaced by a more autonomous author who can consciously stand above 'rich and highly suggestive material' in order to rework it 'into richer and more suggestive material'.[49]

Here the mode of intertextuality that produces tensions beneath the level of the writer's agency is excavated from a deconstructionist Shakespeare *avant la lettre* who can be described in terms reminiscent of traditional bardolatry. Indeed, whenever the term 'intertextuality' is deployed, the resultant creative ingenuity is casually shuttled between that of the revisionist 'author' and the critic. A play such as *As You Like It* may momentarily dissolve the categories of masculine and feminine, but their final reaffirmation that derives from the text's aesthetic structure collapses these cultural distinctions into 'natural' identities, the very textual manoeuvre that Kristeva theorises as the site of an alternative politics,[50] and not simply as a neutral proliferation of meanings.

Lynch's complex critical manoeuvres are replicated at a much lower level in Murray Levith's *Shakespeare's Cues and Prompts* (2007). Levith can acknowledge the multiform nature of Shakespearean texts, but his aim is to identify hitherto overlooked 'sources' embedded in a select number of texts, where the embedding involves a process of 'cuing':

> The present volume examines a number of *types* of Shakespearean intertextual prompts imbedded [*sic*] in and/or cuing selected works: an unrecognised dramatic source from a contemporary play, images likely remembered from a favourite Latin classic, a quasi-mythic narrative, a prompt involving a familiar British national myth and an item of contemporary political interest.[51]

Unfortunately, Levith does not go beyond the process of identification. For example, having identified the 'influence' of Marlowe's *Doctor Faustus* as well as *The Jew of Malta* on Shakespeare's *The Merchant of Venice*, he concludes, rather lamely, that he has 'read *The Merchant of Venice* as a *Faust* play', and that: 'The Faust motif is clearly observable as an *intertext* in *Merchant*, placing characters with choices to make between two worlds, at times exhorted by good and bad angels, or identified with one or another of these worlds and its values.'[52] It is difficult to conclude that the intertext that Levith identifies is anything other than a repetition in one text of its precursor text. There is no indication of the *political* work that the process of intertextuality exposes. Rather, on the problematic matter of the enforced conversion of Shylock he concludes that it merely exposes 'the hellish choice or identification' that involves 'over-concern with the here-and-now, suggested by the vengeful and profit-driven values of Shylock the Jew, who becomes a type of all the "alien-others" despised by the Elizabethan English'.[53] In contrast, 'the Christian choice or identification ... affirms the supposedly Anglican message that the soul and eternity are more important than the body and this life, and that generosity, friendship, love, mercy and sacrifice are the correct values to have on this earth'.[54] Levith disregards Marlowe's representation of the formal properties of *Doctor Faustus*, with the result that he makes of *The Merchant of Venice* a simple morality tale that represses the complex contradictions that the collision of texts exposes, and overlooks entirely the fissures in both plays' symbolic orders that the dramas reveal. The result is an alignment of a revitalised source study with a familiar brand of thematic reading that sucks the politics out of each text and with it the possibility of their dynamic interaction with each other.

Levith does not depart significantly from Robert S. Miola's quasi-Empsonian classification in his essay 'Seven Types of Intertextuality', where he announces:

> The continuum moves from closest approximations to ever freer adumbrations, from conscious, positivistic, and author-directed imitations, through more distant and subtle evocations, to, finally, intertextualities that exist in discourses created by the reader, rather than the writer.[55]

Miola offers a descriptively empirical account of the different kinds of intertextuality, but although he initially mentions Kristeva and Derrida, he refuses to go beyond the different types, nor does he acknowledge the dynamic and interactive politics that is an important element of the concept of intertextuality. Indeed, he shifts his ground from 'conscious, positivistic, and author-directed imitations' to 'intertextualities that exist in discourse created by the reader, rather than the writer'. The shift from 'writer' to 'reader' is, effectively, a move from a writer embedded in history to a reader with access to a library of books. Here the imitation of the Empson of *Seven Types of Ambiguity* conveniently forgets the Empson of *Some Versions of Pastoral*, and it overlooks the dynamics of theatrical performance and what audiences brought to the theatrical experience. For Miola, the scholarly memory is in books, whereas, even if an appeal is made to a historical positivism, the fragmentary, not always accurate, process of recall and its implications for the operations of memory are manoeuvred into the background.

Perhaps the most sustained version of a thoroughly domesticated intertextuality appears, as we have already suggested, in Janet Clare's *Shakespeare's Stage Traffic*. From the outset Clare distinguishes her 'more confined understanding of intertextuality from that of Lynch, ensuring a sustained dramaturgical focus'.[56] She begins, promisingly, with the suggestion that we should regard variant Shakespeare play-texts as having sufficient independence to be treated as 'themselves intertextual, with each version operating within a different intertextual ambit'.[57] The suggestion that 'within the orbit of intertextuality ... plays have evolved in response to other plays' conflates the principle of intertextuality – whose activity cannot be domesticated without rendering the term ineffectual – with a traditional, if not revisionist, source study. Each chapter contains a section entitled 'Intertextualities' that seeks to draw together the texts that Clare nominates. For example, in her chapter 'Troublesome reigns' she pulls together Shakespeare's *King John* and Peele's *The Troublesome Reign of King John*, and asserts: 'Intertextuality is at its most resonant in the transposition of the character of the Bastard from *The Troublesome Reign* to *King John*.'[58] Clare speculates, not unreasonably, that the evidence for the representation of the Bastard in the Folio text of Shakespeare's play suggests that he 'would appear to have built upon the assumption of an audience's prior experience of his stage persona'.[59] It is the case that the two plays are preoccupied with rival claims to the throne, along with the issue of bastardy that was itself a very vexed social and political category in the late sixteenth century. Moreover, Shakespeare expands the role of the Bastard, along with a particular inflection that makes of the character both an outsider *and* a heroic figure. Indeed, the circumstantial revision discloses a complex political contradiction that facilitates a momentary glimpse of an entire symbolic order thrown into disarray by England's challenge to papal authority. At one level the Bastard is in and of society, but at another level he is sufficiently self-conscious to be able to take on the role of critical commentator, something that is minimally presented in Peele's version. By probing this constitutive difference the reader/spectator is offered a glimpse of a political order in process, exposing the manner in which, to appropriate Kristeva's terminology, the text 'is constructed as a mosaic of quotations' and 'is the absorption and transformation of another'.[60] In consequence, as Kristeva observes, 'the notion of *intertextuality* replaces that of intersubjectivity, and poetic language is read as at least *double*'.[61] It seems insufficient, therefore in this context, to simply suggest that 'Shakespeare built upon the dramaturgy of Peele's play'.[62]

Certainly, Shakespeare condenses the opening of *King John* in order to get more quickly to the question of inheritance and the tension between Robert Faulconbridge and Philip, his bastard brother. This adjustment sharpens the focus of the action by drawing together different facets of a patriarchy in crisis, or as Alison Findlay has argued, 'the suspected rebellion against the divine right of husbands mirrors the disappearance of divine right of kingship in the play'.[63] Findlay goes on to suggest that 'the dominant order in *King John* is lacking in true legitimacy',[64] and that Shakespeare uses the figure of the Bastard as part of a sustained 'subversive questioning of patriarchal power'.[65] While, of course, it would be possible to recognise this strain from Shakespeare's text alone, a comparison with Peele's play serves to sharpen its politics, and to expand the play's final lines, placed in the mouth of the Bastard – 'Nought shall make us rue / If England to itself do rest but true!' – to indicate Elizabeth I's own controversial political position. As Findlay observes:

> For England to rest true to itself would be to acknowledge that a woman and a bastard was ruling the country, something highly irregular, even unnatural when viewed from a patriarchal perspective. Sir Richard's patriotism threatens to undermine Elizabeth's government. Alternatively, and more importantly, it raises doubts about patriarchal history and the ideology which produces it.[66]

It would be possible to develop this argument by means of a much more detailed analysis of the intertextual relation between these two plays *and* between them and the historical context that would add further layers of potentially subversive meaning. By identifying the various textual layers, what Kristeva would call the 'mosaic of quotations', and then showing them in interaction with each other, questions concerning the formulation of positionality can be explored, alongside the fissures that open up in what is ostensibly the play's dominant political order. This indicates that we simply cannot separate out the theatrical elements from cultural and political elements. Indeed, what a robust theory of intertextuality does is to expose those areas of the text that may not even be the result of the conscious intention of the dramatist, areas that emerge as a compilation of texts are brought into dynamic interaction with each other.

In her treatment of the relation between *The Troublesome Reign* and *King John*, Clare shuttles nimbly between the two texts, but her unwillingness to grasp the full theoretical implications of the principles of intertextuality forces her back into the vocabulary of traditional source study. Deploying a circumstantial logic, she argues that '*King John* takes its cue from the dramaturgy of *The Troublesome Reign*, adapting its construction, taking over its catalysts, and echoing ideology'.[67] In Shakespeare's presentation of the rival matriarchal figures of Constance and Elinor, what is initiated in the one text is given 'a final ironic profile, as if even in their deaths they are still vying with each other'.[68]

It is indeed the case that Shakespeare provides a combination of 'patriotic, sceptical, and sometimes emotional' commentary, rather than consciously taking over what in Peele's version is the role of a 'patriotic folk hero'.[69] But the Bastard is a special case in that he is the illegitimate son of the Lion-heart and the focus of political resistance to papal authority. He also stands as a rebuke to the principle of hereditary order. In other words, what Clare reduces to a comparison between the formal properties of two texts limits the very 'resonance' that she invokes, in that her focus on the Bastard as a cardinal example airbrushes out of her argument the very process of positionality that is central to the theory of intertextuality, and that makes Faulconbridge an extraordinarily complex, and quite unusual mouthpiece for the intricate politics of the play. It also presupposes a fully conscious author whose relationship to an antecedent text is based unequivocally upon a combination of increasingly sophisticated memorialisation, and critical engagement. While we may identify Peele's text as a synchronic 'resource', the attempt to forge a narrow linear path between Peele and Shakespeare is to fall prey to a selective formalism in which texts become the currency in which interpersonal relationships are identified.

In such arguments, intertextuality is invoked in support of a linear argument that falls back upon variations of the principle of 'influence', and that makes Shakespeare, almost by default, an aesthetically superior dramatist to Peele. That both dramatists draw on similar narratives is not in question. What *is* in question, however, is the con-texts within which the plays are positioned. Issues such as hereditary monarchy, the example of the English rejection of papal authority, the challenge to hereditary monarchy posed by King John himself and the presence of the Bastard, *and* by Arthur as an alternative claimant to the throne, recall the chaotic dynastic struggles of the First Tetralogy.[70] Peter Lake is of the view that in this kind of uncertainty the Bastard's illegitimacy allows him to 'supply the effects of monarchical legitimacy that the usurpation and consequent misdeeds of King John has stripped from the political system, without seeming to undermine for a moment the principles of monarchical legitimacy and hereditary succession upon which the state is about to be re-founded, after the unfortunate detour into illegitimacy represented by John's reign has been concluded'.[71] Whether it is possible to tie all these loose ends up in the way that Lake suggests is a moot point, since circulating round Shakespeare's play is the reality of Elizabeth I's questionable parentage – and her father's challenge to papal authority – that could just as easily have exerted a formative pressure, firstly on the surviving narratives of King John's reign, and secondly on Shakespeare's choice of subject for a play.

The complex interweaving of texts, to which we have only partial access, cannot be reduced to linear patterns on the one hand, or to the domesticated post-structuralist practice of 'allowing a free interplay among texts, including the texts of historical reality (sometimes distinguished as "contexts")'[72] on the other. Hillman invokes Jean Howard's odd conflation of New Historicism and Cultural Materialism as critical tendencies that seek 'virtually to strip literary works of textuality by positing "a hierarchical relationship in which literature figures as a parasitical reflector of historical fact"'.[73] This claim, levelled against two distinct critical practices accuses both of a recidivist Marxism at the same time that it removes from the Bakhtinian concept of 'heteroglossia' its fundamentally political significance. Hillman further cites Howard's curious allegation that both New Historicism and Cultural Materialism 'erase' what she calls 'the problem of textuality', and that it must be enlarged to reveal that both 'social and literary texts are opaque, self-divided, and porous, that is, open to the mutual *intertextual influences* of one another' (my italics).[74] The conclusion that Hillman draws from this is that, 'Such a critical discourse, is capable of accommodating the entire gamut of signifying practices within a shifting pattern of intertextual relations', while at the same time 'retaining its historical consciousness'.[75] What the phrase 'historical consciousness' means in this context is, of course, open to question, since (as in his appropriation of the concept of intertextuality) it is stripped of a form of politics that is explicit in both Bakhtin and Kristeva, and reverts to a vocabulary of influence that leans in the direction of formalism. Indeed, the excavation of a dialogic pressure within the text attests not to an irreducible 'textuality' but to a series of specific, though not always fully recoverable, historical pressures that shape and limit the text's representational investments. The practice of attempting to tease out Shakespeare's 'resources' is located at the very centre of a complex web of representations, some explicitly 'textual' in the limited material sense of the term, and others that circulate, achieve prominence and then fade away as their cultural relevance subsides. Both activities are deeply implicated in informal or circumstantial recollection, and the fragmentation that shows itself from time to time as it flickers across the surface of the text.

We have seen how one line, transposed, partially articulated and changing function in a number of texts, as well as comprising part of the reservoir of commonplace aphorisms, can accumulate meanings that represent nuances of positionality in a play such as *Much Ado About Nothing*. A more extended example in which the density of intersecting narratives is evident and where it is possible to identify a plethora of transformational resources that involve 'an altering of the thetic position – the destruction of the old position and the formation of a new one'[76] – might be *Hamlet*. Geoffrey Bullough suggests that, 'The name Amlotha appears out of the mists of Icelandic antiquity in a quotation from the poet Snaebjorn preserved by Snorri Storlason in his *Prose Edda* (*c.*1230).'[77] He speculates that there may have been 'a legend about an Amleth who assumed madness two or more centuries before his life story was told by the Dane Saxo Grammaticus at the end of the twelfth century'. Bullough then traces briefly the printing history of his *Historiae Danicae* from its appearance in 1514, through a number of editions printed in Basle and Frankfurt, to its translation into Danish in 1575.[78] Saxo Grammaticus's narrative does not appear in English until Sir Oliver Elton's translation, *The First Nine Books of the Danish History of Saxo Grammaticus*, in 1894; there it contains a collection of legends, as well as owing 'something to the Roman legend of Lucius Junius Brutus, who expelled the Tarquins after the rape of Lucrece'.[79] Elements of Saxo Grammaticus's narrative found their way into François de Belleforest's *Histoires Tragiques*, first published in French in 1570, itself the continuation of a collection of tales first begun by Pierre Boiastuau.[80] These overlapping narratives, with significant variations of detail, reappear in the Shakespeare *oeuvre* in both *Hamlet* (1603 and 1605), and in the case of the Roman legend of Lucius Junius Brutus, in the earlier narrative poem *The Rape of Lucrece* (1594). In the case of *Hamlet* there is no certainty that Shakespeare encountered these texts directly, either in Latin or in French. Thus, already, what Bullough identifies as 'sources' for *Hamlet* are clearly not 'origins' but compendia or compilations of other texts, and the number increases in volume and variety as we move closer to the date of the play as other dramatists also incorporate particular motifs into their plays.

The surmised existence of a *Hamlet* prior to 1603 is derived initially from Thomas Nashe's reference in his Preface to Greene's *Menaphon* and to 'English *Seneca* read by candle light [that] yeeldes him faire in a frostie morning, he will afford you whole *Hamlets* manie sentences, as *Bloud is a begger*, and so foorth: and if you intreate, I should say handfuls of tragical speeches'.[81] Nashe's reference to 'manie sentences' pinpoints precisely a tendency to perceive texts, not as organic units, but in term of fragments. Preceding this reference he lumps together 'this kinde of men that repose eternitie in the mouth of a player' with those 'Grammarians, who having no more learning in their scull than will serve to take up a commoditie; nor Art in their brain, than was nourished in a seruing mans idlenesse', who 'feed on nought but the crummes that fal from the translators trencher'.[82] Nashe's 1589 Preface is full of Latinity and commonplace aphorisms, of which the latter find places in

Shakespeare's *Hamlet*. But ironically, as a writer who can 'feed on nought but crummes that fal from the translator's trencher' himself, he goes on to roundly castigate 'Grammarians' who can prostitute themselves by affecting piecemeal learning.

Clearly, a version or versions of a play called *Hamlet* must have been in circulation at some time during the ensuing seven years, since in his anatomisation of 'the Devils Incarnat of this Age', *Wits Miserie and the Worlds Madnesse* (1596), Thomas Lodge characterised 'Hate-Vertue' – who was the son of Beelzebub – as the ghost of Hamlet's father:

> You shall know him by this, he is a foule lubber, his tongue tipt with lying, his heart steeld against charity, he walks for the most part in black under colour of gravity, & looks as pale as the Vizard of ye ghost which cried so miserably at ye Theator like an oisterwife, Hamlet, revenge.[83]

An earlier reference to a performance of the play at Newington Butts in 1594 confirms that a version of *Hamlet* was already in circulation, and that the story of the Prince of Denmark was popularly known well before Shakespeare's version appeared. This earlier version may have been written, it has been suggested, by Thomas Kyd, and Shakespeare may have had a hand in revising it. In addition, Bullough notes some twenty similarities of detail between Kyd's *The Spanish Tragedy* and *Hamlet*, and he speculates further that 'if Q1 [1603] came (however corruptly) from Shakespeare's version prior to Q2 which contained elements from the *ur-Hamlet* later removed, then these verbal links with Kyd might come from his version of the drama'.[84] At work here is Bullough's linear logic in which an '*ur*-text' has to be invented in order to complete the sequence.

In 1926 Sir Israel Gollancz began his account of *The Sources of Hamlet* with a chapter entitled 'An Essay on the Legend', ranging from Snorri Sturlason's *The Prose Edda* (*c*.1230), through Saxo Grammaticus's 'history', itself 'influenced' by Norwegian and Danish 'popular legend, [and] a mass of mythic and traditional lore, [that] still preserved, however obscurely, the memory of the ancient gods and heroes',[85] and also by 'Latin historical writers (such as Bede, Adam of Bremen, and Dudo)',[86] and Geoffrey of

Monmouth, to Irish occurrences of the 'Hamlet' name. In short, the name 'Hamlet' appears in various forms in Icelandic, Danish and Norwegian legend, but is also part of Celtic mythology, and all of this before the appearance of the narrative in Belleforest's *Histoires Tragiques* in a number of editions from 1570 onwards.

Belleforest first appeared in an English translation in 1608 as *The Hystorie of Hamblet*, published by Thomas Pavier, the printer who was no stranger to the texts of a number of Shakespeare's plays.[87] In his utilisation of a quotation from the Q1 version of Hamlet's advice to the players, Jeffrey Masten, extolling the virtues of 'a reconception of collaboration', complains that criticism has continued 'to rely implicitly on the assumption that texts are the products of a singular and sovereign authorial consciousness'.[88] Many of the texts that mention the name 'Hamlet' place it in a mythic setting. Indeed, some also provide more extended narratives, some of whose details recur in the various texts of Shakespeare's play; this points to a process that is much more radical than the idea of collaboration might suggest. Of the fact that versions of the *Hamlet* story were circulating in the late sixteenth century there is no doubt, but bearing in mind Masten's complaint, we would need to extend the principle of 'collaboration' far wider than the suggestion that two or more dramatists might combine their talents to produce a play-script. It is the genesis of the text(s) of *Hamlet* that require us to think as far as possible in strictly diachronic terms, whereas the question of 'collaboration' exerts a synchronic pressure on the text that, unless we are very careful, risks drawing us back into the very 'sovereign authorial self-consciousness' that reinscribes the legitimising figure of the 'author' in the process of textual production.

This is not, of course, to deny the writer agency, or to diminish the power of imagination, rather it is to acknowledge the accumulated layers of textuality that traverse both conscious and unconscious operations in the act of composition. This is to be distinguished from the 'traffic' of the stage, the synchronic movement of contemporary texts with which the dramatist engages. Insofar as it is possible to think in neutral terms of 'origins', the first moment of inscription has some value. But the diachronic pressure exerted by any narrative, or form, or genre, is only of significance if it can be shown to contribute to the production of contemporary meaning, and that it has the capacity to demonstrate their affective power at particular historical conjunctures. A narrative such as that of Saxo Grammaticus's account of Amleth, or the varying versions that appeared subsequently, must have struck a chord with late Elizabethan audiences, and also with the dramatist who is both professionally and personally engaged in developing, revising or innovating upon, the texts that have come down to us. This is a far more complex matter than the image of the writer sitting down in front of a library of books and stitching a script together by means of imitation, paraphrase or embellishment might suggest.

Biographers and critics have consistently drawn attention to the 'fact' that Shakespeare's only son, Hamnet, had died and was buried at Holy Trinity Church in Stratford on 11 August 1596.[89] The Arden 3 editors also note that it is possible that the teenage Shakespeare knew a Katherine Hamlett who drowned in the river Avon at Stratford in December 1579, and that 'this event may have influenced his shaping of Ophelia's death'.[90] In 1585 the twins Hamnet and Judith were baptised and were named 'after Hamnet and Judith Sadler, friends and neighbours who owned a baker's business at the corner of High Street and Sheep Street'; the Sadlers reciprocated by naming their son William.[91]

It is uncertain if, how or why Shakespeare made the explicit connection between 'Hamnet', 'Hamlett' and 'Amleth', or indeed whether the deaths of Katherine Hamlett and some six years later of Hamnet triggered a series of mental associations that culminated in the name of the eponymous hero of *Hamlet, Prince of Denmark*. The connection between what we might call possible personal association and a range of more public stimuli is not easy to fathom; if the resonance of the name 'Hamlet' brought the memory of personal grief and a deep theatricalised anxiety into alignment with each other, it is still difficult to make the imaginative leap between the unfortunate deaths of a neighbour and a son and the convoluted, emphatically pre-Freudian narrative of a regicide, an adultery, madness and suicide, and a series of tragic events involving a complex revenge, culminating in a series of actions that result in the death of the eponymous hero.

To read back the events of the play (in any of its formats) into the personal life of the dramatist would be to posit a disturbing set of familial relations that might excite the prurience of the biographer. Peter Ackroyd does not miss the opportunity with the speculation that:

> In the conditions of Henley Street, however, it would have been inevitable that Anne and her husband slept in the same bed; in this period too there were no properly effective means of birth control. They may have abstained by mutual consent from sexual intercourse. All the evidence suggests that Shakespeare was of a highly sexual nature; it is unlikely that, in his early twenties, he could have abstained without very good reason. The better explanation is also the most obvious one. He was not there.[92]

There would appear to have been a number of stimuli that prompted Shakespeare to produce his version of a story that had both a long history *and* a series of contemporary meanings.

A theatrical version of the play is thought by Park Honan, among others, to have been written by Thomas Kyd 'around 1587'. In addition to the speculation that 'it must have been a source for Shakespeare's later tragedy', he notes with some certainty that this apparent '*ur-Hamlet*' was 'revived at Newington Butts on 9 June, 1594', and that it may have been performed for some thirteen years before Shakespeare's play.[93] But Bullough introduces another element into the growing network of connections with the claim that the links between Kyd's *The Spanish Tragedy* and *Hamlet* are numerous enough to indicate that 'it seems very probable that Shakespeare re-wrote an earlier *Hamlet* (... the *ur-Hamlet*) written either by Kyd or an imitator of Kyd'.[94]

To make the *ur-Hamlet* a repository of all the ingredients of the *Hamlet* texts with which Shakespeare was associated risks descending into improbable fiction. All of the texts that have survived, albeit that in some cases their dating is inconvenient, suggest that a variety of transpositional narratives are associated with the final decade of the sixteenth century. What drew them partially together, firstly in the 1603 quarto and more substantially in the 1605 quarto, is not clear, although what sustained them subsequently appears to be Shakespeare's play. Indeed, Shakespeare had written one Senecan revenge play, *Titus Andronicus*, and the motif of 'revenge' had figured throughout the First Tetralogy of History

Plays, and also in *Julius Caesar* (c.1599). Linda Woodbridge has drawn attention to 'economic unfairness and related legal unfairness reflected in revenge plays' pervasive economic language',[95] and this is precisely the discursive register in which Claudius articulates his private moral dilemma:

> May one be pardoned and retain th' offence?
> In the corrupted currents of this world
> Offence's gilded hand may shove by justice,
> And oft 'tis seen the wicked prize itself
> Buys out the law; but 'tis not so above:
>
> (3.3.56–60)

It is Claudius's venal desire that provokes and drives the play's impulse to revenge, an acquisitive desire that encompasses the crown and all that it sustains. In the last years of Elizabeth I's reign, the execution of Mary, Queen of Scots (thought by some to lie behind Shakespeare's play[96]) was firmly in the past. Moreover, with more local and theatrical memories such as the reference in Shakespeare's play by the actor playing Polonius that he may also have played the role of Julius Caesar in the earlier play, or the recollection in the Gravediggers' scene of the figure of the clown Richard Tarleton, all helped to provide additional material that made the refurbished *Hamlet* narrative thoroughly contemporary. If *Hamlet* is a 'memory' play, then an important category of Shakespeare's resource was a past that extended beyond the scope of the story to embrace a range of events and anxieties that had come together as a focus at the *fin de siècle*. At one level the combination may be regarded as fortuitous, but the contingent interweaving of texts and events, of affect and fantasy – in short, the manner in which they were transposed – may equally be regarded as over-determined. These extra- and intra-dramatic details need to be added to the theatrical traffic that was part and parcel of the competitive life of the late Elizabethan theatre. Plays such as Kyd's *The Spanish Tragedy*, Marston's *Antonio's Revenge* or Chettle's *The Tragedy of Hoffman* deployed dramatic and rhetorical models provided by Seneca, and, as in *Hamlet*, made use of evergreen narratives involving fratricide, regicide, ghosts and female deception. The question here is, of course, to what extent might all of these interlinked

Trafficking in intertextuality 195

pressures – dramatic, theatrical, social, economic, cultural and religious – be regarded as 'intertextual', and, hence, transpositional in the specialised Kristevan, rather than the domesticated, sense of the term.

The structure of the *Hamlet* narrative is anticipated in Book 4 of *The Danish History of Saxo Grammaticus* where it is engraved on the shield of Amleth:

> He also had a shield made for him, whereon the whole series of his exploits, beginning with his earliest youth, was painted in exquisite designs. This he bore as a record of his deeds of prowess, and gained great increase of fame thereby. Here were to be seen the slaying of Horwendil [Old Hamlet]; the fratricide and incest of Feng [Claudius]; the infamous uncle, the whimsical nephew; the shape of the hooked stakes; the stepfather suspecting; the step-son dissembling; the various temptations offered, and the woman brought to beguile him; the gaping wolf; the finding of the rudder; the passing of the sand; the entering of the wood; the putting of straw through the gadfly; the warning of the youth by the tokens; and the privy dealings with the maiden after the escort was eluded. And likewise could be seen the picture of the palace, the queen there with her son; the slaying of the eavesdropper; and how, after being killed, he was boiled down and so dropped into the sewer, and so thrown out to the swine; how his limbs were strewn in the mud, and so left for the beasts to finish. Also it could be seen how Amleth surprised the secret of his sleeping attendants, how he erased the letters, and put new characters in their places; how he disdained the banquet and scorned the drink; how he condemned the face of the king and taxed the queen with faulty behaviour. There was also represented the hanging of the envoys, and the young man's wedding; then the voyage back to Denmark; the festive celebration of the funeral rites; Amleth in answer to questions, pointing to the sticks in place of his attendants, acting as cup-bearer, and purposely drawing his sword and pricking his fingers; the sword riveted through, the swelling cheers of the banquet, the dance growing fast and furious; the hangings flung upon the sleepers, then fastened with the interlacing crooks, and wrapped tightly round them as they slumbered; the brand set to the mansion, the burning of the guests, the royal palace consumed with fire and tottering down; the visit to the sleeping room of Feng, the theft of his sword, the useless one set in its place; and the king slain with his own sword's point by his stepson's hand. All this

was there, painted upon Amleth's battle-shield by a careful craftsman in the choicest of handiwork; he copied truth in his figures, and embodied real deeds in his outlines.[97]

Saxo Grammaticus's model for this is the shield of Achilles from Book 18 of Homer's *Iliad*, which both recuperates and prophesies in a series of complex symbols the details of the conflict between the Greeks and the Trojans.[98] However, the 'careful craftsman' is not, as in Homer, a god, but one who 'copied truth in his figures, and embodied real deeds in his outlines', thereby erasing the contingent stages of its genesis. By the time elements of the *Hamlet* narrative had come down to Belleforest, the models comprised a conflation of biblical and Roman 'Hystory':

> And for that the Hystory (which I pretend to shew unto you) is chiefly grounded upon treason, committed by one brother against the other, I will not erre far out of the matter; thereby desiring to shew you, that it is and hath been a thing long since praticsed and put in use by men, to spill the blood of their neerest kinsmen and friends to attaine the honour of being great and in authoritie; and that there hath bin some, that being impatient of staying till their just time of succession, have hastened the death of their owne parents: as Absolon would have done to the holy king David, his father; and as wee read of Domitian, that poisoned his brother Titus, the most curtius and liberall prince that ever swayed the empire of Rome.[99]

In the one account, a secular mimetic appeal is made to actual events, while in the other, secular and biblical history provide the patterns for the operations of power and the universal positioning of 'authority'. Shakespeare's play alludes through Claudius to a biblical event and continues the motif of 'tragicall history', although the pattern itself of tragic narratives had a literary and oral pedigree in England that preceded Belleforest.

There is no doubt that there were examples readier to hand. John Pickering's *A New Enterlude of Vice Conteyninge the Historie of Horestes* (1567), Thomas Newton's 1581 translation of Seneca's *Agamemnon*, Kyd's *The Spanish Tragedy* and more contemporary 'revenge' plays such as John Marston's *Antonio's Revenge* (c.1599) and Henry Chettle's *The Tragedy of Hoffman* (c.1602) all echo in some ways aspects of *Hamlet*. The distinction that we might make here is between historical antecedents – the diachronic elements of a narrative that feed into a mythologising of 'source' – and the synchronic elements that in their domesticated form comprise 'traffic', with all of the texts from Saxo Grammaticus onwards offering 'snapshots' of a dynamic process. What Shakespeare added to or subtracted from these snapshots, just as what the snapshots themselves added to or subtracted from their predecessors, has often been used to gauge the level of 'originality' and conscious writerly creativity, not to mention the emerging concept of authorship.

There are no ghosts of fathers in Saxo or Belleforest, although in Seneca's *Agamemnon*, Kyd's *The Spanish Tragedy* and Marston's *Antonio's Revenge* there are, while Chettle's *The Tragedy of Hoffman* opens with a clear evocation of the spirit of the hero's dead father, whose body is quickly revealed onstage, hovering in the atmosphere. And all of this is added to by a version of *Hamlet* whose putative existence rested somewhere between Kyd and Shakespeare in some indeterminate relationship. Teasing out the intertextual relations between the actually existing various versions of the stereotypical elements of the Hamlet story is not easy, especially when we take into account the historically over-determined features of each version.

In the face of these variations, perhaps the time has now come to put the question directly: what was it that stimulated Shakespeare to draw together under the aegis of fratricide, adultery and revenge, a story that pulls in the opposite directions of regression, and prophecy, that looks back into the past and extols 'memory', at the same time that it anticipates a future and the new uncertain subjectivities that it promises? Simply to invoke the death of Hamnet as a primary psychological stimulus is to do little more than wrench the process of naming from its primarily domestic setting. Shakespeare had earlier addressed in classical Roman and historical settings elements of revenge and regicide, and he fused them together with issues of outlawed religious practice, matters of inheritance, gender identity, justice and social responsibility, all of which intersected in what we might call the positionality of the hero. This potentially volatile combination of elements exerted their own pressures on both the form and content of the drama, in such a way that both became dynamic points of theatrical focus for the generation, transmission and transposition of meanings in late Elizabethan popular culture.

To take one cardinal motif: all three versions of Shakespeare's play begin with the appearance of the Ghost. The Ghost's purpose is initially unclear, hence the importance of Horatio's lengthy speculation. This is, however, a different kind of ghost from that of either Kyd or Seneca: it represents a subversive force of desire bubbling away in a subterranean region. The Ghost of Old Hamlet represents a past crime to be sure, but his heroic appearance positions him clearly as a heroic king whose words accord with his actions. Unlike, for example, *Agamemnon*, *Thyestes* or even *The Spanish Tragedy* where a specific misdeed is carried through generations, Old Hamlet's 'sins' are generic, and his sojourn in Purgatory is a consequence of his post-lapsarian inheritance. This is of major significance in a play which represents the consequences of divorcing language from action. The memory that the Ghost seeks to activate is recent, and the demand to remember involves a specific obligation to act. Although the son carries the same name as the father, this obligation and the difficulty of its execution will have a direct bearing on the positionality of the Prince and will lead to a tragic revision of the heroic ethos represented by his father. Embedded in the various versions of the underworld that circulated in Kyd, Seneca and obviously more generally in late Elizabethan culture, is Shakespeare's resurrection of a Catholic 'Purgatory', that quasi-geographical space that presents a challenge to the Wittenberg-educated 'Protestant' son, notwithstanding Lodge's association of the Ghost in his brief comments with the progeny of 'Beelzebub'.

Lodge's anatomisation of sublunary 'miserie' and 'madness' serves to moralise a material world populated by devils eager to undermine the structure of a divinely instituted hierarchy.[100] That moral structure is transposed in Shakespeare's play into a secular, historicised domain and cannot, therefore, be easily reduced to Lodge's schema. Indeed, what is clear in Lodge's underworld is problematised in Denmark. Jeffrey Masten is surely correct in his insistence that 'the production of texts is a social process', and he identifies 'a collaborative perspective' as the primary means of acknowledging language 'as a process of exchange' that does not require the commentator to police 'discourse off into its agents, origins and intentions'.[101] As 'abstract and brief chronicles of the time' (*Hamlet*, 2.2.462–3), it is not unreasonable to find a link between dramatisation and a more problematical positionality, between the *mise en scène* of the play and increasingly unstable representations of authority and the subjectivity that is thereby exposed, even if inadvertently. Indeed, what Jonathan Dollimore identifies as 'a condition of radical psychic insecurity' that derives from an early modern sense of 'mutability'[102] is one of the forces that permeates *Hamlet*, and that the play wrestles with but tragically fails to contain:

> an inner dynamic of loss, conflict, doubt, absence and lack, and how this feeds into our culture's obsession with control and expansion – the sense that the identity of everything, from self to nation, is under centrifugal and potentially disintegrative pressures which have to be rigorously controlled.[103]

The motif of revenge contributes to this radical instability since it lays open to question the competence of law and the smooth operations of justice. This was clearly an element of the intertextual network in which Shakespeare's play was enmeshed, and it carries forward the simpler expression of this motif as it appears in the earlier *Titus Andronicus*. It is also a key to a much fuller reading of what happens when 'disintegrative pressures' exceed the instruments by which control seeks to exert its force.

In the case of drama, no less than in the case of the novel, the movement 'of one (or several) sign system(s) into another', to use Kristeva's terms, is no less than a '*transposition* because it specifies that the passage from one signifying system to another demands a new articulation of the thetic – of enunciative and denotative positionality'.[104] This contributes to the problematical subjectivity of the eponymous hero, to what it is only possible to grasp, as the late Francis Barker described, as 'the prince's evasion of a series of positionalities offered to him by the social setting ... the refusal of – or at most, the parodic and uncommitted participation in – the roles of courtier, lover, son, politician, swordsman, and so on'.[105] Where earlier instances of the 'revenge' mode appear comparatively straightforward, singular even, Shakespeare's intertextual engagement introduces a 'mystery' that takes the play far beyond the resolution of the crime of regicide, reaching into the interior of a quasi-Oedipal eponymous hero for an essence that it cannot fully articulate. As Barker puts it:

> At the centre of Hamlet, in the interior of his mystery, there is, in short, nothing. The promised essence remains beyond the scope of the text's signification: or rather, signals the limit of the signification of this world by marking out the site of an absence it cannot fill. It gestures towards a place for subjectivity, but both are anachronistic and belong to a historical order whose outline has so far only been sketched out.[106]

This revision of the grammar of the revenge plot involves an interrogation of a series of issues around questions of politics, of gender, of law, of representation, and of what Steven Mullaney has described as 'Hamlet's affective response', which is taken to be 'relational and social even when the relation is between feigning and feeling real or artificial tears'.[107] All of these issues feed into the problem of articulacy that the embedding of Shakespeare's narrative in a complex intertextual field explores.

Various repetitions that comprise the play's structure, such as that of kings, sons, wives, mothers, parents, children and revengers, all contribute to the critical enlargement of a familiar, and at times more limited, theatrical repertoire. To take an example, the 'madness' associated with Kyd's Hieronimo and Shakespeare's Titus Andronicus is divided in the play between Hamlet – whose madness is frequently feigned: 'I essentially am not in madness / But mad in craft' (3.4.185–6) – and Ophelia, whose actual madness and questionable suicide are caused both by the Prince's rejection of her and her father's death: one effect, shared by two characters, and in very different registers. Ophelia's madness is unselfconscious and mimetic, whereas Hamlet's is strategic and it speaks to one of the positions of woman in the play. Both Ophelia and Gertrude are daughters of Eve, the one manipulated by brother and father, each of whom claims contradictorily that, on the one hand, Hamlet's 'will is not his own' (1.3.16), and on the other, that 'with a larger tether may he walk / Than may be given you' (1.3.124–5). In the case of Gertrude, it is the allegedly feminine submission to an uncontrolled sexual desire, open to deception and forgetfulness, that Hamlet lights on, and in the closet scene she is made to realise these shortcomings:

> O Hamlet, speak no more.
> Thou turn'st my very eyes into my soul
> And there I see such black and grieved spots
> As will leave there their tinct.
> (3.4.85–9)

In her mad ranting, Ophelia inadvertently shares ownership of those 'grieved spots', but unlike Gertrude she is offered no choice about how to erase them. Indeed, her madness and her death are the logical conclusion to a life deprived of patriarchal direction that falls prey to a derangement that Hamlet is forbidden from sinking into.

This is only one side of the contrast with what we might call the Polonius family. The death of the father here leads to insanity and suicide in the case of the daughter, but to the uncontrolled desire for 'pure' revenge in the case of the son. Hamlet cannot sink into a madness that is consequently displaced onto Ophelia, but nor can he follow the path of revenge that Laertes represents since it would violate all the values that he has struggled to uphold. Here the death of a second father opens out an important set of contrasts that raise questions concerning the propriety of revenge. But more than that, the situation reflects back on Claudius the regicide, who, when confronted with the lawless Laertes, advances a tried hegemonic strategy that involves an appropriation of the philosophy of divine right that he has himself already violated.

The entry of the rebellious Laertes is prefaced by an important remark from the unnamed Gentleman that crystallises the play's difficulties with language: 'The rabble call him lord / And, as the world were now but to begin, / Antiquity forgot, custom not known, / The ratifiers and props of every word' (4.5.102–5). Claudius's response exposes a flaw in the ideology of divine right and is a further indication of the affective power and slipperiness of the regal histrionics deployed by another 'player' king:

> Let him go, Gertrude, do not fear our person.
> There's such divinity doth hedge a king
> That treason can but peep to what it would,
> Acts little of his will.
>
> (4.5.122–5)

The intertwining of these separate but related motifs contribute to a radical revaluation of what by the end of the sixteenth century had become a familiar narrative. *Hamlet* does not repeat, but rather it innovates, and it does so by the manner of its critical embedding in a series of extant texts. The result is a novel positioning of the eponymous hero, the wife and mother, the regicide, the figures of sons and daughter, and a revision of the relation between past and present. The production of tragedy involves holding back a complete explanation, emphasising loss rather than complete fulfilment, extolling the operations of a mysterious and unknowable providence, while reaffirming the ineradicable presence of evil in the world. Horatio's warning that Hamlet should be wary of the offer of a duel is met with the latter's dismissal:

> Not a whit. We defy augury. There is a special providence in the fall of a sparrow. If it be, 'tis not to come. If it be not to come, it will be now. If it be not now, yet it will come. The readiness is all, since no man of aught he leaves knows what 'tis to leave betimes. Let be.
>
> (5.2.197–202)

If we add this to the professional theatrical pressures that forced Shakespeare and his contemporaries to look over their shoulders at each other's work, then we can begin to appreciate the complex functioning of the intertextual elements of *Hamlet* and the negotiations of positionality that the play effects whether consciously or inadvertently. Trafficking is the tip of a rather large iceberg that only a theory of intertextuality that recuperates a sophisticated textual politics can reclaim.

This has not, however, deterred scholars from experimenting with the term 'intertextuality', or with expanding its remit. Clearly embedded in any speculation that is based upon the process of recall, are the various operations of memory. In his magisterial study *Memory, History, Forgetting,* Paul Ricoeur follows Bergson in distinguishing between 'habit' and 'memory', between '*mémoire-habitude* (memory as habit) and *mémoire-souvenir* (memory as distinct recollection)'; although, unlike Bergson, he argues that 'habit and memory form two poles of a continuous range of mnemonic phenomena'.[108] Raphael Lyne acknowledges Ricoeur and accepts that '[i]mitation and memory both combine the purposeful and the serendipitous, the structural and the incidental, the personal and the circumstantial'.[109] He then invokes 'cognitive literary theory', a field that 'is united by its interest in the discoveries of experimental psychology as a means of understanding the works of literature'.[110] Lyne candidly acknowledges the distinction between 'the goal of experimental psychology – to find out how the human cognitive system works, *how all minds work, and how they have always worked*' (my italics), and the activity of 'modern literary critics, which is (often) anxiously aware of multiple contingencies, historical and cultural gaps, subjective impressions, and different kinds of indeterminacy'.[111] This is an important distinction that militates against any explanatory inclusivity; indeed, Lyne is forced to admit from the outset that:

> Each work of literature derives from a process of creation, and although this is to a large extent unrecoverable, this may – must – indeed have involved acts of memory.[112]

He takes his lead from Jonathan Culler's account of intertextuality, which moves between a selective account of Kristeva's much fuller notion of the concept in which 'every text takes shape as a mosaic of citations, every text is the absorption and transformation of other texts', and an element of Barthes.[113] This leads Culler to a rather abstract conclusion:

> Though it is difficult to discover the sources of all the notions or expectations which make up the 'I' of the reader, subjectivity is not so much a personal core as an intersubjectivity, the track or the furrow left by the experience of texts of all kinds. To characterise the various levels of *vraisemblable* is to define the ways in which a work can be traversed by or brought into contact with other texts and thus to isolate different manifestations of this textual intersubjectivity which assimilates and naturalises the work.[114]

Of course, much depends upon the weight placed on the concept of 'intersubjectivity' that, as we have seen, Kristeva later went on to refine. But it is this formalist approach that provides Lyne with a point of entry into the sphere of experimental psychology, and from there into the link between intertextuality and the various operations of memory.

Lyne's fascinating treatment of texts is, on the whole, limited to comparisons and contrasts between texts that are designed in the first instance to be read. Hence, his primary focus is on writers such as Jonson and Milton, the Shakespeare of the Sonnets, and Wyatt's 'translations' of Petrarch. In the two chapters that deal with plays, one brings North's *Plutarch* into line with Shakespeare's *Antony and Cleopatra*, where comparisons of detailed elements of Plutarch suggest both the dramatist's close reading of particular passages, and his forgetting of particular aspects of those elements. Of Octavia's speech beginning at 3.4.10, which is paraphrased in North, Lyne observes that it 'has a characteristically memorial shape, whereby a related but absent aspect of the speech fills in the space left by something forgotten'.[115] To be sure, there are elements of Octavia's life that are omitted in Shakespeare, but it is difficult to determine the distinction between 'something forgotten' and a deliberate discarding of detail in the process of selection, even though the link between the shared aspects of the two texts is close. Does Shakespeare have North's *Plutarch* in front of him at this point, and is he recalling imperfectly Plutarch's Latin text? Or is he collating the two? Or is he freely but economically adapting a text that is itself at three removes from the Plutarchian original? Such moments beg more questions than an appeal to cognitive literary theory can satisfactorily answer.

Lyne is very fond of excavating sub-texts as evidenced in his treatment of North's account of the exchange between Menas and Pompey that Shakespeare dramatises in *Antony and Cleopatra* at 2.7.61–84. North's version of the event takes up some seven lines of prose and economically pinpoints Pompey's response to Menas's proposition: '*Pompey* having paused a while upon it, at length answered him: thou shouldst have done it, and neither have told it me, but now we must content us with what we have.'[116] This is how Lyne reads the exchange:

> Pompey struggles to pick up what is being proposed. The basic practical issues have become the heart of the scene, but it takes poetic effort

to get a point across. Communication rermains central as Pompey resists the temptation. Once the idea is – painstakingly – overt, it can no longer thrive.[117]

The Shakespearean version submits to a different reading that gives much greater weight to the final sentence of North's account: 'As for myself, I was never taught to break my faith, nor to be counted a traitor.' This sentiment is launched at the beginning of Pompey's response: 'Ah, this thou shouldst have done, / And not have spoken on't! In me 'tis villainy, / In thee't had been good service' (*Antony and Cleopatra*, 2.7.73–5), but is reiterated at the end of the speech: 'Being done unknown, / I should have found it afterwards well done, / But must condemn it now' (ll. 76–8).

Lyne sees a connection here with *Macbeth*, and with the eponymous hero's 'if it were done, when 'tis done, then 'twere well / It were done quickly' (1.7.1–2). However, a much closer analogy is with Bolingbroke's response at the end of *Richard II* where he conveniently absolves himself of regicide; indeed, when this situation almost repeats itself in *Antony and Cleopatra*, it is the dramatist's recall of the earlier example that allows him to make the connection between an episode in the earlier play and North's account that Shakespeare utilises in the later play. When the new King Henry learns of Exton's murder of Richard, this is his response:

> They love not poison that do poison need,
> Nor do I thee. Though I did wish him dead,
> I hate the murderer, love him murdered.
> The guilt of conscience take thou for thy labour,
> But neither my good word nor princely favour.
> With Cain go wander through the shades of night,
> And never show thy head by day nor light.
> Lords I protest, my soul is full of woe
> That blood should sprinkle me to make me grow.
> (5.6.38–46)[118]

North's Pompey's 'thou shouldst have done it, and neither have told it me' recalls a much fuller political gloss and a series of consequences that Menas's aside fully grasps as he parts company with Pompey. The North sentence triggers a political antecedent whose political contours a largely non-literate audience might themselves have recalled and recognised. Here it would seem that omission owes little to the insights of cognitive literary theory but more to professional and collective cultural memory and the proximity in the public imagination of the larger ethical dangers posed by a Machiavellian politics. By contrast, the issue in *Macbeth* is with speed – the desire to get the assassination of Duncan over and done with – and with the desire to evade the moral and ethical consequences of a particular action through an elision of the imperfectly homonymic 'surcease' and 'success':

> If th' assassination
> Could trammel up the consequence, and catch
> With his surcease, success: that but this blow
> Might be the be-all and end-all, here,
> But here, upon this bank and shoal of time,
> We'd jump the life to come. But in these cases,
> We still have judgement here, that we but teach
> Bloody instructions, which being taught, return
> To plague th' inventor.
> (1.7.2–10)[119]

At this point in *Antony and Cleopatra*, Shakespeare is as much in dialogue with himself as he is with North.

A second example in Lyne's chapter comes with his treatment of Octavia's speech (*Antony and Cleopatra*, 3.4.10–20) as she is torn between the loyalty to her brother Octavius and her new husband Antony. In North we learn more about her extended relationship with Antony, but Shakespeare's 'compacted timeframe', to use Lyne's apposite phrase, omits particular details, and for good reason. The North passage ends with Octavia caught between two extremes such that 'it is uncertain to which of them two the gods have assigned the victory, or overthrow'.[120] Lyne notes that Shakespeare's Octavia paraphrases key points from North but her speech 'also includes new material: the dynamic voicing of her prayers'. His conclusion is that the emphasis upon prayer indicates that the speech 'has a characteristically memorial shape, whereby a related but absent aspect of the speech fills in the space left by something forgotten'.[121]

Here again, there is no evidence to suggest that something has been forgotten, rather it would appear that details have been edited out from the North text. Indeed, what is condensed in North is expanded and personalised in Octavia's speech as her emphasis upon prayer signals the urgency of her plight. In other words, this is what it feels like to be caught between two irreconcilable opposites and to have no power to resolve their differences. In this respect, Octavia is unlike the militaristic Fulvia or the sexually seductive Cleopatra, hence it is important that she should *not* be seen either fulfilling or to have fulfilled a number of female roles that the play traverses.

Lyne expands on this in his treatment of the enigmatic figure of Enobarbus, who can be gruff but who is also capable of inventive poetic narrative. Enobarbus's description of Cleopatra, and of the solitary Antony in the Egyptian marketplace, is rightly described by Lyne as adding 'something personal to the inherited schema: he makes it his schema. Enobarbus remembers more than Plutarch has to offer.'[122] This excess is what Lyne goes on to attribute to 'stories as extending, transforming things',[123] and he is right to suggest that the play disperses 'recalled material across a variety of voices'.[124] But is this not what dramatists do when they dramatise, and in *Antony and Cleopatra*, possibly more than in any other Shakespeare play, representation is filtered through a variety of competing and/or partial perspectives. Lyne ends with a caution:

> Thinking schematically does not always deliver a set of precise characteristics of this or that character. More importantly, it helps an appreciation of the different psychological outlooks through which history passes. Report and memory, deliberate and less deliberate shapings of the truth, all contribute to this play's sharp reflections on history and experience.[125]

Collapsing the play's schema into 'different psychological outlooks', which are implicitly linked to the a-historical operations of the human brain, runs the risk of clouding rather than clarifying the issue. Lyne's reading of intertextuality presupposes a model of recollecting, remembering and forgetting that dissolves the boundary between intention and the unconscious of the artist. We do not know if Shakespeare had ready access to North's *Plutarch*. Unlike Jonson, who did have a library, we can only speculate where

Shakespeare may have got some of his resources from. Were books like this part of the theatre's stock of references? Could Shakespeare have consulted them periodically, and might the model be one closer to adaptation, augmented by the recollection of parts of his own earlier dramatic writing? His scripts were certainly *in* the theatre, and they were saved in pristine condition (if Heminge and Condell are to be believed) from the fire that burned the Globe to the ground in 1613.

Antony and Cleopatra could not be a better example within the Shakespeare *oeuvre* of a 'schematic' play. It recuperates earlier Shakespeare texts, and experiments with the conflict between different geographical settings and the mythologies associated with them. Nowhere is this clearer than in the Fulvia–Octavia–Cleopatra triad where the various roles of 'woman' are specified: ambitious and military Fulvia, whose sexual proclivities Cleopatra bitchily questions – 'Can Fulvia die?' (1.3.59); Octavia, who in proposing the strategic match with Antony is described by Agrippa as one 'Whose virtue and whose general graces speak / That which none else can utter' (2.2.137–8), and who is subject to Caesar's 'power' and is used as a political pawn; and Cleopatra, who uses her sexuality to blunt the force of Roman military power and to undermine its colonial ambitions, as well as its cultural forms. If Rome is the geographical space of an imperial politics, then Egypt pursues politics through poetry; Cleopatra's power lies in an all-embracing fecundity that is capable of affecting and seducing even the most stolid of Romans, and of negating those institutions that have sustained empire. We may perceive here a deliberate shaping of the drama in which no one perspective is allowed from the outset to dominate the narrative.

We return to Lyne's introductory statement and to the notion of imitation and memory combining 'the purposeful and the serendipitous, the structural and the incidental, the personal and the circumstantial'.[126] Despite occasional asides that recognise the operations of the public theatre, Lyne's focus is on literature and on interdisciplinarity as a trafficking of texts, not across the stage, but across the 'mind' of the writer as defined by the dictates of a formal cognitive neural psychology. But while we may impose a modern model on that mind, Lyne's strictures notwithstanding, we are no nearer to accounting for its workings in the culture that shaped it. Indeed, it would appear that we read by imposing quasi-scientific patterns of a modern kind on a creative mind about whose operations we cannot quite be empirically precise. Lyne's final chapter deals with Jonson's *Catiline*; Jonson appears to have had access to a major resource (a library) and to have been the subject of a fully documented, tetchy history of involvement in the technology of print, and with printers themselves, all of which Shakespeare appears not to have had. Lyne bravely maintains a close reading strategy throughout that to some extent leaves the experimental aspects of cognitive psychology behind, but in his Conclusion he revises the statement that he made in his Introduction (my italics):

> Memory is a perennial concern for writers and people in general, and the key themes in this book (patterns of recalling and forgetting) *transcend any historical period*. This is a matter of cultural persistence, also of biological continuities.[127]

So, if we are to understand this correctly, the operations of the early modern brain can be treated a-historically so that comparisons between texts provide a kind of laboratory in which the literary scientist can conduct empirically verifiable experiments. While the secondary literature on the compositional practices of oral poets may teach us much about creative memory and non-literate processes of reception, there is very little analysis of how someone like Shakespeare – positioned between an oral and a literate culture – might have mobilised memory, reading skills and the ready availability of a vital proverbial language in the process of constructing plays. The concept of intertextuality, repositioned as a descriptor of the formal operations of a mind confronted with printed texts embedded in what is otherwise an oral culture, and manoeuvred into a formalist straitjacket, risks sanitising these theatrical scripts of the very 'imperfections' that might contribute towards a closer understanding of the variety of what we would now call the professional life of the early modern theatre and the resources to which it had access.

Notes

1. Robert Weimann, *Author's Pen and Actor's Voice: Playing and Writing in Shakespeare's Theatre*, ed. Helen Higbee and William West (Cambridge, 2000), p. 37.
2. The phrase that Weimann quotes is that of David Scott Kastan, 'The mechanics of culture: editing Shakespeare today', *Shakespeare Studies*, 24 (1996), 34.
3. *Ibid.*
4. Weimann, *Author's Pen and Actor's Voice*, p. 180.
5. Kastan, 'The mechanics of culture', 25.
6. Janet Clare, *Shakespeare's Stage Traffic: Imitation, Borrowing and Competition in Renaissance Theatre* (Cambridge, 2014), p. 1.
7. René Weis, ed., in William Shakespeare, *Romeo and Juliet*, Arden 3 series (London, 2012), p. 124 n. 12.
8. See John Drakakis, ed., in William Shakespeare, *The Merchant of Venice*, Arden 3 series (London, 2010), p. 21 n. 1.
9. William Shakespeare, *Hamlet: The Texts of 1603 and 1623*, ed. Ann Thompson and Neil Taylor (London, 2007), p. 101. The more expanded 1623 Folio version is given to Rosincrance and refers to 'an eyrie of children, little eyases that cry out on top of the question and are tyrannically clappd for't' (2.2.337–9), p. 243. The relevant passages in Q1 and Folio are omitted entirely from Q2 (William Shakespeare, *Hamlet*, ed. Ann Thompson and Neil Taylor, Arden 3 series, revised edn (London, 2016), pp. 289–90).
10. Thompson and Taylor, in *Hamlet* (2016), p. 498 n. 2.
11. Michel Foucault, 'What Is an Author?', *Language, Counter-Memory, Practice: Selected Essays and Interviews*, trans. Donald Bouchard and Sherry Simon, ed. Donald Bouchard (Oxford, 1977), p. 123.
12. *Ibid.*, n. 19.
13. See Mark Kaethler, 'Shakespeare and cognition: scientism, theory, and 4E', *Literature Compass*, 17:3–4 (2020), especially p. 2. https://doi.org/10.1111/lic3.12571.
14. Thomas Kyd, *The Spanish Tragedie* (London, 1592), $C2^r$–$C2^v$.
15. I borrow this phrase from Raphael Lyne, *Memory and Intertextuality in Renaissance Literature* (Cambridge, 2016), p. 3.
16. Cf. George Puttenham, *The Arte of English Poesie* (London, 1589; facs. edn, Menston, 1989), p. 157, for a brief account of '*Parimia* or Prouerb'. See also Quintilian, *The Orator's Education*, ed. Donald A. Russell, Loeb Classical Library, 5 vols (Cambridge, MA,

and London, 2001), vol. 3, bk 8, ch. 5, pp. 407ff., on the topic of 'Sententiae'.
17 Lyne, *Memory and Intertextuality*, p. 8.
18 William Shakespeare, *The Taming of the Shrew*, ed. Barbara Hodgdon, Arden 3 series (London, 2010).
19 William Shakespeare, *Much Ado About Nothing*, ed. Claire McEachern, Arden 3 series (London, 2006).
20 Thomas Watson, *Hecatompathia or Passsionate Centurie of Loue* (London, 1582), sig. F4^r.
21 Philip Edwards, ed., in Thomas Kyd, *The Spanish Tragedy* (Manchester, 1977), p. 29 nn. 3–10.
22 McEachern, in *Much Ado About Nothing*, p. 166n., ll. 242–3.
23 Paul Ricoeur, *Memory, History, Forgetting*, trans. Kathleen Blamey and David Pellauer (Chicago and London, 2004), pp. 58ff.
24 Julia Kristeva, *Revolution in Poetic Language*, trans. Margaret Waller (New York, 1984), p. 59. All quotations will be from this Margaret Waller translation.
25 *Ibid.*, pp. 59–60.
26 Julia Kristeva, *Desire in Language: A Semiotic Approach to Literature and Art*, trans. Thomas Gora, Alice Jardine and Leon S. Roudiez (Oxford, 1980), p. 65.
27 *Ibid.*
28 *Ibid.*, p. 68.
29 Mikhail Bakhtin, *Problems in Dostoevsky's Poetics*, trans. Caryl Emerson, Theory and History of Literature, 8 (Manchester, 1984), p. 183.
30 *Ibid.*, p. 184.
31 *Ibid.*, pp. 184–5.
32 J.M. Coetzee, *Elizabeth Costello* (London, 2004), p. 172.
33 See Michael Riffaterre, 'Compulsory reader response: the intertextual drive', in Michael Warton and Judith Stills, eds, *Intertextuality: Theories and Practice* (Manchester, 1990), p. 61.
34 See McEachern, in *Much Ado About Nothing*, p. 316 n. 94.
35 Ross Chambers, 'Alter ego: intertextuality, irony and the politics of reading', in Warton and Stills, *Intertextuality*, p. 143.
36 Ovid, *The Metamorphoses*, trans. Arthur Golding, ed. John Frederick Nimms (New York, 1965), p. 32.
37 Cf. Jonathan Bate, *Shakespeare and Ovid* (Oxford, 1993), p. 179, where he comments on the acknowledgement in the *Metamorphoses* of 'Jupiter's perjuries and infidelities'. Although he notes the play's 'image of descent from high to low in the context of wooing' that he

identifies with Ovid's narrative of Baucis and Philemon from Book 8 of the *Metamorphoses* (p. 160), nowhere does he mention the passages cited above. Cf. also T.W. Baldwin, *Shakespere's Small Latine and Lesse Greeke*, 2 vols (Urbana, 1944), vol. 1, for references to links between Ovid's *Metamorphoses* and *The Taming of the Shrew* (pp. 68, 71) and Erasmus's introduction of Ovid into the school curriculum (p. 102).
38 McEachern, in *Much Ado About Nothing*, p. 312 n. 45.
39 Toril Moi, *Sexual/Textual Politics*, 2nd edn (London, 2002), p. 165.
40 Richard Hillman, *Intertextuality and Romance in Renaissance Drama: The Staging of Nostalgia* (London, 1992), p. 21.
41 *Ibid.*, p. 22.
42 *Ibid.*, p. 156.
43 *Ibid.*, p. 158.
44 Stephen Lynch, *Shakespearean Intertextuality: Studies in Selected Sources and Plays* (Connecticut and London, 1998), p. 1.
45 *Ibid.*, p. 2.
46 *Ibid.*
47 *Ibid.*, p. 4.
48 *Ibid.*, p. 14.
49 *Ibid.*, p. 115.
50 See Moi, *Sexual/Textual Politics*, pp. 164–5.
51 Murray J. Levith, *Shakespeare's Cues and Prompts* (London, 2007), p. 5.
52 *Ibid.*, p. 17.
53 *Ibid.*
54 *Ibid.*
55 Robert S. Miola, 'Seven types of intertextuality', in Michele Marrapodi, ed., *Shakespeare, Italy and Intertextuality* (Manchester, 2004), p. 13.
56 Clare, *Shakespeare's Stage Traffic*, p. 20.
57 *Ibid.*, pp. 21–2.
58 *Ibid.*, p. 45.
59 *Ibid.*
60 Kristeva, *Desire in Language*, p. 66.
61 *Ibid.*
62 Clare, *Shakespeare's Stage Traffic*, p. 48.
63 Alison Findlay, *Illegitimate Power: Bastards in Renaissance Drama* (Manchester, 1994), p. 27.
64 *Ibid.*, p. 202.
65 *Ibid.*, p. 208.
66 *Ibid.*
67 Clare, *Shakespeare's Stage Traffic*, p. 40.

68 *Ibid.*, pp. 44–5.
69 *Ibid.*, p. 47.
70 But see Ernst Honigmann, ed., in William Shakespeare, *King John*, Arden 2 series (London, 1967), p. lxxii, who argues: 'The Bastard's "rising curve" cannot, of course, be denied. But we are doubtful whether it is integral rather than accidental to the structure.'
71 Peter Lake, *How Shakespeare Put Politics on the Stage* (New Haven and London, 2016), p. 224.
72 Hillman, *Intertextuality and Romance*, p. 22.
73 *Ibid.*, p. 24.
74 Cited in Hillman, *Intertextuality and Romance*, pp. 24–5.
75 *Ibid.*, p. 25.
76 Kristeva, *Revolution in Poetic Language*, p. 63.
77 Geoffrey Bullough, *Nasrrative and Dramatic Sources of Shakespeare*, 8 vols (London, 1957–75), vol. 8, p. 5.
78 *Ibid.*
79 *Ibid.*, p. 6.
80 Stuart Gillespie, *Shakespeare's Books: A Dictionary of Shakespeare's Sources* (London, 2004), pp. 36–40.
81 G.B. Harrison, ed., *Menaphon by Robert Green and A Marguerite for America by Thomas Lodge* (Oxford, 1927), p. 9.
82 *Ibid.*, p. 5.
83 Thomas Lodge, *Wits Miserie and the Worlds Madnesse: Discouering the Devils Incarnat of the Age* (London, 1596), p. 56.
84 Bullough, *Narrative and Dramatic Sources of Shakespeare*, vol. 7, pp. 16–17.
85 Sir Israel Gollancz, *The Sources of Hamlet* (1926; reprinted, London, 1967), p. 17.
86 *Ibid.*, p. 15.
87 *Ibid.*, pp. 166–311, for a full transcription of the translation of the *Hamlet* sections of Belleforest.
88 Jeffrey Masten, *Textual Intercourse: Collaboration, Authorship, and Sexualities in Renaissance Drama* (Cambridge, 1997), p. 20.
89 See Stephen Greenblatt, *Will in the World: How Shakespeare Became Shakespeare* (London, 2004), pp. 288–9, for a convenient account of the person and professional pressures that Shakespeare experienced during 1596.
90 Thompson and Taylor, in *Hamlet*, p. 79 n. 1.
91 Peter Ackroyd, *Shakespeare: The Biography* (London, 2005), p. 95.
92 *Ibid.* This could, of course, explain Shakespeare's absence from Stratford, but an equally plausible explanation might involve Anne's

possible fear of the dangers attendant upon pregnancy. We should not, of course, accept at face value the many depictions of sexual activity in the plays (and poems) – some very brutal and others quite negative – as anything other than instances of the range of patriarchal fantasies for which there was no place in Shakespeare's domestic setting. Nor should we think that Shakespeare's absences from home had any deeper significance than a perfectly acceptable fact of life.

93 Park Honan, *Shakespeare: A Life* (Oxford, 1998), p. 128. See also Bullough, *Narrative and Dramatic Sources of Shakespeare*, vol. 7, pp. 16–19.
94 Bullough, *Narrative and Dramatic Sources*, vol. 7, p. 6.
95 Linda Woodbridge, *English Revenge Drama: Money, Resistance, Equality* (Cambridge, 2010), p. 10.
96 Carl Schmitt, *Hamlet or Hecuba: The Intrusion of the Time into the Play*, trans. David Pan and Jennifer Rust (New York, 2009), pp. 17ff.
97 Oliver Elton, trans., *The First Nine Books of the Danish History of Saxo Grammaticus* (London, 1894), pp. 122–3.
98 Homer, *The Iliad*, books 13–24, trans. A.T. Murray (Cambridge, MA, 1999), pp. 323–33.
99 Belleforest, *Le Cinquiesme Tome des Histoires Tragiques* (1582), Philemon Holland, trans., *The Hystorie of Hamblet* (1608), in Gollancz, *The Sources of Hamlet*, p. 171.
100 Cf. Jonathan Dollimore, *Death, Desire and Loss in Western Culture* (London, 1998), p. 85. Dollimore teases out the dream world of Sir Thomas Browne's *On Dreams* and *Christian Morals*, contrasted with Freud's 'sense of the unconscious as being the place of our repressions, of our other selves (plural) and of forbidden desires which can wreck the socially organised ego' (p. 84), and the containment of 'mutability within an ethical-religious perspective'. Dollimore insists that beyond the comparative stability of Browne's formulation, 'in Elizabethan and Jacobean drama we find an exploration of identity … as necessitating the duplicitous opposite of an authentic honest subjectivity. Time and again in such drama Browne's belief in the ultimate accessibility of true identity is repudiated' (p. 85).
101 Masten, *Textual Intercourse*, p. 20.
102 Dollimore, *Death, Desire and Loss*, p. 92.
103 *Ibid.*, pp. 92–3.
104 Kristeva, *Desire in Language*, p. 60.
105 Francis Barker, *The Tremulous Private Body: Essays in Subjection* (London, 1995), p. 32.
106 *Ibid.*, p. 33.

107 Steven Mullaney, *The Reformation of Emotions in the Age of Shakespeare* (Chicago and London, 2015), p. 61.
108 Ricoeur, *Memory, History, Forgetting*, p. 24.
109 Lyne, *Memory and Intertextuality*, p. 6.
110 *Ibid.*, pp. 6–7.
111 *Ibid.*, p. 12.
112 *Ibid.*, p. 13.
113 Jonathan Culler, *The Pursuit of Signs: Structuralism, Linguistics and the Pursuit of Literature* (London, 1975), pp. 139–40.
114 *Ibid.*, p. 140.
115 Lyne, *Memory and Intertextuality*, p. 169.
116 Cited in Lyne, *Memory and Intertextuality*, p. 167.
117 *Ibid.*, p. 168.
118 William Shakespeare, *The Tragedy of Richard II*, ed. Charles Forker, Arden 3 series (London, 2002).
119 William Shakespeare, *Macbeth*, ed. Sandra Clark and Pamela Mason, Arden 3 series (London, 2015). The echo here is much closer in substance to Claudius's 'O, my offence is rank' (*Hamlet*, 3.3.36ff.).
120 Cited in Lyne, *Memory and Intertextuality*, p. 169.
121 *Ibid.*
122 *Ibid.*, p. 203.
123 *Ibid.*, p. 204.
124 *Ibid.*, p. 205.
125 *Ibid.*
126 *Ibid.*, p. 6.
127 *Ibid.*, p. 239.

5

The nature of con-text

Intertextuality presupposes a radical departure from what Jonathan Culler describes as 'the investigation of sources and influences as traditionally conceived'. Even so, in its more domesticated form it cannot be reduced simply to the Kristevan account of positionality, albeit that this is an important constituent element in its political purchase on the process of signification. To quote Culler again, 'it casts its net wider to include anonymous discursive practices, codes whose origins are lost, that makes possible the signifying practices of later texts'.[1] But this reveals a nostalgia for a past that is, in theory, recoverable through the operations of memory that are assumed to be indispensable to the process of signification, in which the linear and the diachronic are the constitutive structural elements. The relations between past and present that involve the various processes of recall, forgetting and projection shape the present and point towards the future. Cultures accumulate elements of the past in addition to the pressures imposed upon them by the present. All of these elements taken together facilitate the shaping of communal and individual identities, and they contribute to the excavation and reinvigoration of historical models along with the piecemeal discarding of practices that are no longer useful. Whereas intertextuality frequently seeks to establish empirically the relationship between particular texts, the range of material out of which they may be constructed could well pose a challenge to the linear and hierarchical pattern of 'influence' to which the process has often been reduced. In some cases, the link between texts may indicate an equivalence, but where the connection is more than simply formal then a hierarchy of 'text' and 'context' comes into view. It is this problematical connection to which the argument now turns.

As an example, we might consider the figure of 'the Jew' in Shakespeare's *The Merchant of Venice*, who is a compilation of medieval prejudices and onto whom are projected a series of proscribed, but in the circumstances necessary, financial practices. In this play the Jew Shylock advances backwards into a future whose contradictions are only just beginning to be perceived at the end of the sixteenth century in England, but that will later mutate into what we recognise with hindsight as the foundation of capitalism. The figure of Shylock is a complex representation, made up of a series of extant cultural and religious stereotypes that together comprise what it means to be an outsider. These stereotypes form layers, all of which in separate ways continue to feed into the anxieties and prejudices that have outlasted the cultures in which they were originally formulated.

When we think of such composite figures as representations, we are challenged to separate out their constitutive components, whether they are the products of history or those of popular fantasy that find their way into fictional writing, or combinations of both. The issue is complicated even further when what is presented in historical narrative as 'fact' or a stable text, turns out itself to be something that is multi-layered. For example, North's *Plutarch*, which is a translation of a translation, is just such a text; but there are others, as we shall see, where the name disguises what is actually a compilation. Of course, despite our critical obsession with authorship, theatrical texts themselves are nearer to palimpsests than they are to the property of single individuals, although we need to remind ourselves that in the case of writers like Ben Jonson this relatively new model of authorship was beginning to emerge. In the case of the practising dramatist, his (usually his) identity placed him at a meeting point of converging texts, where translation, adaptation, editing and innovating, expanding existing memes, creating new ones, all appear to have been part of the normal practice of composition. Beyond those texts there were other cultural pressures that are less easy to position, even though they may leave textual traces, but that were brought to bear on questions of subject matter, theme and the whole process of representation.

All of this is further complicated when, in the case of a writer like Shakespeare, prior texts *can* be identified, which themselves can be shown to be composite. For example, Holinshed's *Chronicles*, especially the 1587 edition, is a composite text, while in the case of fragmentary quotations ostensibly from other texts, the chain of transmission may not be linear. The difficulty with part of Kristeva's analysis is, as Culler has pointed out, that the tracking down of 'sources with such precision cannot serve as the paradigm for a description of intertextuality',[2] although at no point does Culler refer to her extension of the discussion of intertextuality in her book *Desire in Language* (1980) where a more Bakhtinian emphasis on the fundamentally dialogic and dialectic elements of the literary text is explored.

It is to V.N. Volosinov's little-quoted essay on 'Discourse in Life and Discourse in Art (Concerning Sociological Poetics)' that we now need to turn in order to avoid the possibility of sinking into the kind of formalism that has characterised domesticated versions of intertextuality and obscured the process of discriminating between 'texts' and 'contexts'. Volosinov begins by isolating what he calls 'artistic communication' as a 'special form of social communication' because it 'possesses its own uniqueness' that it is 'the task of sociological poetics' to understand.[3] He goes on to describe this uniqueness as being 'irreducible to other types of ideological communication such as the political, the juridical, the moral, and so on'. Furthermore, he uses the phrase 'aesthetic communication' to indicate 'the basis common to it and other social forms' and to point out the connection between the uniqueness of this particular form of communication and the social conditions that generate it. 'To understand this special form of social communication', Volosinov argues, is 'precisely the task of a sociological poetics'. In this way, the critic avoids what he calls 'the fetishization of the artistic work artifact', which ignores 'the social essence of art'.[4] In a particularly concentrated passage, he explains what the consequences of ignoring the 'social essence of art' entail:

> Those methods that ignore the social essence of art and attempt to find its nature and distinguishing features only in the organisation of the work artifact are in actuality obliged to project the social

interrelationship of creator and contemplator [the artist and the reader] into various aspects of the material and into various devices for structuring the material. In exactly the same way psychological aesthetics projects the same social relations into the individual psyche of the perceiver. This projection distorts the integrity of these interrelationships and gives a false structure of both the material and the psyche.[5]

Post-Althusserian Marxism and Foucauldian discourse analysis have revised considerably the relationship between the classic Marxist categories of the economic base and the superstructure, but what has remained is the clear sense that the artistic text is a special case, inhabiting ideology while at the same time distancing itself from it, deploying rhetorical forms that both replicate ideological positions while at the same time exposing the practices by which they are produced and in which they are inscribed. Volosinov's 'unitary flow of social life' presupposes a singular driving energy, whereas the post-modern perception of the 'social' is more fragmentary and diffuse. That diffusion manifests itself in the variety of representations – not necessarily organic – that drift across and behind the text's surfaces and span the full gamut between the conscious and unconscious investments present in the writer's sensibility and the audience's.

In the Shakespearean text this emerges most obviously in the curious combination of radical and conservative elements, those manifestly teleological conclusions combined with subversive undercurrents that serve to render the plays' endings provisional, and implicitly interrogative, while at the same time mounting a critique of the very ideology within whose aegis the artistic text is shaped. It is here, at those points where the text discloses contradictions with which it cannot cope, that intertextuality has a particular formative role to play, since it is the combined dynamic, diachronic and synchronic space where the social and the aesthetic intersect and interact. The intertext is necessarily a 'locution' which is *'the expression and product of the social interaction of three participants: the speaker* (author), *the listener* (reader), *and the topic* (the who or what) *of speech* (the hero)' (original italics).[6] Like all verbal discourse, it is 'a social event; it is not self-contained in the sense of some abstract linguistic phenomenon, nor can it be derived psychologically from the speaker's subjective consciousness taken in isolation'.[7] Volosinov's rejection of structuralism in favour of an emphasis upon the materiality of language anticipates the Derridean exposure of the category of Saussurean *langue* as metaphysical. But though we may need to revise the identities of Volosinov's 'three participants' in order to accommodate dramatic writing, the phrase 'in isolation' is crucial; he observes:

> Art, too, is just as immanently social; the extra-artistic social milieu affecting art from the outside, finds direct, intrinsic response within it. This is not the case of one foreign element affecting another but of one social formation affecting another social formation. The *aesthetic*, just as the juridical or the cognitive, is *only a variety of the social*.[8]

Volosinov is not concerned to downgrade art here (*'only a variety of the social'*) but to provide it with a framework, 'the extra-artistic social milieu', and not one that can be reduced to what, in another context, Pierre Bourdieu referred to as 'the interpretation of recent events as the end result of initial experiences or ways of behaving',[9] which has for so long underpinned biographies of Shakespeare. Nor should we interpret Volosinov's appeal to 'sociology' as a challenge to some kind of 'transcendental ego' in favour of 'the aggressions of genetic thought incarnated by psychology or by sociology, according to the period'.[10] It is at the point of intersection of 'one social formation affecting another social formation' that a theory of intertextuality of the sort proposed by Kristeva as a distinctive feature of artistic discourse proves valuable. Also, it is here that a theory of contexts comes into its own, even though each intertextual encounter raises a further question implied by the precise contents of the catch-all epithet 'social'. It therefore becomes axiomatic that the dynamic *context* of the text and its intertexts should become part of the complex general pattern of discursive exchanges.

Before the advent of New Historicism the dyad of 'text' and 'context' existed in a clear hierarchical relation. This was something different from what is now the common practice for public figures to claim that controversial statements that they have uttered have been 'quoted out of context', even when the alleged meaning of their utterances is clear and unequivocal. By contrast, and in attempts to situate literary texts in a larger (implicitly and explicitly explanatory) historical framework, generations of editors confronted with variant versions of particular plays have laboured to establish a framework within which to situate artificially stabilised Shakespearean texts. For textual bibliographers the context was primarily printing-house practice, while for others the historical and theatrical contexts functioned as 'background' to what have become and to some extent remain, in the final analysis, fetishised texts.

In 'Shakespeare and the exorcists', a seminal essay that has done much to shape subsequent debate, Stephen Greenblatt begins by lamenting that, 'For a long time the prevailing model for the study of literary sources, a model in effect parcelled out between the old historicism and the new criticism, blocked such a question.' He observes that 'the work's "historical background"' is 'a phrase that reduces history to a decorative setting or a convenient, well-lighted pigeonhole'.[11] Rather, he insists that

> once the differentiations on which this model is based begin to crumble, then source study is compelled to change its character: history cannot simply be set against literary texts as either stable antithesis or stable background, and the protective isolation of those texts give way to a sense of their interaction with other texts and hence of the permeability of their boundaries ... When Shakespeare borrows from Harsnett, who knows if Harsnett has not already, in a deep sense, borrowed from Shakespeare's theatre what Shakespeare borrows back? Whose interests are served by the borrowing? And is there a larger cultural text produced by the exchange?[12]

Greenblatt evidently prefers the phrase 'institutional strategies' to the much more nuanced term 'ideology', and he holds on here to the quasi-structural methodology of cultural anthropology that continues to see in the example the immanent pattern of an organic whole. Moreover, he starts from the position of acknowledging the traditional view that for centuries it has been recognised that 'Shakespeare was reading Harsnett's book, *A Declaration of Egregious Popish Impostures*, as he was writing *King Lear*', and that he may have known personally Robert Dibdale, 'the son of a

Stratford Catholic family linked to the Hathaways'.[13] Greenblatt may be factually correct, but here, as throughout his impressive critical *oeuvre*, one event (the speculation concerning the engagement with Harsnett's book) is seen as the destiny of an 'initial experience',[14] and it might be possible to extend this to the speculations about texts that the dramatist may or may not have encountered as part of his formal education. These caveats notwithstanding, Greenblatt's questions continue to remain pertinent, and the attempts to follow through their implications for 'source' and for issues of context have been sporadic and, in general, theoretically imprecise.

In an essay that began life as a lecture in Western Australia in 1986, was revised for publication initially in 1987 and then which appeared, further revised, in *Learning to Curse: Essays in Modern Culture* in 1990, Greenblatt concludes by quoting (not Althusser, where this formulation first appeared[15]) Anthony Giddens, to whom he credits the observation that 'a concept of textual distanciation [is substituted] for that of the autonomy of the text, so that we can fruitfully grasp the "recursive character" of social life and of language'.[16] This intertextual negotiation is fascinating in itself, but Greenblatt's avowed quarry in this essay is not the Renaissance artistic text, but the interpretative strategies of Fredric Jameson and Jean-François Lyotard, each of whom 'pulls away from a stable mimetic theory of art and attempts to construct in its stead an interpretive model that will more adequately account for the unsettling circulation of materials and discourses that is', Greenblatt argues, 'the heart of modern aesthetic practice'. He concludes with the plea that 'theory' should re-situate itself 'not outside interpretation, but in the hidden places of negotiation and exchange'.[17] Imbricated in those 'hidden places of negotiation and exchange', Greenblatt goes on to suggest, are both the 'historical' conditions of artistic production, and also the preconditions of critical reading. Greenblatt's aim is to attempt to understand 'how the energies were first collected and deployed and returned to the culture from which they came ... but we do so under the terms of our own interests and pleasures and in the light of historical developments that cannot simply be stripped away'. These caveats precede one of Greenblatt's most enduring statements:

I had dreamed of speaking with the dead, and even now I do not abandon this dream. But the mistake was to imagine that I would hear a single voice, the voice of the other. If I wanted to hear one, I had to hear the many voices of the dead. And if I wanted to hear the voice of the other, I had to hear my own voice. The speech of the dead, like my own speech, is not private property.[18]

Nowhere is this caution more pertinent than in the study of the fraught relationship between 'text' and 'background', between the artefact itself and its linkages to that 'unsettling circulation of materials and practices' that Greenblatt seems to want to limit to the suitably imprecise interpretive practices of modern theoreticians.

The involvement of reading theories in the process of textual exegesis is axiomatic, just as the protocols for studying the relations between texts and their histories depend upon the acknowledgement of a principle of 'embeddedness' that changes as historical contexts change. But it is to Francis Barker and Peter Hulme that we owe an important distinction that seeks to disentangle 'context', as it has emerged in literary scholarship and as it appears in the devalued discourse of celebrity culture, from 'con-text', thereby inaugurating a process that permits an important distinction to be made between two different categories of instability.

As we have already suggested, the term 'context' frequently derives its power from its reinforcement of a particular cultural hierarchy whose teleology has much in common with that implied by the concept of 'source'. Asking where the artistic text *came from*, its 'source', is another way of asking the question about the materials from which it is composed, and this question almost always leads to speculation concerning the quasi-religious 'creative' power of the artist. And yet, until 1985, what Barker and Hulme describe as 'the dominant approach within literary study' regarded the text as 'autotelic', which is to say 'a text that is fixed in history and, at the same time, curiously free from historical limitation'. They go on to elaborate: 'The text is acknowledged as having been produced at a certain moment in history; but that history is itself reduced to being no more than a background from which the single and irreducible meaning of the text is isolated.'[19] In his seminal book *Meaning by Shakespeare* (1992) the late Terence Hawkes deployed the example of *The Mousetrap* in *Hamlet* to illustrate the following argument:

> The idea that a play can and inevitably does take part in the affairs of a society requires an abandonment of the notion of the primacy, or, in practical terms, of the existence of any transcendental 'meaning' located within it, able finally to subsume, surpass or determine all others. It calls instead for a recognition of the degree to which all texts are contextualised by history. And that leads in the direction of what might be called a literary pragmatism: the notion that all texts have something in common with *The Mousetrap*. That is, they always take part in historical milieux, whenever and however they are realised, either initially or subsequently. As a result, no final context-free meaning or 'truth' can, or should, or need be assigned to them.[20]

For Hawkes, as indeed for Barker and Hulme, context and context, the shifting historical framework that is over-determined by a specified time itself on the one hand, and the synchronic interactions of the text with other contemporary texts – whether in terms of content or form – are to be distinguished clearly from each other as ways of approaching a text, any text. Indeed, what Barker and Hulme launch in their essay, Hawkes had already begun to develop into what in *Meaning by Shakespeare* became a sustained manifesto for a critical procedure that proffered a challenge, often with extraordinary wit and perception, 'the supposed "authenticity" of the text as a document whose final "meaning" includes unmediated access to the author's intimate being'.[21] What they articulate as 'successive inscriptions' without abandoning that no longer privileged but still crucial originary moment of production, leads them to the term 'con-text', where the hyphen signals the text's engagement with both the moment of its initial inscription as 'an historical utterance', but one that requires a reading 'with and within series of dynamic "con-texts"'; collectively, these combine to represent 'the pre-condition of the plays' historical and political signification, although literary criticism has operated systematically to close down that signification by a continual process of occlusion'.[22] In short, they insist: 'Con-texts are themselves *texts* and must be *read with*: they do not simply make up a background.'[23]

Barker and Hulme turn to two influences on their own thinking. The first is the Volosinov of *Marxism and the Philosophy of Language* (1973), and to the notion of 'utterance'. It is worth pausing over this concept, since what Volosinov defines initially as 'a verbal performance in print' can, *a fortiori*, as Barker and Hulme go on to show, apply to theatrical utterance and to 'verbal communication of any type whatsoever'.[24] No utterance is completely independent, rather it engages dynamically with other elements of communication (original italics):

> Verbal intercourse is inextricably interwoven with communication of other types, all stemming from the common ground of production communication. It goes without saying that [a] word cannot be divorced from this eternally generative, unified process of communication. In its concrete connection with a situation, verbal communication is always accompanied by social acts of a non-verbal character (the performance of labor, the symbolic acts of ritual, a ceremony etc.), and is often only an accessory to these acts, merely carrying out an auxiliary role. *Language acquires life and historically evolves precisely here, in concrete verbal communication, and not in the abstract linguistic system of language forms, nor in the individual psyche of speakers.*[25]

Volosinov's final italicised sentence takes a firm side-swipe at the abstractions of Saussurean structuralism, and also proleptically at more recent movements in the area of cognitive linguistics, thereby undermining the very notion of a modern individualism (the sacred realm of an inner privacy) that the 'new' – or should we say 'neo' – of New Historicism, particularly in its later manifestations, continues to seek to preserve. What Volosinov calls 'the outwardly actualised utterance' is 'an island rising from the boundless sea of inner speech; the dimensions and forms of this island are determined by the particular *situation* of the utterance and its *audience*'[26] (original italics). In their essay Barker and Hulme set out to return the text of Shakespeare's *The Tempest* to the ambit of other contexts that results in a challenge to the critical abstractions that have had a diversionary effect on criticism of the play.

One other co-ordinate informs their approach, and it comes from the post-structuralist account of 'discourse' associated with the work of Michel Foucault. Barker and Hulme argue that while '[i]ntertextuality has usefully directed attention to the relationship *between* texts: discourse moves us towards a clarification of just what kinds of relationship are involved'.[27] They argue that the concept of intertextuality has been 'unable to break out of the practice of connecting text with text, of assuming that single texts are the ultimate objects of study and the principal units of meaning'. Their attraction to 'discourse' is because it 'refers to the *field* in and through which texts are produced', and is 'as a concept wider than the "text" but narrower than language itself [Saussure's *langue*]' because 'it operates at the level of the enablement of texts'.[28] Taking their cue from Foucault, they emphasise that: 'The operation of discourse is implicit in the regulation of what statements can and cannot be made and the forms that they can legitimately take.'[29] Foucault himself makes the point explicitly in the distinction he makes between what he calls 'things' and 'the body of rules that enable them to form as objects of a discourse and thus constitute the conditions of their historical appearance'; he emphasises the distinction thus:

> The analysis of lexical contents defines either the elements of meaning at the disposal of speaking subjects in a given period, or the semantic structure that appears on the surface of a discourse that has already been spoken; it does not concern discursive practice as a place in which a tangled plurality – at once supposed and incomplete – of objects is formed and deformed, appears and disappears.[30]

The phrase 'tangled plurality' is a formal way of describing the *terminus ad quem* of a domesticated intertextuality, although Barker and Hulme follow Foucault in acknowledging that 'the text is in fact marked and fissured by the interplay of the discourses that constitute it', and that this 'interplay' cuts across 'its alleged unity'.[31] They then go on to choose a particular 'ensemble of fictional and lived practices which for convenience we will simply refer to here as "English colonialism"', which 'provides *The Tempest*'s dominant discursive con-texts'.[32]

The Arden 3 editors of the play, Virginia and Alden Vaughan, seek to emphasise the 'rich resources' upon which Shakespeare is thought to have drawn, but insist that the scholarly location of 'likely connections' between the play's 'language and characters and the political, social and intellectual climates in which Shakespeare lived and worked' served 'to mitigate our human tendency to see only the present era's concerns mirrored in Shakespeare's text'.[33] Of course, and as North American scholars, the editors will know that English colonialism has a long history and is a historically specific aspect of the very plurality that inheres in the more general concept of a colonial discourse. Also, if scholarly partisanship is an unavoidable feature of 'our human tendency', then the process of assembling scholarly arguments will *always* be both intentional and as a consequence tendentious. Virginia and Alden Vaughan are at one with Barker and Hulme in seeking to identify the 'rich resources' upon which the dramatist 'drew, consciously or unconsciously',[34] although the discursive field from within which they identify the 'conscious' and the 'unconscious' is tantalisingly unspecific. Barker and Hulme's 'ensemble' captures the plurality that inheres within the discursive field of 'English colonialism' and by so doing guards against any attempt to reduce the discussion to an identifiable single motivating force. Indeed, while Prospero's possession of the island and his relation to Caliban and Ariel are critical, his own back-story, the debate concerning the nature of government, the relationship with his daughter Miranda and the clearly ideological investment in a particular dramatic form all have parts to play in generating a series of distinct affects to which an audience might respond.

These discursive strands and theatrically represented events intersect with each other, but they also recall earlier dramatic versions that Shakespeare was able to call upon in the way of resource. The resulting plurality is derived both from the empirical evidence of the text, combined with the theoretically informed questions that it generates from within the scholarly protocols that are brought to bear as readers (and scholarly spectators) tease out the contradictions that emerge from critique. What the Arden 3 editors ascribe to an irreducible 'human tendency' turns out, in the reading that Barker and Hulme propose, to be a 'textual excess' located in Prospero's 'interrupted masque' that introduces 'a jarring note into the harmony of this supposedly most highly structured of Shakespeare's late plays'.[35] Even in Frank Kermode's Arden 2 edition of the play, the editor recognises the 'apparently inadequate motivation' for Prospero's discomfort at this point in the play, since, according to Barker and Hulme, 'there is no obvious reason why he should so excite himself over an easily controllable insurrection'.[36] Moreover, this allows them to suggest a psychological motivation for Prospero's behaviour whose specificity cannot be easily collapsed into the human tendency of the enquirers. They argue that:

> The excess obviously marks the recurrent difficulty that Caliban causes Prospero – a difficulty we have been concerned to trace in some detail. So, at the level of character, a psychoanalytical reading would want to suggest that Prospero's excessive reaction represents his disquiet at the irruption into consciousness of an unconscious anxiety concerning the grounding of his legitimacy, both as producer of his play, and, *a fortiori*, as governor of the island. The by now urgent need for action forces upon Prospero the hitherto repressed contradiction between his dual role as usurped and usurper. Of course the emergency is soon contained and the colonialist narrative quickly completed. But nonetheless, if only for a moment, the effort invested in holding Prospero's play together as a unity is laid bare.[37]

This is precisely the moment in Barker and Hulme's argument where empirical method and the theory that it generates come together. Even a liberal humanist critic such as Kermode can identify the moment and the discomfort that it causes for the reader, just as he identifies some of the 'colonial' texts upon which the play appears in part to rest. But Barker and Hulme take the matter much further to show how these con-texts are active in what, at various moments in the drama, both contribute to the *production* of contradictions, and provide an artistic resolution to them. At no point is it possible to dismiss their argument as evidence of a scholarly human tendency without challenging not only their reading of the play, but also their reading of those active con-texts within whose cognate discursive fields *The Tempest* is inextricably embedded.

However, Barker and Hulme go on to delineate one more strand in an argument that emphatically parts company with the traditional explanation that hitherto conventional criticism has provided. They note that 'to speak of Prospero's anxiety being staged by *The Tempest* would be, on its own, a recuperative move, preserving the text's unity by the familiar strategy of introducing an ironic distance between author and protagonist'.[38] Even in its recuperative mode, such a staging would risk challenging the generally self-conscious claims made for the play that Prospero and

Shakespeare are one and the same. Barker and Hulme suggest that the challenge is headed off by diverting attention from 'the *crucial nature*' (original italics) of the Caliban sub-plot conspiracy to its formal placement 'in the fully comic mode'. It is this diversion that arrests and neutralises Caliban's 'political claims' by locating the sub-plot, in which he is involved,

> In the convention of clownish vulgarity represented by the 'low-life' characters of Stephano and Trinculo, his conspiracy framed in a grotesquerie that ends with the dubiously amusing sight of the conspirators being hunted by dogs, a fate, incidentally, not unknown to natives of the New World.

They contend that at this point in the play, 'The shakiness of Prospero's position is indeed staged', but that his authoritative version wins out by containing the conspirators 'in the safely comic mode', while at the same time allowing Caliban 'only his poignant and ultimately vain protests against the venality of his co-conspirators'.[39]

In his book *Colonial Encounters: Europe and the Native Caribbean*, published a year after the essay with Francis Barker, Peter Hulme prefaced a chapter on 'Prospero and Caliban' with a statement that effectively reinforced the challenge to traditional accounts of the connection between *The Tempest* and those maritime accounts of explorations of the New World. Hulme dared to question tactfully the way in which connections between the plays and their historical backgrounds were generally treated by biographers and critics: 'Shakespeare's biography has its own fascination, but greater knowledge of his life and acquaintance would not inevitably supply us with greater comprehension of the significance of his plays.'[40] As if this were not enough of a challenge, Hulme went on to dismiss the evidence of the Bermuda Pamphlets, generally claimed to have provided the stimulus for the play, as 'irrelevant', and he expanded his critical scepticism to what he called 'the "source" argument' that 'has similar weaknesses since there can be no incontrovertible evidence for a "source"'. He continues:

> For one thing, close verbal parallels – even identity of wording – could be explained by a common source, perhaps lost, and there is no way of distinguishing between what stands 'in need of' explanation, and

what is simply common coin, part of the language. These difficulties are recognised in the best of the source studies by speaking only of 'probable' and 'possible' sources, a distinction which is to a large degree subjective. So the 'evidence' of source study proves illusory.[41]

To some extent this scepticism explains the tight focus in the 'Nymphs and Reapers Heavily Vanish' essay on the formal properties of Shakespeare's text as a route back to that over-determined assembly of texts, the play's active con-texts, in order to identify what in his book Hulme describes more generally as 'key locations in a text – *cruces* ... where the text stutters in its articulation, and which can therefore be used as levers to open out the ideology of colonial discourse, to spread it out in this text, in an act of explication'.[42]

In the case of *The Tempest*, its formal properties are exposed as being ideologically loaded, hence the importance of the play's 'comic closure', that is regarded as

> necessary to enable the European 'reconciliation' which follows hard on its heels – the patching up of a minor dynastic dispute within the Italian nobility – [that] is, however, itself symptomatic of the text's own anxiety about the threat posed to its decorum by its New World materials.[43]

The materials that have customarily been identified as the text's 'rich complexity' are made to speak more than they know in a reading that treats its con-texts as symptoms. What Hulme went on to identify as a critical delusion is here shown to play an *active* role in performing much more than a gloss on the action of *The Tempest*. Moreover, the discursive field that the play and its contexts inhabit, while possibly not recoverable in its entirety, has left sufficient traces to permit the detection of mechanisms of repression, distortion and displacement that mark early modern European encounters with the New World.

Con-texts have historical antecedents in that they come from somewhere, although the pressures that they exert on each other, and on particular kinds of texts such as plays, are both instrumental and, we might speculate, reciprocal. In other words, theatrical representation might itself provide one of the con-texts for various types of social behaviour and the narrative language that accompanies it. We have many examples of life imitating art, some of them quite horrifying in their effect, but in the same way that books of rhetoric provided models for public speaking, and for engaging with a public, so in early modern England plays could be both mimetic and also prescriptive at the same time. We saw earlier how it was possible for quotations to circulate, and to be transformed by their incorporation in different artistic modes. This is not to suggest, of course, that theatregoers wandered around late sixteenth-century London behaving like Tamburlaine, or Hieronimo, or Falstaff, or Mistress Quickly. But members of an audience could easily pick up, and in surprising ways, on the theatrical resonances of particular rituals. For example, John Foxe's *Book of Martyrs* is full of examples of what we might call 'audience response', full of expressions of affect at the gruesome sights of execution that audience members witnessed. Indeed, as we have suggested, one of the stimuli for Shakespeare's *The Merchant of Venice* (1596–97) has for some time been connected with the execution of Dr Roderigo Lopez, Elizabeth I's Portuguese physician who was accused of plotting to poison her, found guilty and hung, drawn and quartered. The 'history' of Lopez's involvement with both the English and Spanish authorities offers us an exercise in con-textual study, even before we engage with its alleged connection with text of Shakespeare's *The Merchant of Venice* that appeared some four years after the date of Lopez's public execution. Lopez's name first appears in an anonymous tract of 1584, *Leycesters Commonwealth*, which catalogues a series of crimes of the ambitious Earl of Leicester that we are more used to seeing enacted in early Jacobean Tragedy. Leicester was, it is claimed, 'a subject without subjection'[44] who gathered around him those who would do his criminal bidding:

> The Principall instruments, which for this purpose, hee hath had there before this, have beene two Physicians *Bayley* and *Culpeper*, both knowne Papists a little while agoe, but now just of Galens religion, and so much the fitter for my Lords humour: for his Lordship doth always covet, to be furnished with certaine chosen men about him, for divers affaires: as these two Galenists for agents in the Vniversity. *Dee* and *Allen* (two Atheists) for figuring and conjuring: *Iulio* the Italian and *Lopus* the Jew, for poisoning, and for the art of destroying children in

Womens bellies: *Verneis* for murdering: *Dogbies* for *Bawds*: and the like other occupations which his Lordship exerciseth.⁴⁵

This was already the image of Lopez circulating orally in 1584, even though there was no actual evidence to support this negative assessment beyond the reference to the stereotypical declension that began with 'Jew' but quickly incorporated the roles of doctor and poisoner. Lopez was physician first to Leicester, and then from 1581 to the Queen, prospering in the latter role, and in such a manner that might attract envy and a certain skewing of the 'facts'. This important con-text was sustained in William Camden's account of the convoluted plot and of Lopez's last words on the scaffold that raises a number of further questions that are pertinent to the issue of con-text and to the complex network of intertextual connections exposed by an accumulating narrative, some elements of which do not appear to have been borne out by the details provided in *Leycesters Commonwealth*:

> *Lopez*, having been for a long time a man of noted Fidelity, was not so much suspected (save that outlandish Physicians may by Bribes and Corruption be easily induced to become Poisoners and Traitours,) till he confessed 'That he was drawn in by *Andrada* a *Portugueeze* to employ his best and secret Service for the King of *Spain*; that he had received from his intimate Counsellour, *Christophoro Moro*, a rich jewel; that he had divers times thereupon advertised the *Spaniards* of such things as he could come to the Knowledge of; that at length, upon an Agreement to receive 50000 Ducats, he had promised to poison the Queen; and that he had signified as much to the Count *de Fuentez,* and *Ibara* the King's Secretary in the *Netherlands*. *Stephanus Ferreira* confessed 'That the Count *de Fuentez* and *Ibara* had acquainted him both by Letters and word of mouth that there was a plot to take away the Queen's Life by Poison; that he wrote Letters, after *Lopez* his dictating, wherein he promised the same should be effected upon Condition that 50000 Ducats should be paid for the Service; also that *Emanuel Loisie* was secretly sent unto him by *Fuentez* and *Ibara*, to urge *Lopez* to dispatch the matter with all Expedition. *Emanuel* confessed, 'That Count *Fuentez* and *Ibara*, when he had given them his faithfull Promise to conceal the Design, shewed him a Letter which *Andrada* had written in *Lopez* his name about making away the Queen; and that he himself was

likewise sent by *Fuentez* to deal with *Ferreira* and *Lopez* for hastening the Queen's Death, and to promise Money to *Lopez* himself, and Honours and Preferment to his Children.

At the Bar *Lopez* spake not much but cried out, 'That *Ferreira* and *Emanuel* were made up of nothing but Fraud and Lying; that he intended no hurt against the Queen, but abhorred the Gifts of a Tyrant; that he had presented that Jewel to the Queen which was sent him from the *Spaniard*; and that he had no other Design in what he did, but to deceive the *Spaniard*, and wipe him of his Money. The rest spake nothing for themselves, onely throwing the whole blame upon *Lopez*. They were all of them condemned, and after three months put to death at *Tyburn*, *Lopez* affirming that he loved the Queen as well as he loved *Jesus Christ*: which coming from a man of the *Jewish* Profession moved no small Laughter in the Standers-by.[46]

Edgar Samuel has attempted to explain this account by stating: 'Lopez was a Jew, therefore his speech was a dishonest equivocation, which proved his guilt.' He notes that there is no evidence in the Spanish state papers to suggest that Lopez was part of a Spanish plot, but that the intercepted Lopez correspondence 'gives clear evidence that he was a secret Jew and subscribed to the secret synagogue in Antwerp'.[47] Samuel goes on to suggest that Camden may have misreported Lopez's last words, and that he may have said 'I love the Queen as well as I love Our Lord', thereby suggesting that he was 'utterly sincere in his claim to be both loyal to the Queen and God', but that 'because out of habit, he used the equivocal language of a crypto-Jew, he made a deplorably bad impression on the bystanders and later historians'.[48]

The execution of Dr Roderigo Lopez is often linked with Marlowe's *The Jew of Malta*, which was revived in performance shortly after in June and July 1594. The connection with *The Merchant of Venice* seems to have been through the name 'Lopez' and the Latin word for 'wolf', *lupus*, and with Shylock's alleged association with animal 'feeding'; in the court of Venice the unrestrained Gratiano calls Shylock 'thou damned inexecrable dog' (4.1.127), and claims that 'thy desires / Are wolvish, bloody, starved and ravenous' (4.1.136–7). The discursive frame that provides a con-text for Gratiano's utterance is both Ovid's *Metamorphoses*, where the punishment by Jove of Lyceus, King of

Arcadia for sceptical irreverence is to be transformed into a wolf, and also various contemporary tracts on usury where the usurer is compared to a wolf in a long proverbial tradition that can be traced back to classical plays such as Terence's *Eunuchus*.[49] However, although Roderigo Lopez, the Queen's physician, was of Jewish stock, he appears to have converted to Christianity. Camden noted, as we have seen, that Lopez was 'a *Jew* by religion', and although he was 'for a long time a man of noted Fidelity', he was susceptible to bribery and corruption because he was of the company of 'outlandish Physicians' who 'may by Bribes and Corruption be easily induced to become Poisoners and Traitours'. Camden noted that on the scaffold at Tyburn Lopez's affirmation that 'he loved the Queen as well as he loved *Jesus Christ*' was thought to be an equivocation 'which coming from a man of the *Jewish* profession moved no small Laughter in the Standers-by'. Camden's use of the word 'profession' in connection with what he identified as Lopez's equivocation effectively invokes a complex stereotype for which the figure of 'the Jew' both as 'poisoner' and 'traitor' stands, even though he had been 'for a long time a man of noted Fidelity'. The crowd of spectators at his execution who, presumably, were aware of the gossip concerning Lopez, read his declaration as false despite his reputation, since the stereotype they had in mind was that represented in plays like Marlowe's *The Jew of Malta*. In Marlowe's play the prologue Machiavel claims to 'weigh not men, and therefore not men's words'; indeed, his ambitions are fulfilled by poisoning, and he has acquired his wealth by Machiavellian means.[50] In the play, and on the verge of discovery of his having poisoned the inmates of a nunnery, after his daughter's confession, Barabas runs through a number of the accusations levelled against Jews while at the same time enacting a dishonest strategy of survival:

> She has confessed, and we are both undone [*Aside*]
> My bosom inmates! – But I must dissemble.
> O, holy friars, the burden of my sins
> Lie heavy on my soul; then pray you tell me,
> Is't not too late now to turn Christian?
> I have been zealous in the Jewish faith,
> Hard-hearted to the poor, a covetous wretch,
> That would for lucre's sake have sold my soul.

A hundred for a hundred I have ta'en;
And now for store of wealth may I compare
With all the Jews in Malta; but what is wealth?
I am a Jew, and therefore am I lost.
Would penance serve for this my sin,
I could afford to whip myself to death –

(4.1.46–59)

In Marlowe's play the equivocation has the desired effect of initiating a competition between the friars Jacomo and Bernadine for converso Barabas's wealth that he is prepared 'to give to some religious house' (4.1.75). It is quite possible that this was the frame within which the audience of bystanders at Lopez's execution interpreted his 'confession', and that his avowal of dual allegiance to a Christian monarch simply strengthened the popular conviction of his guilt. The possible link with Marlowe's play is that the Lopez affair stimulated a number of performances, even though the play itself was not printed until 1633. Moreover, and given the fact that Machiavelli's *The Prince* did not appear in English until 1640, the series of interlocking stereotypes was kept alive orally within a wide range of active con-texts. All of these con-texts were active when *The Merchant of Venice* appeared in 1597, and adding to the myths surrounding the figure of 'the Jew', Shakespeare revised the Marlovian trope of the equivocating villain to incorporate into it a Christian fantasy whose proverbial life was sustained by an impossibility: the conversion of the Jews.

In the same way that Barker and Hulme identify 'how much of *The Tempest*'s complexity comes from the *staging* of the distinctive moves and figures of colonial discourse',[51] so in *The Merchant of Venice* a different order of complexity is promulgated that takes in racial *and* religious strategies that permit the location of a series of active myths and stereotypes within an actual problematical discursive field. Whereas in Marlowe's play money and a general acquisitiveness permeates the social order from every religious perspective, and where Barabas is only marginally distinctive from his adversaries, that acquisitiveness is more focused in *The Merchant of Venice* where the axis of conflict within the 'discursive performance' of economics is 'trade' and 'usury' and the contradictions that flow from their interaction, while the 'mode of representation'[52] clearly evident in the audience response to the execution of Roderigo Lopez is that of stage comedy.

As David Hawkes has shown, 'economics' during the early modern period involved more than simply the management of money. He traces this back to the Greek term *oikos* ('household') and he begins by observing that: 'Ancient discussions of economics devote considerable attention to the relations between husband and wife, between fathers and sons, as well as to the techniques of slave acquisition and management.'[53] These are the topics covered in Aristotle's *Oeconomica*, and the divisions between 'household' and 'state', in which the former both precedes and takes precedence over the latter, are set out at the beginning.[54] Although the historical conditions of early modern England were not identical to those of Ancient Greece, these same basic divisions reappear in Sir Thomas Smith's *De Republica Anglorum* (1583) that reverses the Aristotelian order by beginning with the definition of kingship and then proceeds to define the 'commonwealth' and the 'household' as coming into existence simultaneously, firstly as a 'societie ... of free men', and then 'a further societie of continuance is of the husband & of the wife after a diverse sorte ech hauing care of the familie'.[55] Hawkes distinguishes between this interpretation of 'oeconomics' and the Ancient Greek chrematistics, which is much closer to the modern practice of 'economics' as the 'the pursuit of exchange-value (money) as an end in itself'.[56] It is perhaps worth observing that the early modern emphasis on the panoply of domestic matters as a substantial support of the state or 'societie' is represented theatrically in the form of comedy.

All of these concerns come together in a number of Shakespeare's plays, but particularly in *The Merchant of Venice*, where social and racial stereotypes, the political organisation of the state, the rule of families (aristocratic and non-aristocratic, and including the servant class) are all represented as elements in a complex socio-religious discursive field of dynamic con-texts. The play opens in Venice, a republic somewhat different from Sir Thomas Smith's 'monarchical republic', and with the melancholic Antonio whose sadness is ambivalent. This scene is followed by the expression of what appears to be a different kind of sadness by Portia, whose dead father continues to control her life. Modern interpretations of

Antonio's sadness have hinged on his repressed homosexual desire for his aristocratic 'kinsman', the Lord Bassanio, who because of his prodigality is clearly unable to manage his own affairs, and who is now in need of financial backing to pursue a marriage with Portia. Although it is not made explicit, Antonio's anxiety seems to come from his mercantile activity insofar as he has no ready capital to risk an investment in Bassanio's venture. Portia's anxiety is more explicit since the providence that governs her life is the 'law' of her dead father, and that law will resurface in the affairs of another 'family' in the play, that of the Jew, Shylock, whose 'Christian name' contradicts his 'profession' as a usurer. The shift from masculine to feminine here as regards anxiety is important, as indeed is the shift from one kind of money-making to another, as we shall see. In each of these, the contradictions that emerge have their roots in the ideologically unstable discourses that are designed to efface them, and the result is an interrogation through discursive performance of the mode of representation itself. It is this tension that makes of the play a 'problem' comedy, a problem that has been exacerbated in modern times by events such as the mid-twentieth-century Jewish Holocaust.

The original performances of *The Merchant of Venice* by the Chamberlain's Men in 1596–97 were embedded in the culture of investment and risk. The company invests in a play in which a central character is, as Theodore Leinwand has convincingly shown, 'locked into thoroughly early modern credit relations',[57] and his adversary is a usurer who emerges out of folk history but who gestures towards an economic future in which he is absolved from the risk of the borrower. The play's language is also embedded in the discursive regime of the usury tracts whose publication increased in volume from the 1570s onwards, where the practice of lending money at interest was persistently vilified as the act of a voracious, animal-like being. In his *General Discourse Against the Damnable Sect of Usurers* (1578), Philip Caesar likened usurers to 'poisoned serpents, to mad Dogges, to greedie Wormes, to Wolues, Beares, and to such other rauening beastes',[58] and his successors continued in this vein, invoking, in the case of Miles Mosse, Aristotle and St Augustine as authorities for their vilification. At the heart of the debate about usury was the issue of money-making and the safeguards that the usurer took to avoid participating in the risk of the borrower. The bond that Antonio makes with Shylock is a 'merry bond', not to be taken as a serious financial transaction, but as we observed in the case of Roderigo Lopez, the alleged tenor of its statement may well be assumed to be equivocal, as Antonio himself suggests:

> [*aside*]   Mark you this, Bassanio,
> The devil can cite Scripture for his purpose.
> An evil soul producing holy witness
> Is like a villain with a smiling cheek,
> A goodly apple, rotten at the heart.
> O, what a goodly outside falsehood hath!
>   (1.3.93–8)

This follows Shylock's invocation of an Old Testament narrative, the story of Jacob and Laban, and initiates a contrast with the New Testament narrative of self-sacrifice that Antonio will later be positioned on the verge of enacting.

Wherever one turns in *The Merchant of Venice* the action is deepened by the presence of one or more dynamic con-texts, ranging from theatrical and dramatis antecedents, to usury tracts, and to both oeconomical and chrematistic concerns. In addition, the intertextual relations that emerge both reveal and reinforce ideologically inflected issues of identity and positionality that carry with them both political and personal significance.

The matter of 'household', which as we have seen in Aristotle and Sir Thomas Smith is crucial to the organisation and administration of the social order, is crucial in Shakespeare's play. In effect there are three households, all with slightly different dynamics, two of which are embedded in the republic of Venice which is the state whose values they replicate.

Let us take Bassanio's aristocratic household first. He is a lord and he is a conspicuous consumer, which is to say that he is not able to reproduce the means by which he lives, and so he borrows money from his kinsman Antonio. It is one of the allegations that Shylock levels against Antonio that he 'lends out money gratis, and brings down / The rate of usance here with us in Venice' (1.3.40–1). We already know that Antonio's 'fortunes are at sea; / Neither have

I money, nor commodity / To raise a present sum' (1.1.177–9), but he also goes out of his way to distinguish between his own financial dealings and those of Shylock:

> Shylock, albeit I neither lend nor borrow
> By taking nor by giving of excess,
> Yet, to supply the ripe wants of my friend,
> I'll break a custom.
>
> (1.3.57–60)

It is at this point that Antonio crosses the line between lending and borrowing within a household held together my mutual love and friendship, and that of Shylock whose household turns out to be disordered at a number of levels. Shylock immediately pounces on the contradiction in which Antonio now finds himself: 'Methoughts you said you neither lend nor borrow / Upon advantage' (1.3.65–6), indicating that, notwithstanding Antonio's antipathy towards his creditor, he is forced by his circumstances to avail himself of the latter's services. The resulting 'merry bond' is fraught with ambivalence, and it is difficult to determine at this point whether the Jew is a stereotyped equivocator *or* whether he intends revenge on his Venetian interlocutor for past insults. The bond has all the indications of a folk motif, but in the now-litigious environment of a Venice where 'strangers' are protected by law, it can become something else. In short, in entering into Shylock's household, which is ruled by chrematistics, Antonio risks compromising the very values for which he claims to stand. Or to put the matter another way, Antonio's mercantilist practice that always relies in the final analysis on a providence that he experiences as serendipity, carries with it an awareness of what is required in a practical sense to alleviate risk, an awareness that from the very outset of the play seems to be at the root of his 'sadness'. In the play he is brought to the brink of realising the risk of entering into an agreement whose terms might be subject to legal scrutiny in a court of law. What appears to be Shylock's change of heart is provoked, as many modern productions affirm, by the disruption in his own household occasioned by the elopement of his daughter Jessica.

The risk that Antonio runs is replicated in generic terms by the risk that Bassanio takes on in his own quasi-mercantile venture to guess the contents of the caskets, while Shylock's financial dealings, which are designed to eliminate risk, are undermined by the elopement of his daughter. While the disorder in Shylock's household is clearly visible, and the audience is expected to register some disapproval at the owner's puritanical ways, Bassanio's household is not free from criticism since it is his capacity for conspicuous consumption (this is not the first time that he has ventured and lost) that is the cause of everything that follows. In short, with friends like Bassanio, Antonio does not need enemies, although both need Shylock as the source of liquid capital.

However, the real contrast in households is with that of Portia in Belmont. Here, and even before the prospect of borrowing money from a usurer has been mooted, Portia's confession that her 'little body is aweary of this great world' (1.2.1) highlights an anxiety that makes of Belmont something less than a fairy-tale world. Nerrisa's response is to give Portia a mini-lecture on the virtues of the Aristotelian mean, as a response to her mistress's frustrating dilemma:

> O me, the word 'choose'! I may neither choose who I would, nor refuse who I dislike, so is the will of a living daughter curbed by the will of a dead father. Is it not hard, Nerissa, that I cannot choose one, nor refuse none?
>
> (1.2.21–5)

The limit placed upon Portia's behaviour is the domestic analogue to those that circumscribe Antonio's business dealings, and the risks are comparable. Equally, Portia is herself the subject of a business risk, articulated both as a financial *and* a romantic prize. For example, Bassanio has already described her as 'a lady richly left' and 'Of wondrous virtues' (1.1.161 and 163), and if he is successful he 'should questionless be fortunate' (1.1.176); Antonio picks this up in his admission that 'Thou knowst that all my fortunes are at sea' (1.1.177). Business and the romance associated with marriage operate within the same discursive field and share the same vocabulary, and limits that are imposed on both generate personal anxiety. And yet this model of the social order is presented in the play as a desirable norm compared with the third household presided over by Shylock.

The nature of con-text

The information that we are given concerning the oeconomical organisation of the households of Bassanio and Portia is limited, but in the case of Shylock it is extensive. The Jew's household mirrors some of the constraints of Portia's except that there is no acceptable way of escaping the constraints they impose upon its members. The Clown seeks to escape, and when his sand-blind father, Giobbe, says that he has brought his son's 'master' a present, his response is:

> I have set up my rest to run away, so I will not rest till I have run some ground. My master's a very Jew. Give him a present? Give him a halter! I am famished in his service. You may tell every finger I have with my ribs.
>
> (2.2.96–100)

Later, Jessica, constrained by the law of a living father, will complain to the Clown that 'Our house is hell, and thou, a merry devil, / Didst rob it of some taste of tediousness' (2.3.2–3). Unlike Portia, she will 'choose' her own partner, but in doing so she will violate the integrity of her father's household by eloping with Lorenzo. The Clown's description, augmented by that of Jessica introduces an additional ambivalence into the oeconomical discourse within which the institution of the household is embedded in the play. The Clown's 'My master's a very Jew' points to the ambivalence of the term 'Jew' in late Elizabethan culture. In all respects *except* in the practice of usury – which is presented as a dubious means of securing one's 'fortune' – Shylock's household intensifies the anxieties that have been exposed in the other households represented in the play. Indeed, all of the households represented in the play, to borrow the formulation that Barker and Hulme use, stage 'the distinctive moves and figures' of domestic discourse. But, although we may agree that there is an 'absence of any direct authorial comment',[59] the accumulation of variations in the performative details outlined between the different households in *The Merchant of Venice* sets up a critical commentary whereby the ideology of the entire discursive field is exposed. In short, the play represents a distillation of the performative elements of a discourse that can move between the oeconomy of the household, and the chrematistic concern with the materialist means to sustain its organisation.

Indeed, when finally Shylock is deprived of his wealth in the Venetian court, he makes exactly this connection:

> Nay, take my life and all, pardon not that.
> You take my house when you do take the prop
> That doth sustain my house. You take my life
> When you do take the means whereby I live.
>
> (4.1.370–3)

In this play, therefore, the Jew is a householder, a possessor of property that places him in certain respects on a par with his adversaries. This serves to open a gap between the *performed* discourse of oeconomica and the ways in which it is *represented* in the play. Portia could easily subvert her dead father's law but she does not; indeed, cross-dressed as a lawyer later she becomes the defender of law against an adversary who, paradoxically, seeks to invoke the law of Venice to uphold what began as a 'merry bond', but what is in essence a practice of dubious legality. On the other hand, Jessica, the subversive daughter, cross-dresses in order to violate patriarchal law and elopes. Her violation, however, is ameliorated because she is one of the main instruments whereby her father becomes a Christian.[60] These adjustments to the representation of the play's domestic discourse result in a nervous provisional ending that seeks to resolve the tensions surrounding the various relationships in the play. The risks to patriarchal authority are not completely alleviated, even though Portia gains a husband by her dead father's means, while the institution of marriage (part of the resolution associated with comic form) is shown to depend upon the fidelity of the partners, both male and female. In the case of Bassanio, Portia and Antonio, providence has looked favourably on their enterprises, but in the case of Jessica the resolution is more the result of concerted (and to some extent outlawed) domestic action, even though it is given a 'Christian' sanction.

There is, however, one dimension of the play that supersedes these domestic concerns, and that is the state of Venice itself. Clearly, Venice as a particular geopolitical space into which the play's range of discursive practices is inserted makes particular demands upon the ways in which they interact. In the wake of performances of *The Merchant of Venice*, sufficient interest appears to

The nature of con-text

have been generated in the idea of the republic as a particular mode of government. Two images of Venice emerged: one of Venice as a necessary stopping-off point in aristocratic itineraries, noted for its art, its architecture, its brothels and its courtesans, and the other of Venice as a threat to England's particular brand of 'monarchical republic' that preserved the various levels of the social hierarchy. In 1599 Lewis Lewkenor's translation of Gasparo Contarini's account of *The Commonwealth and Government of Venice* provided considerable detail of how the Venetian constitution operated. Strangers, it seems, were welcomed and were not discriminated against, and financial dealing was not subject to the same moral strictures that prevailed in England. This is not, however, how Venice is represented in Shakespeare's play. Far from welcoming strangers, or from permitting free and open financial dealing, Shakespeare's Venice exposed the tensions that a mixed republic generated, and its consequences, both at the level of the state and within the household. This is not to say that *The Merchant of Venice* is some kind of thesis play, rather that it must be positioned within that larger constitutional debate that was stimulated by the various evaluations of different kinds of social order that were gathering pace during the last years of Elizabeth I's reign. In Book 5 of Richard Hooker's *The Laws of Ecclesiastical Polity*, published in 1597, which was probably the year in which *The Merchant of Venice* was first performed, ignorance or the wilful repudiation of God, human sensuality and the accumulation of material wealth are associated with atheism:

> The fountain and wellspring of which impiety is a resolved purpose of mind to reap in this world what sensual profit or pleasure soever the world yieldeth, and not to be barred from any whatsoever means available thereunto. And that this is the very radical cause of their atheism, no man I think will doubt which consisteth what pains they take to destroy those principal spurs and motives unto all virtue, the creation of the world, the providence of God, the resurrection of the dead, the joys of the kingdom of heaven, and the endless pains of the wicked, yea above all things the authority of Scripture, because on these points it evermore beateth, and the soul's immortality, which granted, draweth easily after it the rest as a voluntary train. Is it not wonderful that base desires should so extinguish in men the sense of their own excellency, as to make them willing that their souls

should be like to the souls of beasts, mortal and corruptible with their bodies?[61]

Hooker goes on to ask: 'What more savage, wild, and cruel, than man, if he see himself able either by fraud to overreach, or by power to overbear, the laws whereunto he should be subject?'[62] Shakespeare's Jew is, from the perspective of the play's Venetians, inscribed within this discourse whereas Antonio, Portia, and Bassanio are all 'subject' to, and operate within Venetian law. From within the aegis of the play, Venice is a model against which individual behaviour is to be judged, but as a *representation* its ideological features are exposed by comparison with an implied English alternative. Indeed, whatever the pitfalls of monarchy, it almost always emerges during the period as the preferred political form, although comparisons, whether explicit or implicit, inadvertently expose the fissures in its ideology. We are able to recover these fissures at a distance by bringing into play those con-texts that exert dynamic pressure on the representation of these issues in theatrical form. We saw earlier in *Hamlet* how various kinds of repetition served to increase and expose the ideological investments in the various complex elements of the play's discursive framework. The same is true of a comedy like *The Merchant of Venice* where the various domestic and financial concerns of the household are brought into critical alignment with the preoccupations of the republic. All this is embodied in the form of a comedy, and it is to theatrical form as a resource that the argument now turns.

Notes

1. Jonathan Culler, *The Pursuit of Signs: Structuralism, Linguistics and the Pursuit of Literature* (London, 1975), p. 103.
2. *Ibid.*, p. 106.
3. V.N. Volosinov, 'Discourse in life and in art', *Freudianism: A Marxist Critique*, trans. I.R. Titunik, ed. Neal H. Bruss (New York and London, 1976), p. 97.
4. *Ibid.*
5. *Ibid.*, p. 98.
6. *Ibid.*, p. 105.

The nature of con-text 245

7 *Ibid.*
8 *Ibid.*, pp. 95–6.
9 Pierre Bourdieu, *The Rules of Art* (Cambridge, 1996), p. 187.
10 *Ibid.*, p. 188.
11 Stephen Greenblatt, 'Shakespeare and the exorcists', in *Shakespearean Negotiations: The Circulation of Social Energy in Renaissance England* (Oxford, 1988), p. 95.
12 *Ibid.*
13 *Ibid.*, p. 94 and p. 185 n. 1.
14 See also Stephen Greenblatt, *Will in the World: How Shakespeare Became Shakespeare* (London, 2004), where textual details in the plays are systematically linked to earlier 'experiences'.
15 Louis Althusser, 'A letter on art in reply to André Daspre', *Lenin and Philosophy and Other Essays*, trans. Ben Brewster (London, 1971), pp. 223–5.
16 Stephen Greenblatt, 'Towards a poetics of culture', *Learning to Curse: Essays in Early Modern Culture* (London, 1990), p. 159.
17 *Ibid.*
18 Greenblatt, *Shakespearean Negotiations*, p. 20.
19 Francis Barker and Peter Hulme, 'Nymphs and reapers heavily vanish: the discursive con-texts of *The Tempest*', in John Drakakis, ed., *Alternative Shakespeares* (London, 1985), p. 192.
20 Terence Hawkes, *Meaning by Shakespeare* (London, 1992), p. 6.
21 *Ibid.*, pp. 5–6.
22 *Ibid.*, p. 195.
23 *Ibid.*, p. 236 n. 6.
24 V.N. Volosinov, *Marxism and the Philosophy of Language*, trans. Ladislav Matejka and I.R. Titunik (New York and London, 1973), p. 95.
25 *Ibid.*
26 *Ibid.*, p. 96.
27 Barker and Hulme, 'Nymphs and reapers', p. 196.
28 *Ibid.*, pp. 196–7.
29 *Ibid.*, p. 197.
30 Michel Foucault, *The Archeology of Knowledge*, trans. A.M. Sheridan Smith (London, 1974), p. 48.
31 Barker and Hulme, 'Nymphs and reapers', p. 197.
32 *Ibid.*, p. 198.
33 Virginia and Alden Vaughan, in William Shakespeare, *The Tempest*, ed. Virginia and Alden Vaughan, Arden 3 series (London, 1999), p. 37.
34 *Ibid.*
35 Barker and Hulme, 'Nymphs and reapers', p. 202.

36 *Ibid.*
37 *Ibid.*
38 *Ibid.*, p. 203.
39 *Ibid.*
40 Peter Hulme, *Colonial Encounters: Europe and the Native Caribbean* (London, 1986), p. 91.
41 *Ibid.*, pp. 91–2.
42 *Ibid.*, p. 12.
43 Barker and Hulme, 'Nymphs and reapers', p. 203.
44 Anon., *Leycesters Commonwealth: Conceived, Spoken and Published With Most Earnest protestation of all Dutifull good will and affection towards this Realm, for whose good onely, it is made common to many* (London, 1641), p. 29 (sig. E3^r).
45 *Ibid.*, p. 71 (sig. K4^r).
46 William Camden, *The History of the most Renowned and Victorious Princess Elizabeth*, 4th edn (London, 1688), pp. 484–5.
47 Edgar Samuel, 'Dr Rodrigo Lopez' last speech from the scaffold at Tyburn', *Transactions of the Jewish Historical Studies*, 30 (1987–88), 52.
48 *Ibid.*
49 See William Skakespeare, *The Merchant of Venice*, ed. John Drakakis (London, 2010), p. 343 n. 133, and earlier, p. 338 nn. 72–3.
50 Christopher Marlowe, *The Jew of Malta*, ed. N.W. Bawcutt (Manchester, 1978), Prologue, ll. 12, 31–2.
51 Barker and Hulme, 'Nymphs and reapers', p. 204.
52 *Ibid.*, p. 205.
53 David Hawkes, *Shakespeare and Economic Theory* (London, 2015), pp. 3–4.
54 Aristotle, *Metaphysics Books 10–12: Oeconomica: Magna Moralia*, trans. G. Cyril Armstrong (Cambridge, MA, 1935), pp. 327ff.
55 Sir Thomas Smith, *De Republica Anglorum* (London, 1583), p. 12.
56 Hawkes, *Shakespeare and Economic Theory*, p. 4.
57 Theodore B. Leinwand, *Theatre, Finance and Society in Early Modern England* (Cambridge, 1999), p. 16.
58 Philip Caesar, *General Discourse Against the Damnable Sect of Usurers* (London, 1578), p. 4. For a fuller treatment of the usury tracts, see John Drakakis, in *The Merchant of Venice*, pp. 12ff., and for the theatrical and narrative con-texts, see pp. 31ff.
59 Barker and Hulme, 'Nymphs and reapers', p. 204.
60 See John Drakakis, 'Jessica', in John W. Mahon and Ellen Macleod Mahon, eds, *The Merchant of Venice: New Critical Essays* (New York

and London, 2002), pp. 145–64, for a fuller account of the role of Jessica in the play.
61 Richard Hooker, *The Laws of Ecclesiastical Polity*, ed. Christopher Morris, 2 vols (London and New York, 1965), vol. 2, p. 17.
62 *Ibid.*, p. 19.

6

From formula to text: theatre, form, meme and reciprocity

Shakespeare's resources were available to him in a number of forms within two broader categories: historical, through compilations such as Holinshed's *Chronicles*; and classical/historical from writers such as Plutarch (in North's translation) or Suetonius, and of course Livy, and through various translations of Greek and Latin drama.[1] In the case of classical/historical writers, the fascination for the late sixteenth century was that the histories they produced traversed the entire gamut of political institutions. At a more general level, the Greek or Roman past could be shaped to address the preoccupations of the Elizabethan present, but to some extent it could also be used as a means to calculate elements of the future. This was especially true of something like Livy's *History of Rome*, fashioned by Machiavelli into the *Discourses* (but unpublished in English until 1636) that aimed to tease out lessons for the Florentine present by looking into the Roman past. Holinshed provided a more local and ideologically appropriate 'history' of the English past and the aristocratic line it traced into the early modern present. Dramatic and theatrical models offered further resources, including translations of classical plays such as those of Seneca, and an awareness of Ancient Greek models, some of which were subsumed piecemeal (alongside rhetorical texts) into the education system to which a young Shakespeare is very likely to have been exposed.[2] Tracing such resources and identifying them as 'sources' – although to be fair to Bullough, whose categories of 'probable' and 'possible' sources introduce a degree of hesitancy into the process – is, as we have seen, dependent upon a theory of origins that is itself quasi-religious. Also, unlike Enterline, Bullough has no interest in exploring the larger questions of how such texts might shape the schoolboy's emergence as a self ready to occupy a particular place in a symbolic order.[3] It is difficult to gauge the ways in which resources such as these might circulate through the practices of reading or through their effects.[4] Indeed, we have only a circumstantial map of what Shakespeare may have read, and we can only speculate in relation to the attention with which he may have read or the extent to which it shaped a self.

As we shall see, at a basic level there are phrasal and verbal echoes in the texts of the plays, some of which seem, from a modern perspective, like blatant plagiarisms; on other occasions, texts such as *An Interpretation of Dreams* (1576) or Timothie Bright's *A Treatise on Melancholy* (1584) that describe states of mind and what we might call the Elizabethan unconscious, and that find topographical echoes in plays such as *Hamlet* or *Othello*, offer extended narratives of contemporary psychoanalytical thinking that filtered through piecemeal into the dramatic writing of the period. Such texts – though they were, perhaps, analytical by early modern standards – contain what we might call 'creative' elements: mixtures of anecdote, folk wisdom and other non-factual detail. And if we add to this material texts such as Arthur Golding's 1567 translation of Ovid's *Metamorphoses* or Thomas Newton's translation of Seneca's *Tenne Tragedies* (1581) with their pathological violence and dramatic shifts from one state of mind or one predicament to another – and in the case of Ovid, one reality to another – then the circulation of such resources either piecemeal through oral transmission, or, in more detail, print, provided a veritable reservoir of rich material for dramatists looking for models, theatrical forms and appropriate modes of expression. Indeed, it is not difficult to identify writers whose phrasal echoes appear in playscripts of the period, but it is difficult to be certain about the manner and, indeed, the forms in which the wider narratives they contained circulated. Nor should we collapse this enquiry into the question of 'authorship' since in the case of the theatre, and with the notable exception of Ben Jonson, the category appears to have had secondary, if not marginal, significance.

We have seen how the story of *Hamlet* first appeared in early medieval times, and in a 'history' that was not initially English. Saxo Grammaticus's prose narrative was written in Latin and was therefore available only to a very small reading public. Even so, the path it followed into Elizabethan and possibly early modern European culture offers some insight into the processes of adaptation, appropriation and emphasis that the story underwent as it passed from one epoch to the next. To this extent, 'source' as an analytical category becomes less and less relevant, since what is important here is the nature and manner of transmission, processes which, as we have seen, draw texts that show evidence of translation and adaptation into the vertiginous political web of intertextuality. Trafficking may be a convenient empirical term to describe the actual circulation of texts, and especially plays, but it is insufficient, as we saw in Chapter 4, to address the ways in which prose writers, poets or dramatists generated meanings that addressed the various concerns, anxieties and aspirations of the audiences that flocked to see the plays. Moreover, beneath the levels of conscious choice and, indeed, consciousness, other pressures contributed to particular articulations of such resources. That readers and spectators were sensitive to various types of allegorical interpretation is evident from long and intricate texts such as Sidney's *The Countess of Pembroke's Arcadia* (c.1580), Spenser's *The Faerie Queene* (1597) or, in a different, specifically historical register, Sir John Hayward's *The History of Henry IIII* (1597). Indeed, the editor of Sidney's *Arcadia* could pronounce with confidence that 'Shakespeare took the Gloucester plot of *King Lear* from it',[5] while Hayward's 'history' was interpreted as a representation of the relationship between Elizabeth and Essex that drew Shakespeare's *Richard II* into its aegis.[6]

In the case of *Hamlet* it would be a mistake to reduce the various narratives that we find in these resources to a series of rigid structural categories, but the adultery, regicide and revenge progression that appears in Saxo Grammaticus's account of the Amleth story is not dissimilar in terms of content from the preoccupations of Aeschylus's *Oresteia* or Seneca's rewriting of parts of it. Moreover, the shapes that these narratives took resemble isolated events that are laid out in more detail in texts such as Holinshed's *Chronicles*, or the recycling in translation of Livy's *History of Rome*.

As we saw earlier, Peter Lake's lengthy account in his book *How Shakespeare Put Politics on the Stage* (2016) seeks to map the transition from a political narrative fashioned by the professional historiographer onto that of a sequence of Elizabethan plays. His careful account of the contemporary relevance of, for example, Shakespeare's *King John* and its possible entanglement in the fortunes of Mary, Queen of Scots, offers something of a methodology. After rehearsing what he takes to be the likely concatenation of 'facts', which he derives in part from Philip the Bastard's statement that after the death of Arthur, 'England now is left / To tug and scamble, and to part by th'teeth / The unow'd interest of proud swelling state' (4.3.140–54), Lake speculates:

> If we take this to be a statement of the likely consequences of the death of Mary Stuart, then it becomes for the audiences of the 1590s a comment on their current war-torn state, surrounded by enemies, subject to the threat of invasion from abroad and of sedition, division, and rebellion at home. When we add the further fact of John's (and, of course, Elizabeth's) excommunication and deposition by the pope, and their confrontation by the threat of a (papally sponsored) foreign invasion and foreign claimant to the English throne, the case for a very close parallel indeed between the conduct and predicament of John and of Elizabeth is all but clinched. It is surely not going too far to claim that no politically sentient or aware member of the audience at a performance of this play in the 1590s could have failed to note such parallels. We are, surely, dealing here with something rather more intense than the 'atmosphere of contemporary pertinence' imputed to the play by David Womersley.[7]

Lake's account is, of course, plausible, but that it is the Bastard who should pronounce on the state of England cannot easily be tied down exclusively to an event that was, by the time of the appearance of Shakespeare's play, some six or seven years old. Elizabeth's excommunication, and the Catholic claim that she was Henry VIII's illegitimate daughter, might also be what a 'politically sentient or aware member of the audience' perceived, and if so, then the Bastard's statement on a public stage would have been an extremely risky one. Arthur's links with France may seem to narrow the reference down a little, but Lake's revisionist account still does not entirely invalidate David Womersley's more diplomatic assessment of the ethos of the play. Since the publication of Carl Schmitt's 1986 book *Hamlet or Hecuba* that appeared in translation in 2009,

Hamlet has also become the focus of attention with regard to the biography of Mary, Queen of Scots, and that adds something to its plausibility.[8] In a statement that we should treat with care, Schmitt detects a sub-text in the play that he says 'concerns Mary, Queen of Scots':

> Her husband, Henry Lord Darnley, the father of James, was brutally murdered in February 1566 by the Earl of Bothwell. In May of the same year, 1566, Mary Stuart married this very Earl of Bothwell, the murderer of her husband. This was hardly three months after the murder. Here one really can speak of an unseemly and suspicious haste. The question of the extent to which Mary Stuart was involved in the murder of her husband, perhaps even to the point of having instigated it herself, has remained unresolved and disputed to the present day. Mary maintained her complete innocence and her friends, especially the Catholic ones, believed her. Her enemies, above all Protestant Scotland and England, and all devotees of Queen Elizabeth, were convinced that Mary was in fact the real instigator of the murder.[9]

Both Schmitt and Lake choose to emphasise different elements of the Mary, Queen of Scots biography in order to interpret two different Shakespeare plays. Schmitt goes on to ask how the 'outrageous scandal' of the Mary, Queen of Scots story had become 'a taboo at the time for the author of *Hamlet*'.[10] And he answers this by referring to the 'tension and uncertainty' surrounding the last years of Elizabeth I.[11] Both commentators allude to the political instability that is alleged to have informed audience understanding of the contemporary significance of the representation, but beyond that, Schmitt's account aligns historical 'fact' with a structural representation that would (aside from the names of the participants) not have been out of place in a description of Aeschylus's *Agamemnon*. In his account the *details* are not identical, and they respond to elements of Shakespeare's play, but in terms of the *form* of the narrative and its more or less tragic shape, there appear to be close similarities, and his assumption is that both the historically aware modern critic and a contemporary Elizabeth audience would have recognised this.

It is, perhaps, unusual to expect a modern historian and critic such as Schmitt to respond to forms of representation in this way, and it is difficult to determine precisely whether the form itself fulfils a cognitive and heuristic function for him. Hayden White was of the view that 'history' itself comprised a form of representation, and he went on to suggest:

> Whether the events represented in a discourse are construed as atomic parts of a molar whole or as possible occurrences within a perceivable totality, the discourse taken in *its* totality as an image of some reality bears a relationship of correspondence to that *of which* it is an image. It is in these twin senses that all written discourse is cognitive in its aims and mimetic in its means. And this is true even of the most ludic and seemingly expressivist discourse, of poetry no less than prose, and even of those forms of poetry which seem to wish to illuminate only 'writing' itself. In this respect, history is no less a form of fiction than the novel is a form of historical representation.[12]

White later went on to observe that a scientific historiography saw that 'getting the "story" out of "history" was therefore a first step in the transformation of historical studies into a science'.[13] What, then, are we to make of a historiography that, as in the cases of Schmitt and Lake, seeks to reinstate the 'story' and then to align it as 'fact' in a historical sense, as an irreducible element of 'reality' and with the mimetic form in which it is subsequently inscribed?[14] In the case of Lake, 'comprehensibility' rests 'in those true allegories of temporality that we call narrative histories', whereas for Schmitt, 'truth' is located not only in their fidelity to the facts of given individual or collective lives, but also, and most importantly, in their faithfulness to that vision of human life informing the poetic genre of tragedy. In this respect, the symbolic content of narrative history, the content of its form, is the tragic vision itself.[15] This suggests that at a deep structural level historians such as Schmitt and Lake share a project with Shakespeare to the extent that while the dramatist translates history onto the stage, the critical historian simply seeks to reverse the process by naively returning the form to its contents while at the same time importing into the narratives speculations about the kinds of human behaviour that are assumed to inform the myths, the fictions, and the temporal reality that these fictions represent. In short, it is assumed that Shakespeare thinks like a historian, deploying all the resources of allegorisation and irony to which those who claim to be excavating the facts that comprise reality have access. It is, perhaps, worth adding that the erosion of the boundary between the disciplines of history and literature risks in these instances the fictionalisation of fact just as, from the reverse perspective it signals the fact of fictionalisation.

The concern here is not to obscure the distinction between 'historical' and 'fictional' narratives, but rather, as White suggests, to draw attention to what some have considered 'the *proper* way of representing historical events in discourse, inasmuch as such events could be established as displaying the kind of forms met with in traditional story types'.[16] Putting Shakespeare on the stage, to use Lake's formulation, involves the aligning of one form of narrative with another, while at the same time *reversing* the process of transmission. But of course, from the point of view of the practising dramatist, the process of mimesis – of showing 'Virtue her feature, Scorn her own image, and the very age and body of the time his form and pressure' (*Hamlet*, 3.2.22–4) – is filtered through existing models such as the series of theatrical forms from which the players are encouraged to select their script that accords with the actual experience of the crime that a dramatic character like Hamlet hopes to uncover. It is to these forms that our attention should now turn, forms that Shakespeare internalised, adapted, appropriated and innovated upon as he deployed particular models of comedy, tragedy, history and romance in the shaping of his plays. It is in this way that he helped to make theatre history, but not necessarily or entirely in conditions of his own making. It is also important to recognise that what, in retrospect, we identify as genres were actually forms that were themselves in the making during the late sixteenth century when the relatively new technology of the public theatre sought material to satisfy the demands of its audiences.

To take a particular example, a comedy such as *Love's Labour's Lost* (*c*.1595), for which there is no clearly identifiable traditionally conceived 'source', both fulfils and transgresses what we might take to be the 'rules' of Elizabethan comedy that it presupposes. This would suggest that a recognisable comic form was already in existence, one that both dramatist and audience were aware of. We can deduce this from the pattern of comic form that Shakespeare used earlier in *The Comedy of Errors*. Shakespeare's Comedies are primarily domestic, and as we saw in the last chapter, preoccupied with the 'oeconomica' of the household. Almost without exception they are concerned with the frictions between generations, with obstacles and tensions required to be overcome before society can replenish its human resources, and with the provisional resolution of those anxieties that emanate from conflicts between parents and children. But as we saw with *The Merchant of Venice*, and within a much wider and more explicitly political frame in *The Tempest*, those conflicts are embedded in a series of con-texts that extend outwards into society at large.

The immediate and internal con-text within which *Love's Labour's Lost* is embedded is surprisingly political insofar as it is the King of Navarre who forces his aristocratic accomplices to withdraw from society for a period of three years. Navarre goes on to explain his reasons for this edict, in such a way that the process of seeking fame, and of defeating time, is aligned with narrative history itself, as a means of defeating death:

> Let fame, that all hunt after in their lives,
> Live registered upon our brazen tombs,
> And then grace us in the disgrace of death,
> When, spite of cormorant devouring time,
> Th' endeavour of this present breath may buy
> The honour which shall bate his scyth's keen edge,
> And make us heirs of all eternity.
>
> (1.1.1–6)[17]

Navarre's ambitious plan is to outwit man's natural and ultimately unavoidable enemy, but his method of doing so is, paradoxically, to retreat into solitude and withdraw from the very social activities that would guarantee the continuation of human life. Registering 'fame' upon 'our brazen tombs' privileges the technology of writing, but it also separates the technology from the very vital energies that would animate it. Two of his three companions, Longaville and Dumaine, appear willing to give over a life of sensuality and embrace the idea that 'The mind shall banquet though the body pine' (1.1.25), and that 'The grosser manner of these world's delights' should be left to 'the gross world's baser slaves' (1.1.29–30). It is the sceptical Berowne who provides a critique of the oath, and the first 'strict observance' that he objects to is 'not to see a woman in that term' (1.1.16). Already the 'oath', which has the status of a royal decree, is beginning to look a little shaky. Indeed, it unravels as Berowne subjects it to a form of scrutiny that exposes its shortcomings: to withdraw from society and to refrain from exploiting the means to reproduce it and to replace it with an unnatural activity that is nothing more than a form of bodiless patriarchy by proxy. As Berowne puts it, 'Too much to know is to know naught but fame, / And every godfather can give a name' (1.1.92–3). Indeed, the programme of study mapped out by Navarre stands accused of failing in its quest to locate a basic human 'truth' while at the same time destroying a primary organ of perception:

> Why, all delights are vain, but that most vain
> Which, with pain purchased, doth inherit pain:
> As painfully to pore upon a book
> To seek the light of truth, while truth the while
> Doth falsely blind the eyesight of his look.
> Light seeking light doth light of light beguile;
> So ere you find where light in darkness lies,
> Your light grows dark by losing of your eyes.
>
> (1.1.72–9)

Berowne's challenge deploys an amalgam of linguistic forms: paraphrasing, and what Kristeva would call 'quotations', including commonplaces that occur later in Spenser's *The Faerie Queene*, alongside echoes of Cicero's *De Oratore*, and other forms of proverbial language.[18] Both the action and the language in which it is couched constitute an obstacle to be overcome, similar to the kinds of obstacles that require to be overcome in earlier comedies such as *The Comedy of Errors*, *The Two Gentlemen of Verona*, *The Taming of the Shrew* or *A Midsummer Night's Dream*. The *content* might be slightly different in each case, and in this instance explicitly politically charged, but the *form* is common to the majority of Shakespeare's comedies.

What makes *Love's Labour's Lost* exceptional is that the comic impediment to a satisfactory resolution involves not just a violation of a 'natural' order in which events take place in an appropriate time, but a political embassy that at one level brings natural time into direct conflict with seasonal time. In other words, the link between nature and society that Navarre's oath threatens to destroy is precisely what the comic action seeks to restore. The embassy of the Princess of France is politically as well as biologically necessary, as Berowne observes:

> This article, my liege, yourself must break,
> For well you know here comes in embassy
> The French king's daughter with yourself to speak –
> A maid of grace and complete majesty –
> About surrender up of Aquitaine
> To her decrepit, sick and bedrid father.
> Therefore this article is made in vain.
>
> (1.1.131–8)

The immediate threat that the oath poses is to political diplomacy, but more seriously, it poses a risk to language itself. Forswearing such an oath would effectively undermine all those social rituals that depend upon sincerity, veracity and integrity, and that comprise the bedrock of posterity. The play's sub-plot, with Costard's having impregnated the maidservant Jaquenetta, and the Spaniard Don Armado's bizarre courtship, underscores and illuminates Navarre's 'unnatural' enterprise, while at the same time indicating that 'love's labours' rely on the very linguistic stability and sexual interaction that the oath undermines. When oaths are forsworn, courtship – indeed, communication – becomes impossible, and the comic resolution that should be the appropriate conclusion to the labours of love cannot be completed. The narrative conclusion to the play offers a seasonal and provisional 'natural' alternative, imposed upon the mendacious King and his lords, whose conditions, as Berowne ruefully observes, render the process 'too long for a play' (5.2.866).

What is broken symptomatically in this play is what John Kerrigan has identified as the 'binding language' of oaths, that orderly link between narrative and reality that in *Hamlet* along with 'antiquity' and 'custom' comprises 'the ratifiers and props of every word' (4.5.105). In *Love's Labour's Lost* the form's reluctance to sanction a comic resolution demands that the dramatist search for an alternative, one that can survive in the face of an embassy of death that enters personified into the final scene in the form of the messenger Marcadé. The concluding songs of Ver and Hiems reinforce the very seasonal rhythms of nature that it is the function of theatrical art to imitate, thereby compensating for the violation of form. Or to put the matter another way, the dramatist's violation of audience expectation reinforces comic form by pointing to the absence of an indispensable element: 'Our wooing doth not end like an old play: / Jack hath not Jill' (5.2.862–3). Berowne's pleading, however, simply provides more evidence of the need for further education *in society* that the Princess and her ladies prescribe. In the present circumstances the ladies' capitulation, which the rules of an 'old play' demand, would leave all parties subject to the anarchic ravages of time without the protection of social institutions, as the Princess observes:

> KING. Now, at the latest minute of the hour,
> Grant us your loves.
> PRINCESS. A time, methinks, too short
> To make a world-without-end bargain in.
> No, no, my lord, your grace is perjured much,
> Full of dear guiltinesss;
>
> (5.2.781–5)

This postponement of formal closure is uttered against the backdrop of the Princess's father's recent death, and the substitute ending is a kind of wager on the future resolve of the King and his lords whose temporal progress will henceforth be forced to align itself with the inexorable movements of Nature.

Love's Labour's Lost violates the conditions of the very form in which it is cast, and it does so through the invocation and satirising of different artistic forms. For example, convention has it that male lovers write sonnets to their female counterparts. The perjury which the King and his accomplices precipitate involves the oral delivery of their sonnets not to the ladies, but to each other. Set speeches that presuppose and prescribe a particular reaction elicit opposite reactions, and in figures such as Don Armado the language of courtship is comically mangled, and in the case of Costard undermined. But neither the absence of closure nor the various registers in which it might be accomplished clearly remained an issue for Shakespeare; indeed, in plays like *Romeo and Juliet* there is no happy resolution and lovers die, whereas in *A Midsummer Night's Dream*, which answers the ending of *Love's Labour's Lost* directly, 'Jack' *does* get 'Jill' after all obstacles, supernatural and parental, are overcome.

Henry Woudhuysen brusquely glosses over the critical debate over the stimulus for *Love's Labour's Lost* in the group known as 'the School of Night', which Navarre's little academe is thought to resemble. Of course, 'reality' drifts in and out of the play, and Woudhuysen is right to emphasise the flaws in the representational power of language as they emerge. He glosses the exchange that contains Navarre's heraldic reference to 'the School of Night' (4.3.251) as an indication that

> Language cannot express the thing itself, only an image of it: words are approximate counters, convenient signs whose meaning is socially constructed.[19]

What Woudhuysen means by 'the thing itself', as distinct from the language of which it is thought to be 'an image', raises some fundamental epistemological questions. Indeed, Berowne's 'Henceforth my wooing shall be expressed / In russet yeas and honest kersey noes' (5.2.412–13) suggests that Woudhuysen may be inaccurate here, but even the character's clear intention here is undermined by the residual formality of what follows: 'My love to thee is sound, *sans* crack or flaw' (4.3.415). In short, Berowne is unable to shake himself free of all of the formal literary requirements of the lover's discourse. Thus, while the play may include 'approximate counters', as the dramatic characters edge towards representing their experiences, and while it is itself a fabrication consisting of a variety of forms, it attempts in different ways to represent and to advocate a stable 'reality' that, in its own terms, is material insofar as it has material effects. And that advances alongside another, more linguistically inflected, debate about the materiality of language itself that is conducted in laboriously grammatical and rhetorical terms by the pedant Holofernes and Sir Nathaniel.[20]

Love's Labour's Lost interrogates the problem of form, and it does so from within a vocabulary and a discourse of forms that Shakespeare is able to draw on. 'Old plays' provide some of the resources into which Shakespeare manoeuvres particular segments of actual experience. He does this with 'history' in the two tetralogies, in which historical 'fact' is shaped into a causal pattern that is used to explain the trajectory of present time. To this extent, scripts are composed of formal elements that are used to shape, to comment upon, to subvert particular kinds of expression, thereby, in the case of a play like *Love's Labour's Lost*, bringing the domesticity of comedy into contact with larger political questions of national diplomacy, or indeed, of the impetus to historiography. Indeed, these political questions impinge directly on issues of gender in that the Princess and her ladies turn out to be the repositories of power in a society that is nominally patriarchal. This proliferation of forms, and the variations that they embody, intensifies as Shakespeare's own craft develops, and we can, perhaps, see this clearly in his deployment of something like revenge as a structuring motif.

Since the appearance of Fredson Bowers's influential book *Elizabethan Revenge Tragedy 1587–1642* (1940), the stage representations of the act of revenge and its consequences have been aligned with questions of law and the general structure of society. Sir Francis Bacon's famous observation that 'Revenge is a kind of wild justice' is followed by the insistence that: 'For as for the first wrong, it doth but offend the law; but the revenge of that wrong putteth the law out of office.' Bacon continues:

> The most tolerable sort of revenge is for those wrongs which there is no law to remedy; but then let a man take heed the revenge be such as there is no law to punish; else a man's enemy is still before hand, and it is two for one.[21]

He goes on to distinguish between two types of revenge: 'public revenges', which he considers 'are for the most part fortunate', and 'private revenges' that may well have unfortunate consequences.[22] For Bowers, concerned much more with a historical taxonomy of revenge, the origins of revenge lay in the 'vendetta' that emanated from 'the barbarous and unrestricted blood-feud among savage races which lack social machinery for the determination of blood guilt', on the one hand, and on the other 'the personal restricted vendetta marked by the contraction of collective and hereditary punishment'.[23] According to Bowers, revenge is 'extra-legal because there are no laws dealing with it', although its limits are prescribed.[24] He proceeds to tease out the relationship between revenge and what stimulated it, and the law within which an act such as murder attracted 'state punishment'.[25] John Kerrigan has sought to connect the ancient observation of the intrinsic theatricality of the law with forensic rhetoric, but he attributes the longevity of revenge tragedies 'beyond the epoch of their production' to

> retributive attitudes [that] are modified when they enter the realm of law. But they are also machines for producing ethical deadlock: moments of trial within and beyond character in which rhetoric is, in the liveliest sense, an agent of action ... There is no inconsistency in thinking of revenge tragedy as being, to a unique degree, founded in the energies of action and in associating it with some of the most copious, patterned writing of the classical and Renaissance periods.[26]

He goes on to invoke Emrys Jones's suggestion that 'the Roman revenge plays, *Titus Andronicus* and *Julius Caesar*, were influenced by Latin versions of Euripides' *Hecuba* and *Iphigenia in Aulis*', and Louise Schleiner's essay which argues that '*Hamlet* is indebted to one of the Latin translations of the *Orestes* available during the sixteenth century, and that the play is partly based on Jean de Saint-Ravy's Latin rendering of the two-part redaction of *The Oresteia* which was standard in the sixteen century'.[27] Schleiner is very cautious in her formulations, observing that scholarly authorities comparing Greek and Shakespearean tragedy 'have not claimed influence but traced coincidental parallels'.[28] Her cautious argument is prefaced with 'seems' and 'may' as part of the detailed account of likely or possible parallels, and she reverts to Bullough's terms 'sources' and 'analogues', culminating in her account of the churchyard scene in *Hamlet* as either 'sheer invention' or the result of a hitherto unidentified source/analogue since Shakespeare 'seldom sheerly invented anything in the way of plot'.[29]

These additions to the rapidly growing list of 'sources' tend to assume a direct – though sometimes circumstantial – connection between texts, whereas circulation of various models in a variety of ways seems just as likely. What is remarkable is the level of detail that appears to have been habitually sedimented in the minds of writers whose memories were honed to retain such information, whether it was by word of mouth, casual reference, professional discussion, by reading or all of these. The theoretical model that Schleiner deploys is that of a somewhat garbled Kristevan intertextuality that owes as much to Harold Bloom as it does to Kristeva.[30] It is clear that this large list of texts provided models upon which dramatists could draw, in the form of piecemeal cultural inheritance as opposed to being the products of careful print-based literary research. A modern analogue might be the Western film, an increasingly sophisticated fiction that is endlessly open to revision, adaptation and appropriation and that can accommodate a range of issues. Since the 1950s it has managed, like the novel form, to assimilate elements of Shakespeare plots and narratives into its aegis as well as being able to address a range of contemporary political concerns. Indeed, it is the Western that has been most consistent in its appropriation of the structural form of revenge and its association with lawlessness, and the violence generated by a frontier existence. Here, as in the case of revenge tragedy, Kerrigan's 'machines for producing ethical deadlock' continue to thrive, and have migrated further to TV detective series and mafia narratives.

Shakespeare had already begun to experiment with the form and the various memes of revenge tragedy in *Titus Andronicus*, and in the First Tetralogy of History Plays. The most popular and readily available theatrical model was, of course, Thomas Kyd's *The Spanish Tragedy*, thought to have first been performed in 1587, which itself owed much to the classical models that were available at the time. These models were available in print and were used in the secondary education system, but they also circulated in oral form, initially through theatrical performance and further through the collective memories of substantially non-literate popular audiences. *Titus Andronicus* conforms to the conditions laid down by Bacon. Titus is the defender of a Rome that is pathologically violent but relatively civilised compared to the Gothic enemy who, in the form of Tamora, her sons, and her accomplice Aaron, transform it into 'a wilderness of tigers' (3.1.54).[31] When he pleads for his two wrongly convicted sons Quintus and Martius, Titus reminds the judges and senators of his services to Rome:

> Hear me, grave fathers; noble tribunes, stay!
> For pity of mine age, whose youth was spent

In dangerous wars whilst you securely slept;
For all my blood in Rome's great quarrel shed,
For all the frosty nights that I have watched,
And for these bitter tears which now you see
Filling the aged wrinkles in my cheeks,
Be pitiful to my condemned sons,
Whose souls is not corrupted as 'tis thought.

(3.1.1–9)

The stage direction at l. 12 is '*Andronicus lieth down and the Judges pass him by*', and when his son Lucius enters, he reinforces Titus's isolation from the very law that he has laboured to sustain: 'The tribunes hear you not, no man is by, / And you recount your sorrows to a stone' (3.1.28–9). As the horrors mount, authorised indirectly by the very emperor, Saturninus, whom Titus was instrumental in installing, so the latter is forced to resort to Gothic violence in order to seek redress, but not before these experiences have driven him to a madness precipitated by extreme grief. Jonathan Bate has suggested that 'anger' and 'the fate of Lichas at the hands of Hercules (Alcides)', referred to in *The Merchant of Venice*, 'serves as a paradigm for the anger that both Antony and Cleopatra vent upon hapless messengers'.[32] Bate goes on to link 'the idea of destructive *furor*' to Seneca's *Hercules Oeteus* and *Hercules Furens*,[33] although he says nothing about the difference in motivation between Seneca's protagonists and Shakespeare's. Indeed, the difference between the two is that in Seneca's case it is the gods who motivate Hercules/Alcides's 'furor', whereas in Shakespeare, from *Titus Andronicus* onwards, the temperament is contingent upon secular, political and social motivations. The Thyestian banquet Titus prepares for Saturninus and Tamora after having tortured and killed her two sons compares with the worst of Aaron's or Demetrius and Chiron's violence, but not before Tamora and her sons impersonate 'Revenge' and 'Rapine and Murder' before Titus:

Know, thou sad man, I am not Tamora:
She is thy enemy and I thy friend.
I am Revenge, sent from th'infernal kingdom
To ease the gnawing vulture of thy mind
By working wreakful vengeance on thy foes.
Come down and welcome me to this world's light,

> Confer with me of murder and of death.
> There's not a hollow cave or lurking place,
> No vast obscurity or misty vale
> Where bloody murder or detested rape
> Can couch for fear, but I will find them out,
> And in their ears tell them my dreadful name,
> Revenge, which makes the foul offender quake.
>
> (5.2.28–40)

This geographical location of what is, in reality, a psychological landscape, is mapped out in terms of an audacious allegory, in which the criminal Tamora and her sons fabricate what they take to be a narrative closure that is fitting for Titus's 'lunacy' (5.2.70). Perhaps even further, whereas the Ghost of Revenge and Don Andrea in *The Spanish Tragedy* are generated by earthly forces, Shakespeare here produces an even more self-conscious version of a familiar model where the motivation is generated not by the gods but by the play's contingently fabricated plot. Of course, Titus is not fooled into believing in the 'reality' of the pageant, and he beats Tamora at her own game, but her diagnosis of his state of mind is accurate. To this extent Shakespeare references Kyd's *The Spanish Tragedy* where the failure of the law to punish wrongdoing drives Hieronimo to distraction. But there is much more going on in this scene, where both parties are involved in what Jacques Derrida would call 'the feint and trickery':[34] Tamora seeks to feign the identity of Revenge in order to trick Titus, but he recognises her and formulates a counter-plan that exceeds in sophistication the animalistic fury that is associated with the actions of revenge. But here, the human chooses to behave like an animal driven by a somatic energy that under normal circumstances the law would be expected to hold in check. Thus, we can see that already in this play Shakespeare is engaged in a refashioning of the resources available to him, and in adapting existing theatrical models. Indeed, despite what might be seen as the constraints of structure, the treatment of revenge in *Titus Andronicus* demonstrates an element of 'play', in which the representation is embedded in a process of signification that is enabling in its effects. We shall see how enabling the form is in plays that rethink and develop revenge as a driving motif.

We might observe from Shakespeare's plays that revenge can be both a structuring motif, and a relatively casual element in the representation of human interactions. For example, in a comedy that has caused critics some anxiety, *Twelfth Night* (*c*.1601), the sub-plot that begins as a challenge to Malvolio's puritanical restraints on Olivia's household generates a festive counter-movement that begins with Malvolio's put-down of Feste, the clown:

> I marvel your ladyship takes delight in such a barren rascal. I saw him put down the other day with an ordinary fool that has no more brain than a stone. Look you now, he's out of his guard already. Unless you laugh and minister occasion to him, he is gagged. I protest I take these wise men that crow so at these set kind of fools no better than the fools' zanies.
>
> (1.5.79–85)[35]

This provokes the subsequent gulling of Malvolio, and his incarceration, and leads to his asking: 'Why have you suffered me to be imprisoned, / Kept in a dark house, visited by the priest, / and made the most notorious geck and gull / That e'er invention played on!' (5.1.334–8). Fabian reveals the sub-plot, but it is Feste who discloses the motivation and reprises Malvolio's own utterances:

> Why, 'Some are born great, some achieve greatness and some have greatness thrown upon them.' I was one, sir, in this interlude, one Sir Topas, sir, but that's all one. 'By the Lord, fool, I am not mad.' But do you remember, 'Madam, why laugh you at such a barren rascal, an you smile not he is gagged'? And thus the whirligig of time brings in its revenges.
>
> (5.1.364–70)

Malvolio's prescient response, 'I'll be revenged on the whole pack of you!' (5.1.371), inaugurates a cycle of retributory violence that is frighteningly open-ended and that it is doubtful whether Orsino's placatory comments can assuage. Thus, part of the play's festive ethos turns out to be the revenge of time upon the restrictive practices of household management, and the play suggests that this tension is perennial and can only be attenuated by a 'feast of fools' that is both necessary and that is capable of inaugurating a continuous backlash for which generosity of spirit may never be able to compensate.

Revenge crops up briefly in the aftermath of Caesar's assassination in *Julius Caesar*, and is motivated by political difference, but the play that is the most extended meditation on revenge is, of course, *Hamlet*. The play's structure has much in common with Aeschylus's *Agamemnon*: the father killed by his wife's lover, and the son's quest for revenge. But by the end of the sixteenth century this structure had become complicated to the extent that it could be adapted to contain a variety of accretions. While *Titus Andronicus* follows, and innovates upon, the pattern etched out by Kyd, and amalgamates some of its concerns with modified elements of Senecan tragedy, *Hamlet* enters into dialogue with what had become the revenge genre, complicating it by the innovation of an ambiguously motivated regicide that the dead king's son is ordered by the ghost of his father to revenge.

Unlike Kyd's play where the Ghost of Revenge sits above the action, and whose influence on the specifics of plot is made to seem partial, and only occasionally explicit, the Ghost of Old Hamlet is ubiquitous, and his influence on the action is directed through the oaths, doubts and actions of Hamlet himself. *Hamlet* is a play in which the revenger is given a task by a ghost whose identity is in doubt. Stephen Greenblatt has observed that the place of Purgatory from which the ghost of Hamlet's father comes, is treated derisorily in John Foxe's pamphlet *A Supplication for The Beggars* that mocks Sir Thomas More's account of it, and that contradictions laughed away in Foxe's text 'helped make Shakespeare's tragedy possible'.[36] In one sense, Greenblatt is implying a dynamic source for the play, claiming that Foxe made possible a transformation that resulted from 'a violent ideological struggle that turned negotiations with the dead from an institutional process governed by the church, to a poetic process governed by guilt, projection, and imagination'.[37] That the concept of Purgatory should be the basis of 'a violent ideological struggle' during the period is not in doubt, but what Greenblatt misses is the connection between 'suffering and trial' that according to Jacques Le Goff deprives its inhabitants 'of true joy'.[38] Le Goff cites Dante's Pope Adrian V, who observes that the dwellers in Purgatory are compelled to look earthwards by the force of 'justice':

We would not raise our eyes to the shining spheres
But kept them turned to mundane things: so Justice
Bends them to earth here in this place of tears.[39]

For Dante, even in the eschatological space of Purgatory the focus is directed earthwards to the operations of the law and justice. Thus, the inhabitants of Purgatory, contrary to Greenblatt's claim, remain straddled between divine and earthly judgement, where the latter may be open, as Shakespeare's Claudius well knows, to manipulation. Old Hamlet is terrified by the prospect of facing divine judgement 'Unhouseled. Disappointed, unaneled, / No reckoning made but sent to my account / With all my imperfections on my head' (1.5.77–9), while in 'the corrupted currents of this world',

> Offence's gilded hand may shove by justice.
> And oft 'tis seen the wicked prize itself
> Buys out the law; but 'tis not so above:
> There is no shuffling, there the action lies
> In his true nature, and we ourselves compelled
> Even to the teeth and forehead of our faults
> To give in evidence.
>   (3.3.57–64)

Hamlet's enquiry is much wider, of course, but the play accepts no fundamental distinction between the eschatological discourse of Purgatory where the experience of existence is essentially bifurcated and riven with anxiety, and the 'poetry' that, it is claimed, leaves that existence behind. Old Hamlet, Hamlet and Claudius are all caught in the contradictions between the physical, the spiritual and the emotional domains to which the existence of Purgatory draws attention, and that are articulated paradoxically in the higher discourse of poetry.

These important nuances are concentrated in the paradigm of revenge and on the series of comparisons and contrasts that *Hamlet* generates. In one sense Shakespeare's play is a 'memory' play, recalling earlier versions of the narrative, and earlier versions of the paradigm, but also inscribing memory and its temporal scaffolding in the gesture of revenge. That the Ghost's origins are initially questionable does not divest it of the larger judicial con-text in which it is embedded. And it is Bacon's distinction between 'public' and 'private' revenge that permeates the play's dialectic. When the Ghost speaks, he tells how he was poisoned through the ears: 'Thy uncle stole / With juice of cursed hebona in a vial / And in the porches of my ears did pour / the leperous distilment' (1.5.61–4). Editors have failed to identify the nature of the poison referred to here, but its symbolic value is not lost on the Ghost, who explodes the public rumour of his death: 'So the whole ear of Denmark / Is by a forged process of my death / Rankly abused' (1.5.36–8). This is the first critical reference to Claudius's 'process', later to have added to it the possessive and adjectival '*our sovereign* process' (4.3.61, my italics).[40] The poisoning through the ear, and the forgetfulness thereby induced in 'the whole ear of Denmark', represents an attack on the continuous present that incorporates the past into itself associated with the ways in which an oral culture negotiates between past and present, and that a Claudian proto-literary 'rewriting' seeks to eliminate. In *Hamlet*, revenge not only demands a recollection of the past but it also demands public justice for the regicide secreted in its narrative. The Ghost does not tell Hamlet *how* to exact revenge, but he does place conditions upon the act:

> But howsomever thou pursuest this act
> Taint not thy mind nor let thy soul contrive
> Against thy mother aught; leave her to heaven
> And to the thorns that in her bosom lodge
> To prick and sting her.
>
> (1.5.84–8)

It is for Hamlet himself to work through the process and to find a way that will reunite the oral faculty that is the prime means of understanding, and the public action that is appropriate to it. This is the first provisional explanation of the delay in action where the task itself reveals a gap between representation, thought and action that reverberates in the psyche of the eponymous hero.

What follows is a series of father–son relationships where the father is killed and the son (or in the case of Fortinbras, the nephew) is placed in the position of revenger, although no restraint is placed upon him. *Hamlet* begins with news of the invasion of young Fortinbras, whose military ethic appears not quite to resemble that of his father, Old Norway, but who seems bent on revenge (and

From formula to text 269

the repossession of land) in compensation for his father's death. Horatio's long and necessary account of the Old Hamlet–Norway encounter is crucial in order to establish the respect that both chivalric leaders had for the fundamental link between the recording of a military agreement and their personal confirmation of its performative substance through engagement in action and its consequences, but also to provide a political framework for it. At the end of the play this event is recuperated as a means of sustaining Fortinbras's dubious claim to have 'some rights of memory in this kingdom / Which now to claim my vantage doth invite me' (5.2.373–4). What this 'memory' is and exactly how it is linked to the act of revenge is never made explicit in the play, although Fortinbras appears twice before this, once as the manifestation of a political challenge to Claudius's rule, and then later as an exemplar of 'action' in pursuit of something materially insignificant but linked directly to 'honour', which exposes in Hamlet the emotions that are directly connected with the act of revenge:

> Rightly to be great
> Is not to stir without great argument
> But greatly to find quarrel in a straw
> When honour's at the stake. How stand I then
> That have a father killed, a mother stained,
> Excitements of my reason and my blood,
> And let all sleep; while to my shame I see
> The imminent death of twenty thousand men
> That for a fantasy and trick of fame
> Go to their graves like beds, fight for a plot
> Whereon the numbers cannot try the cause,
> Which is not tomb enough and continent
> To hide the slain?
>
> (4.4.55–64)

Thus, while revenge may at times appear in general to be a spontaneous act of passion, here it is a part of a much more complex discourse that traverses the ethical terrain in which honour is embedded. But the action that it generates might just as easily be the product of fantasy, a trick that deludes the actor into thinking that his grave is his bed, disabling him from intuiting the true evaluation of the link between cause and effect. While Hamlet may see this as a spur to action in a purely comparative sense, it points to the complexity of his dilemma that has acted as the brake on his taking decisive action.

The second, and perhaps closer analogy is with Laertes, whose father Hamlet has 'accidentally' killed, and who returns in high dudgeon to demand the truth of his father's death. This is another incident in the play whose motivation derives from contingency *and* from an invisible force that Hamlet himself comes finally to accept as 'Providence'. The 'accidental' death of Polonius is motivated by a meddlesome, bureaucratic temperament that seeks to control events. Paradoxically, he becomes a 'councillor' whose garrulous counsel is abruptly silenced by death: he 'Is now most still, most secret and most grave, / Who was in life a foolish prating knave' (3.4.211–13). On the surface of it, Laertes's situation appears to be a carbon copy of Hamlet's, and this is certainly how it appears in the Q2-F versions of the text, where Act 5 Scene 2 begins with Hamlet's acknowledgement of a divinely over-determined 'rashness':

> And praised be rashness for it: let us know
> Our indiscretion sometime serves us well
> When our deep plots do pall; and that should learn us
> There's a divinity that shapes our ends,
> Rough hew them how we will.
>
> (5.2.7–11)

However, Act 5 Scene 2 begins in Q1 (1603) with an admission that despite the similarities, Hamlet's and Laertes's situations are different even though the intensity of their emotions is not:

> beleeue mee, it greeues mee much *Horatio*,
> That to *Laertes* I forgot myself:
> For by myself me thinkes I feele his griefe,
> Though there's a difference in each others wrong.
>
> (sig. I2ʳ)

Indeed, what Q1 makes explicit here, and what Q2 and the Folio appear to assume, is a form of repetition that, as Gilles Deleuze once observed, 'is never a historical fact, but rather the historical condition under which something new is effectively produced'.[41] The play offers not a proliferation of identical revengers, but distinct examples of different *kinds* of revenge. Laertes's action promises the 'wild justice' identified by Bacon, and we see earlier in the play what that amounts to:

> The ocean overpeering of his list
> Eats not the flats with more impiteous haste
> Than young Laertes in a riotous head
> O'erbears your officers. The rabble call him lord
> And, as the world were now but to begin,
> Antiquity forgot, custom not known,
> The ratifiers and props of every word
> They cry, 'Choose we: Laertes shall be king!'
>
> (4.5.99–106)

Hamlet's analysis of Claudius's polity, offered to his mother earlier at Act 3 Scene 4, is here turned on its head, since everything that the Prince has striven to uphold – indeed, even the language in which he seeks to formulate and reformulate his project – is swept away. Loosened from their moorings in 'antiquity' and 'custom', words here are mere signifiers deprived of all authority and freed from their place in any politically validated hierarchy. The point is emphasised by Claudius's fraudulent appeal to the philosophy of a divine right that he has himself already violated:

> Let him go, Gertrude, do not fear our person.
> There's such divinity doth hedge a king
> That treason can but peep to what it would,
> Acts little of his will.
>
> (4.5.122–5)

Of course, we know this to be a falsehood, since Claudius 'repeats' both the role of the monarch, and the philosophy that authenticates the office, but as in the case of Laertes, the 'historical condition' produces something new that involves the disclosure of the historical realities of power. The object of Hamlet's revenge is an authority that has perverted the law and justice, and the language that upholds political institutions. Laertes's projected revenge, which Claudius has no difficulty in co-opting, is an intention (a 'private' revenge) that is wholly without constraint, and it is this that makes him easy to manipulate. It is at moments like this in the play that it is possible to discern the revenge form and, at the same time, Shakespeare's innovative transformation of its demands.

As an indication of the extent to which the revenge form had developed by the close of the sixteenth century, it is clear that what was formally *exterior* but internally contingent in Kyd's *The Spanish Tragedy* becomes much more *interiorised* in *Hamlet*. That is to say, whereas the Ghost of Don Andrea and Revenge sit above the action and control it in Kyd's play (unbeknown to the protagonist), in Shakespeare's play the action is consciously generated from within the psychology of the protagonist who is explicitly charged with the task of formulating a plan of revenge. It is only because of the death of Horatio, his son, and the failure to secure justice from the very institution that he represents, that Hieronimo is driven to seeking extra-political means of redress. Hieronimo does not question the principle of 'action' nor does he contemplate the link between contingency and metaphysical overdetermination. In contrast, *Hamlet* questions all of these, and the providential force that determines human action is both inscrutable *and* invisible, even though Purgatory is allowed to remain as a provisional, ontologically real destination for the dead. In the face of the challenge that the politically efficacious Claudius poses – he is acknowledged as a 'mighty opposite' – Hamlet interiorises and scrutinises the task he is given, and his questioning forces the delay precisely because the performative power of language itself is reduced to a kind of relativising signification. Unless Hamlet can *make* meaning, then he cannot commit himself to action. His attempts to do so result either in a literal application of the revenge code resulting in an action that is paralysed in the face of a visual encounter of Claudius at prayer, or in a feigned madness that is the displaced form of an interior turmoil. It is only after Hamlet's encounter with the pirates, and his alteration of Claudius's letter to the king of England that he comes to the conclusion that there is a hidden metaphysical design behind the most insignificant of earthly events, and that he has to wait for a suitable opportunity to take a public revenge against Claudius. Here, heroic action of the kind represented by young Fortinbras cannot proceed unless and until its inner workings have been fathomed. Of course, the price of that knowledge is a tragic encounter with the deadly poison that inhabits the material world, an encounter for which Fortinbras has the resolve to challenge. At the end of the play the faculty of memory is reinstated, and the instrument of forgetfulness, Claudius, is dispatched presumably to Purgatory where he will replace Old Hamlet's torment with his own. In the case of Gertrude, Hamlet is instructed to 'leave her to heaven' (1.5.86) and her fate ultimately remains ambiguous.

The revenge form as a meme, a paradigm and a dynamic resource, as a dramatic means of articulating a range of emotions and actions, is refined by Shakespeare, and is something to which he returns regularly. We saw how it appears in both its calculated and spontaneous forms in *Twelfth Night*, and in a play like *The Merchant of Venice* it is regarded by the 'outsider' Shylock the Jew as a distinctive feature of Christianity; there, an appeal to a universal humanity is savagely undercut by initially gesturing to superficial similarities and to a share motivation. But the sting in the tail is that this appeal is accompanied, in Shylock's case, by a mimetic gesture ('we will resemble you in that', 3.1.61) that reduces Christianity to a primary impulse to revenge:

> Hath not a Jew eyes? Hath not a Jew hands, organs, dimensions, senses, affections, passions? Fed with the same food, hurt with the same weapons, subject to the same diseases, healed by the same means, warmed and cooled by the same winter and summer as a Christian is? If you prick us do we not bleed? If you tickle us do we not laugh? If you poison us do we not die? And if you wrong us shall we not revenge? If a Jew wrong a Christian what is his humility? Revenge! If a Christian wrong a Jew, what should his sufferance be by Christian example? Why, revenge! The villainy you teach me I will execute, and it shall go hard but I will better the instruction.
>
> (3.1.53–66)

From a position of theoretical hybridity, Shylock outlines the form that revenge must take, but in the trial scene even his contingently partial literal-mindedness can be undercut. Portia/Balthazar's performative super-literalism trumps Shylock's private revenge with a public revenge whose provisos are enshrined in and validated by Venetian law. The only question here is whether this vaunted superiority is, or is not, ironical in the circumstances.

Where revenge is not the motif that forces the revenger to contemplate its ethics, it is often the result of absolute contingency. Aeschylean and Senecan revenge derives from buried superhuman origins from which they derive their driving force. Aside from a play like *Romeo and Juliet* that emulates this pattern to some extent, the Shakespearean version is one of accumulating but limited contingency, as is partly the case in *The Merchant of Venice*, which inhabits a combination of an 'ancient grudge' and limited and localised motivation. Another example is *Julius Caesar*, in which Marc Antony projects into the future the assassination of Caesar as it develops into an ancient grudge:

> A curse shall light upon the limbs of men:
> Domestic fury and fierce civil strife
> Shall cumber all the parts of Italy:
> Blood and destruction shall be so in use,
> And dreadful objects so familiar,
> That mothers shall but smile when they behold
> Their infants quartered with the hands of war:
> All pity choked with custom of fell deeds,
> And Caesar's spirit, ranging for revenge,
> With Ate by his side come hot from hell,
> Shall in these confines, with a monarch's voice,
> Cry havoc and let slip the dogs of war,
> That this foul deed shall smell above the earth
> With carrion men, groaning for burial.
>
> (3.1.262–75)

This image of political chaos surrounding the act of revenge is repeated with the entry of Laertes in *Hamlet*, and it is a stock rhetorical resource that is capable of providing a lexicon of objective and subjective effects. Shakespeare's exploration of the shapes that this resource can be moulded to fit are much more varied than is evident at first sight.

One further example of the resourcefulness with which this meme can be pressed into service is *Othello* (c.1604). Attempts have been made to squeeze this early Jacobean play into the form of comedy, based on what has been taken to be its 'domestic' content. A.C. Bradley hinted at it in his observation that the atmosphere of *Othello* produces 'those feelings of oppression, of confinement to a comparatively narrow world, and of dark fatality which haunts us'.[42] Bradley had already observed the play's focus on Othello's sexual jealousy that 'converts human nature into chaos, and liberates the beast in man'; he asks:

> What spectacle can be more painful that that of this feeling turned into a tortured mixture of longing and loathing, the 'golden purity' of passion split by poison into fragments, the animal in man forcing itself into his consciousness in naked grossness, and he writhing before it but powerless to deny it entrance, gasping inarticulate images of pollution, and finding relief only in a bestial thirst for blood?[43]

A.D. Nuttall takes Bradley's observations about the focus of *Othello* to an odd conclusion in linking it with 'domestic tragedy', suggesting that the play's 'bathetic domesticity', first noted by Thomas Rhymer in 1693, points to the conclusion that

> Othello's tragedy indeed is strangely – and formally – introverted; it consists in the fact that he left the arena proper to tragedy, the battlefield, and entered a sub-tragic world for which he was not fitted. *Othello* is the story of a hero who went into a house.[44]

What Bradley partially grasps, but what Nuttall overlooks, is the manner in which Othello's sexual jealousy leads to the perversion of a form that Shakespeare has done much, thus far, to establish in its many ramifications: revenge. The play never establishes clearly the reason for Iago's animosity towards Othello beyond the claim that he has been passed over for promotion. Here is the ethos of 'renown and *ressentiment*' that John Kerrigan has ascribed to Elizabethan revenge tragedy,[45] but it is not until Act 3, and after Iago has road-tested his methods, first on Brabantio and then on Cassio, that he approaches Othello. This is, formally speaking, a repetition but with a difference, and its effect on a hero who is a 'split' subjectivity (black *and* white) but who makes judgements that are paradoxically based on a restricted empirical outlook, is devastating in its effects:

> Look here, Iago,
> All my fond love thus do I blow to heaven:
> 'Tis gone!
> Arise black vengeance, from the hollow hell,

> Yield up, O love, thy crown and hearted throne
> To tyrannous hate! Swell, bosom, with thy fraught,
> For 'tis of aspics' tongues.
>
> (3.3.447–53)[46]

This reversion to a pattern of revenge that is more implicit than garrulously explicit in *Hamlet* is pressed even further here as Othello asserts that 'my bloody thoughts with violent pace / Shall ne'er look back / To humble love / Till that a capable and wide revenge / Swallow them up' (3.3.460–3). The problem with this is that the audience is fully aware, as it has been from the start, that Othello has no grounds for revenge, and the tragedy is emphatically *not*, as A.D. Nuttall would have it, that of a hero who went into a house. It is that he is persuaded to espouse a fantasy that the misogynistic and misanthropic Iago has constructed for him, and that is sufficiently plausible to have a wider social appeal. Indeed, even at the point at which he is about to carry out his revenge Othello cannot name its cause even though he is convinced of its truth:

> It is the cause, it is the cause, my soul!
> Let me not name it to you, you chaste stars,
> It is the cause. Yet I'll not shed her blood
> Nor scar that whiter skin of hers than snow
> And smooth as monumental alabaster:
> Yet she must die, else she'll betray more men.
>
> (5.2.1–6)

Hamlet, as we have seen, labours to align word with deed, language with action where the two have been separated by a regicide that removes custom and antiquity from their roles in establishing the veracity of language. In contrast, Othello accepts – as Roderigo, Brabantio and finally Cassio have been persuaded to do – a radical revision of the link between word, object and action, and the result is catastrophic both at the subjective level *and* at the political level where Othello's suicide is acted out as a battle between Venetian and Turk. To those who are persuaded that in this play love is domestic, Othello's suicide should provide convincing evidence that the politics of the *oikos* reflects in miniature the political battle between Venetians and Turks, and that Cyprus provides a necessary con-text within whose aegis Venetian domestic politics requires to be read. We will return to *Othello* in Chapter 7 since the play also demonstrates the malleable use of resource.

King Lear (*c*.1605) offers another interesting example of Shakespeare's use of resources. The play returns to the kind of historical topic that Shakespeare was attracted to in *Hamlet*, and would again be attracted to in *Macbeth* (*c*.1606). Bullough speculates that King Lear 'may have been a creature of Celtic legend',[47] and if so, it raises the question of how this legendary figure escaped from its mythical guise and was transmitted down the ages to the beginning of the seventeenth century and beyond. Catherine Belsey has suggested that the transportability of these narratives can be attributed to the possibility that 'Shakespeare's plays retell these traditional fables with a difference and, in doing so they strike a chord with successive audiences, much as they must have done in their own period'.[48] She goes on to speculate: 'Perhaps, then, the adaptability of Shakespeare echoes the renewability of the fairy tales he reinscribes.'[49] The phrase 'with a difference' reserves for Shakespeare a residual 'singularity' that is important, since the thoughtless relativism that Belsey believes has infected the study of Shakespeare has been in danger of throwing the baby out with the bathwater. Indeed, to redistribute the elements of the Shakespearean text in such a way that it strips him of an authorial identity, is to de-historicise the concept of authorship as it was understood in the early modern period, and to obscure, if not efface completely, the playwright's role in adapting, appropriating, synthesising and creatively transforming particular narratives and the forms in which they circulated. *Hamlet* synthesises a narrative that appears in prose and in the theatre, whereas *King Lear* extends the process insofar as the Lear narrative was available in different forms prior to Shakespeare's version: legend, poetry, prose fiction, historical narrative and drama. It is difficult to determine how many of these forms were active at any one time, just as it is not easy to be certain in what forms Shakespeare may have read or otherwise encountered the story. Nevertheless, and despite Bullough's caution in labelling these various narratives, he is certain that *The True Chronicle Historie of King Leir and his three daughters*, an anonymous play published in 1605, is a 'source' for Shakespeare's *King Lear*, and that it had a long pedigree. My concern is not to disprove Bullough's claim, but to look more closely at the *form* of the anonymous play and to attempt to calculate the level of Shakespeare's innovative approach to a narrative that was already available in a number of versions.

The *True Chronicle Historie of King Leir* is a history play that begins with a royal dilemma: Lear's '(too late) deceast and dearest Queen'[50] has deprived the King of necessary feminine advice: 'For fathers best do know to governe sonnes; / But daughters steps the mothers counsel turnes' (1.[1]19–20). What in the earlier *Mirror for Magistrates* (1574) had been a verse 'story tragicall' narrated in the voice of Cordilla,[51] is recast in the anonymous play as the initial misfortune of Leir's not having had a male 'heyre indubitate' (l. 44). Cordella's failure to participate fully in the game her father has devised results in his disowning of her as a 'bastard Impe, no issue of King *Leir*' (3.311), an appellation that in Shakespeare's play is transferred to the Gloucester sub-plot, and to Edmund. What initially is Cordella's 'tragic tale of my unhappy youth' (7.645) becomes a heroic narrative of the repossession of Leir's kingdom and the restoration of his 'kingly title' (25.2644), along with the defeat of the evil forces of Gonorill and Ragan. Leir duly hands his crown to Cordella, who becomes queen, disinheriting and disowning Gonorill and Ragan in favour of Cordella and the King of Gallia with whom he plans to 'Repose ... awhile, and then for Fraunce' (25.2663). This happy ending in which due credit is given both to his supporters and to the 'heavens' diminishes the narrative's tragic potential, which in other contemporary versions of the story is projected onto the defeated and imprisoned Cordella, who despairs and commits suicide.

In the anonymous play the potential for tragedy is averted in favour of a moralistic, 'fairy-tale' conclusion in which the bad are punished and the good rewarded. The play also dramatises the consequences of a divided kingdom, in which the ensuing chaos is the product of Leir's lack of a male heir. The Gallian king supplies that deficiency as the necessary military support for Queen Cordella, and as the guarantee of peace. But what in this version reduces the play's potentially tragic impact serves to emphasise it in Shakespeare's version of the story.

King Lear (*c*.1605) is a tragedy that draws together a number of threads that are present across a range of Shakespeare's plays.

Lear's tragic error in misjudging his daughters initiates an action in the Aristotelian sense of the term, and the seemingly unpreventable death of Cordelia, along with that of Lear himself, completes it. Throughout the Comedies, and particularly in *Hamlet*, series of overlapping plots are used to expand, comment on and sometimes invert the central narrative, and the double plot involving the parallel fortunes of Lear and Gloucester is characteristic of this strategy. The Gloucester sub-plot, whose 'source' Bullough confidently identifies in *The Countesse of Pembroke's Arcadia* (c.1580),[52] translates into a brutal physicality something that is also metaphorical in the fortunes of Lear. Gloucester has a bastard son, and Lear disowns Cordelia, although the appellation of 'bastard', a feature of the anonymous *Leir* is not repeated. The practical disempowerment of Lear, and the stripping away of his authority and public identity, produces in this case a clearly motivated subjective 'madness' at the same time that it provokes an opportunistic, although inarticulate, 'revenge':

> You see me here, you gods, a poor old man,
> As full of grief as age, wretched in both:
> If it be you that stirs these daughters' hearts
> Against their father, fool me not so much
> To bear it tamely; touch me with noble anger,
> And let not women's weapons, water-drops,
> Stain my man's cheeks. No, you unnatural hags,
> I will have such revenges on you both
> That all the world shall – I will do such things –
> What they are yet I know not, but they shall be
> The terrors of the earth!
>
> (2.2.461–72)[53]

The collapse of the blank verse here directly reflects the collapse into disorder of Lear's mind, and as the Arden 3 editor of the play, R.A. Foakes, indicates, the call is 'for anger appropriate to a male greatness of mind, but it evaporates in the empty and absurd flourish of unimaginable revenges'.[54] This sustained tirade and its extended psychological aftermath expands considerably the perfunctory expression of remorse in the anonymous *Leir* where the unselfconscious king promptly dispossesses himself of his power and authority: 'And here I do freely dispossess my selfe, / And make you two my true adopted heyres' (6.553–4). His daughters' rejection follows some three scenes later, and prompts an equally perfunctory response from a now self-pitying rather than fully introspective Leir:

> This punishment my heavy sinnes deserve,
> And more then this ten thousand times:
> Else aged *Leir* them could never find
> Cruell to him, to whom he hath bin kind.
> Why do I over-live my selfe, to see
> The course of nature quite reverst in me?
> Ah, gentle Death, if ever any wight
> Did wish thy presence with a perfit zeale:
> Then come, my sorrowes with thy fatall dart.
>
> (10.856–66)

Lear's mental torture receives extended treatment in Shakespeare's play, and his reconciliation with Cordelia comes much later than in the anonymous *Leir*.

The True Chronicle Historie of King Leir was performed throughout the 1590s and appeared in print in 1605. Sir Philip Sidney's *The Countess of Pembroke's Arcadia*, which was first published *c.*1580 and in some thirteen editions subsequently, contains a prose version of the Gloucester sub-plot in Shakespeare's play, while its narrative structure echoes elements of the anonymous apocryphal play *Mucedorus*, also popular during the 1590s and published in 1598, which came into the possession of the King's Men in 1610. Sidney's version is set in Gallatia (the king of Gallia appears as Cordella's suitor and future husband in the anonymous *Leir*), and Pyrocles's chivalric companion in Sidney's version is 'Musidorus'. It is clear that by 1611, the presumed year of the performance of *The Winter's Tale*, the stage direction '*Exit, pursued by a bear*' (3.3.57) was an appropriation of the *Mucedorus* stage direction '*Enter Segasto running and Amadine after him, being persued with a beare*',[55] stripped of its context and simply used as a limited plot device. The publication of *King Leir* in 1605, the continued popularity of Sidney's *Arcadia*, the appearance in print of the *Mucedorus*, added to which are the various other aspects of a traditional *Leir* narrative, testify to the ubiquity of a story various aspects of whose form could be moulded into a tragedy. Moreover, the idea of a king who foolishly *divides* his kingdom between two of his three daughters reverses, not without some risk, an extra-theatrical event in which the accession to the throne of the new King James had *united* the kingdoms of England, Wales and Scotland. Also, whereas in *King Leir* Cordella is 'bastardised', it is unlikely that a similar transformation of Cordelia would have been anything other than a risk in Shakespeare's play, given that Elizabeth had been dead only some two years. While we could not, of course, describe *King Lear* as a comedy gone wrong, some of its elements share a domestic concern with other plays in the Shakespeare canon. Thus, Shakespeare appears to have been surrounded by a range of formulaic narratives that he could adapt, ranging from prose chronicles, other plays in the company's repertory, and fiction and poetry. We have only circumstantial evidence to suggest that he actually read what was available in print, although it is more likely that he accessed parts of this material by a combination of means.

One possible avenue to pursue might be the printer James Roberts, who printed a number of the plays and to whose outputs it would be reasonable to assume that the King's Men, if not Shakespeare himself, might have had access. Roberts was responsible for the printing of *The Merchant of Venice* in 1600, and Thompson and Taylor confirm that he printed Q2 *Hamlet* for the publisher Nicholas Ling.[56] In an influential essay entitled 'Shakespeare and the exorcists', Stephen Greenblatt reiterates what since the eighteenth century had become commonplace, 'that Shakespeare was reading Harsnett's book, *A Declaration of Egregious Popish Impostures* as he was writing *King Lear*'.[57] Harsnett's account was printed in 1603 by none other than James Roberts, a year or so before he printed Q2 *Hamlet*. In his Arden 2 edition of *King Lear*, Kenneth Muir itemises what he takes to be Shakespeare's deployment of the nominal, phrasal and thematic echoes of Harsnett's text in both *Lear* and *The Tempest*. But elsewhere he observes, somewhat despairingly: 'It would doubtless be possible to trace the influence of many other books on Shakespeare's work, though the majority of these echoes may do little else than exhibit the working of his subconscious mind and the extent of his reading.'[58] Muir's list in an appendix to his edition of Shakespeare's play makes little distinction between direct quotation from Harsnett's text and language that might easily form part of a publicly accessible discourse, hence his commitment to a vision of a dramatist for whom 'reading', in the sense that we assume, was a primary activity. What we can say here is that the link between the printer James Roberts and the King's Men *may* have provided a conduit through which certain relevant texts passed, and that they may have contributed to a discussion in the playhouse that resulted in some echoes and quotations finding their way into a text such as *King Lear*. Moreover, the value that the company placed on its play-scripts may account for the fact that they survived the fire of 1613 and reappeared in the First Folio of 1623, whereas books (if indeed the company had a small library) may not have done.

Greenblatt accepts many of Muir's working assumptions, but he extends the principle of 'exchange' to the much wider practice of theatrical companies acquiring materials that possessed symbolic value *outside* the theatre. There is no doubting the ingenuity and subtlety of Greenblatt's approach, and it is indisputable that the passage from one domain to another of social practices that are claimed to be inherently theatrical (although in Harsnett's case negatively so) serve to generate new meanings. The question is, to what extent the 'confession of theatricality' that 'for Harsnett, demolishes exorcism' leads to the more general perception that theatre 'is not the disinterested expression of the popular spirit but the indelible mark of falsity, tawdriness, and rhetorical manipulation'.[59] This may have been so for Harsnett, but would a man of the theatre such as Shakespeare have 'read' Harsnett's text in the same way? Granted that Shakespeare would not have been 'disinterested', and even given the fact that the plays contain many negative references to theatre as imposture, it seems unlikely that a successful dramatist would undermine radically the very means by which he made a living. Indeed, there is evidence from within the plays that the opposite might have been the case.

Greenblatt's claim is that what an Anglican bishop charged with investigating exorcism viewed negatively, was part of a legacy upon which the Elizabethan and Jacobean stage depended for its formulae, its stereotypes, its costumes and its thematic content. He argues:

A Declaration of Egregious Popish Impostures takes pains to identify exorcism not merely with the 'theatrical' – a category that scarecely existed for Harsnett – but with the actual theatre; at issue is not so much a metaphorical concept as a functioning institution. For if Harsnett can drive exorcism into the theatre – if he can show that the stately houses in which the rituals were performed were playhouses, that the sacred garments were what he calls 'a lousy holy wardrobe' (78), that the terrifying writhings were simulations, that the uncanny signs and wonders were contemptible stage tricks, that the devils were the 'cashiered wooden-beaten' Vices from medieval drama (115), and that the exorcists were 'vagabond players, that coast from Town to Town' (149) – then the ceremony and everything for which it stands will, as far as he is concerned, be emptied out. And with this emptying out Harsnett will have driven exorcism from the center to the periphery – in the case of London quite literally to the periphery where increasingly stringent urban regulation had already driven the public playhouses.[60]

This is persuasive, but what for Harsnett can be worked up into a metaphor of Catholic subversion (and one with which the theatre itself could be expected to identify) is transformed into the fragments of a discourse whose primary aim is to identify the process of exorcism with feigned 'madness' performed before a select audience in 'at least consecrated places ... that being done publiquely, the weaker sort may have no occasion to suspect the action of fraude'.[61] Harsnett continues, 'Sure all is not well in this exorcising craft, that *iugling*, *turpitude*, and *women*, must be so precisely auoided' (original italics).[62] Edgar's claim to be beset by named devils, often dwelling in Harsnett's female subjects, is also a superstitious version of the feigned madness of Hamlet, for whom exorcism (if we can call it that) is a very different matter altogether. What we are talking about here is a vibrant, and very public discursive currency – a language that inhabits, can articulate and be applied to a wide variety of social experience, that generates its own energy and that circulates in a variety of forms available to the dramatist. What Shakespeare represents here is not necessarily what individuals might have read, but what the community that the theatre serves *is talking about*. Harsnett rehearses a series of plots against Elizabeth, including some thought to have involved

Mary, Queen of Scots, in an attempt to get to the origins of the practices of exorcism. If we add to this Harsnett's potted 'history' of the early origins of dramatic performance, then the Catholic practice of exorcism lends a fearful realism to what was otherwise regarded as an entertainment:

> It was a pretty part in the old Church-playes, when the nimble Vice would skip vp nimbly like a Iacke an Apes into the deuils necke, and ride the deuil a course, and belabour him with his wooden dagger, til he made him roare, wherat the people would laugh to see the deuil so vice-haunted. This action, & passiō had some semblance, by reason the deuil looked like a patible old *Coridon*, with a payre of ghornes on his head, & a Cowes tayle at his breech; but for a deuil to be so vice-haunted, as that he should roare, at the picture of a vice burnt in a pece of paper, especially being without his hornes, & tayle, is a passion exceeding al apprehensiō, but that our old deere mother the Romish church doth warrant it by canon. Her deuils be surely some of those old vice-haunted cassiered wooden-beaten deuils, that were wont to frequent the stages; and haue theyr hornes beaten of with *Mengus* his clubbe, and theyre tayles cut off with a smart lash of his stinging whip, who are so skared with the *Idea* of a vice, & a dagger, as they durst neuer since look a paper-vice in the face.[63]

In his account of exorcism Harsnett is a kind of revisionist source-hunter, whereas Greenblatt undertakes to analyse the cultural discourses within which a highly metaphorised socio-religious practice circulated; and beyond that, the extent to which that practice exacerbated, by an ideological distortion, that of another equally venal institution, the emerging commercial theatre.[64]

The tracing of various narrative and discursive strands in *King Lear*, and the con-texts that serve to extend the range of meanings in which the play is imbricated, provides us with a network of formulae, forms, memes, paradigms and discursive strands, all of which can be thought to be available as resources for the practising dramatist. But there is one further resource: Shakespeare's own dramatic writing and his cumulative experience as an actor and scriptwriter at the service of what was becoming a very successful theatre company. This will be the subject of the next chapter.

Notes

1. See Jonathan Bate, *How the Classics Made Shakespeare* (Princeton and Oxford, 2019), pp. 227–31, where the case is made that 'The Elizabethans were as interested in Seneca the philosopher as they were in Seneca the tragic dramatist' (p. 228).
2. See Lynn Enterline, *Shakespeare's Schoolroom: Rhetoric, Discipline, Emotion* (Philadelphia, 2012), pp. 20–1, which draws our attention to 'the exclusively rhetorical heart of the Latin schoolroom' (p. 21).
3. *Ibid.* Enterline invokes Lacan and Bourdieu as partial theoretical models in locating the 'beginnings' of what she regards as 'the Symbolic's shaping force [which] is promising for a study of early modern masculinity'.
4. See H.R.D. Andes, *Shakespeare's Books* (London, 1903), Stuart Gillespie, *Shakespeare's Books: A Dictionary of Shakespeare's Sources* (London, 2004) and also Robert S. Miola, *Shakespeare's Reading* (Oxford, 2000).
5. Sir Philip Sidney, *Arcadia*, ed. Maurice Evans (Harmondsworth, 1997), p. 9.
6. See John Drakakis, 'Shakespeare as presentist', *Shakespeare Survey*, 66 (2013), 182.
7. Peter Lake, *How Shakespeare Put Politics on the Stage* (New Haven and London, 2016), p. 215. The reference to David Womersley is to his essay 'The politics of Shakespeare's *King John*', *Review of English Studies*, 40 (1989), 497–515.
8. Carl Schmitt, *Hamlet or Hecuba: The Intrusion of Time into the Play*, trans. David Pan and Jennifer Rust (New York, 2009), pp. 16–18.
9. *Ibid.*, p. 16.
10. *Ibid.*
11. *Ibid.*, p. 17.
12. Hayden White, *The Tropics of Discourse: Essays in Cultural Criticism* (Baltimore and London, 1987), p. 122.
13. Hayden White, *The Content of the Form: Narrative Discourse and Historical Representation* (Baltimore and London, 1990), p. 169.
14. See Richard J. Evans, *In Defence of History* (reprinted, London, 2018), pp. 109–11, in which a clear distinction is made between 'sources' and 'discourses'. Evans insists: 'Discourse does not construct the past itself; the most that it is possible to argue is that it constructs our attempts to represent it' (p. 109). He then goes on to argue that 'a historical source is not the same as a literary text' (p. 110), and that in the case of

'statistical series of corn prices or criminal offences' and 'lengthy lists of individuals belonging to this or that organisation', '[t]he conventional tools of literary analysis are of little use in dealing with such materials' (p. 111).

15 See Schmitt, *Hamlet or Hecuba*, pp. 48–9.
16 White, *The Content of the Form*, pp. 169–70.
17 William Shakespeare, *Love's Labour's Lost*, ed. Henry Woudhuysen, Arden 3 series (London, 1998).
18 *Ibid.*, p. 117, ll. 72 and 84–5.
19 *Ibid.*, p. 26.
20 See Margaret Tudeau-Clayton, *Shakespeare's Englishes: Against Englishness* (Cambridge, 2020), p. 140, where the figure of Holofernes is thought to embody 'extravagance' and is consequently 'full of' diverse 'forms'.
21 Francis Bacon, 'Revenge', in *Essays or Counsels Civil and Moral* (London, 1908), p. 19.
22 *Ibid.*, p. 21.
23 Fredson Bowers, *Elizabethan Revenge Tragedy 1587–1642* (1940; reprinted, Princeton, 1966), p. 4.
24 *Ibid.*
25 *Ibid.*, pp. 9–10.
26 John Kerrigan, *Revenge Tragedy: Aeschylus to Armageddon* (Oxford, 1996), p. 29.
27 *Ibid.*, p. 173.
28 Louise Schleiner, 'Latinized Greek drama in Shakespeare's writing of *Hamlet*', *Shakespeare Quarterly*, 41:1 (Spring, 1990), 29.
29 *Ibid.*, 30.
30 *Ibid.*, 48, where the concluding 'theoretical' statement reads like an afterthought.
31 William Shakespeare, *Titus Andronicus*, ed. Jonathan Bate, Arden 3 series (London, 1995).
32 Bate, *How the Classics Made Shakespeare*, p. 226.
33 *Ibid.*, pp. 227–8.
34 Jacques Derrida, *The Beast and the Sovereign*, trans. Geoffrey Bennington, 2 vols (Chicago and London, 2009), vol. 1, pp. 171–2.
35 William Shakespeare, *Twelfth Night or What You Will*, ed. Keir Elam, Arden 3 series (London, 2008). All quotations from the play are from this edition unless otherwise stated.
36 Stephen Greenblatt, *Hamlet in Purgatory* (Princeton, 2001), p. 252.
37 *Ibid.*

38 Jacques Le Goff, *The Birth of Purgatory*, trans. Arthur Goldhammer (Chicago, 1986), p. 353.
39 *Ibid.*, p. 354. See also Dante, *The Divine Comedy*, trans. Dorothy L. Sayers, 3 vols (Harmondsworth, 1955), vol. 2: *Purgatorio*, p. 219: 'For as our eyes would never seek the height, / Being bent on earthly matters, earthward thus / Justice here bends them in their own despight.'
40 For a more detailed discussion of this 'process', see John Drakakis, '*Macbeth* and "sovereign process"', in John Drakakis and Dale Townshend, eds, *Macbeth: A Critical Reader* (London, 2013), pp. 123–52.
41 Giles Deleuze, *Difference and Repetition*, trans. Paul Patton (London, 1994), p. 90. See also Drakakis, 'Shakespeare as presentist', 184–5.
42 A.C. Bradley, *Shakespearean Tragedy*, 3rd edn (London, 1992), pp. 153–4.
43 *Ibid.*, p. 151.
44 A.D. Nuttall, *A New Mimesis: Shakespeare and the Representation of Reality* (London, 1983), p. 134.
45 Kerrigan, *Revenge Tragedy*, p. 172.
46 William Shakespeare, *Othello*, ed. E.A.J. Honigmann, Arden 3 series, revised edn, with a new Introduction by Ayanna Thompson (London, 2016).
47 Geoffrey Bullough, *Narrative and Dramatic Sources of Shakespeare*, 8 vols (London, 1957–75), vol. 7, p. 271. See also James MacKillop, *Myths and Legends of the Celts* (London, 2006), p. 129.
48 Catherine Belsey, *Why Shakespeare?* (Basingstoke, 2007), p. 11.
49 *Ibid.*, p. 12.
50 Anon., *The True Chronicle Historie of King Leir and his Three Daughters* (London, 1605), in Bullough, *Narrative and Dramatic Sources*, vol. 7, p. 337.
51 *Ibid.*, p. 324. The spellings 'Cordilla' and 'Cordell' are used in *The Mirror For Magistrates*, and 'Cordella' is the only form used in *The True Chronicle Historie of King Leir*, the text of which Bullough reproduces.
52 Bullough, *Narrative and Dramatic Sources*, vol. 7, pp. 402ff.
53 William Shakespeare, *King Lear*, ed. R.A. Foakes, Arden 3 series (London, 1997).
54 *Ibid.*, p. 256 nn. 465–75.
55 Anon., *Mucedorus* (London, 1598), sig. A3^v. See also John Pitcher, ed., in William Shakespeare, *The Winter's Tale*, Arden 3 series (London, 2010), p. 143, and J.H.P. Pafford, ed., in *The Winter's Tale*, Arden 2 series (London, 1963), p. 69 n. 58. Pitcher implies that this may have

been a King's Men addition to the scene in *Mucedorus*, and Pafford is non-commital. It is conceivable that what prompted Shakespeare's stage direction was the revival of the play, although the figure of the bear is central to the action of the anonymous play.

56 Ann Thompson and Neil Taylor, 'The quartos', in William Shakespeare, *Hamlet*, ed. Ann Thompson and Neil Taylor, Arden 3 series, revised edn (London, 2016), p. 79. They also speculate on the identity of the printer who printed Q1 (1603), but suggest that it was unlikely to have been Roberts.

57 Stephen Greenblatt, *Shakespearean Negotiations: The Circulation of Social Energy in Renaissance England* (Oxford, 1988), p. 94.

58 Kenneth Muir, *Shakespeare's Sources*, vol. 1 (London, 1957), p. 8.

59 Greenblatt, *Shakespearean Negotiations*, p. 112.

60 *Ibid.*, pp. 113–14.

61 Samuel Harsnett, *A Declaration of egregious Popish Impostures, to with-draw the harts of her Maiesties Subiects from their alleagance, and from the truth of Christian Religion professed in England, vnder pretence of casting out deuils* (London, 1603), pp. 8–9 (sigs B4^v–C1^r).

62 *Ibid.*, p. 9 (C1^r).

63 *Ibid.*, pp. 114–15 (sigs. Q1^v–Q2^r).

64 See *Ibid.*, pp. 14–15 (sig. C3^v–C4^r), where one possessed woman recounted that the exorcist Dibdale, who visited the manor of Denham, believed there to be a 'great store of *Treasure Trouvè* hidden in his said Manor', and that the subsequent 'great walking of spirits about the house' were augmented by 'the deuill himselfe in his Dialogue with *Dibdale*, crying in his deuils roaring voice, that *he came hither for* Money, Money'.

7

The Thorello Plays: Shakespeare, Jonson and the circulation of theatrical ideas

The situating of Shakespearean texts within a framework of narratives, theatrical forms, formulae and con-texts amounts to more than a simple descriptive exercise. In the cases of *Hamlet*, *King Lear* and all of the major tragedies, questions of positionality arise in relation to the eponymous characters, whose own actions raise questions and doubts about what Steven Mullaney has identified as 'any reliable sense of a collective self' that he defines as

> a 'where' rather than a 'what,' a set of places configured as an inhabited social network rather than an ontological or anatomical autonomy. The collective self is where an ontological, anatomical being enters into all of the familial, social, cultural, religious, and political spheres that communicate with it, sometimes to re-interpellate an individual's orientation within the social. It is a matrix held together by affective and ideational and ideological bonds of all kinds, many of them in contradiction with one another.[1]

It is Mullaney's contention that what he calls 'the early modern habitus and social imaginary' contained a number of cultural 'faultlines' that were 'the product of a significant conflict *between* an ideology and something else, whether that "something else" is a particular and idiosyncratic affective investment or a larger, shared structure of feeling'.[2] As part of his explanation of his own usage of the phrase 'structure of feeling', Raymond Williams points to the distinction between Elizabethan and Jacobean plays such as *The White Devil* or *The Atheist's Tragedy* where in the cases of Webster and Tourneur he identifies a contrast 'with plays that had been written only ten years before, in which maximum havoc may be let loose but there is always the concept of an authority which will resolve it, at whatever level of loss'.[3] This is, of course, a different kind of analysis from the sort that prompted T.S. Eliot to claim that after John Donne 'a dissociation of sensibility' set in, and it is a considerable distance from the kind of positivistic, 'scientific' account of the human emotions that we might find in something like Antonio Damasio's *Looking for Spinoza: Joy, Sorrow and the Feeling Brain* (2003) where the avowed aim 'is to explain the brain and body mechanisms responsible for triggering and executing an emotion', and where 'emotions' precede 'feelings'.[4] However, Damasio is forced to concede that there exists a group of *'social emotions* [that] include sympathy, embarrassment, shame, guilt, pride, jealousy, envy gratitude, admiration, indignation, and contempt'.[5] Damasio has very little more to say about 'jealousy', for example, although the kind of response that this emotion was capable of eliciting in Shakespearean drama suggests the presence of a strong cultural component that is well within the purview of Mullaney's account of 'structure of feeling'. What, therefore, is the connection between Shakespeare's representation of the faultline surrounding sexual jealousy, and the concept of 'resource' whose implications we have been pursuing? The answer to this question involves the tracing of a series of links involving Shakespeare as actor *and* as dramatist that will take us beyond the descriptive term 'traffic' and its implications for the process of the interchange that takes place between theatrical texts.

At the end of the 1616 Folio text of Ben Jonson's *Every Man in His Humour*, first acted in 1598 and thought by some to have been recommended to the Chamberlain's Men by Shakespeare himself,[6] the list of 'principall Comoedians' includes a 'Will Shakespeare',[7] who certainly acted in the play.

The year 1598 was an interesting one since it saw the first performance of Shakespeare's *Much Ado About Nothing*, among a clutch of some ten plays that had either, as in the case of *The Merchant of Venice*, been written or were in the process of gestation. Anne Barton, quite rightly, takes the view that if Shakespeare had recommended *Every Man in His Humour* to his fellow sharers in the Chamberlain's Men, then he must have done so having 'recognised, and with characteristic openness of mind, brushed aside the fact that he was supporting a kind of comedy strikingly opposed to the mode he had explored himself in some six or seven Elizabethan plays'.[8] In the Introduction to his edition of *Every Man in His Humour* (Q1), Robert Miola takes a step further in speculating that 'Shakespeare's experience acting in the original *EMI* bore fruit several years later in *Othello* (*c*.1604) – his tale of jealous husbands and innocent wives'.[9] Indeed, in his glossing of the names of the actors, he suggests that the name 'Thorello' 'provides an onomastic link with the lead in *Oth*'.[10] The implication of this suggestion is that the trajectory of influence is linear, and that the 'Thorello' elements of Jonson's play provide a direct link between source and a later Shakespearean text that allows us to understand and to explain the manner of Shakespeare's own mode of composition. It does, indeed, point us to an important and hitherto neglected area that Shakespeare Studies has been prepared to relegate, not without some contempt, to the preserve of 'those carrion-eaters of scholarship'.[11] But it also raises the question of lateral and reciprocal connections for which, as we shall see, the relatively neutral 'traffic' may be too general a term. It also, perhaps, offers us an insight into the microeconomics of the early modern creative mind.

Before embarking on a substantial revision of what appears to have become a discredited activity of primarily pedantic interest, we need to return to some of the issues involved. We have already seen how Geoffrey Bullough categorised influence in his magisterial eight-volume collection *The Narrative and Dramatic Sources of Shakespeare* (1957–75). Throughout, these categories are informed by a preference for linearity, in a quest for what, in a much larger Renaissance context, David Quint has suggested, as we have also seen, leads to 'the artist's individual greatness [that] confers upon him an *originality* which makes him seem to transcend history'.[12] Harold Bloom makes of this struggle an Oedipal drama in which 'the poet-in-a-poet is as desperately obsessed with poetic origins, generally despite himself, as the person-in-a-person at last becomes obsessed with personal origins',[13] and that in order to live, 'the poet must *misinterpret* the father, by the crucial act of misprision, which is the re-writing of the father'.[14] For Bloom this process emerges out of the failure of the Romantics to possess and transform a Miltonic archetype, and he deliberately excludes Shakespeare from the process.[15] Thus, Bloom's Oedipal anxiety thesis has minimal applicability to the circulation of theatrical texts of which the category 'analogue' that Bullough identifies, like 'traffic', gestures only vaguely to what is actually at issue. Nor can we seek too much refuge in the descriptive, apolitical version of intertextuality that, as we have seen, acknowledges a textual plethora while seeking to hang on to a firm sense of 'primary sources', whether or not Shakespeare merely borrowed, exploited or revised them.[16] There were, of course, direct linear connections between texts of this period, but that seems to be but a small part of the complex story that we can unravel in what I wish to label the Thorello Plays. The narrative begins with *The Merchant of Venice* (1596–97) – itself a play that is in a necessarily one-sided dialogue with Marlowe's earlier *The Jew of Malta* (c.1591) and follows Jonson's *Every Man in His Humour* (1598), Shakespeare's *Much Ado About Nothing* (1600) and *Othello* (c.1604), culminating in *The Winter's Tale* (c.1611).

In *Shakespeare's Stage Traffic* (2014) Janet Clare invokes Florio's account of 'borrowing' to suggest that he 'is giving eloquent voice to a theory of intertextuality'.[17] For her, imitation was a routinely encouraged pedagogic practice, and was associated 'with high culture, primarily in relation to classical models', whereas borrowing seems to have veered 'towards a negative register', and was therefore frowned upon. The public theatre, as a popular institution, 'was routinely dependent on borrowing', but it also imitated – indeed, engaged in – the practice of 'taking over blank verse and dramatic patterns' from 'academic drama'.[18] When dramatists such as Ben Jonson in *Catiline* 'extracted from Cicero's orations', they either assimilated the borrowed material or they were guilty of 'patching'; that is to say they could be accused of 'servile borrowing' on the one hand, or, on the other, be lauded for 'accomplished adaptation'.[19] The 'trafficking' that Clare identifies projects these practices into the competitive commercial (but, it must be emphasised, *not* capitalist) world of the Renaissance public theatre, and she continually deploys 'intertextuality' as a general term to identify 'the interaction of texts'.[20] She qualifies Stephen Lynch's attempt to deploy the term to identify the ways in which Shakespeare's 'sources' are embedded in history, opting for 'a more confined

The Thorello Plays

understanding of intertextuality' that aims 'to bring the dynamic exchange between plays into focus, listening to the dialogue they engage in – or their quarrel – as one text enters into a relationship with another'.[21] However, Clare also wishes to include 'plays that Shakespeare could have known only as literary texts, on the grounds that he read them as a playwright with an eye on matters of stage potential and dramaturgy'.[22] Her qualified inclusiveness here is to be commended, and it fences off the lateral interaction between texts from the much larger question of the linear transmission of established 'authorities' that would include Homer, Ovid, Plutarch, Virgil and Dante, as well as the host of classical texts with which from time to time commentators have claimed, not without ample justification, that Shakespeare was familiar.[23] Even so, her theory of intertextuality, as we argued earlier, risks misreading the term. In order to clarify the situation, we need to remind ourselves of Julia Kristeva's usage in her *Revolution in Poetic Language* (1984) that we discussed in more detail in Chapter 4.

Kristeva begins from a definition of 'mimesis' as 'precisely, the construction of an object, not according to truth but to *verisimilitude*, to the extent that the object is posited as such (hence separate, noted but not denoted)'.[24] What mimesis does is to imitate 'the constitution of the symbolic as *meaning*' and as a result 'poetic mimesis is led to dissolve not only the denotative function but also the specifically thetic function of *positing* the subject'.[25] Indeed, mimesis 'pluralises denotation', thereby corrupting the symbolic and its attachments to unitary 'meaning'. In what Kristeva calls the passage '*from one sign system to another*' (original italics), the result is 'an alteration of the thetic position', involving the destruction of the old position and the formation of a new 'enunciative and denotative positionality'.[26] It must be emphasised that this has nothing to do with the question of 'influence' that would leave the issue of pressure more or less passive in the process of textual construction. Indeed, this new articulation of the thetic would require us, in the case of *all* Renaissance dramatists (especially Shakespeare), to abandon the attempt to construct some kind of transcendental ego – the quest of biography – as a passage to some incontrovertible universal truth. To pursue this path would suggest complicity with 'the paranoid moment of the subject defending its unity against the process',[27] where the process itself exposes a heterogeneity of forces that subjectification seeks to regulate. Kristeva opposes a 'logical unity' that is 'paranoid and homosexual' against 'feminine demand, or the hysterical spasm, [which] will never gain a symbolic representation *specific* to itself, but will continue to propose itself as a moment *within* expulsion, within the movement of ruptures and of rhythmical divisions'; for her, the woman's specificity is located in its 'asociality, in the breaking of communal conventions, in a sort of asymbolic singularity'.[28] We can, of course, recognise this phenomenon at work in numerous Renaissance texts.

The point is that 'intertextuality' is not a synonym for either 'source' or 'influence', or even for an apolitical egalitarian lateral circulation of texts themselves. Rather it identifies a heterogeneity that cannot be reduced to unitary meaning or to communication between speaker and addressee in a shared system of communication within an identifiable symbolic order. The practice of prioritising certain texts, while it may disclose the pedagogy required by the symbolic and social order itself, also serves to foreground a patriarchal 'authority' and to expose its fissures. Kristeva contends that when the symbolic order fails to contain or expel those repressed, heterogeneous sub-linguistic energies, in which the subject affirms its 'thetic positioning phase', it loses the capacity to master 'the verbal function'.[29] The result is a foregrounding of heterogeneity, and the exposure of 'the semiotic *chora*' that the process of expulsion, which is 'a-subjective', 'a-familial, a-filial, a-social', resists. It is her contention that 'only movements of social subversion, at times of change or revolution, can offer a field of social action to this process of expulsion'.[30] From this we can confirm that intertextuality goes beyond Janet Clare's commonsense, empirico-historical account of the relationship between texts to expose the ways in which their mutual interaction generates new, alternative and, in some cases, potentially subversive meanings for which the terms 'source' and 'influence' are wholly inadequate. Clare argues that the 'pleasure' stimulated by and 'bound up with the recognition of intertextualities of storyline and genre'[31] is the culmination of a process of comparing the relation between one text and another. Kristeva, however, regards this pleasure as subversive in that it is derived from the challenge and the exposure to critique that these comparisons present to culturally and politically over-determined meanings. But even more, the relation addresses the very process of subjectification that traditional criticism is content to collapse into the banal question of 'authorship'. Added to this, we cannot simply substitute the concept of 'authority' that might be attached to those texts that fall outside the remit of 'narrative and dramatic sources' that constrain Bullough's own frame of reference.

There is a whole range of printed *and* oral material that comprises what we might call the 'culture' of early modern England that together were circulated actively as constituent elements of the larger process of how Elizabethan and Jacobean subjects defined themselves and recognised what Kristeva would label their 'positionalities'. It is precisely this process that Kristeva describes theoretically, but that Mullaney has sought to tease out in more detail under the label of an ideologically specific 'structure of feeling' replete with contradictions. In his own revision of the phrase, Raymond Williams touches on what Mullaney seems to be getting at in the claim that 'authority' could exist and form part of an aesthetic structure – indeed, ultimately lend a teleological shape to it – while at the same time gesturing towards challenges from within the structure to its imperatives. Indeed, we might go further to suggest that texts that were contemporaneous could, intentionally or not, challenge, undermine *and* affirm the very same teleological trajectory within which the elements of the dramatic structure are inscribed.

From the point of view of the practising dramatist, living memory, with its continual refurbishment from the realms of professional experience and the pressures imposed upon it by historically over-determined social, political, domestic and cultural experience, delimits the psychological space in which all of these constitutive elements interacted to produce new texts. As a precursor of the category of Literature, although not ultimately reducible to it, Renaissance theatrical texts have long been thought to have been instrumental in facilitating what Kristeva calls a 'positive subversion of the old universe'. She also asks the question of how Literature condenses 'the shattering of the subject, as well as that of society, into a new apportionment of relationships between the symbolic and the real, the subjective and the objective'.[32] The stage representations of sexual jealousy, the myths that it generates, sustains and subjects to critique, makes it one of those emotions that straddles the boundaries between different realms of personal and social experience, in providing a complex motivation that allows for the entanglement of the pathological, the domestic, the political and the historical in social interaction.

With this very firmly in mind, let us now return to the meanings that might be generated from teasing out some of the connections between the series of texts with which we began. We need also to bear in mind the distinction between the explicitly social investments that culture makes in the production of meanings, and their transposition into the social sphere of particular physical and physiological accounts of the known human world. For example, the Renaissance theory of 'humours' may provide a quasi-medical source (though not in itself a complete explanation) of historically specific human behaviour that neurologists such as Antonio Damasio seem prepared to transform, without adjustment, into a monolithic physiological enquiry into the sources of emotion and feeling as a-historical articulations of the function of the human brain.

We know that Shakespeare acted in Ben Jonson's first version of *Every Man in His Humour*, an Italianate play set not in Venice but in Florence. The play was performed just over a year after the appearance of Shakespeare's own *The Merchant of Venice*, and it is not unreasonable to suppose, firstly, that Jonson was familiar with this play, and secondly, that Shakespeare as an actor was interested in much more than the role of Lorenzo Senior that he is thought to have taken in Jonson's play. Indeed, what Jonson may have appropriated from Shakespeare's play, including the name 'Lorenzo', and, more importantly, what Shakespeare may have retained from acting in Jonson's play, challenges the claim made by Tiffany Stern that 'actors learnt their own fragment in isolation from the story that surrounded it', and that 'for this reason they did not have *a natural sense of the play as a whole*, a fact that was reflected both in the way they performed when together and, I will argue, in the way they revised their lines' (my italics).[33]

Jonson sets his play initially in Florence, the geographical location of Dante and Machiavelli, but he includes as part of the action a sub-plot involving a jealous merchant Thorello and his wife Bianca. Thorello is not a Jew or a usurer, but he is a patriarchal merchant who is obsessed with possessing his wife, whose name, Bianca, Shakespeare appropriates and re-aligns tellingly in *Othello*. On his first appearance, the puritanical Thorello complains about the effect that his profligate brother Prospero is having on his household:

> He makes my house as common as a mart,
> A theatre, a public receptacle
> For giddy humour and diseased riot.
> And there, as in a tavern or a stews,
> He and his wild associates spend their hours
> In repetition of lascivious jests,
> Swear, leap, and dance, and revel night by night,
> Control my servants, and indeed what not?
>
> (1.4.52–9)

We may compare this passage with the more negative account of Shylock's instructions to Jessica to:

> Lock up my doors, and when you hear the drum
> And the vile squealing of the wry-necked fife,
> Clamber not you up to the casements then,
> Nor thrust your head into the public street
> To gaze on Christian fools with varnished faces;
> But stop my house's ears – I mean my casements –
> Let not the sound of shallow foppery enter
> My sober house.
>
> (2.5.27–34)

Both passages are ironical in that they represent onstage puritanical objections to theatrical representation that subverts the domestic economy of the household. Jonson, meanwhile, pulls together Shakespeare's Jew and merchant into one composite figure, and endows him with a pathological jealousy that in effect masks its motivation in a culture of patriarchal possessiveness. Indeed, Shakespeare's clear distinction between mercantile practice and domestic affairs (the economical and the 'oeconomical') is elided by Jonson in the figure of Thorello, whose possessiveness is made a characteristic of his physiological 'humour' that results in a recognisable bent of mind. The 'proof' of Thorello's pathology is not so much demonstrated as asserted in such a way that the social, cultural and pathological overlap. Also, on his first appearance Thorello is concerned with the value and weight of Spanish gold that he has acquired, a task he delegates to his servant Piso whom he praises in the following manner:

> He is e'en the honestest faithful servant that is this day in Florence – I speak a proud word now – and one that I durst trust my life into his hands. I have so strong opinion of his love, if need were.
> (1.4.12–15)

What was in *The Merchant of Venice* a series of separate strands, such as the abortive Portia–Morocco interlude and the merchant–Jew plot, are condensed in Jonson's play in the Thorello–Bianca sub-plot. There are also strands here of what will become the very credulousness of Othello in relation to Iago. These elements will later be transformed and expanded, firstly in *Much Ado About Nothing*, then in *Othello*, where elements of *Every Man in His Humour* and *The Merchant of Venice* are compressed even further; and finally, some will be short-circuited in *The Winter's Tale* where elements of *Much Ado About Nothing* and *Othello* reappear but in different dramatic forms. On each occasion, one or more of the elements in the earlier texts will be rehearsed, repeated, transformed and re-textualised in order to service differently nuanced generic narratives. Initially, the link between Thorello, his gold, his wife and the 'honesty' of his servant Piso are available for radical reworking in other narratives that, in the case of *Othello*, involve a critical recapitulation of names that serves to expand and transform meaning. This kind of innovative reworking sits alongside direct quotations from other texts; for example, in one scene (1.3) Matheo and Bobadilla quote directly from Kyd's *The Spanish Tragedy*, and in another (5.3.295ff.) a quotation from Samuel Daniel's sonnets *To Delia* appears. The invocation of layers of theatrical and literary discourse directs the audience's responses, stimulating judgement through irony and producing satire and ridicule.

In the dialogue between Thorello and Bianca at Act 1 Scene 4 of *Every Man in His Humour*, Thorello reasons that 'where there is such resort / Of wanton gallants and young revellers, / That any woman should be honest long' (1.4.164–6). Here the extension of the insistence upon honesty opens up a range of possible meanings that in *Othello* circulate around both the 'honest' ensign Iago, and the allegedly unfaithful Desdemona. The 'white' Bianca of Jonson's play is transformed and doubled in the ill-fated Desdemona, *and* into the alleged courtesan with whom Cassio has a liaison in the later play, whereas the disturbed Thorello, whose 'head aches extremely on a sudden' (1.4.194), is transformed into the Othello who declares, 'I have a salt and sullen rheum that offends me' (3.4.51). Of course, both these situations draw on the details of a much larger cultural discourse of jealousy and patriarchal possession, and Shakespeare can be seen repeating, recontextualising, expanding and transforming elements from both his earlier *The Merchant of Venice* and Jonson's *Every Man in His Humour* in order to serve different kinds of narrative and dramatic function.

Although we are less certain about how Shakespeare may have encountered Cinthio's *Gli Hecatomithi*,[34] the shaping and reshaping of narrative, extra-narrative and thematic materials offers us insights into how dramatists worked, as well as indicating what they might do with fragments that they could recall to mind and refashion to suit particular purposes. As we move from one text to another, so we simulate critically what we think may have been the actions and dynamics of living memory, as well as postulating what came into the creative consciousness from beneath the level of explicit intention. Even in minute matters of phrasing, sentences, sentiments and observations are seen to move tendentiously from one context to another. For example, Bobadilla's 'I love few words' (2.3.77), ironical in the Jonsonian context of *Every Man in His Humour*, is much more sinister in the mouth of the villain Don John in Shakespeare's *Much Ado About Nothing* that contains an embryonic version of the main plot of *Othello*. Indeed, on his first appearance Don John declares himself to be 'not of many words' (1.1.150), and later he alludes to the very 'humours' that form the staple of Jonson's play:

> I cannot hide what I am. I must be sad when I have cause, and smile at no man's jests; eat when I have stomach, and wait for no man's

leisure; sleep when I am drowsy, and tend on no man's business; laugh when I am merry, and claw no man in his humour.

(1.3.12–17)[35]

Also, in *Every Man in His Humour* the episode involving Bobadilla's purchase of a sword provides a series of lines that are later transformed into a much more politically dangerous narrative in *Othello*; Bobadilla regrets being conned, and draws the sword he has just purchased, to which Lorenzo Junior replies: 'Tut, now it's too late to look on it. Put it up, put it up' (2.3.162–3). Additionally, Stephano seeks to vent his anger on the absent con-man but Prospero calms him with 'It's better as 'tis' (2.3.174); these are identical to the first words that Shakespeare's Othello speaks: "Tis better as it is' (*Othello*, 1.2.6), where it is transformed into a complex ironic comment on the *language* of the protagonist. Moreover, Lorenzo Junior's instructions here to Bobadilla, and to 'Put up your weapons and put off this rage' (*Every Man in His Humour*, 3.4.163), are augmented and transformed in *Othello* where the armed and threatening Brabantio and Roderigo are ordered by Othello to 'Keep up your bright swords for the dew will rust them' (1.2.59).

These phrasal echoes are recollections and embellishments that expand the meaning of what in Jonson seem to be, in part, idiomatic utterances that have limited causal significance, but there are more. For example, in an exchange between Thorello and his servant Piso, the merchant plans to deliver a 'bond' but he is fearful that his house and his wife will be left unguarded when his hell-raising brother Prospero returns with his friends: 'I am a Jew if I know what to say, / What course to take, or which way to resolve' (3.1.37–8). The link between 'Jew' and 'bond' activates the memory of Shakespeare's Shylock, who embodies the full cultural meaning of what it is to be a Jew in the Elizabethan sense of the term. Thorello notes the 'honest' Piso's reluctance to swear an oath of secrecy:

> He will not swear. He has some meaning,
> Else, being urged so much, how should he choose
> But lend an oath to all this protestation?
>
> (3.1.71–3)

But in Shakespeare's later play, Othello expands considerably Thorello's compressed version into a much more detailed speculation:

> Thou dost mean something,
> I heard thee say even now thou lik'st not that
> When Cassio left my wife: what didst not like?
> And when I told thee he was of my counsel
> In my whole course of wooing, thou criedst 'Indeed?'
> And didst contract and purse thy brow together
> As if thou hadst shut up in thy brain
> Some horrible conceit. If thou dost love me
> Show me thy thought.
>
> (*Othello*, 3.3.111–19)

These phrasal echoes and situational appropriations, which are frequently two-way, are part of a wider theatrical discursive field that involves an audience that might be expected to recognise these details and respond dynamically to the shifts and elaborations of meaning that are suggested by revised contexts. In *Every Man in His Humour* there are embedded quotations from Kyd's earlier play, *The Spanish Tragedy*, but the process of quotation or reference that over time became part of the audience's theatrical vocabulary could surely be capable of further embellishment – inversion even – when performances of *The Merchant of Venice* or *Every Man in His Humour* were repeated. In other words, the living memory enshrined in the plays is matched by the accumulated theatrical knowledge of an audience prompted to recall critically, and recognise in some detail, their own experience as regular spectators.

The link between theatrical discourse and the larger social context is important since mimetic import derives from what Kristeva identifies as '*verisimilitude*', which she distinguishes from 'truth'. Thus, the object that mimesis constructs

> is, however, internally dependent on a subject of enunciation who is unlike the transcendental ego in that he does not suppress the semiotic *chora* but instead raises the *chora* to the status of a signifier, which may or may not obey the norms of grammatical locution. Such is the *connoted* mimetic object.[36]

I am aware that Kristeva's concern is to identify a specifically feminist element in the text's unconscious, but her formulation can be extended to apply to any form of disturbance – grammatical or thematic – that then requires some form of accommodation. As Alan Sinfield has suggested, 'All stories comprise within themselves the ghosts of alternative stories they are trying to exclude.'[37] Sinfield's 'dissident reading' is defined as implying the 'refusal of an aspect of the dominant, without pre-judging an outcome' whereby 'it posits a field necessarily open to continuing contest, in which at some conjunctures the dominant will lose ground while at others the subordinate will scarcely maintain its position'.[38] The Thorello plot in *Every Man in His Humour* brings together acquisitiveness (the merchant), the jealous husband (patriarchal possession) and the spotless wife (Bianca), all of which contribute to both an economic *and* a domestic faultline whose tensions an audience could easily recognise.

At the end of Jonson's play, Lorenzo Senior tries to locate his son and he arrives at the door of a brothel at the same time as Bianca, searching for her husband. When Thorello enters, Bianca accuses him of infidelity with a 'huswife' who

> is change,
> She feeds you fat, she soothes your appetite,
> And you are well. Your wife, an honest woman,
> Is meat twice sod to you, sir. Ah, you treacher!
>
> (5.1.39–42)

Bianca's invocation of a patriarchal stereotype in which Thorello appears to be caught in his own pathologically rooted 'appetite' generates a response that reciprocates even as it activates the myth of the jealous husband. His response is to rage, while the baffled Lorenzo Senior exclaims: 'What lunacy is this that haunts this man?' (5.1.59). This is, surely, a blueprint for Othello's behaviour at 4.1.239ff., and for Lodovico's line, 'Are his wits safe? Is he not light of brain?' (4.1.269). Here 'madness' is given an interesting makeover. In the Shakespeare *oeuvre* the triangle of wife–husband–courtesan can be traced back to a set piece in the early *Comedy of Errors*. However, in Jonson's play, and later in *Othello*, the comic moment is subsumed into a tragic plot. In *Othello* the triangle is much more dangerous, where the wife's (Desdemona's) reputation is blackened by the accusation of infidelity and where the alleged courtesan (Bianca) denies by virtue of her name the very stain associated with her profession. Actually, we never know whether or not Bianca is a courtesan since she asserts: 'I am no strumpet / But of life as honest as you, that thus / Abuse me' (*Othello*, 5.1.121–3). This remark is addressed to Emilia, who is herself at times economical with the truth. But as an audience, we are required (as indeed is Othello himself from time to time) to make a judgement on the basis of partial evidence. Indeed, there is only one exception to this general practice, which is the Duke, who in Act 1 Scene 3 refuses to act until he has collated all of the reports concerning the Turks' military objectives.

In such instances as these, the vocabulary of 'source' masks a much more dynamic discursive process in which the material of the fictions themselves is subjected to a critical re-presentation that generates new meanings. *Much Ado About Nothing* occupies an intermediate stage between *Every Man in His Humour* and *Othello* with its balanced centrifugal and centripetal plots. As in the subplot of Jonson's play, the primary issue involves an allegation of female infidelity and male possessiveness within the domestic sphere of formal courtship and marriage. Here, one of the subjects of enunciation is the bastard Don John, who is an anarchic force that constantly threatens the stability of the symbolic order. The 'authority' within the play is the father Leonato, whose precarious control of meaning and whose wilful wrong-headedness is exposed in the face of Claudio's allegation against his daughter Hero. It is the figure of the independent-minded Beatrice who reinforces this distinction, even though at the end of the play she succumbs to patriarchal authority.[39] Perhaps the more subversive figure is Innogen, whose silence potentially undermines completely the patriarchal symbolic order.

In the same way that *Every Man in His Humour* elides the figure of 'merchant' and 'Jew' in the figure of Thorello, so *Much Ado About Nothing* questions the positing of the 'subject' Hero both as the faithful betrothed and as the potential source of anarchic energy externalised in the accusative figure of the bastard Don John.[40] Shakespeare's title, *Much Ado About Nothing*, radically disturbs meaning in its opposition of 'nothing' to 'noting', and in its labelling and dismissal of female genitalia, just as it unpicks the grammar of 'plot' by ascribing responsibility and 'authority' for the solution of the dilemma to the explicitly 'ungrammatical' Dogberry and his fellow members of the Watch. Moreover, while one action seeks to subjugate femininity (and does so completely through the silent figure of Leonato's wife, Innogen), it also exposes a nuanced sexual anarchy involving the figures of Benedick and Beatrice who are returned to the symbolic order (marriage) by the very ruse of deception that had disrupted the Claudio–Hero relationship. Leonato's final 'Peace! [to *Beatrice*] I will stop your mouth. [*Hands her to Benedick*]' (5.4.97–8) restores patriarchal authority at the same time as it reinforces the authority of his earlier gesture of 'resurrecting' Hero and giving her to Claudio. However, this restoration of authority cannot be separated from patriarchal folly that almost causes a 'tragic' conclusion; the power of patriarchy is laid open to question in the play, just as the singularity of masculinity propounded by an unreconstructed Benedick is laid open to question. It is the potential for sexual anarchy, located firmly in the physiology of the female body subjected to the authority of myth that is at issue, and the result of unconstrained female sexual activity is the bastard Don John. But of course, even although the anarchic subject is finally brought to heel, so that we return to the beginning of the play, and to the military victory secured over the forces of sexual anarchy, the restored authority is both provisional and temporary. Don John is captured for the second time, but there is no guarantee that the force he represents will not break free again.

In *Every Man in His Humour*, Thorello's jealousy is pathological, but the pathology is finally corrected when he admits that pathology and physiology are replaced by psychology: 'For this I find where jealousy is fed, / Horns in the mind are worse than on the head' (5.1.431–2). In *Much Ado About Nothing*, in partial contrast, the causes are more explicitly social rather than personal, and are displayed in the flawed rituals surrounding courtship and marriage, although the victims of Don John's deception, and especially Benedick, are required to get a psychological makeover before a comic conclusion can be reached. What is implicit in Jonson's play is explicit in Shakespeare's, and should we require further evidence of the theatrical potential of one of the central concerns of *Much Ado About Nothing*, then we might invoke Jonson's later play *The Silent Woman* (1609) that explored further the ramifications of the myth of a patriarchally imposed female 'silence'.

The Thorello–Othello case offers a condensed version of the ways in which intertextual activity extends beyond the straightforward trajectory of 'influence'. Shakespeare's transformation of the location of the action from an urban, proto-bourgeois environment to the more charged setting of a Venice threatened on all sides, effectively expands the remit of Jonson's drama to provide in *Othello* a trenchant critique of Venice and its discontents, but not before stopping off in *Much Ado About Nothing* to amplify certain of its comic possibilities. Jonson's focus is on character types and how they interact in society, whereas gradually, and through the mediating action of *Much Ado About Nothing*, Shakespeare arrives at a dramatic vision that links the public world of politics with the private domestic world of marital relations. This shows a dramatist working on both his own resources *and* those of a fellow dramatist, refashioning and reconfiguring detail to produce a critical commentary that is capable of expansion in a number of directions simultaneously.

The metathesis from 'Thorello' to 'Othello', and the shift from one etymological origin to another, provides further evidence of a creative expansion of semantic horizon. The root meaning of 'Thorello' derives from the Latin 'tauro', meaning 'bull'. In his *A World of Wordes* (1598) John Florio glosses 'Tauro' as 'one of the twelue signes in heauen called Taurus. Also a little bird being a kind of finch hauing a voice somewhat like a bull. Some call it a bittour.'[41] However, Florio also notes the word 'Ostello', which he glosses as 'an hostel, or mansion, a mansion house'.[42] Astrologically, the zodiacal sign of Taurus appears to have symbolised 'the earth itself in its chaotic state before the almighty ordered the waters to be gathered into one place and the dry land to appear'.[43] What links this symbol of the ocean and its roaring to 'Ostello' and to the household or mansion is the force of jealousy that creates turbulence in what should be a stable social order. The link between household and state is, as we observed earlier, central to Aristotle's *The Politics*, which appeared in translation in

1598 and had been the focus of Sir Thomas Smith's *De Republica Anglorum* (1583). Indeed, Smith identifies the household as a metaphor for government:

> The house I call here the man, the woman, their children, their seruantes bonde and free, their catell, their householde stuffe, and all other things, which are reckoned in their possession, so long as these remaine together in one, yet this cannot be called *Aristocratia*, but Metaphorice, for it is but an house, and a little sparke resembling as it were that gouernment.[44]

The depth of shaping and interactive resonance here requires us to rethink A.D. Nuttall's claim that '*Othello* is the story of a hero who went into a house'.[45]

The point is that Jonson's *and* Shakespeare's texts are already embedded in a series of dynamic con-texts that, once we activate them, expand and complicate their meanings. Such complications increase exponentially as we move from text to text, so that, for example, the primary action of *Much Ado About Nothing* recuperates and expands material that has already appeared in other texts and con-texts. We might say that *Every Man in His Humour* and *The Merchant of Venice* provide *resources* over and above those that we might locate in the plays' con-texts, which mutually nourish each other. Moreover, these contents are developed in different directions in *Much Ado About Nothing* and *Othello* where they undergo shifts from one genre to another. The result is a transposition of detail and a deepening of the issues that exposes a progressive fracturing of subjectivities, the ideologies that sustain them, and the comic and tragic resolutions that result from their representations.

The third major shift is from *Othello* to *The Winter's Tale* (*c*.1611), a play embedded in a series of plays that include *Cymbeline* (1610–11), *Pericles* (1611–12), and *The Two Noble Kinsmen* (*c*.1613). Both *Pericles* and the collaboration of *The Two Noble Kinsmen* contain Prologues that reveal their indebtedness to Gower and Chaucer, respectively, as authorities, although it is in the latter that the Prologue gestures towards a linkage between the venal business of mounting a play and the respectability of connecting with an acknowledged precursor. In a fantasy of association, the playwright occupies the status of the bride in this transaction for whom the first night is problematic. The 'maidenheads' that the Prologue likens to the identities of 'New plays' are subjected to forms of transaction that bear a dangerous resemblance to the behaviour of the courtesan inscribed in the activity of submitting to an audience as bridegroom *and* as 'customer': 'Much followed both, for both much money gi'en, / If they stand sound and well' (Prologue, ll. 2–3).[46] The play's first night is like the bride's first night, which is formally represented in the marriage ceremony of Theseus and Hyppolita that follows, and it is the status of the bride that is problematic:

> And a good play,
> Whose modest scenes blush on his marriage day
> And shake to lose his honour, is like her
> That after holy tie and first night's stir
> Yet still is Modesty and still retains
> More of the maid, to sight, than husband's pains.
> We pray our play may be so, for I am sure
> It has a noble breeder and a pure,
> A learned and a poet never went
> More famous yet 'twixt Po and silver Trent.
> Chaucer, of all admired, the story gives;
> There, constant to eternity, it lives.
>
> (Prologue, ll. 3–14)

The slippage of pronouns here from 'his' to 'her' as the identity of the play shifts gender ascriptions reflects also the interpellation of playwright(s) and audience. But the transposition from 'play' to the experience of loss of virginity, and what that means for the performance as the means of transforming its identity, is central to the institution of marriage as a fundamentally patriarchal transaction. What is retained after the transaction, and what masks the 'husband's pains' (l. 8) is the maid's show of a residual modesty that, as the metaphor develops, feminises the dramatist who has now entered into the venal contract of providing a commodity for money. Nor does the metaphor end there, since caught between two authorities – Chaucer, the 'noble breeder', and the audience as feminised consumer – the play occupies an ambivalent gender status. Thus, beneath the formal ceremony of marriage there lurks a potentially destructive anxiety, laughed off at the end of *The Merchant of Venice*, temporarily avoided in *Much Ado About Nothing*, transformed into tragedy in *Othello*, taking the form of an Oedipal scandal that must be exposed in *Pericles*, and resurrected again in both a potentially tragic and a finally comic resolution in *The Winter's Tale*. Certainly, the relation between *The Two Noble Kinsmen* and Chaucer is one of what Richard Hillman labels 'frankly acknowledged adaptation',[47] but as the evidence from the Prologue suggests, the frank acknowledgement of indebtedness appropriates the name of Chaucer to expose a *difference* between a permanent source – 'where, constant to eternity, it lives' – and the dynamic but unstable life of a play whose very performance is open to an allegation of promiscuity that, according to early Jacobean gender ideology, *always* pursues the newly wedded woman.

The Winter's Tale displays a re-use and a refurbishment of resources that stretches the dynamic interaction of Shakespeare's earlier texts, but also draws other Jonsonian texts into the network. These include the Italianate version of *Every Man in His Humour* (1598, published in quarto in 1601) in which Shakespeare had probably acted, and from which the name 'Thorello' appears to have been transposed into 'Othello', coupled with the merchant's pathological jealousy as motivation, which finds its way into Shakespeare's play. A case can also be made for some kind of structural connection between elements of Jonson's *Volpone* (1605) and *Othello* involving Iago and Volpone, and it may be that the figure of the silent woman in *Much Ado About Nothing* was recalled in Jonson's *Epicoene* (1609). In the absence of firm documentary evidence to suggest links, all we can do is speculate on possible thematic and structural connections, but *The Winter's Tale* elaborates creatively upon aspects of *Much Ado About Nothing* and *Othello*, while gesturing in the direction of some of the other links (especially with Jonson) that have been suggested.[48] However, unlike in *Othello*, where the hero's jealousy builds slowly under the tutelage of Iago, Leontes's jealousy is immediately and very rapidly stimulated by the conversation and the accompanying gestures that Hermione and Polixenes exchange. The trigger is a more generalised version of the misogynistic account of female promiscuity that Iago offers Othello, except that here in *The*

Winter's Tale there is a surprising acknowledgement by Hermione of the historical association of her femininity with sin even within the sacrament of marriage:

> Th' offences we have made you do we'll answer,
> If you first sinned with us, and that with us
> You did continue fault, and that you slipped not
> With any but with us.
>
> (1.2.83–6)[49]

Hermione's pregnancy and the period of time of Polixenes's stay in Bohemia sow doubts in Leontes's mind about his wife's 'modesty'. But what in the earlier plays is the stuff of rumour and gossip is here rearticulated by Hermione herself as a fall into sexuality that contributes to the image of woman as ultimately unknowable, potentially promiscuous and therefore a threat to patriarchal control. This is exactly the sentiment to which Bassanio has recourse in *The Merchant of Venice* when he is confronted with a choice of caskets:

> Look on beauty,
> And you shall see 'tis purchased by the weight,
> Which therein works a miracle in nature,
> Making them lightest that wear most of it:
> So are those crisped snaky golden locks,
> Which maketh such wanton gambols with the wind
> Upon supposed fairness, often known
> To be the dowry of a second head,
> The skull that bred them in the sepulchre.
> Thus ornament is but the guiled shore
> To a most dangerous sea; the beauteous scarf
> Veiling an Indian beauty; in a word,
> The seeming truth, which cunning times put on
> To entrap the wisest.
>
> (3.2.88–101)[50]

In *Much Ado About Nothing*, *Othello* and *The Winter's Tale*, household, mansion and government are disrupted by the activation of the woman's role in this history of the fall and in each case the threat of death hovers above the action. In *Much Ado About Nothing*, Hero 'died but whiles her slander lived' (5.4.66); in *Othello*, Desdemona dies unjustly as the consequence of a fantasy of revenge and cannot be resurrected; in *The Winter's Tale*, Hermione 'dies' but all, including the audience, are led to believe that this death is real. In the initial exchange between Camillo and Archidamus (Sicilia and Bohemia, respectively) the loving friendship between Leontes and Polixenes is outlined but in terms that are proleptically ambiguous; for example, 'They were trained together in their childhoods, and there rooted between them such an affection which cannot choose but branch now' (1.1.22–4). The 'branching' of affection, carefully augmented here in the exchange between the two lords, delicately suggests an alternative form of 'branching' which is an emblematic feature of the cuckold. Archidamus's 'I think there is not in the world either malice or matter to alter it' (1.1.32–3) is a sentiment that can easily be reversed to invoke 'malice' and 'matter', while the switch in conversation to the 'young prince, Mamillius', pinpoints the tension between the hopeful future as a compensatory force for the reality of death:

> It is a gallant child; one that, indeed, physics the subject, makes old hearts fresh. They that went on crutches ere he was born desire yet their life to see him a man.
> ARCHIDAMUS. Would they else be content to die?
> CAMILLO. Yes, if there were no other excuse why they should desire to live.
>
> (1.1.38–44)

Of course, Mamillius will later be sacrificed on the altar of Leontes's jealousy, but not before the sentiments of Camillo and Archidamus have been turned inside out. That process begins in the scene following where Leontes fails to persuade Polixenes to remain in Bohemia, and where he enlists Hermione's assistance.

The play takes the cue of Camillo and Archidamus's reference to the source of the two kings' affection for each other in their childhoods, and having ensnared Polixenes in the ruse of an oath that John Kerrigan has noted involves 'a careful warily quibbling relationship with oaths',[51] Hermione turns to 'my lord's tricks and yours when you were boys' (1.2.60–1). Language itself is already proving to be a rather slippery instrument of communication, and its capacity for suggesting alternative meanings will soon proliferate and in surprising, indeed shocking, directions. For Polixenes, boyhood for both himself and Leontes invokes a utopian existence of 'innocence' that, in retrospect, was free from the stain of the post-lapsarian world:

> We were as twinned lambs that did frisk i'th sun
> And beat the one at th'other: what we changed
> Was innocence for innocence; we knew not
> The doctrine of ill-doing, nor dreamed
> That any did. Had we pursued that life,
> And our weak spirits ne'er been higher reared
> With stronger blood, we should have answered heaven
> Boldly, 'not guilty', the imposition cleared
> Hereditary ours.
>
> 1.2.67–75)

Here Polixenes accepts the fall from Edenic grace and acknowledges the guilt associated with adult responsibility that involves recognition of the potentially destructive force of 'stronger blood' that has both positive and negative connotations. It is not clear how much of this dialogue Leontes hears, but the conversation takes a particular turn with Hermione's tantalising conclusion: 'By this we gather / You have tripped since' (1.2.75–6). What follows is an acknowledgement by Polixenes of a fall into the world of sexual temptation (the 'blood' that requires to be controlled) where the instruments were Hermione and Polixenes's own wife. Hermione blocks off one of the conclusions to be drawn from Polixenes's statement:

> Grace to boot!
> Of this make no conclusion, lest you say
> Your queen and I are devils. Yet go on.
> Th' offences we have made you do we'll answer,
> If you first sinned with us, and that with us
> You did continue fault, and that you slipped not
> With any but with us.
>
> (1.2.80–6)

Leontes's 'Is he won yet?' (1.2.86) suggests that he does not hear this part of the conversation or that his distraction begins earlier with Hermione's 'Come, I'll question you' (1.2.59). If this is so, then the doubt in Leontes's mind has already begun to ferment with

Hermione's offer to release Leontes if he were in the same situation as Polixenes, and her declaration of love for her husband:

> I'll give him my commission
> To let him there a month behind the gest
> Prefixed for's parting; yet, good deed, Leontes.
> I love thee not a jar o'th clock behind
> What lady she her lord.
>
> (1.2.39–44)

Leontes slips back into the conversation, and once Polixenes has been persuaded to stay, the topic switches from the two kings' personal histories to Hermione's successful embassy. But what this exposes is an armoury of feminine wiles that inadvertently drives a wedge between the power of her husband's persuasion and hers. Indeed, what is not clear here is whether her appeal to Polixenes can be interpreted as a flirtation, or as a strategy designed to get results, or a combination of the two. Her admission that 'You may ride's / With one soft kiss a thousand furlongs ere / With spur we heat an acre' (1.2.94–6) is presented as a generalisation applicable to all women on all occasions. On this particular occasion, the link between the present and the past, involving two specific occasions in which Hermione has been active, produces a fatal elision that threatens to diminish the distance between 'husband' and 'friend'.

This is the point at which editors, from Capell onwards, have introduced a stage direction – [*Gives her hand to Polixenes*] – that is positively incendiary and eliminates the very past that thus far the scene has sought to establish. Leontes's 'Too hot, too hot / To mingle friendship far is mingling bloods' (1.2.108–9) initiates an excursion into his own unconscious, as he moves from questioning his own role in Mamillius's parentage to a fragmentary account of fantasy that is in principle not very different from Brabantio or Othello in the earlier play:

> Yet they say we are
> Almost as like as eggs – women say so,
> That will say anything. But were they false
> As o'erdyed blacks, as wind, as waters, false

> As dice are to be wished by one that fixes
> No bourn 'twixt him and mine, yet were it true
> To say this boy were like me. Come, sir page,
> Look on me with your welkin eye. Sweet villain,
> Most dearest, my collop! Can thy dam? May't be
> Affection? – Thy intention stabs the centre,
> Thou dost make possible things not so held,
> Communicat'st with dreams – how can this be? –
> With what's unreal thou coactive art,
> And fellow'st nothing. Then 'tis very credent
> Thou mayst co-join with something, and thou dost,
> And that beyond commission, and I find it,
> And that to the infection of my brains
> And hard'ning of my brows.
>
> (1.2.129–46)

This long passage that charts the psychological degeneration of Leontes exposes the political unconscious of patriarchy. Here signifiers are separated from signifieds, and the result is the encroachment of disordered elements of the patriarchal unconscious into his consciousness, enabling him to make something out of 'nothing'. In this situation, Mamillius is both a regressive symbol of Leontes's own childhood *and* evidence that can support the fantasy of Hermione's infidelity. Indeed the 'nothings' that Hermione's gestures and the 'dreams' stimulate, introduce an instability into both language and gesture that allows Leontes to exchange the 'unreal' for the 'real', fantasy for reality. The process is speedy compared with what happens in *Othello*, where different facets of it are repeated as a result of Iago's devilish strategy before it comes finally to rest on Othello himself. However, Brabantio's dream inhabits the same psychological terrain as Leontes's fantasies, and it is these that cause him to lose faith in Hermione, albeit there is no cause for him to do so.

It is only after the death of Mamillius, and a period of suffering that the audience shares with the penitent king, that Leontes is persuaded by Paulina to 'awake [his] faith' (5.3.95). This allows her to 'make the statue move indeed', and for Hermione to 'descend' and take Leontes 'by the hand' (5.3.88–9). In this, Paulina dismisses the claim that she is 'assisted / By wicked powers' (5.3.90–1), radically revising Hermione's initial invocation of the masculine association of woman with evil. Except that unlike in *Much Ado About Nothing*, where the audience is complicit with the plot to 'resurrect' Hero, in *The Winter's Tale* the 'magic' is ultimately that of the dramatist who can persuade both onstage and offstage audience to 'awake [their] faith' in the performance itself. This reunion of the family and of masculine friendship, cemented by the impending marriage of Perdita and Florizel, takes the play beyond the tragic conclusion of *Othello* and into a realm beyond that of the comic *Much Ado About Nothing*.

I have argued that in a particular group of plays it is possible to discern a series of intertextual relations that extend far beyond questions of 'source' and 'influence', and that show dramatists working and reworking particular details, deepening and complicating their resources in creative ways. The materials of one play reappear transformed in others, and in such a way that they serve to expand meaning and to demonstrate a dynamic interaction between 'resources' that the descriptive term 'trafficking' does not quite encapsulate. Materials pass between writers, where the issue is much more than a question of 'borrowing', and, as in the case of Shakespeare, between plays where ideas, themes, memes and scenarios are revisited, reformulated and transformed to create new perspectives on matters with which the theatre audience can be expected to have some prior familiarity. The resonance of the Thorello sub-plot, in a play that, in part, recuperates elements of *The Merchant of Venice*, expands within the Shakespeare *oeuvre* to take in comedy, tragedy and tragicomedy and to suggest a creative ingenuity that is capable of moulding form to discuss shifts in emphasis and particular faultlines in Elizabethan and Jacobean culture. We can no longer think of 'influence' as an exertion of dominant force on a relatively passive recipient, nor can we think of 'source' as a linear, quasi-religious quest for origins. The play 'in process' is not unlike Kristeva's 'subject in process', involving a making and remaking of material that informs and exposes to view a progress to clarity. The process encompasses both the representation of subjectification *and* the social relations that it sustains, thereby giving us access to the creative (and implicitly political) Shakespearean unconscious.

Notes

1 Steven Mullaney, *The Reformation of Emotions in the Age of Shakespeare* (Chicago and London, 2015), p. 14.
2 *Ibid.*, p. 15. Mullaney borrows the phrase 'structure of feeling' from Raymond Williams, but see Raymond Williams, *Politics and Letters: Interviews with New Left Review* (London, 1979), pp. 156–70, where the phrase is considerably refined and qualified.
3 Williams, *Politics and Letters*, pp. 161–2.
4 Antonio Damasio, *Looking for Spinoza: Joy, Sorrow and the Feeling Brain* (Orlando and London, 2003), p. 29.
5 *Ibid.*, p. 45.
6 Anne Barton, *Ben Jonson, Dramatist* (Cambridge, 1984), p. 44; see also David Riggs, *Ben Jonson: A Life* (Cambridge, MA, and London, 1989), p. 45.
7 Ben Jonson, *The Workes of Beniamin Ionson* (London, 1616), p. 72.
8 Barton, *Ben Jonson, Dramatist*, p. 44.
9 Ben Jonson, *Every Man in His Humour*, ed. Robert S. Miola (Manchester, 2000), p. 65.
10 *Ibid.*, p. 80.
11 Harold Bloom, *A Map of Misreading* (Oxford, 1975), p. 17.
12 David Quint, *Origin and Originality in Renaissance Literature* (New Haven, 1983), p. 4.
13 Bloom, *A Map of Misreading*, pp. 17–18.
14 *Ibid.*, p. 19.
15 Harold Bloom, *The Anxiety of Influence* (London, Oxford and New York, 1973), p. 11.
16 See Stephen J. Lynch, *Shakespearean Intertextuality: Studies in Selected Sources and Plays* (Westport, CT, and London, 1998), p. 3, in which he argues: 'Shakespeare seems consistently to write both with and against his sources, seizing upon and developing suggestions already present in his sources, while complicating his plays with developments that counter and refute his source texts.' Cf. also Murray J. Levith, *Shakespeare's Cues and Prompts* (London, 2007), pp. 3–4.
17 Janet Clare, *Shakespeare's Stage Traffic: Imitation, Borrowing and Competition in Renaissance Theatre* (Cambridge, 2014), p. 5.
18 *Ibid.*, p. 9.
19 *Ibid.*
20 *Ibid.*, p. 18.

21 *Ibid.*, p. 20.
22 *Ibid.*
23 Cf. Ernst Robert Curtius's magisterial *European Literature in the Latin Middle Ages* (Princeton and Oxford, 2013), and also Stuart Gillespie, *Shakespeare's Books: A Dictionary of Shakespeare's Sources* (London, 2004). See also Colin Burrow, *Shakespeare and Classical Antiquity* (Oxford, 2013), p. 92.
24 Julia Kristeva, *Revolution in Poetic Language*, trans. Margaret Waller (New York, 1984), p. 57.
25 *Ibid.*, pp. 57–8.
26 *Ibid.*, p. 60.
27 Julia Kristeva, 'The subject in process', in Patrick Ffrench and Roland-François Lack, eds, *The Tel Quel Reader* (London, 1998), p. 158.
28 *Ibid.*, p. 150.
29 *Ibid.*, p. 142.
30 *Ibid.*, pp. 134–5.
31 Clare, *Shakespeare's Stage Traffic*, p. 26.
32 Julia Kristeva, *Desire in Language: A Semiotic Approach to Literature and Art*, trans. Thomas Gora, Alice Jardine and Leon S. Roudiez (Oxford, 1980), p. 93.
33 Tiffany Stern, *Rehearsal from Shakespeare to Sheridan* (Oxford, 2000), pp. 64–5.
34 See William Shakespeare, *Othello*, ed. E.A.J. Honigmann, Arden 3 series, revised edn, with a new Introduction by Ayanna Thompson (London, 2016), p. 13.
35 William Shakespeare, *Much Ado About Nothing*, ed. Claire McEachern, Arden 3 series (London, 2006).
36 Kristeva, *Revolution in Poetic Language*, p. 57.
37 Alan Sinfield, *Faultlines: Cultural Materialism and the Politics of Dissident Reading* (Los Angeles and Oxford, 1929), p. 47.
38 *Ibid.*, p. 49.
39 Kristeva, *Revolution in Poetic Language*, pp. 57–8.
40 For a fuller discussion of the discursive dynamics of this area of the play, see John Drakakis, 'Trust and transgression: the discursive practices of *Much Ado About Nothing*', in Richard Machin and Christopher Norris, eds, *Post-structural Readings of English Poetry* (Cambridge, 1987), pp. 59–84.
41 John Florio, *A World of Wordes* (London, 1598), p. 414. Florio glosses 'bittour' as 'Bittern: or bull of the bog'.
42 *Ibid.*, p. 25. Cf. also John Florio, *Queen Anna's New World of Words or Dictionarie of the Italian and English Tongues* (London, 1611),

p. 231, which glosses 'Hostello' as 'an hostel, a place of habitation, a mansion-house'.
43 John Barrett, *An Enquiry into the Origin of the Constellations that Compose the Zodiac and the Uses they were Intended to Promote* (Dublin, 1800), p. 26.
44 Sir Thomas Smith, *De Republica Anglorum* (London, 1583), p. 13.
45 A.D. Nuttall, *A New Mimesis: Shakespeare and the Representation of Reality* (London, 1983), p. 134.
46 William Shakespeare, *The Two Gentlemen of Verona*, ed. Lois Potter, Arden 3 series (London, 1997).
47 Richard Hillman, *Intertextuality and Romance in Renaissance Drama: The Staging of Nostalgia* (London, 1992), p. 136.
48 Of course, as one editor of Jonson has suggested, *Every Man in His Humour* resurrects a classical model of comedy. See G.A. Wilkes, *Ben Jonson: Five Plays* (Oxford, 1989), pp. vii–viii, in which the elements of Aristophanes, Plautus and Terence, as well as those of the Tudor Interlude and the Italian *commedia dell'arte* are detected. Jonson seems to have been one of those dramatists who was most conscious of the need to refurbish and bring up to date these 'authorities' and precursors.
49 William Shakespeare, *The Winter's Tale*, ed. John Pitcher, Arden 3 series (London, 2010), p. 156.
50 See Sigmund Freud, 'The Theme of the Three Caskets', *Art and Literature*, The Pelican Freud Library, vol. 14 (Harmondsworth, 1985), pp. 240–4, where the psychology of Bassanio's 'choice' is explained in the following way: 'Choice stands in the place of necessity, of destiny. In this way man overcomes death, which he has recognised intellectually. No greater triumph of wish-fulfilment is conceivable. A choice is made where in reality there is obedience to a compulsion; and what is chosen is not a figure of terror, but the fairest and most desirable of women.'
51 John Kerrigan, *Shakespeare's Binding Language* (Oxford, 2016), p. 446.

8

Shakespeare as resource

In the last chapter we saw how Shakespeare used and re-used some of the resources at his disposal, shifting from comedy to tragedy and finally to tragicomedy, while recalling and refashioning earlier theatrical experience. In her book *Italian Drama in Shakespeare's Time* (1989) Louise George Clubb sets out 'to show the unlimited fertility and transformational capability implicit in each configuration', all of which demonstrate a 'core process: permutation and declension by recombination with compatible units, whether of person, association, action, or design'.[1] Clubb's broader objective is to demonstrate the ways in which various elements of Italian drama found their way from ancient Roman origins into Shakespeare's Comedies, Tragedies and Tragicomedies, and her method is a sophisticated form of source study. There is no doubting the 'history' that Clubb narrates, although a strong case has been made for the influence of Ancient Greek drama, and particularly the plays of Euripides.[2] Such 'additions' swell the volume of sources, but they neither modify nor transform the heuretic model of enquiry that privileges linearity and that regards creativity as what the late Raymond Williams called 'an allegory of the mind of God'.[3] In his book *Shakespeare in Company* (2013) Bart Van Es acknowledges what he calls 'the more partial influence' of Italian comedy on plays like *The Comedy of Errors* and *The Taming of the Shrew*, recognising that both plays come 'much closer to absorbing an established world' that featured Gascoigne's *Supposes*, which was itself a translation of Ariosto's *I Suppositi*.[4] Van Es concludes his opening chapter by observing that: 'The conclusion of *Titus Andronicus* artfully combines, amongst other works, *The Spanish Tragedy*, *The Jew of Malta*, and *Thyestes*.'[5]

Shakespeare as resource 319

By the time of the arrival of Shakespeare in London, the theatre as an institution was thriving and, as we saw in the case of Jonson's *Every Man in His Humour* or Marlowe's *The Jew of Malta* and *Edward II*, there were not only examples upon which Shakespeare could draw, and with which he may have had some practical familiarity, but also an existing repertoire of forms and topics that could provide a basis for imitation or innovation. These were, as Clubb suggests in relation to Italian drama, an ever-expanding storehouse of theatrical formulae available to any developing dramatist. They could simply be imitated and incorporated, or 'contaminated' (*contaminatio*) as in the case of *The Comedy of Errors*, which contains a mixture deriving from Plautus's *Amphytruo* and *Menaechmi*, Gower, St. Paul's *Acts of the Apostles*, and other native English antecedents.[6] Van Es has sought to link as a progression what he calls 'colloquial theatre' with the 'more cultured rhetoric',[7] with the latter having derived, in Shakespeare's case, from a fairly thorough humanist secondary education.[8] That said, Van Es also acknowledges that 'the playwright would, throughout his career, pick up ideas from contemporaries, and borrow wholesale the plots of earlier dramatists'.[9]

However, in the same way that Shakespeare internalised the theatrical devices of others, both 'colloquial' and 'cultured', as his own repertoire of plays grew, so he was also able to mobilise these devices as dramatic and theatrical resources. To those that we identified in Chapter 7 we might add a further list. For example, *Love's Labour's Lost*, *A Midsummer Night's Dream* and *Romeo and Juliet* all imitate and innovate on the comic expectation of a final resolution. In the case of *Love's Labour's Lost* the ending is postponed and the result is a substitute extra-theatrical ending. In *A Midsummer Night's Dream* the comic ending is orthodox, rooting the play's disharmony in the quarrel between Oberon and Titania in the fairy kingdom and then staging an outrageously comic version of the tragic tale of Pyramus and Thisbe that laughs away the tragic possibilities of the two central plots. Finally, in the properly tragic version in *Romeo and Juliet* and contrary to comic expectations, the lovers die, leaving a bereft and sterile older generation to rue their erstwhile mutual hostility.

In the case of *Twelfth Night*, Shakespeare returned to the device of using twin characters that he had previously used in *The Comedy of Errors*, and he returned to material he had used in *The Taming of the Shrew* in the later play *Much Ado About Nothing*. In the case of plays that are never lumped together, his critical view of military heroism that surfaces in the *Henry IV* plays and in *Henry V* is revisited even more critically in *Troilus and Cressida*. Also, in the cases of *Hamlet* and *Macbeth*, for example, the villain in the earlier play becomes the tragic hero in the later one,[10] not unlike the eponymous hero of *Richard III*, and both Claudius and Macbeth internalise at different levels of intensity the ethical and moral dilemmas that arise from their respective ambitions. Perhaps it would be inaccurate to think of these situations as memes since they imitate or further develop already existing character types and/or situations or paradigms that Shakespeare repeats and uses as bases for innovation.

This persistent reimagining and reconstitution of dramatic and theatrical forms is, perhaps, testimony to an unusually vibrant intersection of literary and oral culture, in which examples absorbed in literary (i.e. non-dramatic) narratives could be combined with existing examples from an oral tradition that continued to circulate in various forms. For example, an outline of the life of Coriolanus appears in North's translation of *Plutarch's Lives of the Noble Grecians and Romanes* (1579 and 1595),[11] and later in Philemon Holland's translation of *The Romane Historie of T. Livy* (1600). In his Arden 3 edition of *Coriolanus* Peter Holland argues that Shakespeare 'read Plutarch's "Life" with quite exceptional attentiveness',[12] although Bullough notes some eight occasions when details in North's *Plutarch* do *not* appear in Shakespeare's play. The translations from which Bullough provides excerpts themselves incorporate the opinions of others, and are not themselves entirely stable narratives. Moreover, if Shakespeare had 'read' Philemon Holland's 1600 translation of Livy, we might wonder why his depiction of Coriolanus appears to have overlooked the description of the young Caius Martius as 'a Noble yong gentleman, right politicke of advise, active besides, and tall of his hands, who afterwards was surnamed *Coriolanus*'.[13] Indeed, it would seem that in Shakespeare's play the adult protagonist's childhood is a backward projection.

Shakespeare's Coriolanus is closer to North's 'honest natured man, plaine and simple, without arte or cunning',[14] although a few pages earlier North notes that Tullus Aufidius is reluctant to allow Coriolanus to account to the Volscians for his treatment of Rome 'bicause emongst other things he had an eloquent tongue'.[15] Shakespeare cuts through these inconsistencies and augments his portrait of Coriolanus with what had become by 1607 a familiar critical approach to the theatrical operation of language: either a transparent medium of communication, or the source of dangerous destabilising ambiguity capable of producing a destructive tension between the actor's representation of a dramatic character, and that character's 'inner' life. The issue is present in early Comedies from *Love's Labour's Lost* onwards, and it is central in Tragedies such as *Hamlet*, *Othello*, *King Lear*, *Macbeth* and *Coriolanus*. This concern suggests something more than a theatregram in that it becomes an abiding concern that arises out of a consciousness of the business of theatrical representation, of the actor as a divided subject, and of the emergence of language as a gradually destabilising currency of communication. *Coriolanus* riffs on this just as the Plutarchian Coriolanus is subsumed into the Shakespearean models of power and governance, thereby making the eponymous hero distinctly out of place in a republican Rome whose monarchical past continues to remain within living memory. Also, the Coriolanus that Shakespeare fashions owes as much to the earlier figure of Fortinbras, of whose military exploits Shakespeare is much less critical in the earlier *Hamlet*. Here the mixture of literary antecedents, an already sedimented oral theatre history and a vibrant sense of an extra-theatrical awareness of the instability – one might almost say, commodification – of language, combine to produce a unique combination that the linear model offered by source study, and the restrictive identification of influences does not quite adequately account for.

One further element requires attention: the well-known story of Menenius's fable of 'the belly' that appears in Holland's *Livy* and North's *Plutarch*, but also in Sir Philip Sidney's 'An apology for poetry' (1595) and in William Camden's *Remaines* (1605). According to Sidney, 'the tale is notorious, and as notorious that it was a tale'.[16] Sidney's throwaway comment suggests that this tale was in wide extra-literary circulation, and that it was semi-detached from identified 'source' narratives; indeed, in the manner that we might associate with oral culture, it had a currency beyond its life in print even though both circulated together. In a society that was unstable, a narrative that spoke directly to the manifest anxieties both of the lower orders and the leisured aristocracy could easily become one of those go-to examples at times of crisis. What is 'creative' about Shakespeare's usage is that which Raymond Williams attributes to any artist: 'the process of making a meaning active, by communicating an organised experience to others'.[17] Bullough gathers together a brief array of documents that he labels 'Accounts of Historical Sources'[18] of the kind that, as we saw earlier, Barker and Hulme would radically revise in their label 'con-texts'. As a dramatist seeking to satisfy an eager paying public, the dramatist's own creation of meaning coexisted with the practice of sustaining already circulating meanings with which an audience, possessing its own repertoire of theatrical memories, could bring to the business of understanding.

The scholarly desire to position Shakespeare as a primarily literary writer has often obscured the Shakespeare who, as a practising dramatist, relied also on oral formulae and circulating narratives and anecdotes that could be imitated and contaminated by innovation.[19] Indeed, the preoccupation with seeking to establish how Shakespeare encountered available histories of Rome or Ancient Greece has tended to restrict its lines of enquiry in order to fashion a Shakespeare in its own image. The ingenuity of the literary scholar, now bolstered by the 'evidence' provided by modern technology finds in the composition of Shakespeare's texts an analogy of its own professional practices. The desire to identify external 'sources' tends to obscure resources that are much closer to home, and nowhere is this clearer than in Shakespeare's two Venetian plays, *The Merchant of Venice* and *Othello*, where elements in the earlier play are creatively refashioned in the later play, and which offer additional insights into the process of dramatic composition.

Let us take the figure of Morocco in *The Merchant of Venice*, who appears first in Act 2 Scene 1 and then later in Act 2 Scene 7. The stage direction from the quarto of 1600 reads: '*Enter [the Prince of] MOROCCO, a tawney Moor, / all in white, and three or four followers accordingly.*'[20] Unlike Othello, who does not himself refer to his colour until much later in the play ('Haply for I am black / And have not those soft parts of conversation / That chamberers have', 3.3.267–9),[21] Morocco states his pedigree from the beginning, and in a tone and language that in the later play confirm Iago's description of Othello: 'bombast circumstance / Horribly stuffed with epithets of war' (*Othello*, 1.1.12–13):

> Mislike me not for my complexion,
> The shadowed livery of the burnished sun,
> To whom I am neighbour and near bred.
> Bring me the fairest creature northward born,
> Where Phoebus' fire scarce thaws the icicles,
> And let us make incision for your love,
> To prove whose blood is reddest, his or mine.
> I tell thee lady, this aspect of mine
> Hath feared the valiant; by my love I swear,
> The best-regarded virgins of our clime
> Have loved it too. I would not change this hue
> Except to steal your thoughts, my gentle queen.
>
> (2.1.1–12)

In *The Merchant of Venice* Morocco is an outsider in Venice (and also presumably in Belmont), a 'stranger' who, in accordance with the egalitarian myths that circulated in England about Venice, might be expected to be welcomed. When Morocco appears again in Act 2 Scene 7 he is even more bombastic, and thoroughly egotistical, and he leaves bereft after his failure to choose the correct casket. Portia's parting couplet, 'A gentle riddance. Draw the curtains, go. / Let all of his complexion choose me so' (2.7.78–9), speaks volumes about what we might call the institutional racism of Belmont, just as Venice is institutionally anti-Semitic, despite its vaunted claims to welcome strangers. There is also a larger, more local metropolitan historical con-text for Morocco that I have explored in my Introduction to the play,[22] but the immediate dramatic context is that he follows the rules of the game laid down by Portia's father. In the earlier play we do not know what motivates Portia's father, or what the patriarchal fears (other than the fear of Portia's unruly sexual desire – 'blood') are that the casket game is designed to rein in. In the later play Iago's and Roderigo's miscegenistic vision of Venice is the substance of Desdemona's father's dreams.

When Morocco appears again, in the later play he is a general and not a prince, and he has eloped with Desdemona; we learn from Iago's interaction with Desdemona's father, Brabantio, in more detail what obscene fears Venice harbours in relation to male strangers of colour. The 'accident' that Iago grossly relates to Brabantio is, according to the crestfallen patriarch, 'not unlike my dream, / Belief of it oppresses me already' (1.1.140–1). Clearly, where in the earlier play the dead father, whose rules are sacrosanct, is simply a focus for patriarchal power, in the later play we are given a deeper appreciation of the psychological 'reasons' for asserting patriarchal authority. In *The Merchant of Venice*, violation of patriarchal authority is reserved for the Jessica–Lorenzo sub-plot, and there Jessica's elopement is given a more sympathetic treatment to the point where it becomes, unusually, the instrument of the restrictively patriarchal Jew's ultimate conversion to Christianity.[23] What we see in *Othello* is Shakespeare creatively using and adapting the material from an earlier play to enlarge and expand a popular engagement with republican Venice and the myths that it embodied. In the earlier play he makes use of a range of comic formulae, and the conclusion produces an attenuated form of happiness and unity. In the later play, material that might normally be associated with comedy becomes inverted to sustain a tragedy. In short, and in addition to his absorption and possible appropriation of details from popular non-dramatic fictional narratives, Shakespeare can be seen here to be using at least one of his earlier plays as a 'resource', and the effect that the later play produces in the theatre is enhanced by audience awareness of the earlier one.

This reservoir of material and forms has a larger theatrical context that also subsumes into its aegis the plays of Shakespeare's contemporaries, all of whom share a reservoir of stock characters, situations, paradigms, memes, plot-lines and rhetorical flourishes. In the case of *The Merchant of Venice*, for example, Shakespeare's conversation with the now dead Marlowe's *The Jew of Malta* – although it seems unlikely that such conversations were restricted to this play, given Shakespeare's exposure to a wide range of popular plays by fellow dramatists[24] – along with a longstanding repertoire of characterisations of the figure of 'the Jew' that even in twenty-first-century Western culture has, shamefully, not been eliminated from European popular consciousness, are prominent. The first of Shakespeare's Venetian plays is a comedy and the second a tragedy, the one in which the Jewish outsider is reluctantly assimilated into a Christian community and the other a tragedy where an attempted integration produces irreversibly deadly consequences. If we add to this the details from the various narratives that find their way into these plays then we have a reasonable idea of how Shakespeare assimilated material that was available from within the cultural life of society at large. This also enlarges the picture of how he innovated from his own already generated resources that, as a dramatist working under constant pressure as part of a stable company, he could refashion. At the same time, he could acknowledge his audiences' repertoires as they identified particular stock situations, motifs and quotations, as well as actors whose own theatrical histories could be recognised and recuperated by spectators that might generate a range of additional meanings.[25]

In addition to the repetition of what appear to be the more obvious elements of *The Merchant of Venice* in *Othello*, the inclusion of two minor details at the beginning of the later play go some way to reaffirming that Shakespeare still had in mind aspects of the earlier one. Iago's pornographic description of Desdemona in bed with Othello would appear simply to recall an element of Plautine comedy in pointing up the discrepancy between an 'old' husband and a 'young' wife.[26] But there is much more than that at issue:

> Your heart is burst, you have lost half your soul,
> Even now, now, very now, an old black ram
> Is tupping your white ewe! Arise, arise,
> Awake the snorting citizens with the bell
> Or else the devil will make a grandsire of you,
> Arise I say!
>
> (1.1.86–91)

Iago's phonological simulation of a bestial coupling ('Even now, now, very now') links a dehumanised, aged, libidinal, tragic hero with a 'white ewe', where the appellation 'ewe' ascribed to Desdemona links her homonymically with 'Jew', which, in its Elizabethan spelling, appears in *The Merchant of Venice* as 'Iewe'.

This reminder both of one of the features for which Venice was famed – the hospitality it accorded Jewish people – *and* the episode in the earlier play in which the 'Iewe' Jessica elopes with Lorenzo, draws the two plays even closer together. This is something that modern editors of the play have tended to overlook. Even more puzzling, and completely overlooked by editors, is the following passage a little later, as Iago moves from blank verse to prose and from the analogy of an 'old black ram' to that of a 'Barbary horse':

> Because we come to do you service, and you think we are ruffians, you'll have your daughter covered with a Barbary horse; you'll have your nephews neigh to you, you'll have coursers for cousins and jennets for germans!
>
> (1.1.108–12)

This links the Morocco of *The Merchant of Venice* with Othello, but also with a London sensation of the mid-1590s: John Bankes's talking horse Moroccus. Morocco in the earlier play becomes the 'Barbary horse' in the later play, and the Barbary horse becomes, in Iago's scurrilous discourse, Othello. The accumulation of alliterations begins with the inaccurate 'nephews' (they should be grandchildren) and quickly gathers pace ('coursers for cousins and jennets for germans') while traversing geographically the African continent and the Iberian peninsula (Barbary, jennets and germans).[27] Here Shakespeare alludes to an earlier play while at the same time affirming a series of cultural myths and sexual stereotypes which his eponymous hero both embodies and challenges.

The Merchant of Venice and *Othello* offer us a particularly tight pairing since both plays are set in Venice, but there are other groups of plays where the links are much more circumstantial but show Shakespeare innovating on material that he has used earlier. The trio of *Love's Labour's Lost*, *Romeo and Juliet* and *A Midsummer Night's Dream*, as we have seen, all play with endings. *Love's Labour's Lost* transposes material from the 'literary' Shakespeare into the play, as the King and his fellow courtiers 'invent' sonnets that appear in *The Passionate Pilgrim* (1599).[28] Moreover, the play ends in such a way that violates what are, in effect, the established rules of comedy:

> Our wooing doth not end like an old play:
> Jack hath not Jill. These ladies' courtesy
> Might well have made our sport a comedy.
>
> (5.2.862–4)[29]

The reason for the violation has a great deal to do with the status of language as a medium whose function in the play is to represent truth and the world adequately. When the King seeks to upbraid the Princess for causing him to perjure himself ('The virtue of your eye must break my oath', 5.2.348) the Princess corrects him by radically reconstructing 'virtue':

> You nickname virtue: 'vice' you should have spoke;
> For virtue's office never breaks men's troth.
> Now, by my maiden honour, yet as pure
> As the unsullied lily, I protest,
> A world of torments though I should endure,
> I would not yield to be your house's guest,
> So much I hate a breaking cause to be
> Of heavenly oaths, vowed with integrity.
>
> (5.2.349–56)

A few lines before this serious critique of 'binding language',[30] in a play whose violations of comic form Kerrigan associates specifically with Inns of Court revels, the King's greeting of the Princess with 'All hail, sweet madam, and fair time of day' is met with a telling riposte; '"Fair" in "all hail" is foul, as I conceive' (5.2.339–40) puns menacingly on 'hail', and this grammatical inversion reappears much later in the mouths of the witches in *Macbeth*: 'Fair is foul and foul is fair' (1.1.9).[31] Here a line that begins its life in or around 1595 is still active in the dramatist's memory in 1606.

Love's Labour's Lost mounts a trenchant critique of pedantic language, indeed, of specious courtly rhetoric and regal hypocrisy that is so corrosive that it makes a formal harmonious comic ending involving vows of marriage impossible. In her over-ruling of the King's refusal to admit the pageant of the Nine Worthies at the end of the play, the Princess nominates a formula for comedy:

> That sport best pleases that doth least know how –
> Where zeal strives to content and the contents

Dies in the zeal of that which it presents;
Their form confounded makes most form in mirth,
When great things labouring perish in their birth.

(5.2.514–18)

But the ending of *Love's Labour's Lost* goes much further with the admission of Marcadé, an ambassador of death whose news of the Princess's father's death results in the ridiculous scene beginning to 'cloud' (5.2.716). This is in part what Terry Eagleton calls 'a kind of *comédie noire* or carnivalesque parody',[32] which diminishes the symbolic power of the Nine Worthies at the same time as it displaces onto the lords a sense of the magnitude of their own indiscretions. The penalty that Rosaline imposes on Berowne reinforces a connection between *eros* and *thanatos* that Berowne would wish to keep apart because he thinks the task 'impossible':

To move wild laughter in the throat of death?
It cannot be, it is impossible.
Mirth cannot move a soul in agony.

(5.2.843–5)

Rosaline's response is to outline a principle of reception and to emphasise the social function of laughter: 'A jest's prosperity lies in the ear / Of him that hears it, never in the tongue / Of him that makes it' (5.2.849–51). This is the kind of laughter that encourages the audience to forget death and to place its faith in the diurnal progress from winter to spring embodied in the movement of the seasons from death to regeneration. This complex equation is prompted by the collision of the pageant which fulfils the function of a play-within-the-play, and the ambassador of death.

Two other plays, roughly contemporaneous with *Love's Labour's Lost*, also make use of this formula, but in slightly different ways. *A Midsummer Night's Dream* places less direct attention on the constitutive functions of language and attributes the play's confusions to a petulant deity whose patriarchal authority is denied. Once matters are corrected in the fairy world, then the pairing of the lovers in the earthly world that has already managed with supernatural assistance to face down patriarchal authority conforms to the formal requirements of comedy:

> And the country proverb known,
> That every man should take his own,
> In your waking shall be shown:
> Jack shall have Jill,
> Nought shall go ill;
> The man shall have his mare again, and all shall be well.
>
> (3.2.458–63)[33]

However, the figure of Puck acknowledges a curious commitment to a more threatening darkness than the ending of the play suggests. Already Titania has been forced into a humiliating engagement with an ass, while the mischievous sprite acknowledges the controlling power of 'the triple Hecate's team':

> And we fairies that do run
> By the triple Hecate's team
> From the presence of the sun,
> Following darkness like a dream,
> Are now in frolic;
>
> (5.1.369–73)

Despite the play's formal comic ending, the 'darkness' to which Puck alludes is capable of producing alternatives that are more threatening. This is, perhaps, another version of that collision between laughter and death, between *eros* and *thanatos* that informs the ending of *Love's Labour's Lost*. Also at Theseus's court, not unlike that of the King of Navarre, a curious 'pageant' is performed that provides an alternative to the audience's expectations of a formal comic conclusion; it comprises '"A tedious brief scene of young Pyramus / And his love Thisbe, very tragical mirth"?' (5.1.56–7) that Theseus glosses as 'hot ice, and wondrous strange snow!' (5.2.59). The narrative substance of the play-within-the-play appears in a brief account in Arthur Golding's translation of Ovid's *Metamorphoses*, where the action is set in 'darkenesse'[34] and turns upon Pyramus's mistaking of evidence that his lover Thisbe has been killed. In the hands of the 'rude mechanicals' in *A Midsummer Night's Dream*, just as in *Love's Labour's Lost*, the theatrical mechanics of representation itself are laid open.

Bottom (Pyramus) is unable to sustain the fiction, and in Brechtian manner departs from his assigned role to explain to his audience the very means whereby the play achieves its effects. Similarly, the Prologue (Quince) violates the rules of verse speaking, as Lysander observes: 'He hath rid his prologue like a rough colt; he knows not the stop. A good moral my lord: it is not enough to speak, but to speak true' (5.1.119–21). There is an irony here since Lysander is wholly unaware of the means whereby his own role has been manipulated. Indeed, his exhortation to 'speak true' is thoroughly undermined by what we already know of the means whereby the paired lovers are brought together. Of course, the comic element of the Pyramus and Thisbe performance is *not* in the tale itself, which is concerned with tragic mistaking; indeed, the tale's seriousness is undermined by the comic exposure of the business of representation itself. This distancing of the fable performs a similar function to that of the representation of the Nine Worthies, except that in *A Midsummer Night's Dream* both the onstage and offstage audiences are already assured of a traditional comic conclusion. Night, darkness and the triple Hecate's team notwithstanding, violence and death are kept at bay. Here Shakespeare uses stock theatrical situations and the formulae embedded in them to work through definitions of comedy that involve varying engagements with the troubling entanglement of *eros* and *thanatos*, and we can see him building a repertoire of devices that can be tweaked to fit particular dramatic occasions. Perhaps *Macbeth* looks back to part of the vocabulary of these early plays as 'triple Hecate' morphs later into the Weird Sisters.

While the connection between *Love's Labour's Lost* and *A Midsummer Night's Dream* has not, until Henry Woudhuysen's Arden 3 edition of the play, attracted much critical attention,[35] the connections between the latter and *Romeo and Juliet*, have. As the Arden 3 editor René Weiss observes, recalling the Arden 2 editor of the play, the latter two plays have been regarded as a diptych forming 'different sides of the same coin, tragedy and comedy, Romeo and Juliet / Pyramus and Thisbe as burlesque first cousins'.[36] The dating of the plays is uncertain, although it is generally thought that they are all grouped closely together in terms of composition, indicating that each contains material that might furnish resources for the others. All three share a preoccupation with endings and with particular kinds of teleology. But it is in *Romeo and Juliet* that the reversal from comedy to tragedy is sustained throughout. Under normal formal circumstances the young lovers would be expected to surmount the obstacles to their relationship, except that the 'ancient grudge' referred to by the Prologue has a serious quasi-Senecan inevitability about it. Whereas in *Love's Labour's Lost* and *A Midsummer Night's Dream* the representation of the serious and the potentially tragic are laughed away, in *Romeo and Juliet* the lovers are placed in a position where Romeo's death is the result of an error that in *A Midsummer Night's Dream* Bottom can correct by means of thespian ineptitude. Juliet's is also a heavily symbolic sacrifice that links death and the erotic. Weiss makes the point, correctly, that Shakespeare does not follow the moralistic trajectory of Arthur Brooke's *Tragicall Historye of Romeus and Juliet* (1562), although his theatrical imagination may have been stimulated by a small detail in the Friar's defence of his innocence towards the end of the poem. When the deaths of the lovers are discovered the Friar has in his hands 'the yrons' with which he is accused of having committed the murders:

> As for the yrons that were taken in my hand,
> As now I deeme, I neede not seeke, to make ye understande
> To what use yron was first made, when it began:
> How of it selfe it helpeth not, ne yet can helpe a man.
> The thing it hurteth, is the malice of his will,
> That such indifferent thinges is wont to use and order ill.
> (ll. 2875–80)[37]

On occasions like this it is customary to pause and speculate on the manner of Shakespeare's reading, although if we do that then there is a danger that the conclusion that can be drawn from a comparison might as easily point to Shakespeare's *lack* of originality. In *Romeo and Juliet* the Friar enters at Act 2 Scene 3, '*alone, with a basket*', and is gathering 'baleful weeds and precious-juiced flowers' (2.3.4); he goes on to ponder the economy of Nature:

> O, mickle is the powerful grace that lies
> In plants, herbs, stones and their true qualities,
> For naught so vile that on the earth doth live
> But to the earth some special good doth give,
> Nor naught so good but, strained from that fair use,

Revolts from true birth, stumbling on abuse.
Virtue itself turns vice, being misapplied,
And vice sometime by action dignified.

(2.3.11–18)

Brooke's 'such indifferent thinges is wont to use and order yll' (l. 2880) is in Shakespeare's play worked up to a level of aphorism that can be shown to underpin the entire play; it encompasses the Friar's gathering of herbs *and* the Apothecary's 'culling of simples' (5.1.40) pointing to a moral paradox that resides at the heart of Nature, thereby drawing attention to the contingent elements of the drama, and it inform the deaths of the lovers at the end.

At the end of the play the lovers are free but it is questionable whether their suicidal disposing of themselves is what Eagleton, in a much more general consideration of tragedy, identifies as the 'highest freedom', which is 'to opt for one's own extinction'. Eagleton goes on to suggest that tragic heroism involves a mixture of 'defiance and submission in equal measure, fusing rebellion and authority, will and law, spirit and nature'. He sees tragedy as 'essentially a question of reconciliation',[38] although in the case of Romeo and Juliet the sheer physicality of their love – symbolised in the generally acknowledged *petit mort* of orgasm – is overwhelmed by the irreversible reality of death itself. The presence of the murdered Paris in the tomb with the lovers testifies to the patriarchal 'law' that has brought Romeo and Juliet to this pass. It is not until the two patriarchs, Montague and Capulet, come together at the end of the play that 'reconciliation' is effected, but not before the Duke upbraids them:

> Capulet, Montague,
> See what a scourge is laid upon your hate,
> That heaven finds means to kill your joys with love;
> And I, for winking at your discords too,
> Have lost a brace of kinsmen. All are punished.
>
> (5.3.291–5)

The price that is paid for this reconciliation is the loss of children, as Montague and Capulet exchange golden icons, inanimate statues that are 'poor sacrifices of our enmity' (5.3.304), in a lifeless, sterile world deprived of the capacity to regenerate itself. To some extent the teleology of *Romeo and Juliet* is written against that of *Love's Labour's Lost* where the obstacle to marriage cannot be fitted into the scope of a play, and in the case of *A Midsummer Night's Dream* against an adjustment to the 'means' that are found to reconcile the lovers. Shakespeare will later return to questions of death, reconciliation and, indeed, resurrection, and the theatrical devices that sustain and expand them, in *Much Ado About Nothing* (1600) and, most remarkably, in *The Winter's Tale* (c.1611).[39]

Just as Shakespeare adds to a body of theatrical work, so he accumulates theatrical forms, memes, paradigms, devices and the different kinds of language that will allow him to shape and descant upon existing narratives. This building of resources will allow him to repeat, in his own distinctive fashion, a range of theatrical devices, but also to innovate, to utilise and invent particular dramatic forms that give his plays a distinctive – but perhaps corporate – identity that the claims of 'originality' do not quite address. This is essentially how someone like Shakespeare, who worked primarily within the oral culture of the theatre, would have confronted a variety of literary narratives that had entered into the public domain. By engaging with these different resources, Shakespeare and his fellow writers could impose upon their materials distinctively dramatic shapes, thereby generating a meta-language in which content and form interact creatively. This is all part and parcel of learning one's trade, just as the printing-house compositor learned how to set up a page and to adjust, improve and innovate as and when the occasion demanded. Resource (and resourcefulness) is in these instances the hallmark of professional skill.

Further testimony to the malleability of Shakespeare's resources appears in a trio of plays, two of which we have already identified as showing evidence of sharing particular forms: *Love's Labour's Lost*, *The Taming of the Shrew* and *Much Ado About Nothing*. Each of these plays is concerned with the problematic role of women in the social order. The comic mechanisms are similar in that in each an obstacle is required to be overcome before the social order can settle down. In *Love's Labour's Lost* the Princess and her female companions have the upper hand throughout, and become the instruments whereby the King and his male companions come to some partial understanding of what they have contributed to the impasse that prevents the play from concluding in traditional comic manner. The Princess is on an ambassadorial mission, so the plight of the King it is not simply a question of some kind of neo-Platonic compulsion. Indeed, it is for this reason that the play's intrinsic philosophy of language is so important. Elsewhere in Shakespeare – for example in plays like *As You Like It* – lovers are simply smitten, but in a 'fantasy' play like *The Taming of the Shrew*, where Christopher Sly remains in his metamorphosed form at the end,[40] the failure of what Hodgdon labels 'frame characters' to return seems to her decidedly unorthodox since 'not only does it have *two* fully dramatised scenes that preface "the play proper", but Sly's role creates an expectational (and performative) excess which feeds the desire to see him return'.[41] We shall return to what many critics have regarded as the 'problem' of Christopher Sly shortly, but for the moment let us concentrate on the figure of Kate, who for a large part of the play refuses to adopt an appropriate role in the game that patriarchy has mapped out for her.

Kate is the 'shrew', the obstacle, whose 'taming' is the condition that her father lays down for the marriage of her younger sister Bianca. A suitor is found who will play Kate at her own game and, as Jonathan Bate rightly observes, the relationship between her and Petrucchio is part of a structure in which we are invited to compare it against three others: 'Bianca and Lucentio, Hortensio and his widow' and 'Sly and his offstage wife'.[42] The Folio text of the play tells us nothing about this last relationship, and there is a danger that reading Shakespeare's text against the anonymous *The Taming of a Shrew* (1594), particularly in relation to the latter's epilogue that returns Sly to the waking world, generates the excess that is then projected onto *The Taming of the Shrew*. Perhaps we should speculate further on why there is no Epilogue in Shakespeare's version before seeking explanations of how that absence feeds into the complex textual debates that have surrounded Shakespeare's play.

In 1971 a firebrand Germaine Greer offered an account of the play that today many (including feminists) might find unsettling. The passage is worth quoting in full:

> The submission of a woman like Kate is genuine and exciting because she has something to lay down, her virgin pride and individuality:

Bianca is the soul of duplicity, married without earnestness or good will. Kate's speech at the close of the play is the greatest defence of Christian monogamy ever written. It rests upon the role of a husband as protector and friend, and it is valid because Kate has a man who is capable of being both, for Petruchio is both gentle and strong (it is a vile distortion of the play to have him strike her ever). The message is probably twofold: only Kates make good wives, and only to Petruchios; for the rest, their cake is dough.[43]

Greer's omission of the figure of the Widow is telling, but her evident enthusiasm for the relationship between Kate and Petrucchio fails to register his threats of violence towards her and their ultimate effect. It is perhaps unsurprising that the Christopher Sly of *The Taming of a Shrew* should regard what he has seen as a blueprint for 'taming' his own wife. The title of the chapter in which Greer's comments on Shakespeare's play appear is 'The middle-class myth of love and marriage', although the approving manner in which she describes the Kate–Petrucchio relationship accredits it with a limited veracity beyond the status of 'myth'. The preoccupation of Elizabethan patriarchy with the problem of female resistance, and the interference of an older generation in the sexual behaviour of the younger, may well have been issues that an audience could recognise. But we should also give such an audience credit for distinguishing between the 'fantasy' with which *The Taming of a Shrew* concludes, and the evident refusal to follow its example in *The Taming of the Shrew*. Indeed, as Barbara Hodgdon observes, much of the violence in Shakespeare's play is displaced onto servants, and what she calls 'the vulgarity of oral tradition' is replaced in the play by a series of displacements as the 'potentially violent impulses that Petrucchio harbours get worked out not on Katherine's body, as in folk-tales, but on her clothes – and are displaced further down the social scale when Grumio threatens his subordinate, the lowly Tailor (4.3)'.[44] The difference is between the drunken tinker who may well return home and beat and starve his wife into submission,[45] and the ironic compromise that Kate makes that may, or may not, be out of fear of the power and resolve of her husband. The triptych of Bianca and Lucentio, the Widow and Hortensio, and Kate and Petrucchio all interact with each other to produce meaning. Both Bianca and the Widow ridicule Kate's manifest combination of obedience and subservience, and we are left wondering whether hers is a strategy for survival or a genuine capitulation.[46]

Hodgdon's analysis of the closing stage directions in Quarto and Folio, and her editorial decision to suggest an unresolved formal ending for the exit of Kate and Petruccio,[47] leaves open the possibility of an ironic ending. Also, little has been made of Petruccio's parting comment that condenses sexual meaning and patriarchal anxiety:

> Come Kate, we'll to bed –
> We three are married, but you two are sped.
> 'Twas I won the wager, though you hit the white,
> And being a winner, God give you good night.
> *Exit Petruccio*
>
> (5.2.190–3)

The use of the past participle 'sped' followed by the conditional clause 'though you hit the white' suggests a failure on the part of Lucentio and Hortensio to properly fulfil their sexual obligations in marriage.[48] In other words, although they have 'hit the white' in that they have superficially achieved possession of their wives' sexual parts, they are 'sped' in the sense that their wagering is a form of metaphorical premature ejaculation.[49] Is it possible, also, that their primary interest in money implies the kind of sterility that Aristotle had associated with the 'breeding' of money? This rather concentrated ending of Shakespeare's play is not so much a rejection of the oral folk tradition, but a bringing up to date of its concerns against a backdrop of a reality addressed by *An Homilie of the State of Matrimonie*, with its awareness that the husband should 'yeelde some thing to the woman'.[50] Of course, we do not quite know *what* Petruccio has 'yielded' to Kate, just as we can never be quite sure of the tone of her capitulation.

This concern with endings and with the teleological implications of the dramatic action occurs again in *Love's Labour's Lost* where the Princess and her companions are not so much 'forward' as forthright in their exposure of masculine inadequacy. In this play the attack on language makes an ending dependent on vows impossible. John Kerrigan may be right in his account of the occasion of the play,[51] and he indicates a strand of word-play 'that points to the potential looseness of what is bound in language'.⁵² That 'looseness', however, has many facets, ranging from the possible irony of Kate's superficially moralistic statement of Christian marriage at the end of *The Taming of the Shrew*, through the enforced silence of Beatrice in *Much Ado About Nothing*, to Macbeth's fatal association of the words 'surcease' and 'success' (*Macbeth*, 1.7.4). In *Love's Labour's Lost* the impossibility of a teleologically authenticated ending is far more extreme than the mixture of realism and idealism that leaves doubts in the minds of spectators about the veracity of what they have just witnessed. *Love's Labour's Lost* gives 'some thing to the woman' – a power that frustrates the efforts of their suitors. This provides a counterpoint to the ending of *The Taming of the Shrew* that is ambiguous about the power that Petrucchio finally possesses. *Much Ado About Nothing*, however, unlike the one-sided dynamic of *Love's Labour's Lost*, offers a more balanced form of shrew taming that requires both a masculine *and* a feminine transformation and that shows a dramatist revisiting and revising a theatrical trope that was almost as ubiquitous as that of revenge.

Much Ado About Nothing is predicated upon the desirability of the pliant and silent wife. Leonato's wife, Innogen, who editors have systematically excised from the text as an unrealised thought, represents a silence that is offset by her daughter Hero's victimisation at one extreme and the loquacity of Beatrice at the other. By 1609, when Ben Jonson nervously justified his play *The Silent Woman* with a second prologue, the stage figure of the 'silent' woman was so familiar that it had become a sign of a pathological male fantasy:

> For he knows, poet never credit gain'd
> By writing truths, but things like truths, well feign'd.
> If any yet will, with particular sleight
> Of application, wrest what he doth write;
> And that he meant, or him, or her, will say:
> They make a libel, which he made a play.⁵³

In *Much Ado About Nothing*, that fantasy of patriarchal control unites a predominantly oral folk tradition with a realism that the *Homilie on the State of Matrimony* addresses, with the demands of comic form in which the masculine world – exposed in the figure of

Claudio for its naive and robotic stupidity – to which Benedick nominally belongs, is forced to compromise. Female silence may be the desired condition, and the play represents a silent wife – Innogen – in whose absence editors, male and female, have conveniently colluded. Hero, accused of infidelity before her marriage, is stunned into silence and at the end of the play is given to the very man, Claudio, who had earlier rejected her at the altar, while Beatrice's silence is enforced by patriarchal power. The Arden 3 editor of the play, Claire McEachern, excises Innogen, but restores the Q1 (1600) assignment of the line to Leonato – 'Peace! [*to Beatrice*] I will stop your mouth [*Hands her to Benedick*]' – and augments Theobald's stage direction.[54] The Folio version assigns the line to Benedick, and Theobald has him kiss her. The two printed versions reinforce from slightly different directions the capacity of patriarchy to enforce silence – Innogen should be present onstage at this point to see her daughter become a silent wife – with Benedick being enforced into assuming his masculine role as husband in a distinctly unromantic and, indeed, inept courtship predicated upon denial. The result is a fractionally more egalitarian version of the ending of *The Taming of the Shrew*, with the husband assuming power reluctantly and the wife retaining the propensity for 'forwardness' if her spouse does not quite come up to the mark. This theatrical device offers a variation on a situation that Shakespeare's regular theatre audiences could be expected to recognise from its use in earlier plays that function as resources upon which the dramatist and the company whose members he clearly knew well could draw as occasion demanded. Indeed, as we saw earlier, the situation that appears in *Much Ado About Nothing* was resurrected again in *The Winter's Tale*, although the focus there was on the matriarchal power of Paulina rather than the incompetent but potentially damaging patriarchy that is represented by Leonato in the earlier play.

We have already noted the links between Jonson's *Every Man in His Humour* (1598) and a series of Shakespearean repetitions of some of its elements. But within the Shakespeare *oeuvre* another set of internal connections that link Marlowe's *The Jew of Malta*, Shakespeare's *The Merchant of Venice* (1596–97) and *Othello* (c.1604) suggest that Shakespeare was prepared to rewrite creatively particular elements of the earlier play. Marlowe's play was popular and, according to Henslowe's *Diary*, continued to be performed regularly from 1591 through to June 1596.[55] In his edition of *The Jew of Malta*, N.W. Bawcutt notes (following Henslowe) some eight performances in 1596, the year before which Shakespeare's *The Merchant of Venice* probably first appeared.[56] Bawcutt has little to say about the possible connections between Marlowe's play and *The Merchant of Venice*,[57] but the Arden 2 editor of Shakespeare's play speculates that:

> Shakespeare was probably influenced by Marlowe's *The Jew of Malta*, first performed about 1589. Verbal parallels between the two plays are pointed out in annotations to the text, but more important is the probability that Marlowe's successful portrait of the villain Barabas coloured Shakespeare's conception of a Jew. Abigail, the Jew's daughter who turns Christian, may have played a part in suggesting Shylock's Jessica.[58]

That Marlowe's play was performed regularly – with peaks in 1594, the year of the Lopez affair, and late 1596, either when or just before Shakespeare's play appeared – suggests something a little more than influence. As in the cases of *Tamburlaine* or Kyd's *The Spanish Tragedy* that were regularly performed, and in the case of the latter regularly reprinted, well into the seventeenth century, Marlowe's plays clearly became part of the landscape of both oral and literate culture (both parts of *Tamburlaine* were printed in 1590, although *The Jew of Malta* remained unprinted until 1633). It seems highly likely that Shakespeare's play was in dialogue with Marlowe's and that that dialogue was continued primarily through performance.

But there were two other dimensions to Shakespeare's play that distinguished it from Marlowe's: the shift of geographical location from Malta to Venice, and the foregrounding of the issue of usury. The connection between Venice and usury was a logical one since as an active Mediterranean port it was the geographical centre of trade and finance between East and West, but it was also a locus of Elizabethan fantasy. The term 'ghetto' carries a particular resonance for a modern audience, but in the late sixteenth century it could be both a space of segregation *and* of communication between Jews and Christians. In his book *Flesh and Stone: The Body and the City* in *Western Civilization* (1994), Richard Sennett emphasises the principle of segregation in Venice, and he cites Antonio's comment on commodity and contract in which the latter 'was the key to opening the doors of wealth in this city of strangers'.[59] Sennett continues:

> A real Jewish moneylender lived in the Ghetto the Venetians built for Jews in the course of the sixteenth century. A real moneylender was let out of the Ghetto, situated at the edge of the city, at dawn, where he made his way to the financial district around the Rialto wooden drawbridge near the city's centre. By dusk the Jew was obliged to return to the cramped Ghetto; at nightfall its gates were locked, the shutters of its houses that looked outward closed; police patrolled the exterior. The medieval adage '*Stadt Luft macht frei*' would leave a bitter taste in the Jew's mouth, for the right to do business in the city did not bring a more general freedom. The Jew who contracted as an equal lived as a segregated man.[60]

In many respects Sennett appears to amalgamate the tradition of the 'mythical' Jew of medieval origin with the plight of the European Jew of the late 1930s, although his emphasis on racial difference in Venice that extended to 'Albanians, Turks, and Greeks' suggests a picture that verges on anachronism: 'Christians, *like the Germans*, all were segregated in guarded buildings or clusters of buildings. Difference haunted the Venetians, yet exerted a seductive power' (my italics).[61]

The historian Simon Schama has revised this picture, arguing that: 'The Venice ghetto was not a place of absolute physical segregation, nor were Venetian Jews stripped of all occupations other than the reviled rag trade and moneylending.'[62] Schama notes a vibrant traffic in and out of the Ghetto, even though its 'bridges and gates were closed only at dusk'. Indeed, what he calls 'the universe of Jews' within its confines included 'black Jews (the Jewish *moro*, Moor, often an ex-slave, which could easily have made Othello Jewish. Thus folding two Shakespeare plays into one)'. But he also notes that 'not a few Christian men and women spent more time in the close company of Jewish men and women, *even after the hours of gate and bridge closing*, than was legally permissible' (my italics).[63] Schama's description seems much closer to the historical Venice and harmonises more closely than Sennett's account with the description of Venice and its legal and social structures that appeared in Lewis Lewkenor's translation of Gasparo Contarini's *The Commonwealth and Government of Venice* (1599). Shakespeare's Jew, and later his Moor, both appear to have freedoms in Venice that challenge the inherited prejudices and myths of an English audience, and in the two Venetian plays those prejudices and myths are integral to the tensions of both dramas. What we might now call the 'fake news' generated by myth and prejudice is made to confront a represented reality that seriously complicates the received popular knowledge of the Jew and the Moor as two sides of a carefully nuanced Venetian coin. If, as Sennett observed, 'difference haunted the Venetians', then it also haunted Shakespeare's two Venetian plays and suggested certain structural features that develop from one play to the other.

The Merchant of Venice is uncompromising in its reference on the title page of Q1 to 'the extreme crueltie of *Shylocke* the Iewe'. Name and racial identity here are juxtaposed provocatively, in that 'Shylock' is an English name,[64] rendering what we might call a 'split subject', hence the need for the combination of the name 'Shylock' and the designation 'Jew'. Moreover, Salarino's allegation against Shylock that 'There is more difference between thy flesh and hers [Jessica's] than there is between jet and ivory, more between your bloods than there is between red wine and Rhenish' (3.1.34–6) suggests that either literally or metaphorically the Jew is dark skinned, and is therefore closely related to the unfortunate Morocco, whose earlier appearance and failure in the casket test in Act 2 Scene 7 exposes, as we have seen, a miscegenistic tendency evidently anticipated by the machinations of Portia's dead father. So much for the freedom accorded to strangers in Venice and Belmont. The play does not allow Portia to choose her own partner or, like Jessica, to elope; and where Antonio's anxiety derives from a mercantilist uncertainty about the success or failure of his trading investments, rooted deeply in his Christian faith, Portia's equally debilitating frustration derives from the patriarchal controlling of her 'blood':

> The brain may devise laws for the blood, but a hot temper leaps o'er a cold decree; such a hare is madness the youth, to skip o'er the meshes

of good counsel the cripple. But this reasoning is not in the fashion
to choose me a husband. O me, the words 'choose'! I may neither
choose who I would, nor refuse who I dislike, so is the will of a living
daughter curbed by the will of a dead father. Is it not hard, Nerissa,
that I cannot choose one, nor refuse none?

(1.2.17–25)

Here Portia internalises what in the earlier *A Midsummer Night's Dream* becomes a central structural issue as Hermia and her father clash over the choice of a marriage partner. In *The Merchant of Venice* a series of domestic tensions arise that effectively spread the anxiety until it finally engulfs the newly Christianised Shylock. In the play, the ultimate fulfilment of a Christian fantasy comes, but at a price. Also, the elopement of Jessica provides a contrast with Portia's situation that leads to Shylock's enforced conversion.[65] Already a situation that is partially envisaged in an earlier play is here fleshed out, repeated and expanded into a relatively new area of dramatic enquiry. In *The Merchant of Venice* the myth of an egalitarian state is carefully dismantled, with both the stranger and the Venetian daughter registering at the level of social organisation and psychology political and financial anxieties that the structures of patriarchy and estrangement impose upon both categories of person.

While it is possible to read into the figure of Shylock an identity that the dramatic character may suggest to particular readers,[66] Shakespeare's play is very careful to negotiate a path between Venice's claims for its institutions and financial practices, and the space occupied by a suitably fictionalised outsider who articulates and puts into practice the very sentiments that render him marginal, but who is also given a position from which to mount a scathing critique of his oppressors. It is this structure that is replicated and further sophisticated in *Othello*. There what is present only briefly in the earlier play is expanded to occupy the centre of the tragedy. What does not happen in the Portia–Morocco encounter is fused together with the Jessica–Lorenzo elopement to become the foundation of the Othello–Desdemona relationship that ends in tragedy.

In 1992 Kim Hall drew attention to the manifest presence of the outsider in *The Merchant of Venice*, and the threat posed thereby to every level of Venetian life. Hall noted how the familiar myth of the Jewish 'blood libel' is invoked in the play but in a displaced form to signal fears of colonisation and miscegenation, and she argued that:

> Shylock's reluctance to eat with the Christian displays the fear of 'be[ing] subsumed ... by a hostile host,' but in terms that ratify the reciprocal Christian fear of being consumed by a guest/alien who has been allowed into the home/country.[67]

Hall later went on to observe: 'Shylock gives himself a dual genealogy that associates him with blackness, forbidden sexuality, and the unlawful appropriation of property.'[68] While we cannot be certain that Shylock's blackness was visually represented on the stage, Othello's is. Indeed, both strangers are represented as alien but *necessary* to the financial probity and military wellbeing of Venice. In the one case we observe the process and the consequences of the Jew's forced assimilation into Venice, but his emotional life, such as it is, is contingent upon Venetian pressures that are shown to affect its own indigenous citizens. In Othello's case we see how the hero's psychology is shaped by his interiorising of certain Venetian values that provide an alternative view of the mythical Venice.

The case of Othello is a considerable sophistication of the earlier model, even though the play may have, in part, been stimulated by contemporary metropolitan fears about the influx of, and Elizabeth I's attempts to expel, 'blackamoors'.[69] If Shylock's blackness is metaphorical, and is a product of discourse, there is no mistaking Othello's. The disparity between the 'noble Moor' and his physical appearance could not be more extreme, and it presented a serious challenge to the accepted notion of a 'national identity' that the play projects onto Venice. That the Venetian conception of a national identity is rendered problematical from the outset may be seen in the ease with which Desdemona's father, the patriarchal Brabantio, succumbs easily to Iago and Roderigo's characterisation of Othello; to the allegations that 'an old black ram / Is tupping your white ewe', and that unless the citizens are awakened then 'the devil will make a grandsire of you' (1.1.87–88 and 90), Brabantio retorts, as we saw earlier, with a brief glimpse into the Venetian patriarchal unconscious that is even more revealing than Shylock's exposure of the Venetian behaviour that he confesses to mimicking.

It is a confession of an anxiety that will ultimately kill Brabantio (the first victim) and finally Othello himself, who, through the intermediary of Iago, will inherit the anxieties of his father-in-law. The noble Moor and defender of Venice is gradually persuaded to relinquish all judicious means of arriving at an accurate judgement, as he confronts what he takes to be the split subject of his wife:

> O thou weed
> Who art so lovely fair and smell'st so sweet
> That the sense aches at thee, would thou hads't ne'er been born!
>
> (4.2.67–70)

and:

> Was this fair paper, this goodly book
> Made to write 'whore' upon?
>
> (4.2.72–3)

and finally:

> I cry you mercy then.
> I took you for that cunning whore of Venice
> That married with Othello. You! Mistress!
>
> (4.2.90–92)

This is, of course, an unwitting projection of his own self-division, one that infects the play, just as the alleged courtesan Bianca bears the name that signifies 'white'. It is left to the waiting-woman Emilia (Iago's wife) to expose the plight and behaviour of the 'white ewe' Desdemona as an *effect* that is contingent upon her husband's behaviour:

> But I do think it is their husbands' faults
> If wives do fall. Say that they slack their duties
> And pour our treasures into foreign laps;
> Or else break out in peevish jealousies,
> Throwing restraint upon us; or say they striker us,
> Or scant our former having in despite,
> Why, we have galls: and though we have some grace
> Yet have we some revenge. ...

Then let them use us well: else let them know,
The ills we do, their ills instruct us so.

(4.3.85–102)

This is Shylock's 'Hath not a Jew eyes?' speech, repositioned and domesticated now at the very heart of Venice's sexual politics. The link between 'Jew' and 'female', suppressed in the earlier play, is here brought out into the open and in such a way that it is Venice's patriarchal politics that is a contributory cause of the state's anxieties. Indeed, what at the end of *The Merchant of Venice* is left as a question mark over female constancy, that is a contingent imitation of male inconstancy, is now in *Othello* placed firmly in the domain of a masculine competitiveness that the outsider, Othello, is persuaded to internalise. And when he acts decisively on the visual 'evidence' that Iago fashions for him and kills Desdemona, then he becomes the devil through and through:

> OTHELLO. She's like a liar gone to burning hell:
> 'Twas I that killed her.
> EMILIA. O, the more angel she,
> And you the blacker devil!
>
> (5.2.127–9)

At this point, Iago's initial allegation is fulfilled, and Othello becomes the stereotyped outsider that fuelled the Elizabethan myth of blackness. We saw how in *The Merchant of* Venice the price of assimilation was an uneasy domestication, but, with no chance of assimilation of the outsider who has now become the deed's creature in *Othello*, the play does not and cannot leave it there.

Having murdered Desdemona on the flimsy evidence of the *myth* of female behaviour, where the woman is forbidden to have an independent identity no matter what decisions she might make for herself, Othello then turns on himself. Portia's unruly 'blood' in the earlier play can be contained within the boundaries of marriage that patriarchy controls, even from beyond the grave. And even in the more problematical case of Jessica, the unruly and disobedient woman can be brought into the Christian fold through her marriage to Lorenzo. Modern productions of the play have toyed with representing the psychological effects upon Jessica of her conversion, but the text we have of the play offers very little evidence to sustain this.

In *Othello* the unruly daughter suffers for her decision even though her initial judgement of her spouse strives in the face of her father's implacable opposition to efface the negative effects of his physical appearance. In a manner that anticipates Cordelia in the later play *King Lear*, Desdemona acknowledges what she perceives to be 'a divided duty':

> I do perceive here a divided duty.
> To you I am bound for life and education:
> My life and education both do learn me
> How to respect you: you are the lord of duty.
> I am hitherto your daughter. But here's my husband:
> And so much duty as my mother showed
> To you, preferring you before her father,
> So much I challenge that I may profess
> Due to the Moor my lord.
>
> (1.3.181–9)

If, within the state, the woman occupies a position that is always hybrid – and both Emilia and Bianca indicate the effects of that hybridity within patriarchy – then the outsider displays a much more extreme and consequently more threatening version of this division. In Othello's case the dividing line is between the civilised and the 'barbaric', the Venetian and the Turk. In *The Merchant of Venice* the Jew's 'desires / Are wolvish, bloody, starved and ravenous' (4.1.136–7) and yet he is assimilable into the rituals of a Christian Venice. In *Othello* the eponymous hero enacts a murder that the subsequent enquiry into the truth of Desdemona's wifely duty cannot rectify. In the earlier play the Jew leaves the stage but we are given only the briefest of glimpses into his state of mind. In the later play the hero's self-division is played out in an extraordinary suicide that reveals the psychic life of the outsider forced to struggle with the effects of his own hybrid identity. That struggle is internalised as Othello is made to confront the difference between 'truth' and the myths of femininity that an anxious patriarchal culture generates; indeed, that difference is rearticulated as a military struggle effected on the boundary between Venice and Cyprus, between Venetian and Turk. Of course, Othello is both the Venetian *and* the Turk, a divided Manichean self where the killing of the one must also involve the killing of the other:

> Set you down this,
> And say besides that in Aleppo once
> Where a malignant and a turbanned Turk
> Beat a Venetian and traduced the state,
> I took by th' throat the circumcised dog
> And smote him – thus! *He stabs himself*
>
> (5.2.349–54)

The internal anxieties of a republic that relies upon outsiders to defend its interests are here laid bare. What Venetian institutions seem able to assimilate in the earlier play, thereby displacing negative energies into the domain of a tense domesticity, is in the later play irresolvable, hence the replaying of the concerns of the earlier play as a tragedy in the later one.

Shakespeare's two Venetian plays form a kind of diptych, displacing a range of recognisable Elizabethan anxieties onto the screen of a republic that differed significantly from the 'monarchic republic' that Sir Thomas Smith's *De Republica Anglorum* (1583) describes. The shift from the one play to the other offers us an insight into some of the ways in which Shakespeare deployed resources that he himself had generated, that he could further concentrate and even extend. But the passage from one play to the other opens up a pathway designed, in the words of Robert Weimann, 'to help ensure the play's post-scriptural future'.[70] *The Merchant of Venice* leaves open more or less uncertain futures for the dramatic characters, while *Othello* ends on the promise to loosen the villain's tongue and thereby to begin the play again.

However, in a much earlier and still very influential book, *Shakespeare and the Popular Tradition in the Theatre* (1978), Weimann undertook to trace the emergence of 'popular' theatrical forms in the developing Elizabethan theatre; he was preoccupied, among other things, with the various levels of stage representation and their significance for the engagement of the audience. We have noted in passing how Louise George Clubb's theatregrams described a process of 'contamination and complication, [which] illustrates how theatre came from theatre, self-nourishing, self-reproducing, and evolving'.[71] Weimann's quarry was much broader, both taking on board a linear perspective *and* showing how it evolved in the sophisticated (but still popular) drama of an innovative dramatist such as Shakespeare. In a section late on in the book entitled '*Figurenposition*: the correlation of position and expression', Weimann was concerned to evaluate something much more formal than character; it was 'a more objective understanding of *Figurenposition* – the actor's position on the stage, and the speech, action, and degree of stylization associated with that position'.[72] Initially his focus is upon 'Shakespearean clowns', although this extends to 'the porters in *Macbeth* and *Henry VIII*, the gravediggers in *Hamlet*, Bottom in *A Midsummer Night's Dream*, the nurse in *Romeo and Juliet*, Richard Gloucester, Iago, the Fool, and, partly, Edmund in *King Lear*, Falstaff, Thersites, Apemantus, – and with some reservations – Aaron in *Titus Andronicus*, the Bastard Falconbridge in *King John*, and Autolycus in *The Winter's Tale*'.[73]

What Bart Van Es identifies as the consequence of Shakespeare's consolidation of his position as a member of a stable theatre company, and what Louise George Clubb believes to be the circulating influence of the models of Italian drama, Weimann recognises as the determinant amalgamation of a native English tradition with other pressures. He takes the role of Apemantus in Timon's feasting scene in the late play *Timon of Athens* as a sophisticated version of the morality Vice figure, and he notes that:

> The process of drawing the audience into the play has become inseparable from the development of a complementary perspective that helps refine basic issues and restructure basic positions; at the same time, the process of differentiation between truth and appearance has become part of the dramatic mode itself. Dramatic images of central conflicts achieve a greater depth when subjected both to mimetic representation and self-expressive enactment: for through this mode the audience is drawn into the tensions between the feast and reality between words and their meaning, flattery and criticism, enchantment and disenchantment.[74]

It is possible to trace this device back through Iago in *Othello*, Thersites in *Troilus and Cressida*, Falstaff in the *Henry IV* plays, Shylock in *The Merchant of Venice*, to Richard in *Richard III*, or even to Aaron in *Titus Andronicus*, thereby blurring the clear boundaries that Van Es seeks to impose – not entirely implausibly – upon Shakespeare's *oeuvre*.[75]

One concluding example may serve to illustrate the intertwining of Shakespeare's own resources with those that surrounded him. In Q2 *Hamlet* (1605), the King asks: 'How fares our cosin *Hamlet*?' (3.2.96). The response he gets is:

> Excellent yfaith,
> Of the Camelions dish, I eate the ayre,
> Promiscram'd, you cannot feede Capons so.
>
> (3.2.98–100)

The Folio (1623) revises the lineation, spelling and punctuation, but the word order is identical:

> Excellent Ifaith, of the Camelions dish: I eate
> the Ayre promise-crammed, you cannot feed capons so.
>
> (TLN 1949–50)

The Arden 3 editors note that this derives from a proverb noted by Dent (L505.1) in which it is stated: 'Love is like a chameleon that feeds on air.'[76] Shakespeare had used this striking proverbial saying before in *The Two Gentlemen of Verona*, but an instance of its usage seems to have been much closer to home. Editors and scholars have always commented on Robert Greene's reference in *Greenes Groatsworth of Wit, Bought with a Million of Repentance*, first printed in London in 1592, to Shakespeare as an 'upstart crow'. What they have failed to notice is that in addition to a number of other ideas in this pamphlet, with which Shakespeare may have had some familiarity, there is a reference to the air-fed chameleon. It occurs at the point in Roberto the prodigal's story when he has persuaded his erstwhile brother, Lucanio, to fall for the courtesan Laminia and to consume much of his patrimony in the process.[77] The following outlines the despondent Lucanio's mind at this point in the story:

> In this sorrow he sate down on pennilesse bench: where when *Opus* and *Usus* told him by the chymes in his stomacke it was time to fall unto meat, he was faine with the Camelion to feed upon the aire, and make patience his best repast.[78]

There is, perhaps, not a little retrospective irony in the claims Greene made against routine imitators and borrowers of the language of others, that he should himself not think too deeply about his own borrowings. Moreover, it has been suggested that Greene himself contributed to the text of *Titus Andronicus*, so the two writers may have been more closely acquainted than his waspish denigration of a fellow collaborator would suggest.

Clearly, however, the context of the remark on the chameleon, and the irony, is different in *Hamlet* (Q2 and Folio) from its appearance in Greene's pamphlet. But the sentiment had appeared in John Lyly's *Endymion* (1591), printed the year before Greene's pamphlet and possibly before the appearance of *The Two Gentlemen of Verona*,[79] this time in a less sordid context than that of Greene. On each appearance up to and including Q2 *Hamlet*, the context in which the sentiment was deployed was different, although each innovation carried something of the emotional charge of its predecessor. A garbled version of Shakespeare's usage appears in Q1 *Hamlet*:

> KING How now son *Hamlet*, how fare you, shall we haue a play?
> HAM. Yfaith the Camelions dish, not capon cramm'd, feede a the ayre.
>
> (sig. F3^r)

All usages derive from a common stock that came into Shakespeare's theatrical vocabulary in or around 1591–92 and that he returned to around 1599. To reduce the genealogy to a linear pattern is to diminish the vitality of a proverbial utterance that was alive both in literary parlance and possibly in the living oral language of Shakespeare's audiences. In other words, as with various dramatic forms, situations, theatrical devices and rhetorical ploys, Shakespeare internalised them as part of a developing professional competence, and they were for him a living resource that became his own and that he could recall and deploy as occasions demanded.

Notes

1 Louise George Clubb, *Italian Drama in Shakespeare's Time* (New Haven and London, 1989), pp. 7–8.

2 Tanya Pollard, *Greek Tragic Women on Shakespearean Stages* (Oxford, 2017).
3 Raymond Williams, *The Long Revolution* (Harmondsworth, 1975), p. 22.
4 Bart Van Es, *Shakespeare in Company* (Oxford, 2015), p. 60.
5 *Ibid.*, p. 36.
6 Clubb, *Italian Drama*, pp. 50–1.
7 Van Es, *Shakespeare in Company*, p. 14.
8 *Ibid.*, pp. 3–4.
9 *Ibid.*, p. 27. But see also pp. 79ff., where Van Es argues that there is a dividing line in Shakespeare's career as a writer between the early 1590s and 1594 when he became a 'company man' taking a clear interest in the affairs of one acting company. Van Es isolates particular devices that occur in plays like *Love's Labour's Lost* and *A Midsummer Night's Dream*, the earliest plays post-1594 in which 'the matching and mismatching of parts' (p. 79) figure prominently. However, Shakespeare carried over from this earlier period an interest in endings and other devices that he had deployed from the earlier to the later period.
10 See John Drakakis, '*Macbeth* and "sovereign process"', in John Drakakis and Dale Townshend, eds, *Macbeth: A Critical Reader* (London, 2013), pp. 123–52.
11 See William Shakespeare, *Coriolanus*, ed. Peter Holland, Arden 3 series (London, 2013), p. 33. Holland favours the 1595 edition of North on the basis of 'Shakespeare's confusion of spelling between *Lartius* and *Latius*'.
12 *Ibid.*
13 Geoffrey Bullough, *Narrative and Dramatic Sources of Shakespeare*, 8 vols (London, 1957–75), vol. 5, p. 498.
14 *Ibid.*, p. 545.
15 *Ibid.*, p. 543.
16 *Ibid.*, p. 551.
17 Williams, *The Long Revolution*, p. 49.
18 Bullough, *Narrative and Dramatic Sources*, vol. 5, pp. 553–63.
19 See Van Es, *Shakespeare in Company*, pp. 56ff., which treads a very careful line between the 'literary' and the 'theatrical' Shakespeare. Indeed, the publication of Shakespeare's non-dramatic poetry appears to have skewed the argument in the direction of a primarily 'literary' writer, and Van Es thinks, *pace* Lukas Erne, that 'Shakespeare should not be categorised from the outset a "a man of the theatre"'. He thinks it a possibility that Shakespeare 'took some satisfaction in seeing his plays in print' (p. 74).

20 See William Shakespeare, *The Merchant of Venice*, ed. John Drakakis, Arden 3 series (London, 2010), 2.1.01–2.
21 William Shakespeare, *Othello*, ed. E.A.J. Honigmann, Arden 3 series, revised edn, with a new Introduction by Ayanna Thompson (London, 2016).
22 See John Drakakis, 'Introduction', in William Shakespeare, *The Merchant of Venice*, ed. John Drakakis, Arden 3 series (London, 2010), pp. 85–6.
23 See John Drakakis, 'Jessica', in John W. Mahon and Ellen Macleod Mahon, eds, *The Merchant of Venice: New Critical Essays* (New York and London, 2002).
24 See Van Es, *Shakespeare in Company*, p. 64, for his account of the positioning of *Richard III*, where he argues: 'The play, therefore, is the product of the same material conditions as *Titus Andronicus* and *The Taming of The Shrew* and shares some important structural features with those works.'
25 See William Shakespeare, *Hamlet*, ed. Ann Thompson and Neil Taylor, Arden 3 series, revised edn (London, 2016), p. 334 nn. 90–1. Thompson and Taylor make the point identifying Heminge as Caesar/Polonius, and Richard Burbage as Brutus/Hamlet. What is in the past in relation to the performance of *Julius Caesar* is proleptic in the case of *Hamlet*.
26 See Honigmann, in *Othello*, Arden 3 series, p. 125 n. 87.
27 Cf. Honigmann, in *Othello*, Arden 3 series, p. 127 n. 111. Honigmann traces the link between 'horses' and potential adulterers to the Old Testament book of Jeremiah (5.8). Othello is not an adulterer, and in any case the link appears to be probably more local. This is not to say that the biblical connection would not have occurred to members of an audience steeped in the Bible. It is more likely that the biblical reference comes into its own in the allegation of Desdemona's infidelity later in the play.
28 See G.K. Hunter, 'Poem and context in *Love's Labour's Lost*', in Philip Edwards, Inga-Stina Ewbank and G.K. Hunter, eds, *Shakespeare's Styles: Essays in Honour of Kenneth Muir* (Cambridge, 1980), pp. 25–38.
29 William Shakespeare, *Love's Labour's Lost*, ed. Henry Woudhuysen, Arden 3 series (London, 1998).
30 See John Kerrigan, *Shakespeare's Binding Language* (Oxford, 2016), p. 101. Kerrigan states categorically: 'If you can see why a dramatist so interested in binding language would write *Love's Labour's Lost*, you can also see why he never again let a play be so dominated by oaths.' Perhaps not, but the slipperiness of language into which the

'binding oath' is inserted is present in different forms throughout the Shakespeare canon.
31 William Shakespeare, *Macbeth*, ed. Sandra Clark and Pamela Mason, Arden 3 series (London, 2015). Woudhuysen in his Arden 3 edition of *Love's Labour's Lost* glosses 'hail' correctly but links Shakespeare's usage to its appearance in *The Two Noble Kinsmen*. See William Shakespeare, *The Two Noble Kinsmen*, ed. Lois Potter, Arden 3 series, revised edn (London, 2015), 3.5.99 and p. 237 n. 100, which cross-refers to the line in *Love's Labour's Lost*.
32 Terry Eagleton, *Radical Sacrifice* (New Haven and London, 2018), p. 31.
33 William Shakespeare, *A Midsummer Night's Dream*, ed. Harold F. Brooks, Arden 2 series (London, 1979). All citations from this play are from this edition. Brooks acknowledges that the play may have been composed for a particular occasion (p. lvii) and he links the play with *Love's Labour's Lost* (p. lviii). Kerrigan, *Shakespeare's Binding Language*, pp. 67ff., goes into considerably more detail concerning the occasion of *Love's Labour's Lost*.
34 Ovid, *The Metamorphoses*, trans. Arthur Golding, ed. John Frederick Nimms (New York, 1965), p. 89, l. 114.
35 See Woudhuysen, in *Love's Labour's Lost*, p. 60, where the link with *A Midsummer Night's Dream* and *Romeo and Juliet* is restricted to matters of verse style.
36 René Weiss, 'A Midsummer Night's Dream', in William Shakespeare, *Romeo and Juliet*, ed. René Weiss, Arden 3 series (London, 2012), p. 41.
37 See Bullough, *Narrative and Dramatic Sources*, vol. 1, pp. 359–60.
38 Eagleton, *Radical Sacrifice*, p. 33.
39 See Jonathan Bate, *Shakespeare and Ovid* (Oxford, 1993), p. 119, where he traces what he calls 'a programme for Shakespeare's subsequent Ovidianism', beginning with the Induction of *The Taming of the Shrew*, passing through *Venus and Adonis*, *Titus Andronicus*, *A Midsummer Night's Dream* and *The Merry Wives of Windsor*, 'on the road to Shakespeare's most Ovidian coup, Hermione's statue, so "lively painted" that it comes to life'.
40 *Ibid.*, pp. 121–2. Bate argues that the Folio text of the play is incomplete compared with the anonymous *The Taming of a Shrew* (1594). Meanwhile, Hodgdon, in her Arden 3 edition of Shakespeare's *The Taming of the Shrew*, outlines three editorial possibilities: 'the source theory, the bad quarto theory and the *ur-Shrew* theory' (p. 20).
41 Hodgdon, in *The Taming of the Shrew*, pp. 25–6.

42 Bate, *Shakespeare and Ovid*, p. 121.
43 Germaine Greer, *The Female Eunuch* (London, 1971), p. 209.
44 Hodgdon, *The Taming of the Shrew*, pp. 48–9.
45 Cf. Anon., *An Homilie of the State of Matrimonie*, *The Second Book of Homilies* (London, 1595), sig. Hh3^r–3^{v}ff.: 'But if thou shouldst beat her, thou shalt encrease her euil affections: for frowardnesse & sharp-/nesse, is not amended with frowardnesse, but with softnes and gentleness. Furthermore, consider what reward thou shalt haue at Gods hande: for where thou mightest beat her, and yet, for the respect of the feare of God, thou wilt abstaine and beare patiently her greate offences'. See also Hodgdon, in *The Taming of the Shrew*, p. 53, for a critical comment on the relation between Shakespeare's play and the *Homilie of the State of Matrimonie*.
46 See Bate, *Shakespeare and Ovid*, pp. 121–2, for a comment on the 'contextual irony' generated by Kate's address to the Widow (p. 121), Hortensio's venal approach to marriage and 'Kate's vision of obedience [that] is made to look oddly irrelevant to the reality of marriage' (p. 122).
47 Hodgdon, in *The Taming of the Shrew*, pp. 306–8, and p. 305.
48 See Hodgdon, in *The Taming of the Shrew*, p. 305 nn. 191 and 192.
49 Hodgdon does not go quite this far, and 'sped' does not appear in Gordon Williams's *A Glossary of Shakespeare's Sexual Language* (London, 1997). There is no record of the explicitly sexual connotation of 'sped', but cf. Eric Partridge, *Shakespeare's Bawdy*, 3rd edn (London, 1968), pp. 186–7, which glosses 'speed' as 'to be sexually potent' (p. 186).
50 *An Homilie of the State of Matrimonie*, sig. G5^r.
51 Kerrigan, *Shakespeare's Binding Language*, pp. 67ff.
52 *Ibid.*, p. 92.
53 Ben Jonson, *The Complete Plays*, 2 vols (reprinted, London, 1967), vol. 1, p. 491.
54 William Shakespeare, *Much Ado About Nothing*, ed. Claire McEachern, Arden 3 series (London, 2006), p. 316. McEachern glosses the line and its assignment in n. 97.
55 R.A. Foakes, ed., *Henslowe's Diary*, 2nd edn (Cambridge, 2002), p. 47.
56 N.W. Bawcutt, in Christopher Marlowe, *The Jew of Malta*, ed. N.W. Bawcutt (Manchester, 1978), pp. 1–2. Bawcutt also notes that the play continued to be performed up until 1598 from the evidence of Henslowe's *Diary*.
57 *Ibid.*, p. 44.
58 John Russell Brown, in William Shakespeare, *The Merchant of Venice*, ed. John Russell Brown, Arden 2 series (London, 1972), p. xxxi.

See also Alfred Harbage, ed., *Annals of English Drama 975–1700* (London, 1964), p. 52.
59 Richard Sennett, *Flesh and Stone: The Body and the City in Western Civilization* (London, 1994), p. 214.
60 *Ibid.*, p. 215.
61 *Ibid.*
62 Simon Schama, *Belonging: The Story of The Jews 1492–1900* (London, 2017), p. 120.
63 *Ibid.*, p. 119.
64 Cf. Drakakis, in *The Merchant of Venice*, Arden 3 series, pp. 47–8.
65 See Drakakis, 'Jessica'. But see also Margaret Tudeau-Clayton, *Shakespeare's Englishes: Against Englishness* (Cambridge, 2020), p. 168, where a much more positive view of 'conversion' deriving from St Paul's Epistle to the Ephesians, and linked to *The Comedy of Errors* but not *The Merchant of Venice*, is discussed.
66 See, for example, Sara Coodin, *Is Shylock Jewish?* (Edinburgh, 2017), p. 15. There is nothing inherently wrong with Coodin's presentist readings as presentist readings, although her 'ethical' approach 'implies the presence of the whole person, the composite totality of their intellectual and emotional resources, and a lifelong commitment to the pursuit of an objectively meaningful ideal'. A little more alarming is Coodin's claim that she sees herself 'reflected in [the play's] Jewish characters' (p. 13), as though they are essential and authentic. This mode of reading has been carefully and thoroughly dismantled in Emma Smith, 'Was Shylock Jewish?', *Shakespeare Quarterly*, 64:2 (Summer 2013), 188–219.
67 Kim Hall, 'Guess who's coming to dinner? Colonization and miscegenation in *The Merchant of Venice*', *Renaissance Drama*, 23 (1992), pp. 90 and 95.
68 *Ibid.*, p. 101.
69 Kim Hall, *Things of Darkness: Economies of Race and Gender in Early Modern England.* (Ithaca, 1995), pp. 175–6.
70 Robert Weimann, *Author's Pen and Actor's Voice: Playing and Writing in Shakespeare's Theatre* (Cambridge, 2000), p. 219.
71 Clubb, *Italian Drama*, p. 7.
72 Robert Weimann, *Shakespeare and the Popular Tradition in the Theater: Studies in the Social Dimension of Dramatic Form and Function*, ed. Robert Schwartz (Baltimore and London, 1978), p. 224.
73 *Ibid.*
74 *Ibid.*, pp. 226–7.

75 It is tempting to read Van Es's account of what we might loosely call the 'epistemological break' in Shakespeare's career as a theatrical equivalent of the Althusserian reading of the division in Marx's *oeuvre*.
76 See Thompson and Taylor, in *Hamlet*, Arden 3 series, p. 333 n. 89. They also note the occurrence of this sentiment in *The Two Gentlemen of Verona*, at 2.1.168 and 2.4.25–8. The Arden 3 editor of *The Two Gentlemen of Verona*, Lois Potter, cites the same proverb in that play at 2.1.159–60, but locates it at Dent M226, refers forward to its occurrence in *Hamlet*, but also traces it back to Lyly's *Endymion*: see John Lyly, *Endymion*, in *English Renaissance Drama: A Norton Anthology*, ed. David Bevington *et al.* (New York and London, 2002), p. 104, 3.4.129.
77 See Tudeau-Clayton, *Shakespeare's Englishes*, pp. 177ff., for a much more nuanced account of prodigality.
78 Robert Greene, *Greene's Groatsworth of Wit Bought with a Million of Repentance* (London, 1592), sig. C1ᵛ.
79 Lyly, *Endymion*, p. 104: 'Love is a chameleon, which draweth nothing into the mouth but air, and nourisheth nothing in the body but lungs' (3.4.134–5).

Conclusion: the elephant in the graveyard

In 1816 Samuel Taylor Coleridge published an account of the genesis of his poem 'Kubla Khan', described as 'a vision in a dream. A fragment.'[1] Falling into a drug-induced sleep, he imagined a three-hundred-line poem in which 'all the images rose up before him as *things*, with a parallel production of the correspondent expressions without any sensation or consciousness of effort'. The poem we have is the result of the poet's attempting to reconstruct the totality that he had dreamt, but he was,

> unfortunately called out by a person on business from Porlock, and detained by him above an hour, and on his return to his room, found to his no small surprise and mortification, that though he still retained some vague and dim recollection of the general purport of the vision, yet, with the exception of some eight or ten scattered lines and images, all the rest had passed away like the images on the surface of a stream into which a stone had been cast, but, alas! without the after restoration of the latter![2]

In his book *The Act of Creation* Arthur Koestler recounts this narrative of the genesis of Coleridge's 'fragmentary' poem, although his concern is to point up the prevalence of the poet's 'visual thinking' and its link to 'verbal concepts'. For Koestler, the poet 'thinks both in images and verbal concepts, at the same time or in quick alternation … The dreamer floats among the phantom shapes of the hoary deep; the poet is a skin-diver with a breathing tube.'[3] Coleridge was in little doubt that beneath his powers of recollection there lurked a complete narrative from which the business of everyday life had distracted him. In his attempt to reconstruct this organic original text he succeeded only in recovering 'fragments'. Almost in anticipation of Coleridge's account, William Scott's unpublished *The Model of Poetry* (*c.*1599) offers what is, perhaps, an anecdotal observation of the genesis of Virgil's *Aeneid* that inverts the process in which art was said to augment Nature in the achievement of the poet:

> And then what will they esteem of Virgil, that inimitable glory and prince of poets, seeing it is said that the goodly birth of his *Aeneis* saw not the light, as not being complete, till he was eleven years old, but every moment grew to perfection by the sustenance of art and industry?[4]

Koestler's quasi-anthropological account deviates significantly from Scott's account of the coupling of the poetic imagination and the figuring forth of 'reality', in his claim that in Coleridge's case the poet reverted to 'the pictorial mode'. This plays into the model of a Shakespeare occasionally '*regressing* to an older and lower level of the mental hierarchy',[5] and reverting to Nature as the source of his poetic inspiration, thereby inadvertently implying a version of the classical link between art and reason where the latter seems to involve a failure of memory. Our persistent failure to identify fully the sources of Shakespeare's inspiration, and the resulting plethora of scholarly suggestions that aim to link his texts with earlier texts as cemeterial remains, risks a limiting and limited reconstruction of the bones that are strewn around the elephants' mythical graveyard. The eighteenth-century poet Alexander Pope was under no illusion about the distinction between the dead and the living, or about the perils of attempting to define 'life': 'Like following life thro' creatures you dissect, / You lose it in the moment you detect' (ll. 39–40).[6] Elsewhere, in his 'Essay on Criticism' Pope also had something to say about what we bring as observers to the process of evaluation: 'Fondly we think we honour Merit then, / When we but praise *Our selves* in *Other Men*.'[7]

Pope's strictures emerged from an Augustan sense of organic order and a respect for rules. But the academic study of what lies behind the texts of Shakespeare has not gone very far beyond locating an accumulation of the bones in the elephants' graveyard. Breathing life into them is, as the foregoing chapters have tried to show, another matter altogether, and myths of creation have

Conclusion: the elephant in the graveyard 359

been invoked to account for the phenomenon that we know as 'Shakespeare' at a time when texts were beginning to be thought of as property. Robert Miola's account of *Shakespeare's Reading* (2000) is as good a compendium as any of what, from an empirical investigation, can be traced in Shakespeare's own texts. In his two-paragraph summary of 'Shakespeare as reader' he lists a full variety of authors, some of which have a greater claim to our attention than others. But he then appears to withdraw from this modern idea of 'Shakespeare as reader' to introduce a variety of qualifications and speculations (my italics):

> The term 'reading', *of course*, covers a wide variety of interactions. As a working man of the theatre, Shakespeare *must have* read, consulted, written, doctored, revised, watched, rehearsed, and acted in hundreds of scenes and plays. He worked alone and with other writers and actors; he knew well the repertory of his own company as well as those of the competition. *As we might expect*, he always kept an especially sharp look-out for usable material, sometimes imitating current crowd-pleasers from rival theatres, sometimes reworking an old standby that was *perhaps* gathering dust in the company archives. ... Shakespeare *read plays in print* as well as those being performed on the stages of the inns, courtyards, court, private theatres, and public playhouses that constituted his working world.[8]

Miola is not alone in shuttling between empirically verifiable speculation and baseless assertion; for example, let us assume for the moment that Shakespeare had a 'career' whose elements interlocked in the way that Miola describes. But even if we concede that point, can we be absolutely sure what 'Shakespeare must have read'? And did he 'read plays in print'? We have no way of verifying this suggestion except on purely circumstantial grounds. That he was influenced by plays that he may have seen is plausible enough. For example, Marlowe's *The Jew of Malta*, written around 1589–90 but regularly revived between 1592 and 1596, with some nine performances 'in the first six months of 1596',[9] but not printed in quarto until 1633, was a play with which, as we have seen, Shakespeare was clearly in dialogue in his *The Merchant of Venice* (1596–97).[10]

On the evidence of this encounter, Shakespeare must have had a retentive memory for detail, but to imply that engagements of this kind with an already popular play might have been motivated by the desire to imitate a 'current crowd-pleaser' does not quite do full justice to the critical nature of this interaction. If, for example, the anonymous *Famous Victories of Henry V* put the case for a heroic monarch, then this myth had a wide currency by the time Shakespeare came to write *Henry V*, possibly the play with which the new Globe Theatre opened in the late summer of 1599. Given that printed quartos had a limited public circulation, readership was almost certainly small, a factor that might help to explain the variable survival rates across time of early quartos of Shakespeare's plays. In short, we have no sure way of knowing, except in a very few cases, *what* Shakespeare read or indeed *how* he read. Hence the emphasis placed upon a somewhat slavish adherence to the precepts derived from his secondary education. Did Shakespeare's company accumulate a supply of useful books, possibly unbound, and was reading a communal activity in which the actors as well as the script-writers participated? Answers to these difficult questions might go some way to assisting our understanding of the processes of adaptation, appropriation and emendation to which some of the previously printed materials found their way into Shakespeare's texts. This is emphatically not a question of reassembling the bones in the elephants' graveyard, but of tracking the movements of the live elephant as it traversed an already populated terrain that included oral and printed material, elements of a living tradition and fragments that could be refurbished, updated and appropriated for the present purposes of playing. We may add to that the accumulating fruits of Shakespeare's own efforts, involving his refashioning of earlier motifs and structures. For example, he reformulated in different genres stock situations involving questions of jealousy and deception as they might be traced through Comedies such as *Much Ado About Nothing*, Tragedies such as *Othello* and Tragicomedies such as *The Winter's Tale*. There is also the repetition of stock characters in familiar situations, as in the case of the Duke in *Measure for Measure* or Prospero in *The Tempest*. When we take this wide range of examples into consideration, then we begin to glimpse the active life of the practising dramatist.

Lynn Enterline has scotched the assumption that in the late sixteenth century schooldays were happy days. What she calls 'the discourse of exemplarity' that prevailed in grammar-school culture 'revolved around a master who was the final judge of a boy's worth', but that the pupil's choice was violently curtailed: 'imitate "some piece of an author" well or be beaten'.[11] Jacques's less than flattering depiction of 'the whining schoolboy, with his satchel / And shining morning face, creeping like a snail / Unwillingly to school' (*As You Like It*, 2.7.146–8) comes immediately to mind, along with the fun that Lucentio and Bianca have with Latin translation in *The Taming of the Shrew* (3.1.31–43). It also adds another strand to what is in danger of becoming an overpopulated elephants' graveyard. Enterline's judicious but frank contribution to the increasingly complicated jigsaw of textual and institutional pressures that shaped the dramatist Shakespeare does something to ameliorate the prevailing notion of the eager novice absorbing an education that he knew from an early age he could turn to direct advantage in the public theatre. The implication is that there must have been a clear and direct link between the commercial pressures fostered by a new public institution that perhaps sought to legitimise its activities with occasional reference to literary and rhetorical analogues, and the processes of imitation that were instilled into the schoolboy's thinking. Or to put the matter another way, how can we get from poring over the bones in the elephants' graveyard, to the vitality of Shakespeare's theatrical output? Like literary detectives, we appear to chart the immediate terrain, look for the bodies of ancestors and measure according to a series of formal and historical protocols the signs of their passing. Except that, in this case, we reverse the process since we work back from the animated performance document(s) to the skeletal structures that are thought to support and sustain it. Shakespeare, it would appear, has read what we have read, and he appears to have read in the same ways that we do.

It is perhaps worth pointing out that the elements of a humanist education that scholars have sought to identify in Shakespeare's texts are frequently the source of ridicule in performance. The late Robert Weimann brilliantly uncovered an 'incompatibility between Renaissance poetics and certain traditional forms of performance practice'.[12] Taking Hamlet's advice to the players as a cue, Weimann went on to argue that the tension resulting from this incompatibility points up the difference between 'poetic theory' and 'histrionic practice':

> As the play itself shows, the theoretical dimension of Hamlet's advice cannot and does not discipline the practical side of what the staging of *Hamlet* involves. If anything, Hamlet's precept, his entire notion of how poetic theory and histrionic practice connect, is not binding; rather his recommended poetics is lodged against the foil of what the play has to say about (and is able to do with) relations of language and action, knowing and doing.[13]

The conclusion that we can draw from this is that if Shakespeare was deeply read in humanist poetic and rhetorical theory, then that reading was, at the very least, critical, if not at times oppositional in its exposure of the dichotomy between its perceptual formulations and the practice of performance before an audience, many members of which had not received a humanist education.

We can readily agree with Robert Miola that from the available evidence, Shakespeare's reading was variable. Presumably this means that Shakespeare drew on texts primarily for variable amounts of information. Miola notes, with reference to *Antony and Cleopatra*: 'Shakespeare's reading sometimes shows clearly in his writing, by which we understand a capacity to imitate. We can identify North's *Plutarch* as a book that Shakespeare read, a book that functioned as a source for his play.' But even at that level, he is forced to concede, rightly, that: 'Any complete list of Shakespeare's reading for any single work must always be open-ended, as readers continually hear echoes of new sources.'[14] But if 'one scholar's echo, signalling indebtedness, is another scholar's coincidence, signifying nothing',[15] then the whole question of 'indebtedness' can be reduced to an imprecise form of educated impressionism. The nature of Miola's interest in the sheer scale of the problem and the possible variety of literary bones required to reassemble the living elephant, is candidly acknowledged, but at the root of the problem is the image of Shakespeare as a *reader*. We might readily assent to the notion that, from a strictly empirical standpoint, 'A Shakespearian text registers always a variety of sources – other books read, Shakespeare's own previous writing, the plays of his company and rivals, contemporary literature, recent

Conclusion: the elephant in the graveyard 363

news and events. Reliance on verbal echoes can obscure these rich sources and oversimplify the picture.'[16] Unfortunately, this does not tell us very much. Miola rightly calls out the impressionism that informs much source study but he still hangs on to the concept, and he does not probe the possible connections or the tensions between a new technology such as printing and the more conservative (and hierarchical) pressures of a residual oral culture. At the limited level of content, at least some, possibly much, of what we identify as potentially 'literary' source material may already have had a life in the oral culture of early modern England.

Miola's invocation of the *Star Wars* films to point up a series of cinematographic memes that can be traced back to an earlier film genre, the Western, points to the transmission and transmigration of a popular, non-literary tradition. That some of the original Westerns were based upon novels indicates in part the means whereby a new technology, film, accommodates itself (possibly with a knowing sense of irony) to existing narrative forms. Some of the examples are extreme to the point of ludicrousness, as in the case of early radio, which relied at its inception on some of the visual and organisational traditions of the theatre. And we might say the same about the emergence of popular music that involved imitation, adaptation, appropriation and innovation. Few, if any, white Anglo-American teenagers of the early 1950s had a clue what a line like 'You ain't nothin' but a hound dog' actually meant, or indeed where it came from. And yet, even though they may never have seen them written down, constant repetition enabled the lyrics of Elvis Presley's song to be recited and retained in the popular memory of the burgeoning teenage public long before a retrospective history evolved. Simply invoking tradition does not explain the transmission of artistic forms from one generation to the next, or the level of critical engagement with them. Nor can we say, except in the case of some notable and well-rehearsed exceptions, that Shakespeare only became aware of narratives, memes, structures and existing theatrical forms once they had been written down.

And yet, there continue to emerge dutifully enthusiastic endorsements of Shakespeare's indebtedness to 'the classics'. Jonathan Bate's recent revival of the historian Patrick Collinson's phrase 'republics of letters' seeks to align uncritically, in a way that

Collinson does not, Shakespeare's practice as a writer of theatrical scripts with an alleged desire for 'literary respectability'.[17] As Weimann made abundantly clear, what Bate identifies as 'poesy' comprised a series of classical rules and forms that were up for debate in the popular theatre, suggesting that some kind of conflict between those writers who followed humanist precepts regarding poetic composition and theatre practitioners was well under way by the time that Shakespeare came to write *Hamlet*. That plays such as *Titus Andronicus* or *The Comedy of Errors* might have appealed to classically educated auditors does little more than reverse the avenue of transmission that allowed Shakespeare to purloin the sonnet form for the Prologue of *Romeo and Juliet*, a most un-Petrarchan love story as one might wish to find. The tortured shunting between classical and humanist poetic and rhetorical precepts, and the demands of popular theatre audiences, seems to have left very little room for aspirations to literary respectability despite the acknowledgement of those writers not aligned with the popular theatre who sought to appropriate its outputs for a 'republic of letters'.

The plethora of *Hamlet* narratives alone, accompanied by Weimann's account of the play's critical engagement with the conflict between the literary and the theatrical, demonstrates precisely this, as indeed does the appearance of the Gloucester sub-plot in *King Lear* in Sidney's *Arcadia*. This does not mean that as a businessman (to use a familiar anachronism) Shakespeare did not have his eye to the main chance. Rather, an absorbent memory, sharpened rather than blunted by formal educational training, became the repository of a formidable critical assembly of resources. Although we should be very careful about using the epithet 'professional' in an early modern context, with increasing practice Shakespeare found himself able to do what any competent musician could do once he had mastered his instrument: he could repeat tunes, recall motifs to mind, imitate themes and memes, improvise on existing material and, on a number of occasions, innovate. Unlike the effects of modern information technology, this was not a mechanical 'cut-and-paste' culture in the way that we understand it. Repetition and imitation, maintained the capacity for endless renewal, and was, structurally speaking, as Gilles Deleuze suggests, '*a condition of action before it is a concept of reflection.* We produce something new only on condition that we repeat – once in the mode which constitutes the past, and once more in the present of metamorphosis' (original italics).[18] Shakespeare's resources are emphatically *not* the bones that the literary scholar finds strewn around a mythical elephants' graveyard. They represent in various forms the vibrant movements of the living animal, sensitive to its surroundings and its dangers, innovative in its own way, but threatened by a burgeoning literary culture that over the next four centuries would all but consume Shakespeare.

Notes

1 Donald A. Stauffer, ed., *Selected Poetry and Prose of Coleridge* (London, 1951), pp. 43–4.
2 *Ibid.*
3 Arthur Koestler, *The Act of Creation* (reprinted London, 1971), p. 168.
4 William Scott, *The Model of Poesy*, ed. Gavin Alexander (Cambridge, 2013), p. 10, especially for Horace's combination of 'art' and 'nature' in the making of the poet. Scott goes on immediately to invoke Sir Philip Sidney to describe those poets who 'can endure by no means to be cumbered with many artificial rules, still to defend that the poet needs no art, no nor the reader neither, lest by some mischance he find them to be (as that knight calls them somewhere) poet-apes, that is unreasonable creatures, with a very ridiculous unhandsomeness smocking, rather than imitating, the highest and gracefullest ability of nature and art' (pp. 10–11).
5 *Ibid.*
6 Alexander Pope, 'Moral Essays: Epistle to Cobham', *The Poems of Alexander Pope*, ed. John Butt (London, 1965), p. 551.
7 *Ibid.*, p. 158.
8 Robert S. Miola, *Shakespeare's Reading* (Oxford, 2000), pp. 168–9.
9 See N.W. Bawcutt, in Christopher Marlowe, *The Jew of Malta*, ed. N.W. Bawcutt (Manchester, 1978), p. 1.
10 See John Russell Brown, in William Shakespeare, *The Merchant of Venice*, ed. John Russell Brown, Arden 2 series (London, 1972), pp. xxiv–xxvii, for a detailed rehearsal of the evidence concerning the dating of the play and the conclusion that it 'must have been written in its present form not earlier than August 1596' (p. xxvii).

11 Lynn Enterline, *Shakespeare's Schoolroom: Rhetoric, Discipline, Emotion* (Philadelphia, 2012), pp. 34–5.
12 Robert Weimann, *Author's Pen and Actor's Voice: Playing and Writing in Shakespeare's Theatre* (Cambridge, 2000), p. 154.
13 *Ibid.*, p. 156. See also p. 159, where Weimann detects a tension 'between the wholesome mirror of representation and the distracting requirements of performance practice, between drama as defined by the humanists (editors easily note echoes of Quintilian and Cicero, via Donatus), and theatre as practiced by common players'.
14 Miola, *Shakespeare's Reading*, p. 13.
15 *Ibid.*, pp. 13–14.
16 *Ibid.*, p. 14.
17 Jonathan Bate, *How the Classics Made Shakespeare* (Princeton and Oxford, 2019), pp. 48 and 59.
18 Gilles Deleuze, *Difference and Repetition*, trans. Paul Patton (London, 1994), p. 90.

Bibliography

Ackroyd, Peter, *Shakespeare: The Biography*. London, 2005.
Althusser, Louis, *Lenin and Philosophy and Other Essays*, trans. Ben Brewster. London, 1971.
Andes, H.R.D., *Shakespeare's Books*. London, 1903.
Anon., *Ad Herennium*, trans. Harry Caplan. Cambridge, MA, and London, 1959.
Anon., *An Homilie of the State of Matrimonie, The Second Book of Homilies*. London, 1595.
Anon., *Leycesters Commonwealth: Conceived, Spoken and Published with Most Earnest protestation of all Dutifull good will and affection towards this Realm, for whose good onely, it is made common to many*. London, 1641.
Anon., *Mucedorus*. London, 1598.
Anon., *The True Chronicle Historie of King Leir and his Three Daughters*. London, 1605.
Aristotle, *Metaphysics Books 1–14: Oeconomica: Magna Moralia*, trans. G. Cyril Armstrong. Cambridge, MA, 1935.
———, 'On memory', *On the Soul and Other Psychological Works*, trans. Fred D. Miller Jnr. Oxford, 2018.
Ascham, Roger, *The Schoolmaster*. London, 1579.
Assmann, Aleida, *Cultural Memory and Western Civilization*. Cambridge, 2013.
Bacon, Francis, *Essays or Counsels Civil and Moral*. London, 1908.
Bakhtin, Mikhail, *Problems in Dostoevsky's Poetics*, trans. Caryl Emerson. Manchester, 1984.
Baldwin, T.W., *William Shakespere's Small Latine and Lesse Greeke*, 2 vols. Urbana, 1944.
Barclay, Alexander, *The Ship of Fools*. New York, 1966.
Barker, Francis, *The Tremulous Private Body: Essays in Subjection*. London, 1995.

Barker, Francis, and Hulme, Peter, 'Nymphs and reapers heavily vanish: the discursive con-texts of *The Tempest*', in *Alternative Shakespeares*, ed. John Drakakis. London, 1985.
Barker, Pat, *The Silence of The Girls*. London, 2018.
Barrett, John, *An Enquiry into the Origin of the Constellations that Compose the Zodiac and the uses they were Intended to Promote*. Dublin, 1800.
Barthes, Roland, *Image, Music, Text*, ed. and trans. Stephen Heath. Glasgow, 1977.
Barton, Anne, *Ben Jonson, Dramatist*. Cambridge, 1984.
Bate, Jonathan, *The Romantics on Shakespeare*. Harmondsworth, 1992.
———, *Shakespeare and Ovid*. Oxford, 1993.
———, *How the Classics made Shakespeare*. Princeton and Oxford, 2019.
Belsey, Catherine, *Why Shakespeare?* Basingstoke, 2007.
Benjamin, Walter, *Illuminations*, trans. Harry Zohn. Glasgow, 1970.
———, *Reflections: Essays, Aphorisms, Autobiographical Writings*, trans. Edmund Jephcott. New York, 1978.
Bloom, Harold, *The Anxiety of Influence*. London, Oxford and New York, 1973.
———, *A Map of Misreading*. Oxford, 1975.
———, *Ruin the Sacred Truths: Poetry and Belief from the Bible to the Present*. Cambridge, MA, and London, 1989.
———, *The Anatomy of Influence: Literature as a Way of Life*. New Haven and London, 2011.
Bourdieu, Pierre, *The Field of Cultural Production*, ed. Randall Johnson. Cambridge, 1993.
———, *The Rules of Art*. Cambridge, 1996.
Bowers, Fredson, *Elizabethan Revenge Tragedy 1587–1642*. 1940; reprinted, Princeton, 1966.
Bradley, A.C., *Shakespearean Tragedy*, 3rd edn. London, 1992.
Bright, Timothie, *A Treatise on Melancholie*. London, 1586.
Bullough, Geoffrey, *Narrative and Dramatic Sources of Shakespeare*, 8 vols. London, 1957–75.
Burke, Seán, *The Death and Return of the Author: Criticism and Subjectivity in Barthes, Foucault and Derrida*. 1992; reprinted, Edinburgh, 1999.
———, *The Ethics of Writing: Authorship and Legacy in Plato and Nietzsche*. Edinburgh, 2008.
Burrow, Colin, ed., *The Oxford Shakespeare: The Complete Sonnets and Poems*. Oxford, 2002.
———, *Shakespeare and Classical Antiquity*. Oxford, 2013.
Caesar, Philip, *General Discourse Against the Damnable Sect of Usurers*. London, 1578.

Camden, William, *The History of the most Renowned and Victorious Princess Elizabeth*, 4th edn. London, 1688.
Clare, Janet, *Shakespeare's Stage Traffic: Imitation, Borrowing and Competition in Renaissance Theatre*. Cambridge, 2014.
Clubb, Louise George, *Italian Drama in Shakespeare's Time*. New Haven and London, 1989.
Coetzee, J.M., *Elizabeth Costello*. London, 2004.
Collingwood, R.G., *The Idea of History*. Oxford and London, 1961.
Collinson, Patrick, *The Sixteenth Century*. Oxford, 2002.
———, *The Reformation*. London, 2005.
Coodin, Sara, *Is Shylock Jewish?* Edinburgh, 2017.
Cooper, Helen, *The English Romance: Transforming Motifs from Geoffrey of Monmouth to the Death of Shakespeare*. Oxford, 2004.
Coupe, Laurence, *Myth*, 2nd edn. London, 2009.
Cox, John D., and Kastan, David, eds, *A New History of English Drama*. New York, 1997.
Craig, Hardin, 'Trend of Shakespeare scholarship', *Shakespeare Survey*, 2. 1949.
Crane, Mary Thomas, *Shakespeare's Brain: Reading with Cognitive Theory*. Princeton and Oxford, 2001.
Croce, Benedetto, *Guide to Aesthetics*, trans. Patrick Romanell. Indianapolis, 1965.
———, *A Croce Reader: Aesthetics, Philosophy, History, Literary Criticism*, trans. and ed. Massimo Verdicchio. Toronto and London, 2017.
Culler, Jonathan, *The Pursuit of Signs: Structuralism, Linguistics and the Pursuit of Literature*. London, 1975.
Curtius, Ernst Robert, *European Literature in the Latin Middle Ages*. Princeton and Oxford, 2013.
Damasio, Antonio, *Looking for Spinoza: Joy, Sorrow and the Feeling Brain*. Orlando and London, 2003.
Dante, *The Divine Comedy*, trans. Dorothy L. Sayers, 3 vols. Harmondsworth, 1955.
Deleuze, Gilles, *Difference and Repetition*, trans. Paul Patton. London, 1994.
Deleuze, Gilles, and Guattari, Felix, *Anti-Oedipus: Capitalism and Schizophrenia*, trans. Robert Hurley, Mark Seem and Helen R. Lane. London, 1983.
———, *A Thousand Plateaus: Capitalism and Schizophrenia*, trans. Brian Massumi. London, 1987.
Derrida, Jacques, *Writing and Difference*, trans. Alan Bass. London, 1978.
———, *Specters of Marx*, trans. Peggy Kamuf. New York and London, 1994.

———, *The Beast and the Sovereign*, trans. Geoffrey Bennington, 2 vols. Chicago, 2009.
Dollimore, Jonathan, *Death, Desire and Loss in Western Culture*. London, 1998.
Drakakis, John, 'Trust and transgression: the discursive practices of *Much Ado About Nothing*', in Richard Machin and Christopher Norris, eds, *Post-structural Readings in English Poetry*. Cambridge, 1987.
———, 'The Plays of Shackerley Marmion (1603–39): A Critical Old-spelling Edition.' Unpublished PhD thesis, University of Leeds, 1988.
———, 'Shakespeare as presentist', *Shakespeare Survey*, 66. 2013.
Drakakis, John, and Townshend, Dale, eds, *Gothic Shakespeares*. London, 2008.
———, eds, *Macbeth: A Critical Reader*. London, 2013.
Duncan-Jones, Katherine, and Woudhuysen, Henry, eds, *Shakespeare's Poems*, Arden 3 series. London, 2007.
Eagleton, Terry, *Radical Sacrifice*. New Haven and London, 2018.
Edgar, Samuel, 'Dr Rodrigo Lopez' last speech from the scaffold at Tyburn', *Transactions of the Jewish Historical Society*, 30. 1987–88.
Edwards, Philip, Ewbank, Inga-Stina, and Hunter, G.K., eds, *Shakespeare's Styles: Essays in Honour of Kenneth Muir*. Cambridge, 1980.
Elton, Oliver, *The First Nine Books of the Danish History of Saxo Grammaticus*. London, 1894.
Enterline, Lynn, *Shakespeare's Schoolroom: Rhetoric, Discipline, Emotion*. Philadelphia, 2012.
Erasmus, Desiderius, *Essential Works of Erasmus*, ed. W.T.H. Jackson. New York and London, 1965.
Erne, Lukas, *Shakespeare as Literary Dramatist*. Cambridge, 2003.
Evans, Joan, *A History of the Society of Antiquaries*. London, 1956.
Evans, Richard, *In Defence of History*. Reprinted, London, 2018.
Fevbre, Lucien, and Martin, Henri-Jean, *The Coming of the Book*, trans. David Gerard. London, 1984.
Findlay, Alison, *Illegitimate Power: Bastards in Renaissance Drama*. Manchester, 1994.
Florio, John, *A World of Wordes*. London, 1598.
———, *Queen Anna's New World of Words or Dictionarie of the Italian and English Tongues*. London, 1611.
Foakes, R.A., *Henslowe's Diary*, 2nd edn. Cambridge, 2002.
Foucault, Michel, *The Archaeology of Knowledge*, trans. A.M. Sheridan Smith. London, 1974.
———, *Language, Counter-Memory, Practice: Selected Essays and Interviews*, trans. Donald Bouchard and Sherry Simon, ed. Donald Bouchard. Oxford, 1977.

Fox, Adam, *Oral and Literate Culture in England 1500–1700*. Oxford, 2000.
Freud, Sigmund, *Introductory Lectures on Psychoanalysis*, vol. 1, ed. James Strachey and Angela Richards, Pelican Freud Library. Reprinted, Harmondsworth, 1978.
———, *The Psychopathology of Everyday Life*, vol. 5, trans. Alan Tyson, Pelican Freud Library. Reprinted, Harmondsworth, 1978.
———, *Art and Literature*, ed. Albert Dixon. Harmondsworth, 1985.
———, *The Unconscious*, trans. Graham Frankland. Harmondsworth, 2005.
Fulke Greville, Lord Brooke, *The Remaines Being Poems of Monarchy and Religion*, ed. G.A. Wilkes. Oxford, 1965.
Garber, Marjorie, *Shakespeare's Ghost Writers: Literature as Uncanny Causality*. New York and London, 1987.
Genette, Gérard, *Palimpsests: Literature in the Second Degree*, trans. Channa Newman and Claude Doubinsky. Lincoln, NE, and London, 1997.
———, *Paratexts: Thresholds of Interpretation*, trans. Jane E. Lewin. Cambridge, 1997.
Gillespie, Stuart, *Shakespeare's Books: A Dictionary of Shakespeare's Sources*. London, 2004.
Gollancz, Israel, *The Sources of Hamlet*. 1926; reprinted, London, 1967.
Greene, Robert, *Greene's Groatsworth of Wit Bought with a Million of Repentance*. London, 1592.
Greenblatt, Stephen, *Shakespearean Negotiations: The Circulation of Social Energy in Renaissance England*. Oxford, 1988.
———, *Learning to Curse: Essays in Early Modern Culture*. London, 1990.
———, *Hamlet in Purgatory*. Princeton, 2001.
———, *Will in the World: How Shakespeare Became Shakespeare*. London, 2004.
———, *The Swerve: How the Renaissance Began*. London, 2011.
Greer, Germaine, *The Female Eunuch*. London, 1971.
Grimalde, Nicolas, *Marcus Tullius Cicero: Three Bokes of Duties*. London, 1556.
Gurr, Andrew, *Shakespeare's Opposites: The Admiral's Company 1594–1625*. Cambridge, 2009.
Hall, Kim, 'Guess who's coming to dinner? Colonization and miscegenation in *The Merchant of Venice*', *Renaissance Drama*, 23. 1992.
———, *Things of Darkness: Economies of Race and Gender in Early Modern England*. Ithaca, 1995.
Halpern, Richard, *The Poetics of Primitive Accumulation: English Renaissance Culture and the Genealogy of Capital*. Ithaca and London, 1991.

Halsey, Katie, and Vine, Angus, eds, *Shakespeare and Authority*. London, 2018.
Harbage, Alfred, *Annals of English Drama 975–1700*. London, 1964.
Harrison, G.B., ed., *Menaphon by Robert Greene and A Marguerite for America by Thomas Lodge*. Oxford, 1927.
Harsnett, Samuel, *A Declaration of egregious Popish Impostures*. ... London, 1603.
Havelock, Eric, *Preface to Plato*. Cambridge, MA, and London, 1963.
Hawkes, David, *Shakespeare and Economic Theory*. London, 2015.
Hawkes, Terence, *Shakespeare's Talking Animals: Language and Drama in Society*. London, 1973.
———, *Meaning by Shakespeare*. London, 1992.
Helgerson, Richard, *Forms of Nationhood: The Elizabethan Writing of England*. Chicago and London, 1994.
Herford, C.H., Simpson, P., and Simpson, E., eds, *Ben Jonson*, 11 vols. Oxford, 1963.
Hill, Thomas, *The Moste pleasaunte Arte of the Interpretation of Dreames*. London, 1576.
Hillis Miller, J., *Fiction and Repetition: Seven English Novels*. Cambridge, MA, 1982.
Hillman, Richard, *Intertextuality and Romance in Renaissance Drama: The Staging of Nostalgia*. London, 1992.
Hinman, Carlton, ed., *The Norton Facsimile of the First Folio of Shakespeare*, 2nd edn. New York, 1996.
Hiscock, Andrew, *Reading Memory in Early Modern Literature*. Cambridge, 2011.
Homer, *The Iliad*, trans. A.T. Murray. Cambridge, MA, 1999.
Honan, Park, *Shakespeare: A Life*. Oxford, 1998.
Hooker, Richard, *The Laws of Ecclesiastical Polity*, ed. Christopher Morris, 2 vols. London, 1965.
Howard, Jean E., and O'Connor, Marion F., eds, *Shakespeare Reproduced*. New York and London, 1987.
Hulme, Peter, *Colonial Encounters: Europe and the Native Caribbean*. London, 1986.
Hutson, Lorna, *Invention of Suspicion: Law and Mimesis in Shakespeare and Renaissance Drama*. Oxford, 2007.
———, *Circumstantial Shakespeare*. Oxford, 2015.
James, Heather, *Shakespeare's Troy: Drama, Politics and the Translation of Empire*. Cambridge, 1997.
Jeanneret, Michel, *Perpetual Motion: Transforming Shapes in the Renaissance from da Vinci to Montaigne*, trans. Nidra Poller. Baltimore and London, 2001.
Jones, Emrys, *The Origins of Shakespeare*. Oxford, 1977.

Jonson, Ben, *The Workes of Beniamin Ionson*. London, 1616.
———, *The Complete Plays*, 2 vols. Reprinted, London, 1967.
———, *Every Man in His Humour*, ed. Robert S. Miola. Manchester, 2000.
Kaethler, Mark, 'Shakespeare and cognition: scientism, theory, and 4E', *Literature Compass*, 17:3–4. 2020. https:/doi.org/10.1111/lic3.12571.
Kastan, David Scott, 'The mechanics of culture: editing Shakespeare today', *Shakespeare Studies*, 24. 1996.
Kerrigan, John, *Revenge Tragedy: Aeschylus to Armageddon*. Oxford, 1996.
———, *Shakespeare's Binding Language*. Oxford, 2016.
———, *Shakespeare's Originality*. Oxford, 2018.
Kiséry, András, *Hamlet's Moment: Drama and Political Knowledge in Early Modern England*. Oxford, 2016.
Koestler, Arthur, *The Act of Creation*. London, 1971.
Kojève, Alexander, *The Notion of Authority (A Brief Presentation)*, ed. François Terré, trans. Hager Weslati. London and New York, 2014.
Kristeva, Julia, *Desire in Language: A Semiotic Approach to Literature and Art*, trans. Thomas Gora, Alice Jardine and Leon S. Roudiez. Oxford, 1980.
———, *Revolution in Poetic Language*, trans. Margaret Waller. New York, 1984.
———, 'The subject in process', in Patrick Ffrench and Roland-François Lack, eds, *The Tel Quel Reader*. London, 1998.
Kyd, Thomas, *The Spanish Tragedie*. London, 1592.
———, *The Spanish Tragedy*, ed. Philip Edwards. Manchester, 1977.
Lake, Peter, *How Shakespeare Put Politics on the Stage*. New Haven and London, 2016.
Laplanche, J., and Pontalis, J.-P., *The Language of Psychoanalysis*, trans. Donald Nicol-Smith. London, 1985.
Le Goff, Jacques, *The Birth of Purgatory*, trans. Arthur Goldhammer. Chicago, 1986.
Leinwand, Theodore, *Theatre, Finance and Society in Early Modern England*. Cambridge, 1999.
Levith, Murray J., *Shakespeare's Cues and Prompts*. London, 2007.
Lewis, Rhodri, *Hamlet and the Vision of Darkness*. Princeton and Oxford, 2017.
Lodge, Thomas, *Wits Miserie and the Worlds Madnesse: Discouering the Devils Incarnat of the Age*. London, 1596.
Lucretius, *De Rerum Natura*, trans. W.H.D. Rouse. Cambridge, MA, 1982.
Lukács, George, *The Theory of the Novel*, trans. Anna Bostock. London, 2006.

Lyly, John, *Endymion*, in *English Renaissance Drama: A Norton Anthology*, ed. David Bevington *et al*. New York and London, 2002.
Lynch, Stephen J., *Shakespearean Intertextuality: Studies in Selected Sources and Plays*. Westport, CT, and London, 1998.
Lyne, Raphael, *Memory and Intertextuality in Renaissance Literature*. Cambridge, 2016.
MacKillop, James, *Myths and Legends of the Celts*. London, 2006.
Maguire, Laurie, and Smith, Emma, 'What is a source? Or how Shakespeare read his Marlowe', *Shakespeare Survey*, 68. 2015.
Mahon, John W., and Macleod Mahon, Ellen, eds, *The Merchant of Venice: New Critical Essays*. New York, 2002.
Margaroni, Maria, '"The lost foundation": Kristeva's semiotic *chora* and its ambiguous legacy', *Hypatia*, 20:1. Winter, 2005.
Marlowe, Christopher, *The Jew of Malta*, ed. N.W. Bawcutt. Manchester, 1978.
Marrapodi, Michele, ed., *Shakespeare, Italy and Intertextuality*. Manchester, 2004.
Masten, Jeffrey, *Textual Intercourse: Collaboration, Authorship and Sexualities in Renaissance Drama*. Cambridge, 1997.
McEachern, Claire, *Believing in Shakespeare: Studies in Longing*. Cambridge, 2018.
Miola, Robert S., *Shakespeare's Reading*. Oxford, 2000.
Moi, Toril, ed., *The Kristeva Reader*. Oxford, 1986.
———, *Sexual/Textual Politics*, 2nd edn. London, 2002.
Moretti, Franco, *Distant Reading*. London and New York, 2013.
Muir, Kenneth, *Shakespeare's Sources*, vol. 1. London, 1957.
———, *The Sources of Shakespeare's Plays*. London, 1977.
Mullaney, Steven, *The Reformation of Emotions in the Age of Shakespeare*. Chicago and London, 2015.
Newton, Thomas, *Seneca, His Tenne Tragedies*, ed. Charles Whibley, 2 vols. London, 1927.
Nietzsche, Friedrich, *Untimely Meditations*, trans. R.J. Holingdale. Reprinted, Cambridge, 1990.
Notopoulos, James, 'Mnemosyne in oral literature', *Transactions of the American Philological Association*, 69. 1938.
Nuttall, A.D., *A New Mimesis: Shakespeare and the Representation of Reality*. London, 1983.
Ong, Walter J., *Orality and Literacy: The Technologising of the Word*. London and New York, 1982.
Orgel, Stephen, *The Authentic Shakespeare and Other Problems of the Early Modern Stage*. London, 2002.
———, *Spectacular Performances: Essays on Theater, Imagery, Books and Selves in Early Modern England*. Manchester, 2011.

Ovid, *The Metamorphoses*, trans. Arthur Golding, ed. John Frederick Nimms. New York, 1965.
Patterson, Annabel, *Shakespeare and The Popular Voice*. Cambridge, 1989.
———, *Reading Holinshed's Chronicles*. Chicago and London, 1994.
Partridge, Eric, *Shakespeare's Bawdy*, 3rd edn. London, 1968.
Pollard, Tanya, *Greek Tragic Women on Shakespearean Stages*. Oxford, 2017.
Pope, Alexander, *The Poems of Alexander Pope*, ed. John Butt. London, 1965.
Puttenham, George, *The Arte of English Poesie*. London, 1589; facs. edn, Menston, 1989.
Quint, David, *Origin and Originality in Renaissance Literature*. New Haven, 1983.
Quintilian, *The Orator's Education*, ed. Donald A. Russell, 5 vols. Cambridge, MA, and London, 2001.
Radcliffe, Ann, *The Mysteries of Udolpho*, ed. Bonamy Dobrée. Oxford, 1988.
Raleigh, Sir Walter, *The History of The World*. London, 1614.
Ricoeur, Paul, *Memory, History, Forgetting*, trans. Kathleen Blamey and David Pellauer. Chicago and London, 2004.
Riggs, David, *Ben Jonson: A Life*. Cambridge, MA, and London, 1989.
Sanders, Julie, *Adaptation and Appropriation*, 2nd edn. London, 2016.
Schama, Simon, *Belonging: The Story of the Jews 1492–1900*. London, 2017.
Schleiner, Louise, 'Latinized Greek drama in Shakespeare's writing of *Hamlet*', *Shakespeare Quarterly*, 41:1. Spring, 1990.
Schmitt, Carl, *Hamlet or Hecuba: The Intrusion of Time into the Play*, trans. David Pan and Jennifer Rust. New York, 2009.
Scott, William, *The Model of Poesy*, ed. Gavin Alexander. Cambridge, 2013.
Sennett, Richard, *Flesh and Stone: The Body and the City in Western Civilization*. London, 1994.
Shakespeare, William, *The Winter's Tale*, ed. J.H.P. Pafford, Arden 2 series. London, 1963.
———, *King John*, ed. Ernst Honigmann, Arden 2 series. London, 1967.
———, *The Merchant of Venice*, ed. John Russell Brown, Arden 2 Series. London, 1972.
———, *A Midsummer Night's Dream*, ed. Harold Brooks, Arden 2 Series. London, 1979.
———, *Hamlet*, ed. Harold Jenkins, Arden 2 series. London, 1982.
———, *The Complete Works*, ed. Stanley Wells and Gary Taylor. Oxford, 1986.

——, *Titus Andronicus*, ed. Jonathan Bate, Arden 3 series. London, 1995.
——, *King Lear*, ed. R.A. Foakes, Arden 3 series. London, 1997.
——, *Othello*, ed. E.A.J. Honigmann, Arden 3 series. Walton-on-Thames, 1997.
——, *The Two Gentlemen of Verona*, ed. Lois Potter, Arden 3 series. London, 1997.
——, *Love's Labour's Lost*, ed. Henry Woudhuysen, Arden 3 series. London, 1998.
——, *The Tempest*, ed. Virginia and Alden Vaughan, Arden 3 series. London, 1999.
——, *King Henry the Sixth Part 1*, ed. Edward Burns, Arden 3 series. London, 2000.
——, *The Tragedy of Richard II*, ed. Charles Forker, Arden 3 series. London, 2002.
——, *Pericles*, ed. Suzanne Gossett, Arden 3 series. London, 2004.
——, *Much Ado About Nothing*, ed. Claire McEachern, Arden 3 series. London, 2006.
——, *Hamlet: The Texts of 1603 and 1623*, ed. Ann Thompson and Neil Taylor. London, 2007.
——, *The Norton Shakespeare*, 2nd edn, ed. Stephen Greenblatt, Walter Cohen, Jean Howard and Catherine Maus. New York and London, 2008.
——, *Twelfth Night or What You Will*, ed. Keir Elam, Arden 3 series. London, 2008.
——, *King Richard III*, ed. James Siemon, Arden 3 series. London, 2009.
——, *The Merchant of Venice*, ed. John Drakakis, Arden 3 series. London, 2010.
——, *The Taming of the Shrew*, ed. Barbara Hodgdon, Arden 3 series. London, 2010.
——, *The Winter's Tale*, ed. John Pitcher, Arden 3 series. London, 2010.
——, *Romeo and Juliet*, ed. René Weis, Arden 3 series. London, 2012.
——, *Coriolanus*, ed. Peter Holland, Arden 3 series. London, 2013.
——, *Macbeth*, ed. Sandra Clark and Pamela Mason, Arden 3 series. London, 2015.
——, *The Two Noble Kinsmen*, ed. Lois Potter, Arden 3 series, revised edn. London, 2015.
——, *Hamlet*, ed. Ann Thompson and Neil Taylor, Arden 3 series, revised edn, 2 vols. London, 2016.
——, *Othello*, ed. E.A.J. Honigmann, Arden 3 series, revised edn. London, 2016.
Sidney, Sir Philip, 'An apology for poetry', *English Critical Essays XVI–XVIII Centuries*. London, 1961.

———, *The Old Arcadia*, ed. Katherine Duncan-Jones. Oxford, 1985.
———, *Arcadia*, ed. Maurice Evans. Harmondsworth, 1997.
Sinfield, Alan, *Faultlines: Cultural Materialism and the Politics of Dissident Reading*. Los Angeles and Oxford, 1992.
Smith, Bruce R., *The Acoustic World of Early Modern England: Attending to the O-factor*. Chicago and London, 1999.
Smith, Emma, 'Was Shylock Jewish?', *Shakespeare Quarterly*, 64:2. Summer, 2013.
Smith, Thomas, *De Republica Anglorum*. London, 1583.
Smith, William George, *The Oxford Dictionary of English Proverbs*, revised by Sir Paul Harvey. Oxford, 1948.
Spenser, Edmund, *The Faerie Queene*, ed. A.C. Hamilton. London, 1977.
Stauffer, Donald A., *Selected Poetry and Prose of Coleridge*. London, 1951.
Stern, Tiffany, *Rehearsal from Shakespeare to Sheridan*. Oxford, 2000.
Streete, Adrian, *Protestantism and Drama in Early Modern England*. Cambridge, 2009.
———, *Apocalypse and Anti-Catholicism in Seventeenth-century English Drama*. Cambridge, 2017.
Taylor, Gary, and Lavagnino, John, eds, *Thomas Middleton: The Collected Works*. Oxford, 2010.
Tillyard, E.M.W., *The Elizabethan World Picture*. London, 1943.
Tóibín, Colm, *House of Names*. London, 2017.
Tudeau-Clayton, Margaret, *Shakespeare's Englishes: Against Englishness*. Cambridge, 2020.
Van Es, Bart, *Shakespeare in Company*. Oxford, 2015.
Vickers, Brian, ed., *Shakespeare: The Critical Heritage, vol. 1: 1623–1692*. London, 1974.
Volosinov, V.N., *Marxism and the Philosophy of Language*, trans. Ladislav Matejka and I.R. Titunik. New York, 1973.
———, *Freudianism: A Marxist Critique*, trans. I.R. Titunik, ed. Neal H. Bruss. New York, 1976.
Warton, Michael, and Stills, Judith, eds, *Intertextuality: Theory and Practice*. Manchester, 1990.
Watson, Thomas, *Hecatompathia or Passionate Centurie of Loue*. London, 1582.
Webster, John, *The Duchess of Malfi*, ed. John Russell Brown. London, 1964.
Weimann, Robert, *Shakespeare and the Popular Tradition in the Theater: Studies in the Social Dimension of Dramatic Form and Function*, ed. Robert Schwartz. Baltimore and London, 1978.
———, *Author's Pen and Actor's Voice: Playing and Writing in Shakespeare's Theatre*. Cambridge, 2000.

White, Hayden, *The Tropics of Discourse: Essays in Cultural Criticism*. Baltimore and London, 1987.
———, *The Content of the Form: Narrative Discourses and Historical Representation*. Baltimore and London, 1990.
Wilkes, G.A., *Ben Jonson: Five Plays*. Oxford, 1989.
Williams, Gordon, *A Glossary of Shakespeare's Sexual Language*. London, 1997.
Williams, Raymond, *The Long Revolution*. Harmondsworth, 1975.
———, *Marxism and Literature*. Oxford, 1977.
———, *Politics and Letters: Interviews with New Left Review*. London, 1979.
Wilson, John Dover, *What Happens in Hamlet*. Cambridge, 1935.
Wilson, Thomas, *The Art of Rhetorique*. London, 1585.
Womersley, David, 'The politics of Shakespeare's *King John*', *Review of English Studies*, 40. 1989.
Woodbridge, Linda, *English Revenge Drama: Money, Resistance, Equality*. Cambridge, 2010.
Yates, Francis, *The Art of Memory*. Reprinted, London, 2010.

Index

Ackroyd, Peter 193
Aeschylus 16, 130, 132, 250, 252, 276
Andes, A.H.R. 1–2, 18, 22
architextuality 67
Aristotle 4, 13–14, 35, 74–5, 90, 148, 158, 236–8, 305, 336
Ascham, Roger 2, 23, 25, 39,
Assmann, Aleida 5, 8–9, 15–16, 18–19, 46–7
authority 16, 21, 45, 49, 53–5, 57–9, 62–3, 79, 82, 84, 86, 89, 98–9, 102, 107, 112–16, 119, 136, 138, 143–4, 147–9, 151, 153, 164, 175, 184, 186–7, 196, 199, 242–3, 271, 279, 290, 294–5, 303–4, 324, 328, 332, 372

Bakhtin, Mikhail 173–5, 187–8, 218
Barclay, Alexander 96–8
Barker, Francis 34, 80, 199, 223, 229
Barker, Pat 130, 132, 140
Barthes, Roland 61, 63–4, 203
Barton, Anne 290
Bate, Jonathan 13, 16–17, 33, 158, 263, 334, 363–4
Bawcutt, N.W. 339

Beaumont, Francis, and Fletcher, John 141, 180
Belleforest, François 71, 79, 189, 191, 196–7
Benjamin, Walter 103–4
Bergson, Henri 38, 202–3,
Bloom, Harold 51–3, 55, 58, 176, 262, 291–2
Bourdieu, Pierre 156–7, 220
Bowers, Fredson 260–1
Bradley, A.C. 274–5
Braudel, Fernand 68, 73
Bright, Timothie 74, 76, 249
Brooke, Arthur 331–2
Brown, John Russell 118
Browne, Sir Thomas 147–8, 214
Bullough, Geoffrey 18–19, 24, 34, 42–61, 64, 71–2, 78, 81, 94, 100, 102–5, 109, 117, 157, 188–90, 193, 248, 261, 277, 279, 291–2, 295, 320, 322
Burke, Seán 135, 145, 150–1
Burrow, Colin 3, 5, 7, 28–31, 53–4, 120
Burton, Robert 74

Caesar, Philip 237
Camden, William 8, 11, 21, 232–4, 321
Chambers, Ross 176

Chaucer, Geoffrey 28, 50, 66, 105, 134, 136–7, 306–8
Chettle, Henry 64, 79, 194, 196–7
Cicero 2, 12, 25–7, 36, 40, 48, 94, 266, 292
Clare, Janet 64–5, 73, 78, 165, 168, 184, 292, 294
Clubb, Louise George 30, 40, 318–19, 347–8
Coetzee, J.M. 175
Coleridge, Samuel Taylor 19, 44–5, 357–8
Collingwood, R.G. 44, 83
Collinson, Patrick 16, 145, 363–4
Contarini, Gasparo 77, 243, 341
Cooper, Helen 109
Cotton, Sir Robert 11, 21, 47
Craig, Hardin 43, 51, 82, 102, 113, 126, 175
Crane, Mary Thomas 9–10
creativity 44, 57, 99, 197, 318
Croce, Benedetto 42–3, 44, 45, 57, 82, 83, 86, 87, 93–4, 102, 134
Culler, Jonathan 203, 216, 218

Damasio, Antonio 290
Dante Alighieri 266–7, 293, 296
Deleuze, Gilles 23–4, 69, 83, 110–11, 156–7, 158, 270, 364
Derrida, Jacques 107–9, 131, 142, 183, 264
Dollimore, Jonathan 199

Eagleton, Terry 328, 332
early modern 3–4, 8, 12–13, 16–18, 21–2, 30, 35, 67, 70, 74, 76, 93–4, 103–4, 111, 114, 116, 121, 132, 135, 137–8, 140, 145, 164, 166, 199, 209, 230–1, 236–7, 248–50, 277, 289, 291, 295, 363–4
theatre 59, 166

Empson, William 183
Enterline, Lynn 248, 360–1
Erasmus, Desiderius 2, 24–6, 95–8, 115
Erne, Lucas 99
Euripides 2, 16–17, 90, 130, 132, 133, 261, 318
Evans, Joan 11, 295

Findlay, Alison 185
Florio, John 118, 292, 305
Foakes, R.A. 279
Foucault, Michel 63–4, 66, 88, 141–4, 167–8, 225–6, 370
Fox, Adam 4, 6, 14–16, 37–8, 45–6, 138, 241
Fox, John 27, 231, 266
Freud, Sigmund 20, 52, 55, 70, 106–7, 109–12, 142, 144–6, 172–4, 192, 214

Garber, Marjorie 144–6, 157
Genette, Gérard 67–8, 70, 73, 78, 89
Giddens, Anthony 222
Gillespie, Stuart 22, 29, 127
Golding, Arthur 50, 108–9, 112, 177, 249, 329
Gollancz, Sir Israel 71, 190
Gower, John 50, 66, 105, 138, 306, 319
Greenblatt, Stephen 25, 52, 53, 64, 98, 165, 221–3, 266–7, 281–2, 284
Greene, Robert 64, 189, 349–50
Greer, Germaine 334–5
Greville, Fulke 111
Guattari, Félix 24, 69, 110–11

Hall, Edward (Chronicles) 3, 43
Hall, Kim 342–3
Halpern, Richard 49, 84
Havelock, Eric 13, 23, 47

Hawkes, David 236
Hawkes, Terence 7, 17, 66, 112–14, 223–4, 236
Hayward, Sir John 250
Helgerson, Richard 20, 30–1, 34, 37, 49–50
Hill, Thomas 74–5
Hillis Miller, J. 157–8
Hillman, Richard 179–80, 187–8, 308
Hiscock, Andrew 12, 23, 37
history 6, 7, 9, 14–15, 19, 28, 34, 42, 44, 52–3, 59, 68, 73–4, 79–80, 82, 92–4, 100, 104, 112, 115, 132, 156, 166, 173–4, 180, 183, 189–90, 193, 207, 209, 217, 221, 223–4, 227, 231, 248–50, 253–5, 259, 278, 284, 291–2, 309, 318, 363
  biblical 196
  cultural 58
  folk 237
  history plays 33, 43, 118, 262
  history of ideas 55, 142
  linear 59, 174
  literary 33
  oral 12
  patriarchal 185
  pre-history 24, 104
  sacred 99
  theatre 321
  universal 96
Hodgdon, Barbara 171, 334–6
Holinshed, Raphael 8, 17, 27–8, 43, 52, 218, 248, 250
Holland, Philemon 320
Homer 3, 16, 28, 49, 66, 115, 130, 133, 158, 196, 293
Honan, Park 1–2, 5, 193
Hooker, Richard 243–4, 372
Howard, Jean 187–8

Hulme, Peter 34, 80, 90, 223–30, 235, 241, 322
Hutson, Lorna 17, 22, 30, 38, 49
hypertext 68–9, 71, 89, 181

ideology 33, 36, 51, 99, 100, 102, 178, 185, 186, 201, 219, 221, 241, 244, 289, 308
intertextuality 22, 60–5, 79, 164–220, 226, 250, 292–4

Jeanneret, Michel 101
Jenkins, Harold 149, 158
Jones, Emrys 2, 24, 28, 32, 55, 261
Jonson, Ben 7, 132–4, 142, 217, 249, 290, 292, 296, 298–9, 337–8

Kerrigan, John 17, 114–15, 119, 151, 257, 261–2, 275, 310, 327, 336
Kiséry, András 134–5
Kojève, Alexander 54–5, 84, 86
Kristeva, Julia 61–2, 65, 67, 70, 172–5, 182–3, 185, 188, 195, 199, 203, 211, 216, 218, 220, 256, 262, 293–5, 301–2, 314
Kyd, Thomas. 71, 73, 149, 168, 170, 190, 193, 262, 266

Lake, Peter 33–4, 52, 55, 187, 250–4
Lascelles, Mary 18
Le Goff, Jacques 266
Leinwand, Theodore 237
Levith, Murray 61–2, 182–3
Lewis, Rhodri 13–14, 38, 76–7
Lewkenor, Lewis 77, 243, 341
linearity 20, 34, 60, 69, 76, 98, 115, 147, 291, 318
literacy 12, 13, 65, 128, 135, 165

382 Index

Livy 250, 320–1
Lodge, Thomas 43, 181, 190, 198
Lopez, Roderigo 166, 231–6, 238, 339
Lucretius 74, 95, 97–8
Lynch, Stephen J. 60–1, 180–2, 184, 292
Lyne, Raphael 203–9

Machiavelli, Niccólo 29, 206, 234, 235, 248, 296
Maguire, Laurie 104–8, 112
Margaroni, Maria 70
Marlowe, Christopher 47–8, 50, 104–7, 109, 112, 126, 133, 166, 182–3, 233–5, 292, 319, 324, 338–9, 354, 359
  Dido, Queen of Carthage 104, 105, 106
  Doctor Faustus 182–3
  Edward II 166, 319
  The Jew of Malta 47, 84, 166, 182, 233–4, 292, 318–19, 324, 338–9, 354, 359
  Tamburlaine 231, 339
Marston, John 194, 196
Marx, Karl (Marxism) 10, 67, 73, 102, 104, 107–8, 187, 219, 224
Masten, Jeffrey 120–1, 139–41, 191, 198
McEachern, Claire 31, 171, 316, 338
meme 109, 118, 123, 155, 166, 169, 217, 262, 273, 274, 283, 314, 320, 324, 333, 363–4
Middleton, Thomas 120
Miola, Robert 183, 291, 359, 362–3
Moi, Toril 178
Moretti, Franco 68, 73, 80
Mosse, Miles 237
Mowat, Barbara 137–9, 150

Muir, Kenneth 18–20, 22, 24, 55–6, 281–2
Mullaney, Stephen 116, 200, 289–90, 295
Mystery Plays 2–3, 32
myth 8, 12, 21, 24, 61–2, 69, 95, 103–4, 112, 123, 132, 136–7, 235, 253, 277, 296, 302, 304, 323–4, 326, 335, 340–3, 345–6, 358, 360, 365
mythic law 190, 305
mythology 100, 120, 179, 182, 191, 197, 208

Nashe, Thomas 65, 138, 189
new historicism 52, 187–8, 220, 225
old historicism 221
Nietzsche, Friedrich 6, 9, 157–8
North's *Plutarch* 204–7, 217, 248, 330–1, 362
Nuttall, A.D. 275–6, 306

Oldcastle, Sir John 27
Ong, Walter 13
orality 4, 12, 14, 75, 112, 123, 135, 165
Orgel, Stephen 134, 142–3, 147, 164
Ovid 2, 50, 52, 54, 66, 105, 108–9, 112, 148, 171, 177, 233, 249, 293, 329

Patterson, Annabel 7, 28, 33–4, 36, 37, 40
Paul, H.N. 18
Pavier, Thomas 71, 191
Plato 13–14, 23–4, 47, 58, 93, 99–100, 103, 114–16, 147–8, 291
Plautus 2, 46, 118, 319
Pollard, Tanya 16, 38

Pope, Alexander 56, 266, 358
post-modern 24, 132
Prouty, Charles 18, 118, 261, 308
Puttenham, George 48, 64–5, 84, 88, 210

Quint, David 49, 57–9, 93, 99–100, 103, 114–16, 147, 291
Quintilian 2, 8, 13, 17, 26, 210

Raleigh, Walter 56–7
Raleigh, Sir Walter 94–8, 100, 104, 134
Renaissance 42, 45, 56–8, 64, 70, 98–9, 104, 118, 134, 222, 261, 291–6, 361
Rhymer, Thomas 275
Ricoeur, Paul 14, 202–3

Saxo Grammaticus 71, 79, 189–90, 192, 195–7, 249–50
Schama, Simon 340
Schleiner, Louise 261–2
Schmitt, Carl 251–3
semiotic chora 62, 87, 183, 294, 301
Seneca 26, 50, 52, 73–5, 81, 189, 193, 194, 196–8, 248–50, 263, 266, 274, 331
Sennett, Richard 339–41
Shakespeare, William
 1 Henry IV 27
 1 Henry VI 138
 2 Henry IV 27, 136
 Antony and Cleopatra 204–6, 207–8, 362
 As You Like It 23, 60, 136, 145, 181, 334
 The Comedy of Errors 46, 254, 302, 318, 319, 364
 Coriolanus 320–1
 Cymbeline 306

 Hamlet 29, 71, 72, 73, 78, 79, 81, 100, 107, 109, 112, 118, 134, 144, 145–9, 151–2, 157–8, 166, 189, 190–4, 196, 199, 202, 223, 249, 251–2, 254, 266–74, 281, 320, 321, 348–50, 364
 Henry V 145, 320, 360
 Henry VIII 348
 Julius Caesar 81, 145, 194, 261, 266, 274
 King John 184–5, 186, 251, 348
 King Lear 18, 60, 117, 118, 157, 221, 277–8, 281, 284, 346, 348
 Love's Labours Lost 59–60, 116, 117, 118–19, 121–2, 123, 255–60, 327–8, 330–1, 333, 336–7
 Macbeth 18, 28, 74, 117, 157, 205, 206, 277, 320, 327, 348
 Measure for Measure 18, 360
 The Merchant of Venice 46, 47, 52, 66, 70–1, 78, 105, 110, 166, 182, 217, 231–2, 235–6, 238–44, 263, 273–4, 281, 292, 296–9, 301, 306, 308, 322–4, 325–6, 338, 339, 341–3, 345–6
 A Midsummer Night's Dream 50, 74, 123, 256, 259, 319, 326–7, 328–31, 333, 342, 348
 Much Ado About Nothing 18, 31, 154–6, 168, 170, 176–9, 188, 292, 298–9, 302, 303–4, 305, 306, 308, 314, 320, 333, 337–8, 360
 Othello 75, 77, 81, 117, 157, 249, 274, 275–7, 291, 297–8, 300, 303, 306, 308, 313, 322, 324, 325–6, 337, 343–7, 360
 The Passionate Pilgrim 120, 121, 326

Shakespeare, William (cont.)
  Pericles 60, 138, 145, 306, 326
  The Rape of Lucrece 189
  Richard II 166, 205, 250
  Richard III 4, 320
  Romeo and Juliet 46, 123, 165, 258, 274, 319, 326, 330–3, 348, 364
  The Taming of the Shrew 74, 169–70, 256, 320, 333, 334–6, 338, 361
  The Tempest 105, 106, 225, 227–30, 281, 360
  Timon of Athens 348
  Titus Andronicus 158, 193, 261, 263–4, 348–9, 364
  Troilus and Cressida 18, 28, 320
  Twelfth Night 265–6, 273, 319
  The Two Gentlemen of Verona 136, 256, 349–50
  The Two Noble Kinsmen 136, 306, 308
  The Winter's Tale 60, 280, 292, 298, 308, 310–14, 333, 348, 360
Sidney, Sir Philip 21, 39, 129, 250, 280, 285, 321, 364–5
Sinfield, Alan 128, 302
Smith, Bruce R. 7
Smith, Emma 104, 107
Smith, Sir Thomas 79, 236, 238, 306, 347

Sophocles 16, 73, 130, 132, 133
Spenser, Edmund 10–12, 24, 250, 256
Stern, Tiffany 32, 41, 296, 316
Suetonius 26, 248

Taylor, Gary 120, 149
Thompson, Ann 29, 40, 78, 91, 149, 161, 162, 167, 210, 213, 288
Tillyard, E.M.W. 51, 102–3
Tóibín, Colm 130–3, 140
Tomkiss, Thomas 12
Tourneur, Cyril 289

Van Es, Bart 318–19, 348–9
Vaughan, Alden 226–7
Vaughan, Virginia 226–7
Virgil 50, 105, 133, 148, 293, 358
Volosinov, V.N. 218–20, 224–5

Watson, Thomas 170–3, 176
Webster, John 117–18, 289
Weimann, Robert 153, 164–6, 347–8, 361, 364
White, Hayden 253–4
Williams, Raymond 92, 289, 295, 318, 322
Woudhuysen, Henry 116, 259, 330
Woodbridge, Linda 194

Yates, Francis 8, 13, 18, 35

EU authorised representative for GPSR:
Easy Access System Europe, Mustamäe tee 50,
10621 Tallinn, Estonia
gpsr.requests@easproject.com